W9-DFO-207

REPRESSION AND RECOVERY

REPRESSION AND RECOVERY

MODERN AMERICAN POETRY AND THE POLITICS OF CULTURAL MEMORY, 1910–1945

CARY NELSON

PS
310
.M57
N45
1989

THE UNIVERSITY OF WISCONSIN PRESS

KBS

For Paula

The University of Wisconsin Press
114 North Murray Street
Madison, Wisconsin 53715

3 Henrietta Street
London WC2E 8LU, England

INDIANA-
PURDUE
LIBRARY
WITHDRAWN
FORT WAYNE
8-17-92
P

Copyright © 1989
The Board of Regents of the University of Wisconsin System
All rights reserved

5   4   3   2   1

Printed in the United States of America

Bob Brown, "Art," copyright © 1959 by Eleanor Brown. Malcolm Cowley, "A Poem for
May Day" ("The Last International") from *Blue Juniata: A Life* by Malcolm Cowley.
Copyright © 1941, copyright renewed 1968 by Malcolm Cowley. Reprinted by per-
mission of Viking Penguin, a division of Penguin Books USA, Inc. Sol Funaroff, "Fire
Sermon," copyright © 1932 by *New Masses*. Langston Hughes, "Come to the Waldorf-
Astoria," copyright © 1931 by *New Masses*.

Library of Congress Cataloging-in-Publication Data
Nelson, Cary.
    Repression and recovery : modern American poetry and the politics
of cultural memory, 1910–1945/Cary Nelson.
        352 pp.   cm. — (The Wisconsin project on American writers)
    Includes bibliographical references.
    1. American poetry—20th century—History and criticism.
2. Modernism (Literature)—United States.   I. Title.   II. Series.
PS310.M57N45   1989   89-40264
811'.5209—dc20   CIP
ISBN 0-299-12340-5

10-12-92

CONTENTS

ILLUSTRATIONS

PREFACE

Repression and Recovery: Modern American Poetry and the Politics of Cultural Memory is a prolegomenon to what I imagine to be a series of future projects—for both myself and others—about American poetry from 1910 to 1945. It is thus not a complete history but rather an overview of the problematics of writing one and a provocation to reexamine what remains the dominant story of modern poetry. It is also an effort to revise our notion of the social function of poetry, an effort grounded in a series of rereadings of marginalized or forgotten poets—particularly women, blacks, and writers on the left—and in a theoretical discussion of poetry's cultural status as a discourse among others. The book proceeds at once by way of a continuing meditation on the assumptions underlying the way modern literary history has been written and by way of brief comments on a large number of modern poets, many of whom are now rarely reprinted, read, or even acknowledged in criticism on the period. My reflections on literary history include critiques of our received views of modernism as well as an analysis of the problematics of both canon formation and the continuing effort to expand the canon so that it includes a wider number of neglected writers. Finally, *Repression and Recovery* is also a Marxist and poststructuralist analysis of the difficulties and temptations inherent in reading modern poetry at a moment when we are beginning to realize some of what we have lost of our cultural heritage. I do not, however, view these theoretical commitments as the components of a seamless metadiscourse but rather as mutually corrective impulses.

Repression and Recovery is obviously addressed to all those—both inside and outside academia—with a special interest in its subject matter. Like most university press books, it will be particularly relevant to those academics who are themselves writing in this area. Indeed, those of us who study and analyze modern poetry are gathered together in the collective "we" that recurs throughout the book. I have worked, therefore, to address that audience directly, urging them to interrogate the social meaning of the work they do.

Readers will notice immediately that the book is not divided into chapters. Along with a number of other somewhat unconventional elements of the book—from decisions about who will count as an American poet to decisions about what poets to group together and what texts to emphasize—this choice is deliberate. I am aiming first of all to counteract the familiar groupings that chapter divisions would likely entail. A single, continuous essay proved the best way to suggest the interpretive fluidity of the wide range of poetry published during this thirty-five year period. It should also encourage people to read the main body of the book in one day, an experience that should not only demonstrate the frequent historical simultaneity of much of modern poetry's diversity but also help readers see relations between discourses that we have too often struggled to keep separate.

I have included a large number of illustrations in the book, both because they are discussed in the text and because they represent a significant part of what we have forgotten of the context and impact of modern poetry. Many of these illustrations have not been reproduced since they were first published. In most cases, the books, pamphlets, song sheets, and journals now exist only in private collections or in rare book rooms in a few libraries, so people will have little opportunity to see the originals. This book is thus in part an effort to disseminate these images again, to give them another opportunity to do productive work in our culture.

Whenever I give the dimensions of the original, the width precedes the height. All dimensions are in inches. Unless otherwise noted, the originals are in the author's collection. In order to balance readers' need to situate themselves temporally against the risk of overwhelming the book with dates, I have placed poets' birth and death dates in the text but relegated most dates of journals to the index. The notes give special emphasis to describing the primary and secondary material available on the lesser-known writers and artists mentioned in the text. In some cases, so far as I can tell no published biographical information exists.

A number of people have been kind enough to read the book with care at various stages of its composition. Nina Baym, Ed Brunner, Leon Chai, Alice Deck, Ed Folsom, Michael Greer, Lawrence Grossberg, David Minter, and Robert Parker read early versions and helped give the project direction. Joanne Wheeler has been a continual resource for discussions of the historical issues at stake in the period. Frank Lentricchia, Mary Loeffelholz, Andrew Ross, and Paula Treichler read the manuscript toward the end and persuaded me to pursue numerous issues further than I would have on my own. Karen Ford and Jeff Hendricks each read the manuscript both early and late with the kind of thoroughness that only shared intellectual commitments can make possible. Both Allen Fitchen and Jack Kirshbaum at the University of Wisconsin Press have been resourceful in bringing the book toward publication.

The book was begun during a year at the University of Illinois Center for Advanced Study. The research was made much easier because of the cooperation of the staff at the rare book rooms at the University of Illinois and the University of Wisconsin. The Ewing C. Baskette Collection at Illinois and the Marvin Sukov collection at Wisconsin have both been essential to the book. The photo services departments at both campuses worked hard to produce excellent results from originals that were often difficult to photograph. The cost of reproducing the illustrations was shared by the English Department, the College of Liberal Arts and Sciences, and the Research Board at the University of Illinois. A number of rare book rooms and special collections at other libraries provided help at crucial moments: the Amistad Research Center at Tulane University; the Moorland-Spingarn Research Center at Howard University; the Director of Kent Library at Southeast Missouri State University; the Schomberg Center for Research in Black Culture in New York; the Kenneth Spencer Research Library at the University of Kansas; the Hoover Institution at Stanford University; and Special Collections Departments at Ohio State University and the University of Washington. A number of rare book dealers, including Beasley Books in Chicago, Cornerstone Books in New Haven, and Serendipity Books in Berkeley have been industrious in locating copies of books I needed. For all of this assistance I remain genuinely grateful.

REPRESSION AND RECOVERY

INTRODUCTION

I t is the problem of history at its most intractable that I need to confront in this thirty-odd year impertinence of the calendar, a period roughly coinciding with what we call the modern period in American poetry. Whether I choose it to be the case for this project or not, a book on modern poetry necessarily engages history as a palimpsest of two durations—then and now, the earlier period that is overtly "under consideration" and the current period, uneasy about its potentially apocalyptic destiny but so far uncertain about its concluding date, in which I am writing. Neither time in fact is unitary; moreover, these two periods both construct and erase one another in the writing and reconstruction of history. For what and who we are now is already in part a result of what we no longer know we have forgotten. And our understanding of the poetry of these thirty-five years is, among other things, a cultural construction explainable by way of several stories that can be told about the subsequent suppression of history, in the broader sense, along with some of *its* literature, as part of the construction and institutionalization of the narrow disciplinary integrity of academic literary history. These relationships will work themselves out in any literary history of the period. The key choice is thus to decide whether to address such historical issues more directly.[1] That is what I try to do here.

I will raise a number of difficult questions about literary history—some very much a part of current debates, some less familiar—and provide suggestions about how to seek appropriate, necessary, and yet altogether provisional answers to questions that cannot actually be settled. The challenge in thinking through the interpenetration of present and past in literary history is not to master the problem, or even to identify all its components—for neither goal is achievable —but rather to decide how to proceed in the midst of problems that can be acknowledged and clarified but not fully resolved.

The focus for this reflection on how we do literary history is my contention that we no longer know the history of the poetry of the first half of this century; most of us, moreover, do not know that the knowledge is gone. Indeed, we tend to be unaware of how or why such a process of literary forgetfulness occurs, let alone why it occurs among the very people who consider themselves the custodians of our literary heritage. Custodians, of course, concern themselves not only with conserving the past but also with selectively disposing of much of it, though the two impulses become deceptively conflated in the imagination of academic disciplines—so that a self-congratulatory process of conservation remains primarily in view.

There is now, however, a renewal of interest in the problematics of literary history, a renewal whose background merits mention here. As the prestige of philological research and textual scholarship began to decline, practitioners of literary historiography sought to separate their enterprise from "literary criticism" and thus to position themselves to take on those interested claims for rigor that had been freed for rearticulation.[2] Thereafter, through the critical revolution of the 1960s and 1970s, up until the early 1980s—the period when both theory and the counterreaction to theory were disseminated throughout the humanities and social sciences—the study of literary history in America remained a rather privileged and stable terrain. Relatively untouched by changes in other literary fields, it occupied the peculiar discursive role of a retreat from contemporary historical pressures and a reserve of secure antitheoretical convictions. The discourse of literary history seemed an intellectual, personal, and institutional alternative at once to the complications of theory and to the vicissitudes of politics; it was something we already knew how to do, an intellectual pursuit whose theoretical questions were either nonexistent or already settled. Despite more complex and actively contested models of literary history in European scholarship—one thinks especially of Lukács—writing literary history here retained the image of an activity entailing a set of tested procedures embodying disinterested and ethically resplendent thoroughness. Like the New Critics of the 1930s through the 1950s, the newer theoretical critics too—so conservative literary historians would repeatedly insist—knew little of history and cared still less for the diligence and objectivity necessary to find anything out. History, or so the underlying logic of historical scholarship suggested, was simply *there to be known* for those scholars willing to do the appropriate work. But a number of forces combined to make this confident, positivist vision both of the scholarly gaze and of the past itself increasingly impossible:

First, the political movements of the 1960s linked the ethics of academic disinterestedness with an unwillingness to engage in contemporary political processes and with a conservative resistance to compelling pressures for social change. A purported intellectual stand about the past was actually a way of living in the present while trying to avoid, deny, or resist its pressures. Moreover, competing versions of national history were in considerable conflict: from thinly idealized versions of manifest destiny promoted by a series of national governments to critiques of imperialism from the left during the Vietnam war, from continually circulating myths of national progress to reconstructions of the country's continuing history of racism. Thus the sense that "history," or at least any narratives we tell in its service, is never simply given but is always politically, rhetorically, and institutionally constituted, became increasingly prominent in public life.

Second, the theoretical movements of the period, particularly structuralism, made much of their deliberate conceptualization of and sometimes disregard for an exclusively linear model of history, providing thereby at once a convenient target for traditional critics and, more subversively, evidence for the intellectually manipulable nature of the record of historical time, for the uneasy recognition that our understanding of history could be radically reordered according to different spatial models.[3]

Third, newer critical movements, from Black Studies work growing out of the civil rights movement to feminist theoretical work growing out of the feminist movement, demonstrated that the literary and social history we promulgated as sufficient in fact suppressed an immense amount of writing of great interest, vitality, subtlety, and complexity—writing, indeed, if one feels the need to argue the case on these grounds, of demonstrably high quality. Literary history thus told a selective story substantially constituted by its cultural presuppositions and restricted by its ideological filters. Finally, work by historians on the tropological nature of historical narration, and by the new Marxism with its revived versions of totality, made the figurative and metaphorical character of historical writing increasingly apparent.

Literary history could hardly withstand these pressures indefinitely. Indeed it is surprising that it has taken so long for people involved in contemporary theory to begin criticizing and rethinking our assumptions about how literary history has been, should be, or even can be written. We are now beginning to recognize that literary history as a modern academic endeavor is a special institutional project to be consciously (if imperfectly) separated from literary history as it may actually have taken place. The polymorphous production of literature is never recoverable in its entirety. The discourses of literary history are no less open, interpretive, problematic, and indeterminable than the knowledge and insight generated, the writing produced, in the close reading of texts. Moreover, unlike a reading of one poem, the discourse of literary history has no limited, pregiven, firmly established textual corpus we can imagine to be the certain ground of its knowledge. We can never be certain what kinds of texts should be included within or excluded from "literary history," let alone what their number might be. Literary history always risks becoming an infinite subject.

Three specific problems with typical literary histories may nonetheless be identified. First, literary history is often implicitly construed as a centuries-long competition to enter the official canon and be taught in literature classes, a concern that was often not central to writers or to their audiences. Second, the term "literary history" is itself a curious one, for the two words—"literary" and "history"—collaborate to disguise the substantial absence of each other's presence in the enterprise as we have known it. Thus the New Critics were at pains to point out that "literary history" generally omitted and obscured what was specifically *literary* about poetry and fiction, the textual qualities that distinguish literary language from other discourses. It may now, however, be more crucial to argue that literary history is typically (and improperly) detached from history as it may be more broadly construed—not only the familiar history of nations but also the still less familiar history of everyday life. Third, literary history is generally addicted to narrative presentations that ignore diversity when it cannot be fitted into a coherent historical sequence. But textual and social difference and diversity may be irreducible phenomena. The full range of modern poetries is so great that it cannot be persuasively narrativized in any unitary way. The textual field of modern poetry is a countervailing force to any consistent, uncontradictory presentation of its development. No single story can be told about modern poetry and its varied audiences that is even marginally adequate.

In existing histories of twentieth-century poetry, each of these tendencies creates both specific and systemic distortions. Considerable damage can be done by unqualified devotion to a single master narrative. A 1986 book on modern American poetry ends with the following global (and exclusive) declaration: "Again, what is American Modernism? It is the long writing of the long poem."[4] While it has for some time been recognized that a number of modern American poets turned to the long poem after the first phase of their careers, there are many others who never worked in this form. Apparently, they are not to count as modernists. To be in thrall to a single historical narrative, moreover, is to miss the benefits that come from juxtaposing multiple, competing narratives. Just as useful and pertinent as this narrative of modernism as the long poem would be a narrative of the interplay between formal innovation and social critique. Or one could write the story of modern American poetry as a long struggle over how women are to be represented in poetry.[5] Williams and Pound would play major roles in that story—Williams with his naive and conventionalized sexism, Pound's being perhaps more insidious—but these roles are different from those they play in the story of the long poem. As it happens, the master narratives we have been given so far tend to be heavily exclusionary and distinctly interested politically.[6]

The modern American poetry we have been most likely to encounter for some time—the poetry most regularly anthologized, taught, reprinted, read, and written about—is the poetry of a limited number of figures that many (though certainly not all) academics

now consider to be the major poets of the period, including Robert
Frost (1874–1963), T. S. Eliot (1888–1965), Ezra Pound (1885–1972),
Wallace Stevens (1879–1955), and William Carlos Williams (1883–
1963). Of course this list is itself a recent historical product. Yet
once an author is accepted as a major figure in the canon, it is easy
(especially for those who neither lived through nor contributed to
the process of canonization) to believe it was always so. In Stevens'
case, his claim for a place in the essential canon of academic modernism did not begin to be staked out until the late 1950s and did
not become "apparent" to all of us—or at least apparent enough
to be hotly debated—until the 1960s. Williams arrived even later.
Always crucial to other poets, his work was not written about extensively by scholars until the late 1960s and was not widely valued
in the academy until the 1970s.[7] Indeed, for those, like me, who
were reading and writing about Williams in the late 1960s, his current prominence in the academic version of modernism still seems,
paradoxically, at once a major victory and a goal that may remain
unachievable. My generation has made an investment in Williams'
academic marginality and thus, for us, he will probably always be
somewhat outside the official canon. The process by which poets
like these are elevated and others marginalized or forgotten is increasingly being questioned and challenged; in part, it has come to
be regarded as immensely biased and repressive. For the period of
1910–1945 was an enormously productive and diverse one in American poetry. One of my purposes is to further the project—begun by
many other critics—of recovering some of that diversity.

Yet one never actually "recovers" the thing itself. Literary history
can never have in view, can never hold within its intellectual grasp
or even merely in its gaze, some level of sheer, unmediated textual
facticity, let alone any stable system of signification. History and
its artifacts are always reconstructed, mediated, and narrativized.
Though I therefore resist an overarching narrative I will resort to
explicitly narrativized passages. Moreover, before I claim that I have
written a thoroughly decentered and postmodern book, I should add
that, although there is no one master thesis here, a cluster of related
arguments recur throughout. And there are no doubt narrative effects
of my prose of which I am unaware and over which I have exercised

no control. Indeed, I would agree with those who argue that there is no descriptive and denominative discourse that is nonnarrative. Nor is this a neutral feature at the local level of any discourse, for it means that all histories are interested.

As an anthropologist argues, the process of revising our stories about the past answers to the needs of current institutions:

> In the intervening years, some slogans have become risible, some words have become empty, and others too full, holding too much cruelty or bitterness to modern ears. Some names count for more, and others that count for less are due to be struck out. The revisionary effort is not aimed at producing the perfect optic flat. The mirror, if that is what history is, distorts as much after revision as it did before. The aim of revision is to get the distortions to match the mood of the present times. . . . When we look closely at the construction of past time, we find the process has very little to do with the past at all and everything to do with the present. Institutions create shadowed places in which nothing can be seen and no questions asked. They make other areas show finely discriminated detail, which is closely scrutinized and ordered. . . . To watch these practices establish selective principles that highlight some kinds of events and obscure others is to inspect the social order operating on individual minds.[8]

This analysis captures the dynamic of the institution of literary studies and applies to my own revisionary effort as well. If it is unrealistic to imagine we could transcend these determining forces, it is possible to become significantly—though imperfectly and discontinuously—aware of them. When interest in marginal authors is ascending again, we recognize how rapidly the institution of literary studies spreads out an artist's work to give it extraordinarily detailed attention. Polemical overviews of a writer's career appear first, and they make it possible to publish elaborate, "finely discriminated" readings of individual works. The space of our literary memory shifts and realigns, not only to accommodate forgotten literary works but also to accommodate new interpretive discourse. The process also works in reverse. During the McCarthy era of the 1950s, many people destroyed their copies of political books and magazines from the 1930s. The institution of literary studies cooperated and eliminated the names of political poets from the ongoing conversation of the discipline. Like the leveling movement of the sea, the weight of our cultural memory closed over this part of our heritage, turning it into a shadowed place where nothing could be seen. Only a few books worked against this tendency.[9] Literary studies as a whole instead devoted itself to establishing the limited canon of modernism.

This is equally true of our perception and understanding of all texts, all poems. One literally never sees a poem on a page in and of itself alone; it is always a function of the assumptions and urgencies of our psychology, our critical models, our disciplinary aims and defenses, and our own historical moment. Nothing that we can say or think about a poem is free of social construction. If the "thing itself" were available to us, it would have no meaning whatsoever. There is no perceptible, unmediated, unconstructed zero degree of literary materiality that serves as a consensual basis for interpretation. Even what is to count as a poem has to be decided before the words in white space will have any meaning. More than seventy years after the onset of the modernist revolution, this first, inescapable generic question remains essentially as controversial as ever, not only for modernism but also, as any reader of book reviews can testify, for the poetry of our own day as well.

But keeping the thoroughly constructed nature of literary perception practically and usefully in mind is quite another matter, especially in a project like this that is driven by a series of moral imperatives, such as the desire to revive suppressed literary traditions. Indeed, the very delusion that one has gotten closer to (even arrived at) the productive, determining, and contested relations in which literature came to be written can itself be politically and discursively productive. Such impulses will lead here, as they have led elsewhere, to some neglected texts being read again. But the illusion that one has reached a level of secure and permanent textual or historical knowledge is best resisted.[10]

Yet there have been moments—especially when I take pleasure in a book or magazine that most people now writing about modern poetry have never seen—when I feel I have broken through the interested forgetfulness of decades, divested myself of present interests, and established an authentic relationship with a discourse from the past.[11] In response to such fantasies, however, I would counter with what Roland Barthes says about literary evaluation in the opening pages of *S/Z*: "what evaluation finds is precisely this value: what can be written (rewritten) today."[12] Yet if writing literary history necessitates enacting our own historical moment it also offers the possibility of coming to know more of our place in history, at least to the extent that its discursive conditions are apparent in the texts we need and value and are able to reinterpret and promote anew. To argue that such knowledge—provisional knowledge of our own time—is either trivial or contaminating, preferably to be rejected in favor of some more permanent truth, is, curiously, to deny any significance to our own historical moment or to our lives within it. On the other hand, recognizing that the will to recover certain texts is historically produced can lead us to see how our literary "taste" is not a superficial phenomenon but one embedded within the productive relations of our history, one that points to the nature of our time and to the contemporary relations between choice and constraint. To write criticism is thus, in Barthes's words again, to decide "which texts would I consent to write (to re-write), to desire, to put forth as a force in this world of mine" (p. 4). Literary history is never an innocent process of recovery. We recover what we are culturally and psychologically prepared to recover and what we "recover" we necessarily rewrite, giving it meanings that are inescapably contemporary, giving it a new discursive life in the present, a life it cannot have had before. A text can gain that new life in part through an effort to understand what cultural work it may have been able to do in an earlier time, but that understanding, again, is located in our own time. If the effort to understand past cultural projects can only become authentic when we demonstrate that we have transcended our own historical entanglements, then such efforts will never be authentic. Though one cannot ever stand outside this hermeneutic circle or even decisively identify its components, one can nevertheless begin to accept the existence of its constraints and thus, at least intermittently, to recognize their pertinence.

The necessarily contemporary nature of what is recovered of the past is apparent not only in our own preferences but also in the recovery projects that helped shape the modernist period. This was the period, for example, when a reasonably accurate edition of some of Emily Dickinson's poems was published for the first time. Her unconventional style was honored and partly preserved in the 1914 edition of a selection of her poems because we were finally culturally prepared to see it as a meaningful innovation. In the process, she was seen as a precursor of modernism—Amy Lowell and others saw her specifically as an early imagist—and her poetry was reread in the context of a cultural revolution she could hardly have forseen herself.

Yet in "recovering" a text, in urging others to join the process of rediscovery and new valorization, we often imagine we might succeed in placing a text permanently on the social stage of literariness. But that is not really something we have ever had the power to accomplish. Everything, in time, is lost, forgotten, or repressed anew. Even if a text remains in the foreground of the literary history we continue to retell and revise, it will be reinterpreted and embedded in new cultural contexts and thus in time inevitably acquire meaning that bears no relation to the bases of our own interest; judged by any standard of meaning, tested against any demonstrable notion of identity, it will have become another text. Even if our interpretations do survive for a time, even if our textual priorities continue to have influence, that will not be because they are valid or intrinsically persuasive but because they happen, usually unpredictably, to remain pertinent to either changed or similar institutional and historical circumstances. Yet none of this presents us with a catastrophic level of uncertainty, for none of it prevents us from giving a text value in our own time.

This measured language may mask the substantial difficulties this position can generate. A recent book on nineteenth-century American fiction argues convincingly that a properly historical understanding of literary texts should be based on articulating the cultural work they were designed to do in their own time. The author acknowledges, however, that a reconstruction of this sort is "as much determined by the attitudes and values of the interpreter as is the explication of literary works."[13] Her "reading of the historical materials," she adds, grows "directly from the circumstances, interests, and aims that have constituted me as a literary critic" (p. xiii). The problem, not just for this critic but for all of us, is how to proceed so as to remain true to this recognition. How does one register this double historical awareness as one writes? Can one sort out and deal with (or even regularly acknowledge) the multiple historical determinations at work in one's own critical prose? It is actually quite difficult to put in practice the recognition that objective historical knowledge is impossible. In many ways that is something we do not yet know how to do.[14]

Yet the last thing a politically committed criticism needs to do—perhaps the major temptation it should avoid as we near the end of this relativistic century—is to reassert a stable, positivistic sense of the availability of historical facticity and adjudicable literary meaning. Of course many modern poets, both on the right and on the left, believed they knew the truth of history. But that is one way we may differ from those earlier generations. Among the lessons to be learned from the fulcrum events that helped propel us into postmodernity—from the Holocaust to Hiroshima—is that the truth of history is literally unspeakable. History, indeed, is unspeakable in both senses of the word; it is horrific and unutterable. The singularity of these events puts them beyond description, beyond the capacities of a language contaminated with prior uses. No familiar metaphors—no metaphors we can endure—are tolerable as representations of our historical ground. Yet any commentary, paradoxically, also seems an unacceptable, new, and false construction, a trivializing supplement to a primary meaning we can neither grasp nor reproduce. The reality of these events is incontestable, and they seem decisive in a way that exceeds anything preceding them. But because no words can confirm their meaning they come to stand as irrefutable mute testimony to the inadequacy of language. And as the experiences of the Holocaust and the possibility of global nuclear war penetrate all of postwar existence, we realize they have other general lessons to teach us. After contemplating history's most elaborate social investment in mass murder and the knowledge that we have the capacity to destroy all life on the planet, we realize there is nothing that can be adequately named and comprehended. All meaning is inauthentic. *Nowhere* can the full text of history be established. Any discursive layer of facts we peel off for analysis inevitably distorts and betrays that whole whose essential character is beyond our understanding.

Since literary texts appear to be physically self-contained and stable on the page, we often persuade ourselves their meaning is decidable as well. We can certainly struggle usefully over what those texts mean to us; for texts previously ignored or belittled, our greatest appreciative act may be to give them fresh opportunities for an influential life. That discourse can include new constructions of the cultural work those texts may have done in their own time. But such reflection after the fact takes place in language that serves our needs and interests, language that would often be substantially unintelligible to earlier readers. Indeed, few of us would be eager actually to speak from within the certainties of the modern period. Would we wish again to proclaim Stalin's innocence, as did a number of poets of the period? Would we wish to be fully at one with Pound's economic and social views? Would we wish literally to take up Vachel Lindsay's project of describing Springfield, Illinois, as the golden city of the future? It is worth recognizing just how appalling it would be to recover such authorial intentionality so thoroughly as to lose ourselves in it. It is not merely that such readings would seem incredibly restricted but also that we would find the subject positions they entail intolerable. On the other hand, would it be useful to block speculation about Lindsay's aims and limit our understanding of his poetry to the experience of those who attended his readings? To ignore Pound's political beliefs? To deny ourselves the opportunity to share the poetic celebration of the unfulfilled and impossible proletarian revolution? Of course there are other subsets of the literary past of which we might imagine ourselves to be in possession. But neither the experience of authors nor the experience of past audiences for literature would be satisfactory forms of self-knowledge for us, even if we could recover them. I emphasize this because one component of a belief that the past can be recovered intact is often a tendency to idealize it unreflectively.

Yet some of the most successful efforts to open up the canon over the past two decades have exhibited just this kind of false confidence

about the appeal, availability, and certifiability of historical knowledge. We have too often heard claims that the experience of past generations—authors and readers—could be fully known to us and once
again mean for us what they have meant for others before us. Too
often we have been urged to feel again what authors felt in the 1920s
or 1930s. Too often we have set out to "recover" the semiotic effects
of texts from between the two world wars. Of course it may be that
the project of putting forgotten or suppressed texts in circulation
again required this sort of partly unreflective and untheorized zeal.
It may have been impossible to resist the complacently (and often
unconsciously) racist and patriarchal consensus among scholars of
American literature while simultaneously calling the epistemology
of that resistance into question. And the effects of opening up the
canon are certainly altogether to be preferred over the consensus that
prevailed beforehand. Without that effort to open up the canon large
numbers of readers of modern literature would still feel disenfranchized. Our culture would be substantially more impoverished. And
books like this one would not exist.

But now that the hegemony of the racist and patriarchal canon
has been partially exposed and discredited—it remains a potent but
wounded cultural presence—it may be possible to complicate our
notions of textual recovery. We have a different cultural environment for revolutionary self-reflection and self-critique than we had
twenty years ago. Even if we are still reading and teaching only a
small part of our modern heritage, the moral and historical grounds
for rethinking the canon have been firmly established. And theory
has simultaneously made a more provisional style of argument both
welcome and desirable. A move to problematize the project of opening up the canon can thus be seen as an alliance with theory rather
than an admission of weakness. It is time to recognize that the semiotics of this new textual environment do not replicate an earlier
system of meaning. We have put many texts into circulation again,
but they circulate in ways that are both familiar and unexpected.
Some meanings are recovered; others are new. But we cannot expect
to distinguish these kinds of meaning decisively. The total, mobile,
differential system of articulations belongs to our time alone.[15] To
accept that fact—and to work consciously within that recognition—

is to to take responsibility for the social meaning of the more varied textual past disseminated among us again.

This argument about the necessarily plural and overdetermined nature of efforts to reconstruct the past suggests that one of my opening metaphors—"a palimpsest of two durations, then and now" —is actually oversimplified. The palimpsest of overlaid durations is much more complexly layered. It is a like a continuing series of lap dissolves in film, in which each image, only briefly separated from those that precede and follow it, is itself a synchronic picture of a moment in time and its reconstitution and evaluation of the whole historical past.

At least in the modern literary era, moreover, there is no clear "then" and "now" except as these values are filtered through a series of literary histories that stretch across the years at issue. Here the writing of literary history is continuous with literary production. Histories of modern poetry began to be written in the midst of the modernist revolution. We continue to write them, but it is of doubtful utility to fantasize that, say, *Tendencies in Modern Poetry* (1917) by Amy Lowell, *The New Era in American Poetry* (1919) by Louis Untermeyer, *New Voices: An Introduction to Contemporary Poetry* (1919) by Marguerite Wilkinson, *First Impressions: Essays on Poetry, Criticism, and Prosody* (1925) by Llewellyn Jones, *A Survey of Modernist Poetry* (1927) by Laura Riding and Robert Graves, *A History of American Poetry: Our Singing Strength* (1934) by Alfred Kreymborg, *Negro Poetry and Drama* (1937) by Sterling Brown, *The American Way of Poetry* (1943) by Henry Wells, or *A History of Modern Poetry: 1900–1940* (1946) by Horace Gregory and Marya Zaturenska are now secure in their status as time-bound documents of literary history, "primary" texts in poetics—passionate expressions of local commitment that require our interpretive intervention before they can speak to readers of the present—while the critical histories of our own day are "secondary" (and potentially more objective) works of scholarship that communicate without interpretive mediation.[16] There is no metaphysical moment when the blade of conceptual objectivity cuts through literary history, dividing a merely lived past from a rigorously self-aware and disinterested present. Nor is there a gradual evolution from poetic expression to scholarly knowledge. Literary history is never written from the vantage point of a secure and stable distance. It is always written in the midst of—and constituted by—the multiple social determinations of literariness. We can never be anything other than participants in the stories we are driven to tell.

Indeed, we are embedded in a selective remembering and forgetting that often makes for considerable self-delusion, not only about what we know of our own past but also about who we are. A preliminary sense of what we have forgotten or suppressed, and are only now ready to "know" again differently may be obtained by reading the chapter titles of the 1946 Gregory and Zaturenska *History*:

PART I: THE "TWILIGHT INTERVAL"
William Vaughn Moody and His Circle—Three Poets of the Sierras: Joaquin Miller, Edwin Markham, George Sterling—The Barefoot Boy of Indiana: James Whitcomb Riley—A Note on the Poetry of George Santayana—Four Women of the "Twilight Interval": Reese, Guiney, Crapsey, and Teasdale—"La Comédie Humaine" of E. A. Robinson—A Note on Stephen Crane

PART II: THE "POETIC RENAISSANCE"
Harriet Monroe and the "Poetic Renaissance"—The Horatian Serenity of Robert Frost—Ezra Pound and the Spirit of Romance —Amy Lowell, Literary Statesman—The Islands of H.D.— The Postimpressionism of John Gould Fletcher—A Formal "Objectivist": William Carlos Williams—The Heritage of "The Yellow Book" and Conrad Aiken—Three Middle Western Poets: Masters, Lindsay, and Sandburg

PART III: THE 1920's
Donald Evans: Preface to the 1920s—Edna St. Vincent Millay and the Poetry of Female Revolt and Self-Expression—Elinor Wylie and Leonie Adams: The Poetry of Feminine Sensibility— "The Romantic Traditionalists": William Ellery Leonard, Louis Untermeyer, Robert Hillyer, and Mark Van Doren—Marianne Moore: The Genius of "The Dial"—The Harmonium of Wallace Stevens—Three Poets of Brattle Street: E. E. Cummings, John Wheelwright, Dudley Fitts—John Crowe Ransom, Allen Tate,

Robert Penn Warren, and a Note on Laura Riding—The Negro
Poet in America—Robinson Jeffers and the Birth of Tragedy—
T. S. Eliot, The Twentieth-Century "Man of Feeling" in American
Poetry

PART IV: THE 1930's
The National Spirit of Stephen Vincent and William Rose Benét,
With Notes on Lola Ridge and Muriel Rukeyser—Archibald
MacLeish and the "Invocation to the Social Muse"—The Lost
Generation of John Peale Bishop—The Critical Realism of Kenneth
Fearing—Hart Crane: Death and the Sea

William Carlos Williams and Wallace Stevens, neglected or forgotten thereafter for a time by academic critics, have chapters of
their own. Edna St. Vincent Millay is recognized as a partly feminist,
rather than merely romantic, figure, a perspective we forgot or suppressed but are now remembering and enriching in ways appropriate
to our historical conditions. Amy Lowell is credited as a "literary
statesman," a status we have long reserved for Pound. A number of
other figures now usually marginalized but being rediscovered and
reinterpreted—Wheelwright, Jeffers, Fearing—are given high visibility. And others, like Moody, whom we should read again, are given
salutory emphasis. Of course we are unlikely to find Gregory and
Zaturenska's essays satisfactory, since they do not include the kind
of close textual analysis we now demand. But their sense of what
individual poets one might value—and in what terms—is remark-
ably close to perspectives we have struggled to recover and recreate
in terms appropriate to our historical context, perspectives we often
erroneously imagine we are inventing for the first time.[17] Moreover,
their chapter titles alone show that Gregory and Zaturenska are not
burdened by the restricted canon that has largely controlled our view
of modern poetry.

*Repression and Recovery: Modern American Poetry and the Poli-
tics of Cultural Memory* should help explode the canon's more narrow versions of literariness that still dominate discussions of American modernism. That is partly the aim of the distinctly limited kind
of quotations I will provide. I rarely quote complete poems and make
no claim to have chosen the single best or most representative pas-

sage by a particular poet. This decision highlights a problem built into any effort to revive interest in little-known figures. A single poem by Eliot no longer has to represent, by synecdoche, the whole of his career; a stanza from *The Waste Land* will not be taken as accounting for *Four Quartets* as well. But what about Abraham Lincoln Gillespie or the Baroness Else von Freytag-Loringhoven? A poem by either of them is immediately taken not only as representing everything they did but also as their entry in the contest to determine who will be included in the canon. Though the fragmentary quotations I use cannot eliminate the tendency to take such passages as representative, as tests of excellence and potential interest, they can ensure that the evidence will seem insufficient, thereby foregrounding the issue and making the problem a self-conscious one. I want to resist the tendency toward decisive canonical judgments because my aims are different: to suggest the range of voices, styles, and discourses at work in the period, to point toward rather than wholly represent their writing practices, to provide possible entrances into their work, to raise interest in rather than settle the status of these poets, to identify poetry that may be able again to do useful cultural work in our own time. And finally to propose a general reconsideration of the relations between poetry and the rest of social life.

MODERN AMERICAN POETRY AND

THE POLITICS OF CULTURAL MEMORY

1910–1945

n the received version that all of us know, twentieth-century poetry took a while getting started. One could argue, however, as many have argued who have seen the origins of our modernity recede under interpretive pressure, that a significant amount of modern American poetry—including poetry by Walt Whitman, Emily Dickinson, and Stephen Crane—was written before the century began. Moreover, a long tradition of political poetry continued to flourish in important subcultures and in moments of national crisis before it came to full fruition in the Harlem Renaissance and in the widely politicized 1930s. Except in accounting for poets displaying strong links with Romanticism or with the European styles of the 1890s, however, the dominant model tends to see modern poetry as making a decisive break with the past. Thus one is led to imagine that writers and readers of the first decade of the century spent their time in a kind of cultural and ontological limbo: waiting for modernism to begin.[18]

Alternatives to this version of early twentieth-century poetry—in which the birth of formally experimental modernist poetry is considered the only story worth telling—often take a still more dangerous route: constructing a contest between an aesthetically ambitious but distinctly elitist and apolitical modernism and a tired, sentimental tradition of genteel romanticism. Once our image of the period is contained and structured this way—once our sense of the discourses at work is limited to these choices—it is easy to feel that experimental modernism deserved to win this battle, for it is difficult to recapture the knowledge that these were not the only forces in play. But in fact they were not.

Of course no reading of modern American poetry is complete without a sense of the traditions Eliot, Pound, Williams, and others were reacting against, without a sense of how restricted the options for publication seemed when they first began to write.[19] Yet poets themselves often simplify the work of their contemporaries and their predecessors and categorize them as enemies or allies so as to gain an energizing sense of opposition and collaboration. But there is no reason why we should continue to ignore a variety of differences unacknowledged at the time. And there is certainly no inherent reason for us to oversimplify conflicts whose complications were acknowledged. Yet schematic, two-part contest models are a recurrent feature of the way we write literary history, not only of modern literature but also of many other literary periods. This pattern of recurrence ought to suggest that these binary models have as much or more to do with the discourse of literary historiography—with its aims, interests, and cultural functions—as with the field of differences in the literary past itself. Such melodramatic oppositions facilitate writing literary history by foregrounding conflicts that can easily be presented in narrative form; they then develop from gradual emergence through sustained conflict to victory or defeat for various combatants. In the process they often block our awareness of other past conflicts that can speak productively to our historical situation; thus they always suppress difference and variety, typically in quite specific and politically pointed ways. What's more, such models operate very efficiently, creating a logical structure that *seems* complete: a self-sufficient, balanced rhetorical system whose components can address one another indefinitely.

Employed to construct the history of modern poetry, this system appears to account for (and do justice to) all the poetry of the period. The genteel tradition thereby effectively absorbs all the American poetry written between the death of Whitman and the modernist explosion of 1912 and thereafter. A formally experimental but politically disengaged modernism in turn absorbs the varied and often politically focused discourses of the following decades. Yet other vital poetries and other engaged audiences for poetry were also at work. We have begun (with varying thoroughness and degrees of visibility) to reevaluate some of this partly forgotten poetry—including black poetry, poetry by women, the poetry of popular song, and the poetry of mass social movements—thereby giving those texts new connotations appropriate to our time, but the process has only begun. Much remains to be revived and resemanticized, rediscovered texts must be disseminated to wider audiences (some recovery projects remain quite marginalized), and we will have to realize that recovering forgotten and excluded traditions entails more than a series of individual additions to the canon. The whole way we do literary history and the role that literary history plays in shaping both our cultural memory and our present options need to be rethought. As one critic wrote in 1983, making an argument that the profession has not yet been ready to heed, "the major issue is not assimilating some long-forgotten works or authors into the existing categories; rather, it is reconstructing historical understanding to make it inclusive and explanatory instead of narrowing and arbitrary."[20]

As one begins to reread both poets now classed as minor and poets essentially written out of the story of modern literature, one discovers, for example, that traditional forms continued to do vital cultural work throughout this period. Far from being preeminently genteel, poetry in traditional forms was a frequent vehicle for sharply focused social commentary. Poets were thus often quite successful at making concise, paradigmatic statements about social life. Freed from the need to provide extended analysis or support a thesis with detailed evidence, poetry instead could highlight both the most basic structures of oppression in the culture and the fundamental principles that positive change should observe. Countee Cullen's (1903–1946) "Incident" (1925)—a widely known poem by a poet generally viewed as relatively minor because of his preference for traditional forms— describes a black child's encounter with a Maryland resident:

> Now I was eight and very small,
>   And he was no whit bigger,
> And so I smiled, but he poked out
>   His tongue, and called me, "Nigger."
>
> I saw the whole of Baltimore
>   From May until December;
> Of all the things that happened there
>   That's all that I remember.[21]

"Incident" hardly says all there is to say about race relations in America, but it does point with notable economy to its continuing human cost. The violation of this childlike form by the word "Nigger" is more disturbing and effective than its appearance in a modernist collage would be. Moreover, the very innocence of the form makes the poem's pathos a productively self-conscious burden for contemporary readers. Much the same argument could be made about Mike Quin's "How Much for Spain?" (1937). Quin (1906–1947), now essentially a forgotten writer, was perhaps the quintessential Communist party poet, for he was ready to produce a poem about almost any current cause.[22] Here, however, he manages a straightforward and rather powerful text that is at once a pragmatic vehicle for loyalist fund raising and a call to remember the price some have paid for their idealism. A typical private paralysis about commitment is contrasted with those who publicly committed everything they had:

> The long collection speech is done
> And now the felt hat goes
> From hand to hand its solemn way
> Along the restless rows.
>
> In purse and pocket, fingers feel,
> And count the coins by touch.
> Minds ponder what they can afford
> And hesitate—how much?
>
> In that brief, jostled moment when
> The battered hat arrives,
> Try, brother, to remember that
> Some men put in their lives.

Published in *The Daily Worker* in 1937, Quin's poem was part of a broad effort here and throughout left culture to intensify support for the loyalist forces in Spain. Both in *The Daily Worker* and in other journals, highly accessible poems like Quin's coexist not only with poems that are much more complex rhetorically but also with poems embodying modernist formal experimentation. Indeed, one of the striking things about the gradual emergence of modernist forms in American protest poetry—from Arturo Giovannitti's prose poems of 1914 to Anna Louise Strong's free verse of 1919 to Lola Ridge's and Charles Reznikoff's imagist poems about immigrants in American cities, on through to the poets of *We Gather Strength* (1933) —is the lack of a sense of a radical break with the past. The thematic continuities in this hundred-year-old American tradition are so strong that a sense of opening out and diversification, of thematic conservation and formal variation, overrides the adversarial model of modernism wholly rejecting the more formal traditions in American poetry. The strong, common political commitments in this poetry turn the coexisting traditional and experimental forms published in journals and anthologies into a dialogue rather than a competition to be won. It was not, to be sure, always a peaceful dialogue. Poems designed for a mass audience were sometimes faulted for their naïveté, while complex modernist experiments were sometimes castigated for ignoring the needs of a mass audience. And the rhetoric of the genteel tradition and the rhetoric of modernism were often counterpointed in the work of individual poets. Nonetheless, an uneasy coexistence did persevere into the 1940s, and that is not the story we have chosen to tell about the development of modern poetry. Moreover, the anthologies and journals of the period suggest that the terms of the struggle between tradition and innovation were rather different than we have come to believe.

An overview of modern poetry offers a particularly appropriate occasion for rethinking both the prevailing versions of literary history and their underlying assumptions, for it is striking that, even for so recent a period, much is already forgotten even among specialists in this area. Despite our collective professional tendency to congratulate ourselves for dramatically opening up the canon in the past twenty years, where modern poetry is concerned there remains a great deal of interesting work that is largely ignored. Comparing the range of poets discussed in *Repression and Recovery* with the course syllabi collected in the 1983 *Reconstructing American Literature* will suggest how inadequate even recent revisionist efforts have been in representing the diversity of modern poetry.[23]

This partly reflects the tendency for people challenging the canon

to work within only one alternative tradition. We have specialists recovering the experimental modernism of journals like *transition* and
The Little Review, reversing the pervasive exclusion of women from
the canon, reviving interest in minority poets whose work was either
forgotten or never published, and rereading the almost universally
suppressed political poetry of the period.[24] These essential projects
should retain some discursive and political autonomy. A partial autonomy helps give them coherence and visibility. But their potential
to force a rethinking of the cultural forces that brought about such
interested blindness will be significantly curtailed if they remain
mutually exclusive commitments. We need alliances among people
working on these projects—and mutual critique by those engaged
in different subcultural recovery efforts—if the institution of literary studies is to be pressed into reexamining its assumptions.[25] Such
mutually critical alliances will not only have practical political but
also theoretical effects; thus comparisons between these projects
will demonstrate that it is misleading to imagine there has been a
uniform dominant culture and a single, excluded, alternative modern literary tradition. That merely reproduces the contest model
with different combatants. We need a sense of how diverse competing discourses were repeatedly realigned and reconfigured, how the
field of the literary was both constituted and divided against itself.
The only risk here is that the integrity of alternative traditions will
be challenged when they are seen to occupy a variety of shifting
and sometimes contradictory positions. But the potential gain is a
discipline less inclined to reproduce itself unreflectively and more
inclined to examine its cultural role.

Such a project can only be hinted at in these pages. I would not
want to suggest that any book could recover all the productive relations between the interesting poetries of the period. Indeed I omit
discussion of the work of a considerable number of poets very much
worth reading again. Furthermore, I emphasize the recovery of poetry
written from a left perspective, since I consider its broad exclusion
from literary history to be particularly instructive and I am interested in seeing what cultural work it can do in the present. In the
end, all the poetry from 1910–1945 merits reexamination, even the
genteel poetry of the mass circulation magazines, for it too helps

A. Miguel Covarrubias' jacket for Langston Hughes's first book of poetry, The Weary Blues *(1926).*

B. *Louis Lozowick's design for the frontispiece and jacket of* Unrest: The Rebel
Poets' Anthology for 1930, *edited by Ralph Cheyney and Jack Conroy, the second
of three such annual collections. The editors' names are listed in small type on
the jacket. Sixty-three poets are included. Roosevelt University Library.*

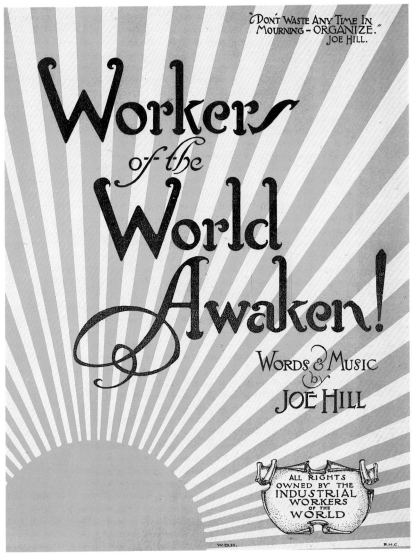

C. The cover to the IWW song sheet version of Joe Hill's "Workers of the World Awaken" (10½ × 13½, 1918). The quotation in the upper-right corner of the illustration comes from a telegram that Hill sent to IWW leader Bill Haywood just before Hill was executed in 1915. Baskette Collection, UIUC.

D. Alice Halicka's cover (7½ × 11) for the September 1923 issue of Broom, an international magazine of literature and art edited by Harold Loeb and others from 1921 to 1924. First published "by Americans in Italy," it later moved to Germany and then to New York. Sukov collection, UWM.

E. Edward Nagle's cover for the October 1923 issue of Broom *(7½ × 11). Broom's
contributors included Sherwood Anderson, Maxwell Bodenheim, Malcolm Cowley,
Hart Crane, E. E. Cummings, T. S. Eliot, John Gould Fletcher, Else von Freytag-
Loringhoven, Marianne Moore, Lola Ridge, Isidor Schneider, Wallace Stevens,
Gertrude Stein, Jean Toomer, and William Carlos Williams. Sukov collection,
UWM.*

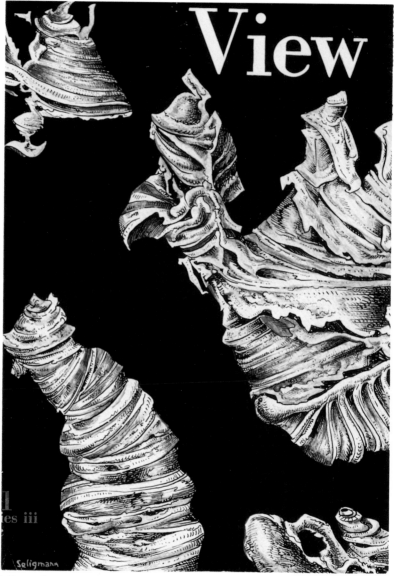

32

F. Kurt Seligmann's cover (9 × 12) for the April 1943 issue of View, an international
magazine of art and literature edited by Charles Henri Ford and published in New
York from 1940 to 1947. Sukov collection, UWM.

G. One panel (5¾ × 8½) of Weinold Reiss's endpapers for Alain Locke's anthology The New Negro *(1925), which included poetry by Countee Cullen, Angelina Weld Grimké, Langston Hughes, James Weldon Johnson, Claude McKay, Jean Toomer, and others.*

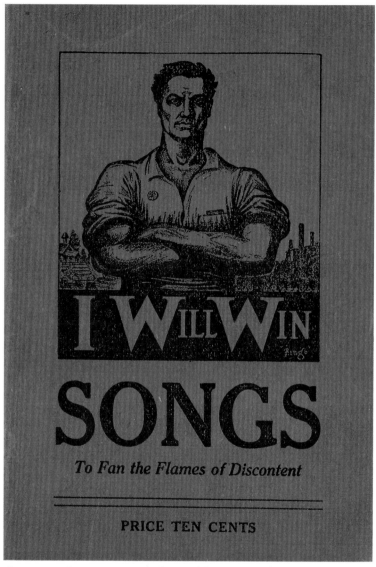

H. The cover to the twenty-second edition of the IWW's Little Red Song Book (1926). Illustration by Ralph Chaplin. The IWW's initials are used as the first letters of the words "I Will Win." On the title page, the subtitle is "Songs of life—from the mine, mill, factory, and shop." Chaplin's illustration was also printed in the August 4, 1917, issue of Solidarity and used as the cover to his 1946 pamphlet The General Strike for Industrial Freedom. Baskette Collection, UIUC.

define the cultural meaning of poetry. In its own way it may prove reactively and defensively modern.

It is remarkable how rapidly we lost the rich literary and social heritage of modern poetry. By the 1950s a limited canon of primary authors and texts was already in place. The names in the canon continued to change, but a substantial majority of interesting poems from 1910–1945 had already been forgotten. Academic critics had come to concentrate on close readings of a limited number of texts by "major" authors. University course requirements were increasingly influential in shaping the market for new anthologies. And the professorate, largely white and male and rarely challenged from within its own ranks, found it easy to reinforce the culture's existing racism and sexism by ignoring poetry by minorities and women.[26] Much of modern poetry was either out of print and no longer available in bookstores or never published in book form and thus forgotten in journals no longer being published. As the dominant social functions of poetry began to change in the 1940s, some poets found it difficult to publish their work.[27] Other poets, such as Mina Loy and Marsden Hartley, never made much effort to promote their own poetry, rarely sending poems to journals and showing relatively little need to assemble and publish books. That did not, however, mean they were any less committed to their writing. We tend to ignore evidence that promotion by oneself or others plays a role in building careers, preferring to assume it is the best poets, not necessarily those who are most ambitious or most widely publicized, who retain long-term visibility.

As a result of these and other factors, modernism came to be seen in part as an oppressive burden—the unassailable, unrepeatable achievements of a few masters. And it was not only literary critics who felt this way. Poets also believed they couldn't compete with the major modernists, that modernism left them no resources to exploit on their own. "We had been born too late," Hayden Carruth would write, "the great epoch of 'modern poetry' was in the past; its works, which we desperately admired, *The Waste Land*, *Lustra*, *Harmonium*, *Spring and All* and so many others, had been written long ago and had exhausted the poetic impulse. Nothing was left for us to do." For Paul Carroll it seemed "all of the major poetic discoveries and innovations had been accomplished." As W. D. Snod-grass argued, "that originally revolutionary movement had become something fixed, domineering and oppressive." For Robert Lowell, it was the "bitter possibility" that we were "the uncomfortable epi-goni of Frost, Pound, Eliot, Marianne Moore, etc." Richard Howard saw these poets as "certain enormous creatures like dinosaurs that crawl around on the earth's surface"; it was best to "try to keep out of their way."[28] We might describe such observations as a "reading" of modern poetry, but only if we give that word its broadest cultural resonance. For it is not merely a narrow reading of a group of texts. It is a reading of the literary past that helps sustain an entire vision of the contemporary world.

Yet this was our culture's perspective on modern poetry, not an incontrovertible fact of modernism itself. It reflects less the heritage and burden of modernism than the curtailed cultural space left open for poetry in the dominant culture of the early 1950s. If one begins to reread the whole range of modern poets, one finds so much in-teresting work out of print and forgotten, so many careers cut short or carried on without wide recognition, so many movements or in-dividual experiments derailed by literary politics or historical pres-sures, so many competing styles and projects, that modern American poetry seems less a fixed series of achievements than a fluid field of both fulfilled and unfulfilled possibilities, a continuing site of un-resolved struggle and rich discursive stimulus. Over and over again work never fully tested in its own time offers itself to us to see if it might yet do valuable work in ours. Writing about modern poetry means remaining open to that possibility. For we will be making judgments on that basis whether we admit it or not.

I would argue that the 1950s vision of modern poetry as ruled over by a small group of unapproachable giants—though influenced by Eliot's and Pound's criticism—has nothing whatsoever to do with the textual field of modern poetry itself. It is partly a powerful and blinding retrospective illusion, a highly determined reconstruction of the past by a later literary culture. The oppressive weight of the past that many poets felt was not something the past did to us but rather something we, as a culture, did to ourselves. We were driven, it seems, to preserve our past in an intimidating and attenuated form.

The collapsing of modern poetry's wild diversity into a hypostatized combat between literary titans mirrors the most simplistic of 1950s North American political world views. It resembles the ideological strategy of those who promoted a vision of a world contest between freedom and communism, the United States and the Soviet Union, with most of the world's diverse cultures simply invisible to us. That was how we reconstructed our recent literary heritage as well. But the modern heritage is richer and more variable than that; it can speak to us of possibilities not yet fully tried, not just of aesthetic and political opportunities completed, disproven, or closed off.

But it will not suffice to search for what we can now recognize as powerful poems excluded from the canon because of racial, sexual, aesthetic, or political biases. Although poets continue to be rejected on those grounds, these are not the only kinds of exclusion that influence our conception of American literature. Nor do individual adjustments to the canon necessarily lead us to recognize the general ideological structures undergirding the process of canonization or to confront the canon's problematic cultural effects: the ways in which the history of canonization is pervasively racist, sexist, and anti-intellectual; the way modern canon formation reinforces a romantic ideology of timeless individual achievement and a disdain for lived experience; or the way the canon polices our notions of literariness and the social functions of poetry.

The canon as it now exists serves as much to prevent (or at least to discourage) us from reading certain kinds of texts—particularly texts marked as disruptively political—as to ensure that what we have judged to be the best literature will continue to be read. It maintains a limited and apolitical notion of poetry in part by decreasing the chance that people will read poems that provide counter-examples. The canon, moreover, is linked with all the psychological, institutional, and economic mechanisms that reward us for studying the poetry most valued by the dominant culture. In excluding certain kinds of poetry from the dominant sense of the poetic—a notion particularly dependent on the canon's selection of admired and approved poetic discourses—we also thereby include within or exclude from poetry a whole range of cultural functions. A canon that chooses between William Carlos Williams' elegant love poem "Asphodel,

That Greeny Flower" and Langston Hughes's socially critical "Let America Be America Again" and makes such a choice a general principle of selection and exclusion quickly mounts very different views of what poetry is and should be; it also helps determine how poetry is to be articulated to all other elements of social life. The canon is not only a model of a particular culture's notions of literary quality; it is a guide to how literature should engage such matters as sexuality, politics, race, religion, and individuation. This becomes a decidedly anti-intellectual force when its results are fixed and unchallenged, since a stable canon tends to close the process of interrogating these cultural relations. They become naturalized, given features of our received notions of literariness. The canon suggests that both literary quality and the nature of literature's social relations are always already substantially decided, rather than being sites of continuing struggle and negotiation.

Also crucial are ideological linkages between the discourses of literary history and the processes of canon formation and transmission. If we suppose that historical research is mainly devoted to pursuing and explicating the best writing, we will miss much writing that helped shape both American history and American literature. We will also devalue and decontextualize much of what our generation judges to be the major literature that deserves to be canonical. But little is gained if, instead, we construe literary history as providing the context and background for the great literature of the past. Then a hierarchical distance opens between those canonized texts and the productive literary and social relations in which they were once embedded. When political and social history, along with "minor" literature, becomes mere background for our most idealized works, the relations between foreground and background acquire structural and ideological effectivity.[29]

Yet as the field of literariness is presently constituted, these structural relations are instrinsically incoherent. The distinction between major and minor literature is convincing only because it is unthought. Under even minimal reflective pressure the category of minor literature becomes impossible or radically destabilizing. When the concept is thought again, when such literature is read instead of being ignored, the category of minor literature becomes genuinely interesting. Yet until recently neither our teaching nor our writing brought this to pass very often. For the canon keeps minor literature elsewhere, outside textbooks, outside the textual domain of elaborate close readings. Set against literature at its most prestigious, minor literature provokes (and sometimes celebrates) a series of paradoxes: literature before literature, literature that is less than literature, literature that is unbecoming to literature, literature that has ceased to be literature, literature that will never become literature. As a category suggesting major literature in potentia, minor literature remains that which—but for the drag of circumstance—might have been major. When we read marginal works so as to understand major ones, to reconstruct historical contexts, we intrude a contaminating social materiality into the imaginative domain of literariness. Minor literature is thus an epistemological threat to the socially constructed transcendence of literary excellence. It amounts to a risky type of deflationary interpretation, a way of reading major literature that diminishes its idealized status. Nor is a continuum between minor and major literature a risk-free alternative; minor literature needs to be excluded as pathologically real, historical, and contingent. "Minor literature" is a contradiction in the imaginary of the profession: an impossible and obscene conjunction of determined facticity and imaginative freedom. The canon polices this epistemological threat, ensuring that if minor poetry actually becomes wholly "literary" it will cease being "minor."

So long as the distinction between minor and major literature is believable, the texts in the canon seem not only to encapsulate but also to master and transcend the essence of their historical moment. And that dynamic is articulated to a series of oppositions—such as spirit versus flesh, high culture versus popular culture—that devalue history and elevate the works in the canon. A national project to maintain the hegemony of the dominant culture thus comes into play, as we thereby marginalize or suppress alternative visions of American culture, homogenizing an idealized vision of American life by way of a limited notion of literary excellence. Canon formation and writing literary history thus feed into each other and become conservative, even reactionary, political forces, with potential for significant impact both on how the literary community participates in public life and on the general values of the culture. Working together, canon formation and literary history reaffirm that the dominant culture is the best that has been thought and said, sanctioning the silencing of minority voices and interests not only in the classroom but also in the society at large.

The canon, then, is not simply a neutral container for excellence. Even if we recognize that value judgments are entirely contingent, more remains at stake than the historical nature of literary excellence. The canon is also a network of aesthetic assumptions and social biases—and implicit cultural and economic priorities—built into and reinvoked by the range of texts it includes. The canon thus helps establish a metaphysics, a politics, and an ethics. It promotes certain cultural ideals and trivializes others. If, as one critic argues, "canons play the role of institutionalizing idealization," if they "preserve rich, complex, contrastive frameworks, which create . . . a cultural grammar for interpreting experience," if they demonstrate how "the very concept of imaginative ideals requires a dialogue between empirical conditions and underlying principles"—if canons can establish a limited number of texts as primary sources of a culture's images of political and interpersonal value—then it is even more damning that sexist, racist, and ethnocentric principles of canonical selection (and a narrow vision of political opposition) are inherent in the way "canons themselves may form the very society they lead us to dream of."[30] And these restrictive aims are sustained by all the canonizing discourses and institutions: from book reviews to scholarly journals, from normalizing critical histories to anthologies and reference works, from student handbooks and class reading lists to graduation requirements that emphasize "major" authors, from faculty hiring priorities to tenure decisions that privilege certain authors and disparage others, from convention programs to publishers's lists. Thus we never really encounter the canon in its hypothetical unmediated form of a ranked series of literary texts. We deal with the canon through a mutually articulated network of pedagogical and professional discourses. The power of the canon—and its ability to coopt efforts toward change—is in this complex web of texts and institutional practices. Yet as the kinds of texts included in the canon change, the nature of the canon can undergo some change as well, though not as much as one might wish. There is, however, significant potential for an unstable canon to open spaces for alternative discourses critical of the fundamental process of canon formation.

In challenging and expanding the canon—and problematizing its place in literary studies—we need to learn how to value, almost recreate, not only poetry we can now recognize as aesthetically compelling (the criteria for which are always changing and always ideological) but also poetry of significant historical and cultural interest. This distinction is not a dependable mechanism for permanently evaluating poetry but rather a working category designed, for this historical moment, to guarantee exposure to different kinds of texts and to destabilize distinctions between quality and historical relevance by making them self-conscious. Identifying texts of historical interest will trick us into personal and institutional change and multiple textual allegiances we might otherwise resist. This process will establish varied cultural roles for literariness—as opposed to a single, dominant notion of literariness overseen by the academy—and different, even contradictory, subject positions from which literariness can be valued. For literature can serve a variety of partial roles—not only for different subcultures but also for the same individual within different social and institutional settings—and we can occupy those roles without assuming they need to absorb our entire being or treating some as illegitimate. Indeed, this book is partly a record of the way my own reflections about the issue of historical interest have changed my taste in poetry.

Consider one example of a text we can place, for working purposes, primarily into the category of historical interest. In October 1941, Edna St. Vincent Millay's dramatic poem, *The Murder of Lidice*, written at the request of the Writers' War Board, was performed on the National Broadcast Company radio network and widely reported in the press. In rather simple, deliberately accessible ballad-like form, it retells the story of the Nazi extermination that June of the village of Lidice, Czechoslovakia, suspected of having briefly sheltered Reinhard Heydrich's assassins. (Heydrich was deputy chief of the Gestapo.) If the poem is mentioned today at all, it is typically dismissed as doggerel; critics tend to feel that it is badly written and that it debases the poetic function in its willingness to serve the state. This was, moreover, a role Millay filled more than once; her 1940 poem against isolationism, *There Are No Islands Any More*, was published as a separate book with the motto "Lines written in passion and in deep concern for England, France, and my own country"; her "Poem and Prayer for an Invading Army" was actually read over the radio as the Allied armies were landing in Normandy and then published as a separate pamphlet.[31] Whatever its interest, *The Murder of Lidice* clearly depends, for any claim it might have had then or now, on its relation to the major historical events of its day and on its public reading as a historically contextualized occasion.

Published as a book the following year,[32] *The Murder of Lidice* is pulled conceptually in two directions: toward giving a few of the victims (primarily one hypothetical family) specific names with at least rudimentary individual identities and toward a more generalized, mythic retelling that casts the poem as a folk tale. In the portion of the narrative that follows the second impulse, Heydrich sniffs at the village doors in the guise of a vampirous wolf. It seems clear that this form, unlike a comparably polemical prose report, is better suited to a symbolically choral performance by the American public. We are offered subject positions among those who might recite the poem. As a ritually repeatable poem, unlike a factual prose report that might be read only once, it is also potentially repeatable in fact. That, of course, was the point: to warn us, in the midst of the war, that this could happen in the United States as well if the war were lost. The poem's performance collectively reenacts our moral outrage and our danger. Thus *The Murder of Lidice* raises interesting issues about the special public functions of poetry in periods of historical crisis. It is also linked with all the political poetry addressed to a mass audience in America—from the abolitionist poetry of the mid-nineteenth century through the poetry of Whitman, Lindsay, Sandburg, and Hughes. It is not the noble task of literary history to tell us we need not trouble ourselves to read *The Murder of Lidice*. If we wish to achieve some mixture of distance and identification in our relation to the politically persuasive poetry of our own moment, if we wish to know what poetry might have meant to its varied audiences in the past and to remain open to its different cultural functions in the present, we need to know the history of the genre in our own culture.

That motive alone would justify our reading a poet rather more marginal than Millay: one H. H. Lewis (1901–1985), briefly known as the "Plowboy Poet" of Missouri. In Lewis's case, we are not dealing with minor work by a poet still read and admired but with a poet, like Quin, whose work is nearly extinct. A few of his poems are typically included in collections devoted exclusively to radical literature of the 1930s, but he is never included in general anthologies of modern poetry and is rarely cited in critical books on modern literature. A few brief articles on his life or work have appeared over the years, including Jack Conroy's essay "Poet and Peasant" published in *Fantasy* in 1933, but Lewis—like many of the politically engaged poets from 1910 to 1945—has no entry in the *Oxford Companion to American Literature* and David Perkins' 1200-page *A History of Modern Poetry* nowhere mentions his name.

Yet Lewis was quite visible for a time. He published in a surprising number of journals, including *The Left, The Rebel Poet, The Anvil, Hinterland, Scope, Blast: A Magazine of Proletarian Short Stories, New Masses, Poetry,* and *American Mercury.* He also issued four twenty-five cent pamphlets of his collected poems, which were available by mail from the poet himself: *Red Renaissance* (1930), *Thinking of Russia* (1932), *Salvation* (1934), and *Road to Utterly: Poems Written By a Missouri Farmhand and Dedicated to Soviet Russia* (1935) (figs. 1–2).[33] The four pamphlets were all published by Ben Hagglund, a Minnesota farmer who bought a second-hand printing press and some broken lots of used type and began printing little magazines and radical poetry on his farm in the late 1920s. Lewis's fifth pamphlet, *Midfield Sediments,* had reached proof stage, and a collection of poems and songs, *We March Toward the Sun,* at least had a formal cover printed, but both projects collapsed under the economics of the Depression.[34] Like the work of many modern poets, these pamphlets are now out of print; scattered copies are available only in a very few rare book rooms at university libraries, most of which will not copy them for patrons at other schools. It is thus difficult to read his poems without travelling to other libraries. But for a brief moment of history—a few years in the 1930s—he was a notable

figure. From 1930 to 1936 his work was reviewed in such publications as *Western Poetry*, *The Industrial Democrat*, *Earth*, *The Rebel
Poet*, *The New Republic*, *The Daily Worker*, *New Masses*, *Fighting
Miner*, and the *Moscow Daily News*. Translations appeared in Russia
and Japan. *New Masses* included him in its long list of contributing
editors and regularly featured his name on the cover when they published his work. This most public phase of his career largely closes
with the poems he published in *The New Republic* and *Poetry* in
1938, the same year that he won the Harriet Monroe Award for Lyric
Poetry. As Alfred Kreymborg reported, Lewis made one more appearance back East, arriving in New York with a large quantity of poems
in 1942.[35] He gave a public reading, borrowed a suit so he could have
his picture taken, placed a poem in *Poetry* and a number of poems in
The Daily Worker, and then retreated to his one-room house in Cape
Girardeau, Missouri, to live, unknown except to his correspondents
and neighbors, for the last forty-three years of his life.

If we have lost Lewis and others like him, it is partly because his
poetry does not generally display the surface indecision and ambivalence that many critics since the 1950s have deemed a transcendent,
unquestionable literary and cultural value. From that perspective,
the ideal political poem is W. H. Auden's 1937 *Spain*, a poem tortured by the impossibility of making a clear commitment to either
side in an imperfect world. Because it reinforces the English profession's ruling ideology of political indecision lived out in uneasy
inner anguish and external inaction, Auden's poem is often taken to
be *aesthetically* superior. In *Spain* no material choices can embody a
humanism uncontaminated with violence and thus there are no decisive distinctions to be drawn in the political world.[36] Yet for Lewis
such distinctions are often easy. Some would argue that his poetry
is therefore too simple, though the political, social, and aesthetic
issues it raises are as complex as culture itself. But his political subject matter does threaten the disciplinary conviction that literature
is a wholly independent cultural domain. Yet these judgments are
all interested and compromised, not neutral. They define not only
an attitude toward literature but also a highly determined position
about what role the advocacy of literariness will play in society.

Lewis perfectly embodies the academic's nightmare of the politi-

1. John C. Rogers' linoleum block design for the cover of H. H. Lewis's poetry pamphlet Thinking of Russia *(1932). Black on a grey background. Lewis Archive, Southeast Missouri State University.*

2. John C. Rogers' design for the front (right) and back (left) of H. H. Lewis's poetry pamphlet Salvation (1934). Black and red on a white background. Lewis Archive, Southeast Missouri State University.

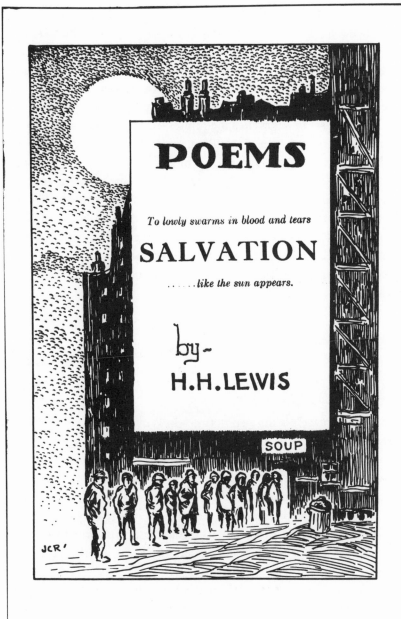

cal, for he is not only willfully crude and polemical but also wholly self-conscious. He is thus a hybrid figure—a poet who chooses (instead of being duped into) the straightforward rhetorical character of his oppositional politics; for this he represents an unacceptable contradiction. Indeed, by all accounts Lewis was a difficult man who was more likely to quarrel with the Communist party than to follow its lead. At his best, Lewis writes a compressed, sardonic poetry based in unqualified conviction. Capitalism he defines as "livelihoods at war." All national flags, he writes, are mere rags, "flagrags . . . a vision of war and more wars" (TR, 6). Lewis's is a poetry urging action, a poetry mixing practical skepticism ("metaphysics can result / In either a Christian or an Atheist cult") with renewed belief. In his playful "Thinking of Russia," America's whole history collapses for a moment under pressure from the merciless, willfully childish pun in the third line; it is as if the country is not worthy of a better conceit:

> I'm always thinking of Russia,
> I can't keep her out of my head,
> I don't give a damn for Uncle Sham,
> I'm a left-wing radical Red.   (TR, 1)

His more elaborate poems—sometimes in Whitmanesque long lines —are often, it seems to me, unsuccessful, at least when Lewis abandons the strong rhythms of his short stanzas, loses touch with his sense of humor, and lets the contesting rhetorical strands in his work become clotted. Throughout his work, however, issues are raised that retain their force today: the unfairness of the economic system, the vulnerability of the small farm, the untrustworthiness of nation states. From other modern poets he learns a willingness to coin words and a freedom in using dialect; to the farmer "plowin' undah cotton," he observes "He needs tuh luhn dat cotton / Ain't really meant fuh clo'es" (RU, 12) but rather for profit within a system benefitting the few. Lewis often uses simple, traditional forms, not only because he wants to communicate clearly but also because he is disrespectful of all pretensions and because traditional forms place him in more direct confrontation with the dominant culture.

He is also capable of offering complex theory in a wholly accessible form. Here is his witty, instructive version of the argument that consciousness is determined by material conditions:

> Here I am
> Hunkered over the cow-donick,
> *Earning* my one dollar per
> And *realizing*,
> With the goo upon overalls,
> How environment works up a feller's
> pant-legs to govern his thought.   (*TR*, 12)

The single best essay on Lewis's work—the only essay that deals substantively with his poetry—remains William Carlos Williams' "An American Poet," published in the November 23, 1937, issue of *New Masses*, the year after Williams had reviewed Lewis's work in *Poetry*.[37] Williams quotes lines he admires, applauds Lewis's fervor, and urges all of us to consider Lewis's inexpensive printing and distribution methods. But he also points implicitly to what later generations would lose in forgetting Lewis: "Without saying that Lewis is important as a poet . . . I will say that he is tremendously important as an instigator to thought about what poetry can and cannot do to us today."

To lose Lewis from our cultural memory—a process literary historians have almost universally facilitated rather than resisted—is to flatten and homogenize the past, to deprive ourselves of some of its pleasures and some of its constitutive tensions and possibilities. We thereby establish ourselves in a more impoverished and restricted present. Lewis, moreover, while a unique figure, is emblematic of all the political poetry we no longer know we have forgotten. If Williams is correct, we need Lewis not only as readers or writers of poetry but also as American citizens. Otherwise, arguments about what political work poetry can or cannot do are carried on in ignorance about what political poetry already has done in the recent past. We cannot lose Lewis and other poets like him without both falsifying our history and losing part of ourselves, without having our present cultural and personal options curtailed, without cutting ourselves off from some potentially liberating and politically significant forms of verbal advocacy and social satire. To forget the conditions of our own historical existence, to forget how poetry has intervened in history in the past, to ignore what it is in American culture and in academic life that has led us to repress that knowledge, is thus to miss seeing a series of possible present actions simply evaporate, leaving no trace in our sense of what it is possible to do. Literary history, then, is deeply implicated in the ideological formulation and obliteration of cultural memory and in the process of establishing our current rhetorical and political options; its role is hardly merely that of conserving the past.

If the loss of Lewis helps deprive us of the strategic value of a political irreverence linked to popular wisdom, it is another kind of wisdom that we lose in failing to read the political poetry of the first decade of the century. William Vaughn Moody's (1869–1910) turn-of-the-century poem "On a Soldier Fallen in the Philippines" alone can suggest how an earlier political poem might alter the blindness of the contemporary moment. Unqualifiably opposed to U.S. armed imperialism in the Philippines, Moody nonetheless manages to distinguish between the ordinary soldier and official policy. "Let him have his state," Moody writes, "Give him his soldier's crown," for "he did what we bade him do." He will "never guess / What work we set him to":

> Let him never dream that his bullet's scream
>   went wide of its island mark,
> Home to the heart of his darling land where she
>   stumbled and sinned in the dark.[38]

The honors—"Let the great bells toll," Moody writes—therefore, are hollow, and they are hollowed out here by a poem that uses conventional forms to undermine conventions of patriotism. But Moody also manages to see the common soldier as a victim of the culture's ideology, rather than as a figure of evil. That was a distinction, notably, that neither the poets writing about the Vietnam war in the 1960s and 1970s nor the left in general was able to make. In well-known antiwar poems by poets like Robert Bly, Galway Kinnell,

Denise Levertov, and others the ordinary soldier is almost always a figure of unqualified evil.[39] I would not want to claim that Moody's poetry alone could have awakened us to the class realities at issue in getting soldiers into the infantry during Vietnam, but it clearly offers a perspective that might have helped.

There are some academic practices we should change if we want to preserve the texts that prompt discussion of such issues. If, for example, literary history continues mainly to evaluate texts for the canon, we may recover some forgotten poets, but we will probably resist large-scale rereadings of our literary past, thinking that individual cases are all that matter. We will also continue the risky practice of reassigning some careers to oblivion, thinking that the objective quality of a poet's work is all that is at stake in such cultural erasures. We should instead take it as axiomatic that texts that were widely read or influential need to retain an active place in our sense of literary history, whether or not we happen, at present, to judge them to be of high quality. Our tendency to regard the taste of the past as quaint merely establishes our own time-bound position, not our ideal judgmental capacity. But reading what past generations have valued is not the only way we need to interrogate our own biases. We also need to reevaluate precisely those texts we habitually mark as mediocre. A second axiom, then, can be stated baldly: we should always read what people assure us is no good. Finally, we need to rediscover poets whose work is no longer even mentioned in most literary histories.

These principles should be central to the writing of literary history. For literary history should continually question the institutional memory of the discipline. It should resist acquiescing in the loss of any portion of our heritage. And it needs continually to ask a series of questions: What have we entirely forgotten and why? How has the selectivity of our literary memory facilitated and inhibited (and been directed by) our development as a culture? How might both the present and the future be altered if we rediscover the literature we have lost? That is not to say we can remember everything that has been written, or give equal weight to everything we do remember, any more than I have given equal weight to all the poets mentioned here. But we can resist the two dominant ways we explain the selectiveness of our literary memory—naturalizing the hierarchical ranking of poets or congratulating ourselves for those biases we do recognize.

If, as I stated earlier, it is impossible simply to "recover" a text —since no text can be unproblematically and thoroughly present in the culture's memory, since texts are not available either to consciousness or to cultural institutions in an unmediated form, and since we resemanticize what we do recover—it is now necessary to add, as my title suggests, that we cannot simply and unproblematically forget a text either. First, no texts are merely erased from our memory in a neutral and nonideological fashion. There are no innocent, undetermined lapses of cultural memory. The possibility of their erasure may initially be set in motion by their being stigmatized or scandalized (whether as outrageous, trivial, or inferior), and the scandal itself—even if it is no longer linked to exemplary texts— often remains in place as part of the institutional structure of what we do remember. In any case, both what we remember and what we forget are at once interested and overdetermined. Properly speaking, an absolute distinction between full recall and mere forgetfulness is impossible, since they are inextricably linked to each other. It is the collaboration between literary history and canon formation that makes this whole process of cultural recollection and forgetfulness seem seamless and uncontradictory.

As the discipline has operated for many years, literary history serves essentially as the gatekeeper for canon formation. Feminist and minority scholars have begun to challenge where the gates are placed and open them wider. But the gates are still there. Nor does the paradoxical notion that multiple alternative canons can coexist as options in the culture—a liberal fantasy that disguises the actual struggle for dominance—do anything to alter the restrictive role that canons play. Though canons have served different functions at different historical moments—and not all textual canons have even been preeminently "literary"—for a number of historical conditions canons have proved reactionary, repressive, and resistant to change. Thus it would be most useful for us if literary history and canon formation were separated more distinctly and became contesting cultural forces, with canon formation recognized as necessarily cen-

tripetal and elitist and literary history typically centrifugal and de-
mocratizing. Their present relation is one of unthought dependency,
with each providing unreflected support and grounding for the other.
The canon establishes and limits what would otherwise be the infinitely undecidable textual base of literary history, what has been
called the "potential canon"[40]—a universe of writing in which not
only the quality of literary works but also the validity of the concept of literariness is at risk—a vast body of writing more likely to
provoke anxiety than curiosity among literary academics. Literary
history, in turn, "proves" the primacy of the texts in the canon, nar-
rativizing their superiority, foregrounding their prominence among
both lesser works and the vicissitudes of history. Each discourse pro-
tects the other from the risk of recognizing its inherent intellectual
instability; each thus turns the other into a ritualized and substantially anti-intellectual activity.

The interlocking structures of canon formation and literary historiography have not, however, been equally weighted, despite a continuing tradition of aggressively alternative literary histories. For
some time theirs has been a relation of dominance in which the perspective and ideology of the canon prevails. If this were not the case,
if the writing of literary history and the process of canon formation
were mutually compensatory discourses, we would have seen very
different sorts of literary histories being written over the past several
decades. Authors given greater attention would not have their prominence treated as a fact of nature; the history of their reception would
be part of any evaluation, not a separate (and marginalized) field of
study. "Minor" authors would not be complacently dismissed. Literary historians would consider it their responsibility to try to write
sympathetically about, on behalf of, much of the literature they encountered.[41] Literary history under these conditions would almost
certainly not devote most of its space to explications of works by
what are judged to be the major authors, a practice that amounts to
little more than a celebratory chronological staging of the canon. Instead, literary history would tend to dissolve the canon in a range of
alternative discourses.[42]

We would be better served, then, if literary history and canon formation were openly hostile to one another, or at least if they were

competitive discursive traditions engaged in a dialectical relation of
conscious critique, instead of being the interlocking, mutually sup-
portive structures of the discipline. The values of the canon would
then be continually under pressure in literary historiography. Evaluation would be uncertain, a category for self-scrutiny, not a site for
fixed determinations.[43] If we want a field that is open to intellectual
challenges, canon formation and literary historiography should cul-
tivate a productive antagonism. This requires that both discourses
imagine themselves to be defending their own boundaries, that both
see themselves as threatened projects, that each sees it as essential
to counter the cultural impact of the other.[44]

In this hypothetical model of more consciously dialectical relations between literary historiography and canon formation, the two
discourses would still be deeply entwined.[45] But they would inter-
act by way of an aggressive dialogue rather than through shameless
collaboration. Since they would be energized by their active engagement with one another, by the effort to correct each other's excesses
or delusions, they would still be interdependent. Thus we cannot
simply demonize the canon and idealize literary history. They do
not have the mutually exclusive, self-sustaining discursive character that could justify establishing such a fixed opposition between
them. Moreover, even a revitalized literary history can never fully
achieve its democratic aims. Conversely, the effects of the canon
have not been entirely negative, since it has kept certain texts in
circulation. However bound up those texts are with hierarchy, their
full range of semiotic effects cannot be accounted for in terms of
their involvement in the repressive hegemony of the dominant culture. Nor can the publicity the canon offers be credited with all the
effects literary texts have within the culture. Canonized texts are
often recaptured by revolutionary interpretive practices, just as they
are often lost to more conservative readings. And noncanonical texts
play important roles outside the academy. Finally, twentieth-century
literary historiography is hardly an exemplary instance of reflective
and self-critical praxis.

The canon is thus not likely to be eliminated, and we will continue to make evaluative judgments (as I have continued to make
them here), though the aesthetic assumptions the canon embodies

will change as other kinds of texts are valued once again.[46] By virtue of what it includes and excludes, the canon will reflect both the best and the worst of a given culture: its interests and ambitions, its capacity for self-critique, its ideals, its delusions, its blindnesses, what it knows about itself and what it represses. But the canon should always be considered a transitory construct, one to be questioned, not just defended, though it will resist impulses that undermine its authority. To maintain that critique, again, canon formation and writing literary history need to be in continual crisis, challenging rather than reinforcing one another. For it will never suffice to aim for a wholly redeemed and democratized canon; the canon is fundamentally irredeemable. It never will be a primarily democratic force in the culture. To do away with the canon, however, we would have to challenge hierarchy and dominance in the culture generally, for the two are widely interconnected. That the profession of literary studies reflects these pervasive rhetorical structures is not surprising; it is surprising rather that we should imagine ourselves independently capable of extricating literature from the cultural semiotics of power and evaluation.

Another reason I recognize that hierarchical, canonizing cultural impluses cannot so easily be swept away is that I realize I have a number of internally canonized and devalued texts. Moreover, there are texts I regret finding relatively unable to do vital cultural work for current audiences. I would be pleased to urge people to reread, say, Max Eastman's (1883–1969) or John Reed's (1887–1920) poetry, but I cannot.[47] Despite his revolutionary politics, Eastman remained trapped in a genteel, idealized notion of the poetic. His work may now have interest only as a symptom of the cultural restriction of poetic discourse. Reed presents different problems. With the exception of his Whitmanesque "America 1918," first published in *New Masses* in 1935, his forced rhymes and histrionic poses now have little to offer. Yet I would also historicize my impulse to defend poems I do admire. I have no illusion that my views, even if persuasive to others, will hold forever. Nor do I imagine that claims about quality put me in touch with a realm of transcendent truth. "Excellence" speaks to what we value now, to texts we are capable of cathecting, celebrating, and reading with care. It is a contemporary structuring of the domain of literariness, a structuring that is necessarily political and ideological. While we might be comforted or challenged by imagining a culture in which the domain of literariness would not be hierarchized, such a culture is not the one in which we live and work.[48]

The most thorough modern hierarchizing of the domain of literariness is the canon prior to the concerted critique of the past twenty years. That recognition leads one critic to argue in another context that a "canon is not a literary category but a category of power."[49] But this suggests that literature exists apart from its institutionalization, that it survives despite all odds as an unsullied domain meriting unqualified idealization. I would argue instead that the canon structures literariness in terms of power; it does not so much overpower as *empower* literature in a particular (and selective) way, investing it with restricted but effective social meaning by giving it differential relations with the culture's other hierarchically elevated categories. If power is a constitutive structuration of literariness that gives it meaning, then power is inextricably bound up with literature. Power is an effect of that structuration, not an intrusive independent force. There exists no pure, socially uncontaminated "literature" in an ideal but vulnerable elsewhere that can be invaded by the canon's will to power. The canon at once empowers and disempowers, enhancing certain literary texts and capacities and suppressing others, both in terms of literature's internal hierarchizations and in terms of the social domain. Thus the canon speaks to and for other structures of power in the society. But then so too does every other way of granting meaning to literary texts. No purely literary categories exist; there are merely different ways of constructing the textual and social domain of literariness. The canon is thus not an extraliterary category. Although it is worth trying to imagine what literary life would be without a formal, institutionalized canon, it is not realistic to think we can easily make that change. We might, however, be able to adopt local, pragmatic, and temporary canons.

If I were putting together a reading list for a course on modern poetry—a course that would include other kinds of texts besides poetry—I would have some poems in mind as essential reading. I would not be willing to compile a list of the best American poems, but there are poems I would defend and want to share with others. But my notion of what is essential is contingent and temporary; it is an estimate of what is most pertinent to current negotiations between our shifting self-knowledge and the partly visible materials of the past. Our estimate of what is essential for us to read will thus change as our political circumstances change. My current reading list would include, among other texts, Gertrude Stein's "Lifting Belly," an unstably dialogic poem that seems at once to accumulate and deconstruct connotative effects, and Langston Hughes's marvelously polyphonic *Ask Your Mama* (1961), among the crowning texts of his career.

In reaching beyond the conventionally expanded canon of the 1980s—a canon that would be more likely to include Hughes's "The Negro Speaks of Rivers" and Stein's "Susie Asado"—to embrace these longer and less stable texts, however, we encounter several ironies. Placing these poems in a competition for dominance alters their cultural meaning and rearticulates them to values they might otherwise have some potential to resist. Nor does it altogether help, alternatively, to mark their otherness within the canon's hierarchical space, for an elitist impulse inheres in singling them out as the best feminist and minority poems. Opening the canon to a limited number of minority poems does not merely change the canon but also enlists an oppositional poetry in a hierarchizing, exclusionary cultural project. At the least, canonizing these texts means that others are less likely to be read. But the compromising effects also extend to affiliations with all the culture's dubious idealizing values. Even when claims about quality grow out of feminist and minority efforts to open up the canon, they may embody other unexamined biases and thus facilitate continuing ideological closure. Women minority scholars, for example, have pointed out that the canon of major black writers was largely male and thus substantially sexist. Thus even an expanded canon should not represent the whole range of works we read and teach and value. Seemingly ephemeral literature that once empowered large numbers of readers, significant subcultures, or a few key writers is equally important; this should remain a criterion for our attentiveness to poetry's place in contemporary culture. For poetry not traditionally part of modern literary history has sometimes played a powerful role in changing American lives.

One striking case is the *Little Red Song Book*, as it is widely known, published by the IWW (Industrial Workers of the World). Legendary among labor advocates and on the left in general, this essential booklet is basically invisible in English departments. Yet the *Little Red Song Book* includes some of the famous songs by Joe Hill (1872?–1915) that contain phrases that have since entered the American lexicon.[50] In his most famous song, "The Preacher and the Slave," Hill sardonically assures us we need not worry about social conditions on earth, since we will be rewarded when we die:

> Long-haired preachers come out every night,
> Try to tell you what's wrong and what's right;
> But when asked how 'bout something to eat
> They will answer with voices so sweet:
> > You will eat, bye and bye,
> > In that glorious land above the sky;
> > Work and pray, live on hay,
> > You'll get pie in the sky when you die.

Based on small song sheets that had been distributed by the union, an early edition of the songbook was published in 1909, but it was soon revised and expanded, selling hundreds of thousands of copies before World War II.[51] It remains in print today. Officially titled *I. W. W. Songs* or *Songs of the Workers* and subtitled "To Fan the Flames of Discontent" or "On the Road, in the Jungles, and in the Shops" (Pl. H, figs. 3–4)—the title and subtitle varied over the years—the four-by-five-and-a-half-inch booklet typically included from fifty to eighty songs in about sixty pages. It was designed as a deliberate cultural intervention. In addition to the songs, it supplied photographs of IWW martyrs and brief prose lessons: "There can be no democracy in a world ruled by industrial despots"—"for every dollar the parasite has and didn't work for there's a slave who worked for a dollar he didn't get."

Although Hill often composed his own music, most of the songs

I.W.W. SONGS

TO FAN THE FLAMES OF DISCONTENT

We Are
In Here
For YOU

You Are
Out There
For US

Remember!

GENERAL DEFENSE EDITION

▼

PUBLISHED BY

I. W. W. PUBLISHING BUREAU
1001 W. MADISON STREET, CHICAGO, ILL.
U. S. A.

3. *The cover to the fourteenth (1918) edition of the* Little Red Song Book *(4 × 6). As the title suggests, the covers were often dark red, though some covers were printed on brown or blue card stock. This cover had black type on a red background. The central illustration, by Ralph Chaplin, was reprinted from the August 4, 1917, issue of* Solidarity. *A great many IWW members were in prison awaiting trial when this edition of the song book was published. Carl Sandburg collection, UIUC. It was also used as the illustration for the small leaflet version of Chaplin's prison poem "To My Little Son," where it serves as a self-portrait.*

4. *The cover to the twenty-fourth (1932) and twenty-seventh (1939) editions
of the* Little Red Song Book. *Printed on both red and brown backgrounds.
This illustration was adapted from Robert Edmond Jones's poster and
brochure advertising the famous 1913 Paterson Strike Pageant at Madison
Square Garden. Baskette Collection, UIUC.*

in the *Little Red Song Book* are set to well-known existing melodies, a practice reinforced through much of the nineteenth century in American labor songs. Here, however, this had a double purpose. First, it ensured that people could sing many of the songs whether or not they read music. But it also had a more subversive aim: to empty out the conservative, sentimental, or patriotic values of the existing songs while replacing them with radical impulses. People in one sense, therefore, already knew the songs they would encounter in the *Little Red Song Book*, but they knew them falsely. The contrasting titles alone suggest the countervailing value systems. "Silvery Colorado" provides the music for "The Tragedy of Sunset Land," a title that retains the landscape metaphor but makes it negative rather than complacently idealized; "Take It to the Lord in Prayer" becomes "Dump the Bosses off Your Back," turning patience into impatience and replacing religious consolation with practical action; "Meet Me Tonight in Dreamland" is rewritten as "The White Slave," offering a brutal economic realism in place of the fantasy of idealized human relations. Sometimes the confrontation between the two songs continues throughout the text. "The Battle Hymn of the Workers" rewrites "The Battle Hymn of the Republic" while retaining many of its phrases: "Mine eyes have seen the vision of the workers true and brave . . . Their hosts are marching on." "The Banner of Labor" aims to give "The Star-Spangled Banner" a more pertinent and aggressive politics: "And the BANNER OF LABOR will surely soon wave / O'er the land that is free from the master and slave." These texts can help reopen the whole question of the political use of traditional verse forms, for the aim here is radically to resemanticize existing cultural traditions. Rather than adopt cubist dislocation as a way to resist the complacent world of the bourgeoisie, the authors of these songs mount an opposition from within the commonplace forms of the culture, thereby winning back both tradition and common sense from their articulation to conservativism. Notably, the IWW often included several poems in the song book, thus further unsettling the generic status of the collection. In the end, the *Little Red Song Book* is not only an irrepressible site of popular resistance but also evidence of a celebratory popular pleasure in poetry's satiric capacity to undermine bourgeois values. It is a witty, culturally self-conscious class pleasure that breaks through the high culture/low culture division in these songs.

Uniquely aware of the power poetry and song had to raise consciousness, build union membership, generate solidarity, and offer individuals discursive sites in harmony with the general values of the movement, the IWW also often placed illustrated poems on the front page of its newspapers. Three poets in particular—Ralph Chaplin (1887–1961), Arturo Giovannitti (1884–1959), and Covington Hall (1871–1951)—became identified with the IWW, built strong popular reputations, and have remained important to those interested in labor history and culture.[52] All were notably activist poets—so activist in fact that it is difficult to find comparable careers in North America now, though there are poets elsewhere in the world who combine writing with revolutionary action. Hall edited *The Lumberjack* during the violent struggle to organize timber workers in Louisiana and Texas in the years before World War I and simultaneously founded a secret terrorist organization for black-listed workers. Giovannitti was active in the Italian Socialist Federation, edited the radical newspaper *Il Proletario*, and helped organize the famous textile strike in Lawrence, Massachusetts, in 1912. Accused of murder by the state authorities as a way of taking him out of action, he was later tried and acquitted. Chaplin edited the IWW's *Solidarity*, designed covers (Pl. H, fig. 3) and drew cartoons for a number of IWW publications, and wrote "Solidarity Forever," the song that is virtually the anthem of the American labor movement. Chaplin was one of 113 Wobblies subjected to a mass trial in 1918. In an atmosphere of hysteria created by the government, he was convicted of over a hundred crimes despite the lack of any evidence other than inflammatory IWW publications; he spent a year in Chicago's Cook County Jail and five years in the Federal prison at Leavenworth.[53]

Bars and Shadows: The Prison Poems of Ralph Chaplin was published in 1922, including his famous "Mourn Not The Dead" that urges us instead to "mourn the apathetic throng . . . who see the world's great anguish and its wrong / And dare not speak!" But an earlier book, *When the Leaves Come Out and Other Rebel Verses* (1917) probably presents Chaplin at his best—combative, exhilarated with the possibility of radical action, uncompromising in his class antagonism: "Go fight you fools . . . Stand by the flag . . . Lay down your lives for land you do not own."[54] Some of these poems were also issued in little illustrated pamphlets, including *Salaam, Too Rotten Rank for Hell*, and the little multiauthor, eleven-poem pamphlet *The Rebel Poets* (fig. 5), which included Chaplin's "The Red Feast" and Sandburg's "Jaws."[55] The conflicting visual styles of *Too Rotten Rank for Hell* (fig. 6) suggest some of the verbal tensions in this sort of work, as the roughly sketched editorial cartoon on the cover competes for priority with the formal art nouveau design by Chaplin that decorates the opening of the poem.

Like Chaplin, Hall was also at his best when most confident and irreverent. Only a few of his many hundreds of poems are collected in his books, including *Songs of Rebellion* (1915), available by mail from the poet or the poet's printer, as H. H. Lewis's pamphlets would be twenty years later, *Rhymes of a Rebel* (1931), and *Battle Hymns of Toil* (1946), which continued to be sold by the IWW for many years after its publication. The opening stanzas of "The Curious Christians" are typical of his antiestablishment fervor:

> For "Jesus' sake" they shoot you dead,
> They fill you full of gas and lead;
> They starve your body, stunt your soul,
> Then pray to God to "Make you whole."
>
> They stand for war; with fervent breath
> They bless the instruments of death;
> They flap the flag, they shout for blood,
> Then weep beside the crimson flood.[56]

Giovannitti also wrote poems in a high rhetorical mode, a number of which were published in the *Liberator* in the 1920s, but his most interesting work is probably the prose poetry he published in *Arrows in the Gale* (1914) and thereafter. Using much the same form that Sherwood Anderson would soon adopt, Giovannitti worked to give specific spaces of confinement and liberation deep symbolic resonance for the culture as a whole. His characteristic irony is thus underwritten by a faith in utopian alternatives. "One Against the World" is a powerful antiwar poem:

THE
REBEL
POETS

Let other critics kill with curses
We sneak around with sawed-off verses;
And when with bard-shot we have filled 'em
Our victims never know what killed 'em.

Kieth Preston

Hand-set and Privately Printed
by a superfluous Printer
Price 10 cents

5. *The cover and title page of the pamphlet anthology* The Rebel Poets *(c. 1917). Baskette Collection, UIUC.*

TOO ROTTEN RANK FOR HELL!

Dedicated to "willierandolphhearst"

The Devil stood, as a Devil should,
  Near a pit of burning coals,
And without a word his red imps
  stirred
  A stew of dead men's souls.

And the caldron hubbled and bub-
  bled and boiled,
  And the red imps hurried and
  scurried and toiled.
And the vapors were whirling and
  curling that coiled
  From the stew of dead men's
  souls.

6. The cover and first page of Ralph Chaplin's pamphlet Too Rotten Rank for Hell (*c. 1917*). Baskette Collection, UIUC.

65

THEY SAID: Leave the plow in the furrow, leave the pruning hook
in the bleeding branch awaiting the virgin vigor of the graft;
leave the hammer on the anvil; leave the saw on the plank, the
awl on the last, the needle in the cloth, the bobbin in the loom,
the trowel by the wall, leave the unfinished task of peace and
welfare and love for the joy and promise of all men, and go to
war, sturdy lad, go to war. Your country needs you.[57]

"The Walker," first published in an IWW pamphlet, is an allegory
based on Giovannitti's own time in prison awaiting trial:

Wonderful is the supreme wisdom of the jail that makes all think
the same thought. Marvelous is the providence of the law
that equalizes all, even in mind and sentiment. Fallen is the
last barrier of privilege, the aristocracy of the intellect. The
democracy of reason has leveled all the two hundred minds to
the common surface of the same thought.
I, who have never killed, think like the murderer;
I, who have never stolen, reason like the thief.[58]

These are not, moreover, the only texts that destabilize the accepted generic and cultural divisions in modern literary history. To
take another case, when we include Langston Hughes's (1902–1967)
spiritual-, blues-, and jazz-influenced poetry in the canon, it becomes
intellectually indefensible to exclude (as nonliterary) lyrics by, say,
Gertrude "Ma" Rainey (1886–1939) or Bessie Smith (1896–1937).[59]
The distinction is maintained by claiming that Hughes merely uses
blues rhythms as the raw material for the higher activity of poetic
creation and thus that his poetry in no way blurs the distinction
between poetry and popular music. In fact, if Zora Neale Hurston
(1891–1960) is correct, Hughes sometimes appropriated passages
from such sources virtually unchanged. And one might argue that
the jacket to The Weary Blues (Pl. A) offers Hughes's book to us
not as a text with hierarchical or even differential relations to the
blues tradition (and certainly not as a high cultural improvement
on the blues) but rather as a direct continuation of the tradition, as
a collection of blues lyrics inviting accompaniment on the piano.
Moreover, the piano player's exaggerated fingers capture the double

consciousness of the blues; they suggest at once crabbed weariness or melancholy and a leap into rapture.

If the challenge to the canon's view of the privileged, culturally self-sufficient status of literariness implicit in Hughes's poetry is not widely recognized, it is because the current, somewhat more inclusive canon amounts to a form of liberal pluralism whose contradictory assumptions have not been confronted by the institution of literary studies. Real change in the canon begins to occur when the contradictions it embodies become great enough and sufficiently recognized so that people feel they cannot get along without working on them, talking about them, debating them. We may now have reached that point. Jostled together in the expanded canon's virtual space are texts with widely varying implications for our notions of both literariness and the social formation. By restricting literary study to the close reading of individual texts, however, New Criticism would have us serenely traverse these differences without setting them against each other or questioning their challenges to the norms of academic life. Indeed, the institutions of literary study have tended drastically to restrict the subject positions available for those interested in valorizing literary texts, a tradition that makes poetry useless to many and often politically irrelevant.

This ideology of "the poetic" is maintained in part by the repetition of the long-standing general insistence that poetry has no relation to "the popular." The bathetic, sentimental, conventionally religious strain in the idealization of the poetic—a strain fully informing the modern academic study of literature—is thereby kept not merely at a distance but actually invisible. Poets are canonized in part according to how they support this position, how they contain and mediate raw feeling and structure their whole relation to everyday life. Of course the subject matter of ordinary life enters modern poetry quite prominently, but it is offset by a higher degree of formal distanciation. Williams' "The Red Wheelbarrow" is perhaps the locus classicus of the risk in modern poetry that the distinction between form and the everyday will collapse.[60] Mainstream academic criticism often works hard to reinforce the separation between the poetic and the everyday. Notably, criticism of black literature has often aimed at exactly the reverse process, reaffirm-

ing and strengthening poetry's relation to lived experience and to
the cultural struggles in which ordinary people find themselves embedded. To the extent that minority criticism of minority literature
reinforces or celebrates literature's function of heightening everyday life and focusing social critique, it is easy to understand why
some minority writers and scholars resist the co-optation of their
work by the academy. Mainstream white literary criticism tends to
deny those very political and social connections. In ways that most
English professors cannot comprehend, the effective suppression of
popular art forms—in our case, jazz, the political poetry of mass
social movements, and song—and the rejection of the uses to which
nonacademic audiences put literary texts are explicit expressions of
class relations. The lives and experiences of disenfranchized populations, insofar as they intersect with poetry, are rejected as inferior or
irrelevant to the best of cultural history. English professors should be
pressed to explain why, for example, the poetry sung by striking coal
miners in the 1920s is so much less important than the appearance
of *The Waste Land* in *The Dial* in 1922.

Some of the more narrowly ideological grounds of the canon begin
to become apparent. If we fault Carl Sandburg's (1878–1967) studies
of working-class types for failing to present fully realized individual
human beings, this may suggest more about the power that romantic
humanism has over our sense of poetry than it does about Sandburg's
project. "The working girls in the morning are going to work," he
writes, "long lines of them / afoot amid the downtown stores and
factories, thousands with little / brick-shaped lunches wrapped in
newspapers under their arms"; "the muckers work on . . . pausing
. . . to pull / Their boots out of suckholes where they slosh"; the
fish crier "dangles herring before prospective customers evincing a
joy identical / with that of Pavlowa dancing," his gestures obliterating the high art / popular culture distinction.[61] If we reread Sandburg's work in terms appropriate to our own intellectual milieu—
these are not terms Sandburg would have used himself—then we
can say that, like many activist poets, he aimed in part to articulate
and humanize certain socially constituted subject positions, to depict types not individuals. In so doing, he would make these types
available to a popular audience, not so they could be regarded with

self-congratulatory empathy but so they could be reoccupied with a newly politicized self-awareness. Critics who fault him in this endeavor may feel uncomfortable with the argument that what we are as people may have more to do with our socioeconomic status than with any unique individuality we may possess.

Finally, when literature is provisionally contextualized—both within its own broader history and within American social history as a whole—some of the more well-known failures in modern poetry become as interesting as the established successes, and some nearly forgotten poets become genuinely exciting again. Indeed, we need to stop thinking of artistic failure as a statement only about individual tragedy or the weaknesses and limitations of individual character and begin to see it as culturally driven, as a complex reflection of social and historical contradictions, as the result of the risks of decisions made in a network of determinations. In that context Vachel Lindsay's (1879–1931) doomed fantasy of a truly public and participatory democratic poetry becomes, say, as important to our sense of the culture as T. S. Eliot's virtually decisive co-optation of modernism in *The Waste Land*.

In Lindsay's case, it is partly his failure to achieve his impossible ambitions—ambitions extracted from ideals circulating in the culture at large—that is his gift to future generations. Nowhere are the contradictions more marked than in the extraordinary *Village Magazine*, the illustrated book Lindsay designed himself and distributed for free in Springfield, Illinois. The first edition was published in 1910, but the book was substantially expanded in both length and physical format for the second edition of 1920. My own preference is for the striking third edition of 1925, with a dark red cover and a page size of just over nine by twelve inches. Illustrated with witty cartoons, elaborate illuminated letters at the opening of prose passages, and full-page drawings that mix Victorian, art nouveau, and art deco elements, *The Village Magazine* also recalls Blake by virtue of its illuminated poems and poems in Lindsay's holograph.

Intended to help the residents of Springfield imagine their city transfigured by a popular, democratic will to make it an ideal practical and spiritual setting, *The Village Magazine* unfortunately showed that Lindsay did not have a clear or effective grasp of how to reach a

popular audience with his whole visionary project. The magazine is
a kind of exquisite compost of contradictory elements. Urging "bold
arts that simple workmen understand," it also promotes an improbable and inaccessible mystical vision of Springfield "with the censers
of the Angels swinging over it," a vision that most people, simple or
not, will find either empty or incomprehensible.[62] When the illustrations are decorative, playful, or straightforwardly populist, however,
and not tied to Lindsay's arcane mystical politics, they can be quite
successful, and the prose, where Lindsay can work out the multiple
impulses in his ambivalent mission, is often genuinely powerful.
Regrettably, however, Lindsay printed none of his most successful
poems here—neither the poems for which he had become famous
nor the experimental poems he was writing in the 1920s—but instead chose his most naïve and genteel efforts. Risking far more in
committing himself to the literal regeneration of his local setting
than Williams and Olson would do later in their more narrowly literary reconstructions of Paterson, New Jersey, and Gloucester, Massachusetts, Lindsay also guarantees a more anguished project. Urging
the rejection of materialistic values, he also rejects all overtly political positions—"What has an orchard of Johnny Appleseed to do with
either capitalism or socialism?"—and thus relegates poetry to the
sort of vague inspiration that is guaranteed to have little chance of
motivating people either to change their lives or to see their circumstances differently. Lindsay's poetry here suggests in part how the
Whitmanesque democratic project will fail if it accepts the political
and aesthetic constraints of the genteel tradition. Ironically, Lindsay
does try to intervene in daily life—more directly than many of his
contemporaries, with his famous walks across the country and with
his effort to distribute his poetry to the general public for free—but
with a poetry in which everyday life has no place. Not only Lindsay's
sense of democratic possibility but also the psychological, political,
and aesthetic constraints that sometimes limit his effectiveness are
drawn from the surrounding culture. His career is embedded in its
time and becomes more relevant to us if we acknowledge that.

Concentrating on a limited number of major figures emphasizes
the heroism of individual achievement or the equally romantic tragedy of individual failure. Yet most poets work within a contextu-

alized sense of what is possible rhetorically: what innovations are made available to them by the work of their contemporaries; what tendencies are to be emulated, transformed, or resisted; what issues it seems necessary (or unimaginable) to address; what cultural roles have been won over or lost for poetry. If we want to restore a more full awareness of the discourses at work in this period, we need to regain a broader sense of the range of poets publishing in books, journals, and newspapers. New discursive tendencies—like imagism, the modernist experiments with verbal collage, or the poetry of minority resistance and cultural self-definition—are often established by a considerable number of poets, only a few of whom may survive the canon's restrictive vision. As a result, we lose the complex play of similarity and difference, stimulation and competition, that shapes the discursive options for poets.

If we shift attention from the poets of the canon and return to the journals of the period to find, say, the range of markedly experimental and avant-garde projects in progress in the second and third decades of the century, the most obvious difference is in the number and variety of poems being published. Although comparisons between the dismantling of representational forms in the visual arts and field effects in poetry are by now commonplace in essays on the aesthetics of modernism, the diversity of types of verbal collage has become partly invisible. Experiments in cubist dislocation are taken in numerous different directions—mimetic, mythic, personal, pop cultural, and socially critical. In that context, the dadaist and surrealist dislocations of Baroness Else von Freytag-Loringhoven (1874–1927, a German national who was part of the American scene for a time), which were never collected in a book and which ranged from miniature effects that explode imagism's long institutionalized referential claims ("be drunk forever and more / with lemon appendicitis") to long poems in an exclamatory style ("Chiselled lips harden—shellpale skin coarsens—toadblood OOZES in reddish pale palms"), make the verbal risks other poets were taking seem almost tame.[63] As the debates of the time demonstrate, the baroness, who was also a sculptor and an artist's model and who used her own body as a stage on which to perform dadaist cultural experiments, succeeded in going beyond what many otherwise innovative poets found tolerable.[64] But that was not her only contribution, nor the only thing we have lost in eliminating her from the foreground of literary history. What we have lost is a full sense of the political and cultural functions served by such aggressively disruptive poetic experiments. Freytag-Loringhoven and other women poets clearly found the new experimental techniques essential to a self-conscious critique of gender.

In a series of idiosyncratically gothic love poems published in *The Little Review* from 1919 to 1921, Freytag-Loringhoven dramatizes the cultural construction of sexual difference by hurling the sexes disruptively together. I "know a man," she writes in one of these, "harsh mouth—harsh soul . . . why should EVERY ONE fingertip YEARN to touch a frozen body"?[65] Like many of her poems, it develops by repeating and varying a cluster of phrases separated by dashes and punctuated by exclamation marks. The poems open at a peak of intensity and yet their energy typically increases as the phrases reform and implode on one another, with capitalized passages often taking over toward the end. "THERE IS A WIRE OF CONTACT IN THAT FLAME-FLAGGED CASTLE OF ICE." Her frequent archaisms effect a kind of inner violence on ordinary language and on the accepted models of sexual difference.

Freytag-Loringhoven's reflections on gender were by no means consistent or easily recoverable, but that is part of their power. In her long prose poem "Thee I call 'Hamlet of Wedding-Ring'—Criticism of William Carlos William's 'Kora in Hell' and why . . ." she targets the contradictions in male identity: "Inexperience shines forth in sentimentality—that masqueraded in brutality: male bluff" and "Thus to formula—male brute intoxicated bemoans world— (into that he never stepped)," but in poems like "MINESELF—MINE-SOUL-AND-MINE-CAST-IRON LOVER" she mixes ecstatic erotic overtures ("His hair is molten gold and a red pelt") with rage at the repressive limitations of male character—its defenses and its fear of contact: "He is hidden like the hidden toad." But even these classifications disintegrate in the face of the complex displacements carried out by her odd diction.

Equally radical and equally concerned with sexual difference is Mina Loy (1883–1966). Like Freytag-Loringhoven, she sometimes commits herself to an unconventionally dichotomous view of sexual difference and sometimes mocks and undermines it. Her diction is often idiosyncratic and oblique as well, though, unlike Freytag-Loringhoven, she works less with sheer excess than with intricately controlled ironies. In her case, it is important to read her work—including her long poems—aloud, so that her strategic pauses have the desired effect of multiplying divergent connotations and producing self-conscious irony. Despite their widely different styles, both these poets destabilize gender identities by exaggerating the received associations of maleness and femaleness. As one begins to credit that aim as a central project of modernism, Loy's unpredictable, brilliantly inventive antiromantic love songs take on a central role in defining the modernist sensibility:

> Spawn   of   fantasies
> Silting the appraisable
> Pig Cupid   his rosy snout
> Rooting erotic garbage
> 'Once upon a time'—[66]

Throughout the thirty-four "Love Songs," first published in *Others* in 1915 and 1917, Loy's erotic imagery is at once deflating and affectionate. It also manages to be both sexually explicit and ambiguous: "Shuttle-cock and battle-door / A little pink love / And feathers are strewn." In her most ambitious poem, "Anglo-Mongrels and the Rose," she turns these antiromantic vignettes of interaction between the sexes into a critique of the relations between the hierarchies of national culture and the hierarchized oppositions of gender. Her intricate debunkings of English upper-class culture link the impoverished ideals of empire with an imperial self whose sexuality is an attenuated caricature:

> Early   English   everlasting
>   quadrate Rose
>   paradox-Imperial . . .
> Rose of arrested impulses
> self pruned

of the primordial attributes
— A tepid heart   inhibiting
with tactful terrorism
the (Blossom) Populous
to mystic incest with its ancestry
establishing
by the divine   right of self-assertion
the post-conceptional
virginity of Nature.[67]

Equally innovative and surprising are the intricately theorized provocations of Abraham Lincoln Gillespie (1895–1950). Finally gathered into a book thirty years after his death, his texts are a conflation of pop culture and reflections on the nature of language; they define another of the outer limits of modernist experimental writing.[68] These passages, from his 1928 "Textighter Eye-Ploy or Hothouse Bromidick?," suggest that postmodernism was with us earlier than we usually admit. Gillespie collapses clichéd phrases into single, highly self-conscious words, combines words to coin new terms designed to sensitize us to language's capacity to motivate us and structure our consciousness, and in general satirizes the unconscious, determining power of verbal culture:

sweettrustmisery-Eyed hurtbyherMan-Woman
motherready-responsewarmth
cashregisterAnnote dissemINFO . . .
tender-regretreminiscEcho LETTUCE-crunch . . .
The necessity of 'impressionistic' begin-the-incarceration-
of-Grammar changes in Language-functivity may seem
    questionable.
A further step, then, is to suds a Fels-Napth at the
Express-Shirt of precipiThinking, commence-examining its
PhraseFront for Wot's-it-matter-how-much-the-Reader-is-
Overt Insulted bleedpleadCommunicate.[69]

Scattered through Gillespie's work as well are strikingly contemporary propositions about the problematics of interpretation. "Reading

Modern Poetry," published in *1933: A Year Magazine*, anticipates reader response criticism in declaring that "PUBLISHED POEMS BE-LONG HENCEFORTH TO THE VERY-READER'S ADLIB-REACT." A poem's meaning can no longer be controlled by the author's wretched, single-minded, godlike interpretive tyranny ("AwThor-Won-mond-interptyronny").[70] Moreover, like Loy, he recognizes that, when his positions run counter to the culture's commonplace wisdom, he cannot trust the received and connotatively contaminated language in which he works. Thus the witty difficulty of his style is a deliberate struggle with the assumptions of the culture and the predispositions of his readers.

As we begin to fill out our sense of the period, we realize that these works—along with the dadaist poems published by Walter Conrad Arensberg (1878–1954), the series of poems on death written by Walter Lowenfels (1897–1976) ("the skeleton only / of what the poem had eaten away"), the irreverent, self-consciously staggered lines of the final section of *Twenty-Five Poems* by Marsden Hartley (1877–1943, a painter who exhibited with the Blaue Reiter in Berlin in 1913 and who experimented with fauvism and expressionism), and the experimental poems from 1920–1930 collected in Kenneth Rexroth's (1905–1982) *The Art of Worldly Wisdom*—are all as necessary to our sense of the historically available verbal resources as, say, the now relatively familiar collage effects of *The Cantos* of Ezra Pound.[71] And the past few pages have only touched on some of the most obviously experimental poets whose work has been substantially forgotten. For the anonymous or essentially anonymous poems distributed as part of the mass social movements of the past century—from the poems distributed in rural areas by the Populist presses of the 1890s to the poems passed out on street corners during the strikes that convulsed major cities through the first third of the twentieth century—are as crucial to our self-knowledge as a people and to the development of some of the major traditions in modern poetry as are the poems we can connect with the careers of individual poets.

In the period at hand there is in fact an almost inconceivable variety of poetry at work in the culture. A kaleidoscopic passage across book titles, manifestos, and brief quotations gives some sense of the range of poetries in the period. By 1910, Gertrude Stein, Carl Sandburg, Ezra Pound, Vachel Lindsay, and William Carlos Williams had published their first (though not yet characteristic) books.[72] Edwin Arlington Robinson (1869–1935) was entering the final phase of his immensely productive career. Within a few years, several of the central discourses of modernism were already pervasively at work. In 1912, for example, Alfred Steiglitz's *Camera Work* published reproductions of paintings by Henri Matisse and Pablo Picasso, along with essays on their work by Gertrude Stein (1874–1946); Stein's pieces were offered as evidence of the postimpressionist spirit in prose. Harriet Monroe's *Poetry*, founded in Chicago in 1912, printed Pound's imagist principles in 1913. "Use no superfluous word," he warned, "no adjective, which does not reveal something," and, in a famous phrase, defined an image as "that which presents an intellectual and emotional complex in an instant of time. . . . It is better to produce one Image in a lifetime than to produce voluminous works." He went on to give specific advice about rhythm and line breaks: "Don't chop your stuff into separate *iambs*. Don't make each line stop dead at the end, and then begin every line with a heave. Let the beginning of the next line catch the rise of the rhythm wave, unless you want a definite longish pause."[73] That same year Stein's highly influential experimental prose poems, *Tender Buttons*, appeared in print:

A DRAWING
The meaning of this is entirely and best to say the mark, best to say it best to shown sudden places, best to make bitter, best to make the length tall and nothing broader, anything between the half.

WATER RAINING
Water astonishing and difficult altogether makes a meadow and a stroke.

A SOUND
Elephant beaten with candy and little pops and chews all bolts and reckless rats, this is this.

A TABLE
A table does it not my dear it means a whole steadiness. Is it likely that a change.

> A table means more than a glass even a looking glass is tall. A
> table means necessary places and a revision a revision of a little
> thing it means it does mean that there has been a stand, a stand
> where it did shake.[74]

Traversed by referentiality, haunted by it, in effect, because it is
structured as a series of definitions or titled entries, *Tender Buttons*
is also a writing space that displays a much wider range of linguistic
functions. Thus the sequence of entries can also be read as a random
sequence of compositional units, a contrapuntal dialogue, or a demonstration of the disseminative force of writing. The passage following "WATER RAINING," for example, may invoke psychological responses—amazement and incredulity—to the phenomenon of falling
water or suggest perhaps a visual "meadow" formed by sheeting rain.
But it can be taken as a response to the sound of the words as well. "A
SOUND" is at once a condensation of a circus or a zoo—"elephant
beaten with candy"—and a fantasy response to the sound of rain, perhaps itself a delayed reading of "WATER RAINING," which occurs
some seventeen entries earlier in the original text. But "A SOUND"
is also a playful paean to the sound of words and the reckless dissemination of meaning—"little pops and chews all bolts and reckless
rats"—to the "this is this" of her writing as it progresses on the page.
Distributing these and other effects across the surface of her writing, Stein blocked any single recuperative effort and thus demolished
assumptions about intentionality and the control of meaning.

But equally important modern innovations were taking place
where meaning was more narrowly controlled. Thus 1913 was also
the year when a remarkable theatrical event combining art and
politics took place. Aiming both to publicize and do fund raising for
the IWW-organized silk workers strike in Paterson, New Jersey, John
Reed wrote and directed an extraordinary pageant that was performed
at Madison Square Garden on June 7. A cast of 1,200 people, among
them workers and labor organizers, reenacted the main events of the
strike, including the walkout, the attack by the police, the funeral
of a worker, and a finale in which the cast sang the "Marseillaise."
A financial failure, despite its audience of 15,000, because of the
extravagance of some of the surrounding events, the pageant was a
considerable cultural and artistic success.[75] Unknown to most liter-

ary academics, it would nonetheless remain an inspirational model of revolutionary art for decades to come.

And in 1913 as well what remains the most important single art exhibit in American history opened in New York, the Armory Show (officially, the International Exhibition of Modern Art). The Armory Show introduced American poets to postimpressionism, cubism, expressionism, and futurism; the impact was almost immediate. *Camera Work* published Mina Loy's "Aphorisms on Futurism" the following year. "LOVE the hideous in order to find the sublime core of it," she wrote, "the Future is only dark from outside. *Leap* into it— and it EXPLODES with *Light*."[76] Responding in part to the provocations of Marinetti and the Italian futurists, while distancing herself from their sexism, Loy helped establish one characteristic form of the American poetic manifesto: a series of exclamatory aphorisms with insistent but highly metaphoric and unstable demands on our attention.[77] It initiates the declamatory metaphor, exploding in the heart of the ordinary logic of proclamation.

These impulses were rapidly both consolidated and advanced in the stunning journal *291*, which published but twelve issues in New York from March 1915 to February 1916. Juxtaposing manifestos, satire, and a remarkable range of verbal and visual experimentation, *291* demonstrated that self-conscious formal displacement put all the arts in a relation of revolutionary dialogue. Responding in part to the visual poetry Guillaume Apollinaire had begun to publish in France—Apollinaire's "Voyage" was reprinted in the first issue of *291*—the Mexican artist Marius De Zayas designed several pages of poetry and prose poetry to push the manipulation of the space of the page still further (fig. 7). If Apollinaire reproduced the discontinuous, simultaneous aural space of international modernity in "Ocean-Letter" (1914), and if the futurists showed that typographic arrangement could make the space of the page explode outward from a field of conflicting forces, De Zayas's 1915 settings for the collage and prose poetry of Katherine N. Rhoades (1895–1938) and Agnes Ernst Meyer (1887–1970) demonstrated that the textual space of the page could be stretched and turned upon itself, that its planes could diverge and intersect, that its volume could be sculpted. We have learned to credit this kind of inventive experimentation with the space of the page to Europe, but here it is in an American magazine in

1915. The Meyer and De Zayas 1915 "Mental Reactions" (fig. 7) turns the poem into a kind of roller coaster ride or textual pinball machine. We are propelled back and forth between different elements of the page; thus the relationships between the elements of the text remain unstable. Typography adds another element of defamiliarization, as "MYSELF" in elongated capitals becomes as much of a commodity as "PARFUM ULTRA PERSISTANT." Moreover, as with Loy's and Freytag-Loringhoven's poetry—the former's work already appearing in journals, the latter's due in a few years—Rhoades, Meyer, and others in *291* found these decomposed and radically rearticulated visual and verbal collaborations to facilitate the deconstruction of the culture's received notions of gender. In "Mental Reactions" the visual dislocations have the effect of counterpointing the conventions of male and female identity and the partial critique of them implicit in the poem's self-consciousness.[78] These effects were further enhanced by the dramatic format of *291*; its pages, nearly nineteen inches high, made each poem into a full poster. Finally, its juxtapositions of drawings and texts made for formal analogies of line, curve, and volume that remain provocative today.[79]

By this point, other major impulses in modern poetry were well established. Imagist poems, for example, had begun to appear in journals like *Poetry*, *The Egoist* (from London), and *The Little Review* and in collections like Pound's *Des Imagistes: An Anthology* (1914) and Amy Lowell's annual *Some Imagist Poets* (1915–1917). H. D. (Hilda Doolittle, 1886–1961), Lowell (1874–1925), and John Gould Fletcher (1886–1950) published volumes of their own versions of imagist poetry. Although he would have a later reincarnation as a conservative southern agrarian, at this point, with *Irradiations— Sand and Spray* (1915) and *Goblins and Pagodas* (1916), Fletcher was the ideal representative of imagism's less widely recognized, loosely descriptive, and impressionistic mode. His subjects include "the swirling of the seamews above the sullen river," "the iridescent vibrations of midsummer light," the "trees, like great jade elephants" that "chained, stamp and shake 'neath the the gadflies of the breeze" and

> Flickering of incessant rain
> On flashing pavements:

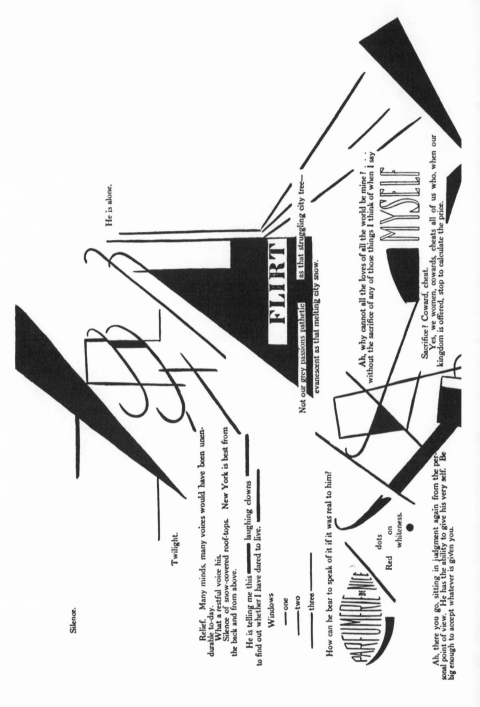

Silence.

Twilight.

He is alone.

Relief. Many minds, many voices would have been unendurable to-day.
What a restful voice his.
Silence of snow-covered roof-tops. New York is best from the back and from above.

He is telling me this —— laughing clowns to find out whether I have dared to live.

Windows
—— one
—— two
—— three

How can he bear to speak of it if it was real to him?

FLIRT

Not our grey passions pathetic as that struggling city tree— evanescent as that melting city snow.

Ah, why cannot all the loves of all the world be mine? without the sacrifice of any of those things I think of when I say

MYSELF

Sacrifice? Coward, cheat.
Yes, we women, cowards, cheats all of us who, when our kingdom is offered, stop to calculate the price.

Ah, there you go, sitting in judgment again from the personal point of view. He has the ability to give his very self. Be big enough to accept whatever is given you.

PARFUMERIE

Red dots on whiteness.

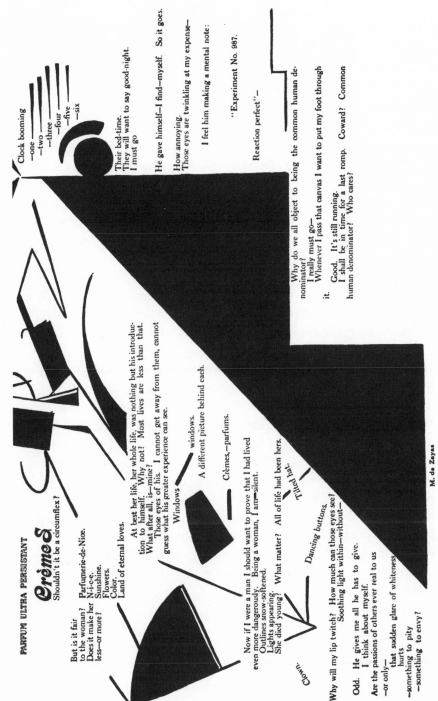

7. Agnes Ernst Meyer and Marius De Zayas, "Mental Reactions," *291*, No. 2 (April 1915). The original page is about 19 inches high. UIUC.

> Sudden scurry of umbrellas:
> Bending, recurved blossoms of the storm.[80]

He was also capable of indulging himself in "lacquered mandarin moments" and "crimson placques of cinnabar." With his tendency to echo the writerly excesses of the 1890s, Fletcher is already outside the tradition of imagist precision and restraint. But the group title of imagist is even more problematic for Amy Lowell and H. D. Subsequent scholarship, indeed, perhaps following Pound's inclinations, has sometimes used the term imagism as a restrictive label to limit our awareness of the power and range of women's writing. Lowell's work, in fact, soon became too diverse to be classified in any single movement. With H. D., even in the early poems there is too much throttled self-expression displaced onto nature, too much rhythmic invention, for her work to fit easily within imagism's more regularly anthologized mode of pictorial detachment. "Hurl your green over us," she calls to the sea in "Oread," "cover us with your pools of fir."[81] The presence of the speaker here, calling up a force out of nature and intensifying it, enlisting descriptive imagery in a vatic psychological demand, removes "Oread" from any of the conventional paradigms of imagism. Passages like this in H. D.'s work provoke a whole series of displacements and reversible oppositions. If nature is sexualized, psychologized, and placed in a dynamic, transformative relation with the speaking subject here, the same images invoke demands made of a lover and of the subject's own unconscious. Yet the dynamic psychological torque in this work does not justify assimilating H. D. to the expressive subjectivity we have long associated with lyric poetry. We are not simply in the presence here of a discourse of resplendent or imperiled identity. It hearkens toward an anonymous, sacralized voice, a ritual incantation, in which a transgressive otherness breaks through the discourse of identity. That is partly how we can understand the sense in "Oread" that the body is an animate landscape of vital forces. We cannot choose between such readings in H. D.; these semantic possibilities are simultaneously concentrated in and disseminated by her language.[82] What is clear, however, is that we cannot cast her poetry in the mold of disinterested description. Imagism's more familiar pictorial mode, on the other hand, we can represent with Charles Reznikoff's (1894–1976) descriptions of spring and moving water, in lines typically *not* anthologized, since Reznikoff is not generally included in the official pantheon of imagist poets: "The stiff lines of the twigs / blurred by buds"—"the ceaseless weaving of the uneven water."[83] Reznikoff's imagism, however, is also complicated by other impulses, both psychosexual ("I have not even been in the fields, / nor lain my fill in the soft foam") and social ("knights . . . laughing / at prisoners whose bellies soldiers open, pulling the / guts into basins."[84]

During the same time, Robert Frost also published his first two books, *A Boy's Will* (1913) and *North of Boston* (1914); Vachel Lindsay issued the poems for which he is best known, *General William Booth Enters Into Heaven and Other Poems* (1913) and *The Congo and Other Poems* (1914); Edgar Lee Masters (1868–1950) published *Spoon River Anthology* (1915); and Sandburg collected his *Chicago Poems* (1916), which had been introduced to readers of *Poetry* in 1914. The opening lines of "Chicago," with their strikingly varied rhythms, need to be quoted, for they can serve as a historical anchor for every subsequent effort—throughout the century—to rewrite the social meaning of poetry by importing traditionally "unpoetic" material into it. Here, perhaps surprisingly, Sandburg achieves his revolutionary effect by clustering one Whitmanesque long line with four short epigrammatic lines using devices familiar from the history of epic poetry—from formulaic epithets to personification:

> Hog Butcher for the world,
> Tool Maker, Stacker of wheat,
> Player with Railroads and the Nation's Freight Handlers,
> Stormy, husky, brawling,
> City of the Big Shoulders[85]

A few years later, Sherwood Anderson (1876–1941) published his often effective, Whitmanesque poems contrasting industrialized culture with the land, *Mid-American Chants* (1918), a book now rarely read in part because Anderson is classed as a writer of fiction. The tendency to identify writers with only one genre regularly draws attention away from some of their work, even with "major" authors.

But *Mid-American Chants* does not actually fit well in any genre. Indeed, like many modernist texts that include prose poems—from Stein's *Tender Buttons* to Toomer's *Cane* to Williams' *Spring and All*—it resists the institutional urge to categorize and thus succumbs to the relative marginality to which blurred genres are repeatedly assigned:

> I am pregnant with song. My body aches but do not betray me. I will sing songs and hide them away. I will tear them into bits and throw them in the street. The streets of my city are full of dark holes. I will hide my songs in the holes of the streets.
>
> All of the people of my time were bound with chains.[86]

Fourteen years later, in *The Kingdom of Smoke: Sketches of My People* (1932), one of the notable efforts at writing poetry for a working-class audience, Stanley Kimmel (c.1894–1982) would echo some of Anderson's populist rhetoric—as he would echo Lindsay in a number of his poems—with the coal miners of Southern Illinois in mind:

> God of the prairie, my people have lost their kingdom. They are captives in a land that once belonged to them. It is time for new men to come up out of the underground. It is time for my people to gather in the fields and break the chains that have been fastened upon them. . . . I have come up out of the underground to picture the story of my people upon a canvas of smoke.[87]

It is not that the works of these poets lie outside modernism but rather that it is constituted differently within them. Frost, for example, adopted traditional forms but resolutely used colloquial language and the subject matter of everyday life; for that he was recognized as a modernist and credited (even in *The Masses*) as having a revolutionary impact. But there are other levels at which Frost's textuality is inescapably modern; his apparently straightforward verbal surfaces begin to disintegrate under the slightest interpretive pressure and the poems become widely, if not infinitely, interpretable. Of course certain elements of Frost's poetry work against that kind of recognition. The tightly controlled forms seem to master the pervasive thematic treatment of doubt and irresolution. Often consolations are offered to us. But other forces erode these stabilities, from his affection for Dickinsonian riddles to strategic self-deflations. If some of his poems engage and thus appear to privilege religious questions, we realize from most of the rest of his poetry that Frost in fact does not believe, and thus that the apparent local resolution may be disingenuous. The Frost we are increasingly inclined to read, the Frost appropriate to our intellectual moment, not necessarily to all others, appears to be this Frost whose poems undermine their own surface wisdom. In "The Rabbit-Hunter" the final parenthetical admission that he himself has no comprehension of death suddenly deflates the preceding stylistic and structural confidence. "In Hardwood Groves" offers natural process as something one can be confident in, but then the speaker appears to be repelled by its power over him.

In summary, then, despite the fiction that imagism was a coherent movement with Pound's "In a Station at the Metro" as its defining text, one actually has multiple (even conflicting) versions of the imagist poem—from compressed, restrained observation to extended play with elaborate description to evocations of moments of psychological stress. Moreover, in the so-called imagist period in modern American poetry, we also see populist poems celebrating American life, a restrained and universalizing regionalism, radical experiments with verbal collage, and poems on the bankruptcy of American culture. And in February 1919, in Seattle, Washington, a peaceful strike beginning in the shipyards brought the city to a standstill. A poem written by one Anise, actually the pen name of Anna Louise Strong (1885–1970), was published in the *Union Record*, a newspaper that regularly carried Anise's poems and placed them prominently in a special box:[88]

> What scares them most is
> That NOTHING HAPPENS
> They are ready for DISTURBANCES.
> They have machine guns . . .
> But this SMILING SILENCE
>   Is uncanny . . .
> It is the garbage wagons

That go along the street
Marked "EXEMPT
by STRIKE COMMITTEE." . . .
And the three hundred
WAR Veterans of Labor
Handling the crowds
WITHOUT GUNS,
For these things speak
Of a NEW POWER
And a NEW WORLD
That they do not feel
At HOME in.

Close to prose, except, like many modern poems, for its line divisions, the poem makes use of capitalized words for both rhetorical emphasis and to imitate a sign on a truck. Additional indentations add a level of irony. It is, in short, a self-conscious, ironic, politically aggressive modern poem with significant historical meaning. Anise's specialized use of free verse narrative becomes more distinctive after reading a series of her poems in the actual format in which they were printed in the newspaper (figs. 8–9). In these two poems, "Damned By a Name" and "The Property Man," a series of three bold-faced periods separates each line and makes each line an individually staged unit. In other poems she uses exclamation marks or dollar signs between each line, though the symbol chosen remains the same throughout each individual poem. The argument of the poems thus paradoxically builds despite this forced formal repetition, which makes for a distinctively witty and self-conscious presentation of each line. Similarly, the frequent but irregular use of capitalized words—sometimes to honor terms she values, sometimes to mock concepts we take for granted that she wants to deride, and sometimes for simple emphasis—has the effect of spreading an unpredictable, unstable, wry self-consciousness across the whole surface of the language. A number of Anise's poems were reprinted in the *New York Call*, giving them some influence in the East as well, and a selection were gathered into a distinctive nine-by-six-and-a-half-inch oblong book titled *Ragged Verse* (c. 1920). They represent a

THE PROPERTY MAN
By Anise

In the Chinese theater
They have a person
Called the PROPERTY MAN,
Who stays on the stage
ALL the time.
He hangs up the SUN
When it is NEEDED,
Or he puts up the MOON
For a night scene
Between lovers.
He furnishes chairs
And tables and ladders
Whenever the characters
WANT them.
He is always the SAME,
Whatever the TIME
Or PERIOD
Or COSTUMING of the play,
He trots around
In the same clothes
With the same smile
Of superior cynicism,
Knowing
That all times and changes

And all the high sounding
ORATORY'
Is only ILLUSION
Played around objects that he
PUTS UP
Or PULLS DOWN.
The Chinese audience
Considers him INVISIBLE
And have trained themselves
NOT to observe him
For so LONG
That most of them now
Don't even SEE him.
There are folks who say
That we have such a creature
STALKING in our MIDST
And that all our world
Is just a STAGE,
And when
Our POLITICIANS
Make great GESTURES
Or indulge in splendid
CONTROVERSIES,
Or when our noble judges

Punish the guilty
And set free the oppressed,
As always happens in
The best of plays,
They say it is an ILLUSION
And that the REAL OBJECTS
Are PUT UP
Or PULLED DOWN
By an invisible creature,
Whose acts condition
All ACTORS.
Who is himself the SAME
In all ages,
Smiling the same smile
Of superior cynicism
At the virtuous platitudes
That cover HIS activities.
Some folks have called him
The "invisible government,"
But I think
The Chinese gave him
A simpler, truer name
When they called him
The "PROPERTY MAN"!

8. Anise (Anna Louise Strong), "The Property Man," from the Seattle Union Record (May 24, 1919).

key moment in the development of modernism and in its extension to a working-class audience. They also link free verse and the use of ordinary speech rhythms with an oppositional politics in a way that would seem decisive if her work were not largely forgotten. The adjective in her title refers not only to the ragged right margins and to the ragged surface produced by her capitalized words but also to a ragged, unruly mass revolutionary impulse.

Other forms of political and linguistic self-consciousness were simultaneously at work elsewhere in the culture. Dadaist and surrealist poems began appearing in journals. One would shortly see Lola Ridge (1871–1941) write in empathy with specific immigrant

DAMNED BY A NAME
By Anise

It was a good scheme
But they called it
By a BAD NAME
And that killed it!

I.
The war department
Started the plan
Of SHOP COMMITTEES
In their arsenal
At Rock Island,
And last September
The department announced
That remarkable improvement
In EFFICIENCY
Had resulted
These shop committees'
THEN
Somebody called it
SOVIETISM!
And that finished it!
For an attack begun
On the war department
And its little scheme—
And recently

They announced that they
Are GIVING it UP!

II.
In the Leavenworth prison
They started a plan
Of SELF-GOVERNMENT
Among the PRISONERS,
Hoping to make MEN
Out of WRECKS,
Instead of making WRECKS
Out of MEN!
The system WORKED!
And DISCIPLINE
Was better,
The breaking of rules
Almost STOPPED,
The prisoners learned
To MANAGE themselves,
Which is the first lesson
In MANHOOD
And in CITIZENSHIP!
Then somebody called it
"The prison SOVIET"!

And some ignorant senators
In Washington,
Who know nothing whatever
About men's SOULS,
Except what strings to pull
To get VOTES—
Denounced the war department,
And the self-government plan
STOPPED!
And the men are now
Like CAGED BEASTS
Beaten and hounded
And BRUTALIZED!

III.
Who was the guy who said:
"What's in a name?"
I guess he never had heard
Of Bolsheviks
And soviets,
For those little names
Have such wondrous power
They can be used to damn
ANY good thing."

9. Anise (Anna Louise Strong), "Damned by a Name," Seattle Union Record (March 6, 1920).

populations in the cities (*The Ghetto and Other Poems*, 1918) and Eliot consolidating a universal ruined modern landscape in *The Waste Land* (1922). Marianne Moore's (1887–1972) first two books, *Poems* (1921) and *Observations* (1924), were published at this time as well, establishing what would prove her unending and exemplary ambivalence toward language—meticulously arranging its very dispersal in quotation and description, paradoxically pursuing intricately nuanced disavowals of the self.

By then, the Harlem Renaissance had begun its sudden and prolific period.[89] Grounded in the long history of black culture in America, it was made possible not only by diverse theoretical writing by Booker T. Washington (*Up from Slavery*, 1901), W. E. B. Du Bois (*The Souls of Black Folk*, 1903), and others, but also, in part, by an unusual social configuration. Both during the war and after, blacks in the rural South were actively recruited by northern industries. They moved North in large numbers, thereby infusing Harlem with a substantial amount of southern black culture. There were also productive, influential, and disputatious relations with Marxist and socialist politics and cultural theory, many more options for publishing (especially once the federal government ceased its World War I suppression of black magazines), some patronage by interested whites (most of which did not survive the worldwide economic collapse of the 1930s), and the kind of conjunction of opportunity and social dislocation that often generates a need to write.

Claude McKay's (1890–1948) *Harlem Shadows* (1922) gave black anger new specificity and a much greater rhetorical range. Although McKay was out of the country during the height of the Renaissance, his poetry served an important and distinctive cultural function: demonstrating that poetry could offer condensed, uncompromising, emblematic versions of pervasive racial conflicts. And that is a function, moreover, that his poetry can still serve for us; indeed, his use of anger as both an aesthetic resource and a source of psychic integration anticipates the Black Arts movement of the 1960s. McKay is often faulted for his decision to struggle within the constricted sonnet form, but these criticisms generally miss the possibility that he was not only trying to demonstrate that black poets could master traditional forms but also, like other political poets, working to destabilize those forms from within. His poetry can at least open the possibility that we will never again be able to assume the sonnet form guarantees us the consolations of the dominant culture. It is sometimes precisely the unresolvable conflicts between the connotations of a received form and the new anger it contains that make his poetry interesting. Moreover, there is no reason to treat McKay's poems as though they were entered in a contest to determine the one true form of poetry appropriate to the Renaissance. The diversity of this period is part of its legacy to us. Some of his poems—including the famous "If We Must Die" and "Baptism"—are sufficiently abstract so that they can be rearticulated to an embattled heroism in any context, racial or nonracial. But in others, such as "Mulatto," first published in *Bookman* in 1925, the rage of a racially divided consciousness cannot be disentangled from its social causes:

> There is a searing hate within my soul,
> A hate that only kin can feel for kin,
> A hate that makes me vigorous and whole,
> And spurs me on increasingly to win.
> Because I am my cruel father's child . . .[90]

James Weldon Johnson's (1871–1938) anthology *The Book of American Negro Poetry*, with an important preface urging black poets to find new forms to express their experience, appeared the same year as McKay's *Harlem Shadows*. Langston Hughes began publishing poetry based on blues and jazz rhythms in journals like *The Crisis* and *Opportunity*. These impulses were soon consolidated in a series of books: Countee Cullen's *Color* (1925), *Copper Sun* (1927) (fig. 10), and *The Black Christ* (1929) (fig. 11); Hughes's *The Weary Blues* (1926) (Pl. A) and *Fine Clothes to the Jew* (1927); Johnson's *God's Trombones* (1927); and a number of anthologies, including Alain Locke's *The New Negro* (1925), with its classic introduction, Charles S. Johnson's beautifully designed and illustrated *Ebony and Topaz* (1927), and Cullen's important poetry anthology *Caroling Dusk* (1927). *Caroling Dusk* remains helpful in recalling many poets who are now marginalized and in stimulating comparisons and contrasts across the discursive space of Renaissance poetry.

The New Negro, however, may be the most indispensable book of the period. It demonstrates not only the widest ambitions of the Harlem Renaissance but also its multiple and differential achievements across all cultural domains: essays, drama, poetry, fiction, music. From Weinold Reiss's stunning, highly stylized mauve endpapers in an African motif (Pl. G)—endpapers that simultaneously make this cultural connection the framing device of the volume and set up a complex series of celebratory historical and cultural displacements from an African heritage to contemporary American style—and Reiss's sensitive, confident portraits—fourteen of them in color in the original editions—to the dynamic block prints by Aaron Douglas and the reproductions of African masks and sculptures, *The*

New Negro also shows the centrality of the graphic arts in the Renaissance. What Weinold Reiss captures in his endpapers is a mediated, ironic, self-conscious exoticism.[91] It is an explicitly contemporary rearticulation of African materials, not an essentialist claim of immediate and instinctual identity across cultural, historical, and geographical boundaries. The very wry playfulness of the style honors complexity and difference. Interestingly, although Aaron Douglas's powerful totemic cover for *Fire!!* (fig. 28) is a rather different sort of cultural statement, its decorative elements and figure/ground reversibility include a related element of deliberate play.

Related impulses carry over into a surprising number of the volumes of poetry of the period. Aaron Douglas did eight illustrations (and a jacket) for Johnson's *God's Trombones*, using an art deco style that was both decorative and suggestively symbolic. Indeed, in Douglas's prints the familiar radical diagonals of the deco style take on a series of specific cultural meanings: as vectors of black aspiration and ambition, as the leading edges of the emerging Renaissance cultural bricolage, as transcendentalizing recognitions of black suffering.[92] Charles Cullen's internal illustrations for *Color* and *Copper Sun*, recalling Beardsley's work in the 1890s, give the poems a self-conscious emblematic force that helps counter their occasional naïveté.[93] Cullen's masterful cover illustration for *Copper Sun* (fig. 10), its criss-crossing beams of light stretching across the front and back jacket, depicts at once a multilayered scene of racial conflict and a dynamic, confident gestalt that signals the book's cultural ambitions. Overall, the jacket creates a rich tapestry of varieties of blackness. Partly reflecting Charles Cullen's own mysticism, the illustration is also a complex gathering of mythic and historical figures that looks back to the poet's first book and foreshadows the opening section of this one. Many of the figures are racially or sexually ambiguous, so that such differences are marked but also implicitly destabilized or transcended. On the front, three figures with the lean bodies of dancers stand together in a posture that suggests the ambiguities of an elegant culture grounded in a history of bondage. For we may take them as performing a dance step or bound together against their will. On the upper right of the back panel, a tiny lynched figure hangs from a tree; beneath it a dark crucifix is carried across a field,

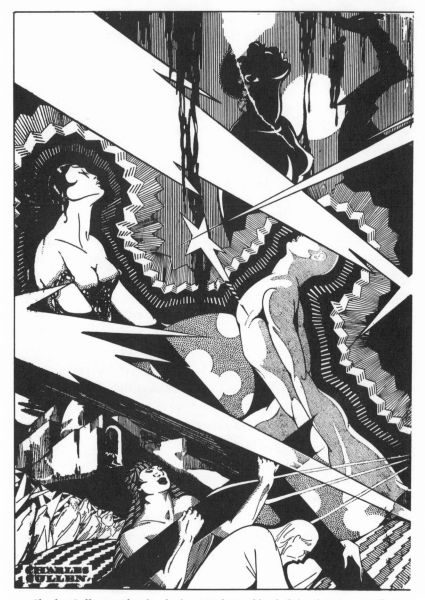

10. Charles Cullen's jacket for the front (right) and back (left) of Countee Cullen's Copper Sun *(1927). Black and white, except for the title and author's name, which are copper in color.*

thereby reinforcing a connection both Cullen and Hughes would invoke repeatedly in the figure of the Black Christ.

That connection becomes stronger still in Cullen's *The Black
Christ* (1929). Cullen's point, reinforced by the jacket of his book, is
not that Christ and all the lynched black men are identical but that
they are now linked together in multiple relationships of similarity
and difference. Charles Cullen's checkerboard cover (fig. 11) gives
this notion visual realization by making the two panels reciprocal
and equally weighted but different iconic forms. The jacket is composed of alternating square panels of a white Christ, crucified, with
bolts of lightning crossing the sky behind him, and a black man,
lynched from a tree. The checkerboard effect is reinforced by the fact
that the backgrounds of the illustrations alternate between light and
darkness. But powerful diagonals link the two kinds of images to
form a nexus of intersecting cultural meanings. Falling rain, tears,
or blood makes the cover as a whole one scene, as if viewed through
the multiple panes of a single window. In that light, the two images
form a reciprocal act of interrogation, in which racial and religious
guilt and expiation, as well as comparable cultural indictments, are
forever bound together. Yet the two images are not identical. Christ
is empowered by the dominant diagonal and vertical lines in the
image. The black figure is enclosed in soft curves that shape a cameo
of victimage. This relationship is complicated, however, by the extraordinary frontispiece by Charles Cullen that opens the book.
There the lynched black man is installed at the base of the crucified
Christ. The image is filled with radiating beams of light that flow
not from the white Christ above but from the Black Christ below.

In other cases, text and illustration are designed to be fully inte-
grated. Cullen's decorated borders for Charles Cullen's *Ballad of the
Brown Girl* (1927) and Prentiss Taylor's illustrations and borders for
Hughes's *The Negro Mother and Other Dramatic Recitations* (1931)
contribute to coherent verbal and visual projects whose elements are
not really separable. Taylor's opening illustration (fig. 12), surprisingly, simultaneously anchors the poem's political sentiment, with
his elegant conflation of a black soldier with a partial evocation of
a hovering Black Christ, and makes the poem's specific historical
irony (that blacks fought in a war to defend a freedom they never

11. Charles Cullen's jacket for Countee Cullen's The Black Christ *(1929). Black against pale gray, except for the type, which is in red.*

THE COLORED SOLDIER   1

A dramatic recitation to be done in the half-dark by a young brown fellow who has a vision of his brother killed in France while fighting for the United States of America. Martial music on a piano, or by an orchestra, may accompany the recitation — echoing softly, Over There, There's a Rose That Grows in No-Man's Land, Joan of Arc, and various other war-time melodies.

THE MOOD	THE POEM
Calmly	My brother died in France — but I came back.
telling	We were just two colored boys, brown and black,
the story.	Who joined up to fight for the U. S. A.
Proudly	When the Nation called us that mighty day.

12. Prentiss Taylor's design for the first page of Langston Hughes's The Negro Mother and Other Dramatic Recitations (1931). The poem continues on the next two pages. Four of the poems were also issued as long illustrated broadsides.

ing upon these studies is the assumption that there is no fundamental difference in the behavioral principles determining
originality and problem solving behavior generally. Both involve
the evocation of relatively uncommon responses, otherwise the
situation would not be called a problem or the behavior original.
This is especially apparent in connection with Maier's two-string
problem. Maier (1931) considers the pendulum solution to be a
consequence of productive thinking whereas other solutions
represent reproductive thinking. As indicated elsewhere (Maltzman, 1955) these problem solving behaviors do not involve
fundamentally different laws as demanded by Maier, but only a
difference in the extent to which initial response hierarchies are
modified. Furthermore, as far as can be determined this also is
the basis that Maier used for distinguishing reproductive from
productive solutions. The former solutions were given by his Ss
upon the initial presentation of the problem. Only after these
solutions were given and the Ss were told to find still another
solution, which happened to be the pendulum solution, did
Maier call it productive thinking. The empirical basis for the
distinction between reproductive and productive thinking, then,
was the probability of occurrence of the solution under his experimental conditions. The pendulum solution was relatively
uncommon and is original in this sense.

Several studies have attempted to determine, with some
success, whether verbal responses necessary for the solution of a
subsequent problem are present in the initial response hierarchy
of Ss (Saugstad, 1955; Saugstad & Raaheim, 1957; Staats, 1957).
The determination is made by obtaining word associations to
objects later found in the problem situation. Responses necessary for the solution of the problem are presumably uncommon,
have a low probability of occurrence in the initial response hierarchy. An association procedure has also been used to determine
the uncommonness of responses evoked in the initial response
hierarchy and their relation to subsequent success in the two-
string problem (Maltzman, Brooks, Bogartz, & Summers, 1958).

A series of experiments by Judson, Cofer, and Gelfand
(1956) is a limiting case of the use of textual responses in facilitating "productive" problem solving or originality. They employed
the two-string problem as the test and rote learning as the training situation. Instead of attempting to increase the occurrence of

uncommon responses during training and determining their transfer effects in the test situation, they induced directly the response chain necessary for a pendulum solution to the problem. A group form of the two-string problem was employed, and the Ss were required to write as many solutions as possible to the problem of grasping both strings simultaneously. The design of the experiment was to prompt a pendulum solution to the problem by presenting an experimental group with different lists of words, one of which contained the relevant response chain "rope," "swing," "pendulum." Additional control groups were employed receiving word lists including none of these words, one or all three but each in a different list. In this study as well as in two replications, the experimental group was superior to the control groups, although the differences were not always statistically significant. A further qualification is that these results hold only for men. No reliable differences were obtained among women in the various conditions. An analogous experiment was conducted employing a group form of Maier's hat rack problem, and comparable results were obtained. These studies suggest that repeated evocation of the critical words during rote learning increased the probability of their occurrence in the problem situation which in turn led to an increased frequency of the desired problem solution.

Another related study has been reported by Flavell, Cooper, and Loiselle (1958). Their study was designed to demonstrate that "functional fixedness" could be reduced by evoking uncommon responses to an object during a pretest period. In one respect it is more pertinent to the problem of producing relatively nonspecific transfer than the studies by Judson, Cofer, and Gelfand (1956), because the responses evoked during the pretest period were not the appropriate ones in the subsequent test problem. However, for our purposes the experiment suffers the limitation that it does not show an actual facilitation of problem solving performance but only a reduction in "functional fixedness."

A series of studies by Maltzman, Brooks, Bogartz, and Summers (1958) combines features of both of these experiments (Judson et al., 1956; Flavell et al., 1958) by evoking uncommon textual responses during a pretest period which are not involved in the problem solution in any obvious manner. Evidence of facilitation was obtained under these conditions. A screwdriver and a block of balsa wood were the objects available for use in the problem situation. Only the screwdriver was sufficiently heavy to serve as a weight permitting a string to swing in pendulum fashion. In the first experiment a control group was given the test problem without any pretraining. Lists of unusual uses for a screwdriver, balsa wood, and string were read by the experimental group before they performed in the problem situation. None of the uses referred to operations involved in the experiment. It was nevertheless found that the experimental group solved the problem significantly faster than the control group, and these results held for both sex groups. Additional experiments with modifications in the lists of unusual uses also obtained reliable differences between experimental and control Ss, but typically in the case of women and not the men. Many variables in this experimental situation are in need of further analysis. However, the inherent lack of reliability of the two-string problem as a test and the difficulties involved in obtaining experimental control over the relevant variables in the situation suggest that more fruitful studies of originality and problem solving generally should employ another type of experimental situation. Also, with respect to the study of originality, test problems of this sort usually involve uncommonness of response only by inference or by definition. A more direct measure of originality would be highly desirable.

CURRENT STUDIES OF ORIGINALITY TRAINING

Because they seemed to meet the desired requirements, tests of originality of the kind developed by Guilford (1950) and his associates (Wilson, Guilford, & Christensen, 1953) as well as earlier writers (Hargreaves, 1927; Slosson & Downey, 1922) were chosen for a more detailed experimental analysis of variables involved in training originality by Maltzman and his associates (1958, 1960).

In the first experiment in this series (Maltzman, Bogartz, & Breger, 1958) the Ss were run individually. All of the subsequent studies were conducted in group form. A modified free association procedure was employed in which the stimulus words were selected on the basis of their restricted response hierarchies. Since a relatively small number of different responses are evoked by the stimuli, a high degree of communality occurs among their responses. A control group received an initial list of 25 words to which they gave free associations and a different final list of 25 words to which they gave free associations. This was followed by the Unusual Uses Test of originality (Guilford, 1950). The latter test consists of a series of names of six common objects for which S must give different uses other than their common everyday use.

An experimental group received the same treatment except that the initial list was presented five additional times with instructions to give a different response on each repetition. A second experimental group was treated in the same fashion except that E said "good" after every approximately fifth uncommon response during training. Each of these three groups was subdivided prior to the introduction of the free association test list. Half the Ss in each condition were instructed to try to be as original as possible, and half were told nothing. Each of these subgroups were further subdivided prior to administration of the Unusual Uses Test and instructed to be as original as possible. These latter instructions may have been redundant, if not confusing, since the written instructions to the test already implied as much.

Originality measures were obtained for performance on the free association list by determining the frequency with which the responses to each stimulus word occurred. The mean frequency of his associative responses was taken as each S's originality score. Thus the lower the score the more uncommon are S's responses on the average. The total number of unique responses given to the items was taken as the measure of originality on the Unusual Uses Test, where a unique response was defined as a use occurring only once in the sample. Results of the experiment showed that both training and instructions produced a significant increase in originality on the free association test list. What is more, the experimental subgroups receiving training in addition to instructions were significantly more original than the control group receiving instructions alone, indicating that the training may produce its effects independently of instructions to be original. Results obtained from the Unusual Uses Test were ambiguous, yielding a significant triple order interaction where the experimental subgroup without originality instructions was significantly more original than its control group. However, results on the Unusual Uses Test from subsequent experiments have consistently shown reliable training effects.

Despite the above evidence indicating that the training procedure facilitated originality, additional information is needed to determine precisely what characteristics of the procedure are responsible for the effect. Differences between the experimental and control groups may have been due to the difference in number of stimulus words presented, number of responses evoked, number of different responses evoked, etc. The fact that different responses were evoked by the same stimuli may be neither necessary nor sufficient for an effective training method. Additional research was therefore conducted in an attempt to isolate the relevant variables.

In one study (Maltzman et al., 1960) the control condition and the experimental condition without verbal reinforcement or instructions to be original were again employed. The latter group received instructions to give a different response to each presentation of the same stimulus word. For convenience they will be called the standard control and experimental conditions, respectively. Two additional experimental groups received lists of 125 different stimulus words, the same number as the repetitions of the initial list for the standard experimental group. One group received high frequency count stimulus words while the other group was presented with relatively low frequency count words (Thorndike & Lorge, 1944). This procedure equated the experimental groups for the total number of different responses. They differed in that the responses all occurred to different stimulus words in the new experimental conditions whereas different responses occurred to the same stimulus words in the standard experimental condition. Another control group was added which received the same number of repetitions of the initial list as did the standard experimental group, but these Ss were instructed to try to give the same response at each repetition of a given stimulus. This condition would aid in determining whether the number of responses per se, or the number of different responses, is the relevant variable influencing test performance.

Results from the free association test of originality showed that the three experimental groups did not differ significantly from each other and the two control groups did not differ significantly. But each of the experimental groups was significantly more original than each of the control groups. On the Unusual Uses Test the standard experimental group did significantly better than all the other groups. The two experimental groups receiving different stimulus words during training did not differ from the standard control group, while the new control condition was significantly less original than each of the other conditions.

The results from this experiment indicate that under some conditions the evocation of a relatively large number of different responses to different stimuli may increase originality to the same extent as the method of repeated evocation of different responses to the same stimuli. However, the two methods apparently differ in the extent to which they produce transfer effects, as indicated by the significant difference between the two methods on the Unusual Uses Test. These results show that the evocation of different responses to the same stimuli is an important aspect of the standard experimental procedure, although arousal of many different responses by different stimuli is also effective, within limits.

The significant loss of originality by the new control group was not entirely unexpected, and shows that a training technique can significantly decrease as well as increase originality, a result which is of theoretical interest as well as suggestive for classroom practices. Exactly why the effect should appear on the Unusual Uses Test and not on the preceding free association test is not clear, and is a problem that requires further experimental investigation.

Another experiment (Maltzman et al., 1960) was designed to further explore possible relevant variables and alternative procedures for facilitating originality.

The standard control and experimental conditions were again employed. Another experimental condition was given repeated presentation of items from the Unusual Uses Test in order to determine whether the effectiveness of the training procedure is limited to only certain kinds of materials. This was accomplished by presenting the list of six items a total of six times with instructions to give a different use prior to each repetition. A different kind of training procedure was employed with a third experimental group. They were presented with a booklet consisting of 125 different pairs of words. The Ss were instructed to indicate the member of each pair which goes more readily with the stimulus word orally presented to them. The same stimulus words and number of repetitions as employed with the standard experimental conditions were administered. Each pair of words were unique responses to the stimulus words selected from the previously established norms. A fourth experimental group was given the word pairs and asked to indicate which member of each pair they thought to be more familiar. The stimulus words were not presented. Results of the free association and Unusual Uses Test showed that the standard experimental condition was significantly more original than the other four groups on both tests, while the other groups did not differ significantly from each other.

In one of the new conditions uncommon responses were evoked as textual responses following the stimulus words. In the other condition only the textual responses occurred. These conditions were introduced in order to determine whether the uncommon responses must be evoked by the stimulus words in order for the training to be effective. The fact that these groups were significantly less original than the standard experimental group suggests that, at least with the training and test materials employed, uncommon responses must be evoked as intraverbal responses by the stimulus words if there is to be an increase in originality in the test situations.

Since the experimental condition which received original training with items from the Unusual Uses Test failed to show a significant training effect, another experiment was conducted to determine whether the failure was due to an inadequate amount of training. Four conditions were employed in this study receiving different amounts of training. None of the groups showed a significant increase in originality on the free association test when compared with the standard control condition.

Results from the latter experiment and one condition from the previous experiment showed that training with unusual uses items in the same fashion as word association materials does not produce a comparable increase in originality. Thus the method of repeated evocation of different responses to the same stimuli does not work with all materials.

A basic assumption of our approach is that, if original behavior can be induced to occur repeatedly through some training procedure, it will increase in its frequency of occurrence in new situations. If this condition is not met, transfer of originality to new situations cannot occur. Inspection of the unusual uses training data indicated that an appreciable increase in originality did not occur during training. In the case of training with free association materials a marked increase does take place.

Another experiment was conducted in which different groups received 0, 1, 5, or 10 repetitions of the initial word association list before testing on another word association list and the unusual uses. A significant trend was evidenced on both originality tests, with a single repetition of the training list producing a significant increase in originality (Maltzman et al., 1960).

On the basis of the current dearth of relevant information, we can only speculate as to why training with unusual uses failed to induce an increase in the uncommonness of the responses. One hypothesis that may be offered is based upon the apparent relatively limited number of different uses available for each item. Given the instructions to write a different use to each repetition of an item and the inability of Ss to do so with a different operant, they respond with essentially synonymous uses repeatedly, a condition, as we have already seen, not likely to facilitate originality.

If, as we have assumed, originality can be learned according to the principles of operant conditioning, then the effects of originality training should be of the same kind as those ordinarily obtained in experimental studies of learning. One of the gross characteristics of learning is that the behavioral changes produced by reinforcement persist for some time, are not relatively transistory. Increased originality induced by the training method previously described should therefore also persist. An experiment designed to investigate this property of originality training has been conducted, and positive results have been obtained (Maltzman et al., 1960). Using the standard control and experimental conditions of the previous experiments, a delay of approximately one hour was interposed between the training and test situations for a control and an experimental group, and a delay of two days for another control and experimental group. A significant training effect was obtained on the word association and the Unusual Uses Test of originality.

These results show that the effects of originality training persist to a significant degree for at least two days, under the given experimental conditions. We may conclude from these results and that of the previous experiment that the standard experimental procedure for training originality produces some kind of learning.

RELATION OF ORIGINALITY TRAINING TO LEARNING TO LEARN

Originality training studies of the kind reviewed here and learning to learn studies (Duncan, 1958; Harlow, 1949; Morrisett & Hovland, 1959) have the common characteristic of producing relatively nonspecific transfer effects. Training on given stimuli transfers to other stimuli in the absence of any obvious opportunity for the operation of primary stimulus generalization. Despite the apparent similarity between the results of training in learning to learn and those discussed here, differences in the experimental operations and the kind of behavior induced in these procedures suggest that different principles are involved in these situations.

The learning to learn procedure involves the learning of a great many different discrimination problems. Different stimuli are presented repeatedly until S has learned a differential response to a criterion or has received a given number of trials. The responses are not varied and uncommon responses are not reinforced, nor can they be, because a specified response is correct. Under these conditions Ss show a progressive decrease in the number of trials required to learn new discrimination problems. In originality training, on the other hand, variability of response is induced. Repeated presentation of the same stimuli and reinforcement of a specific predesignated response likewise does not occur in originality training. In learning to learn, the stimuli vary from problem to problem, but the responses do not. In originality training and test situations the stimuli and the responses vary. Thus the two procedures differ in terms of the operations employed to induce nonspecific transfer. Furthermore, the interpretations offered by Duncan (1958) in his comprehensive study of learning sets at the human level do not appear applicable to originality training. The acquisition of observing responses, habits of looking at details of stimuli, etc. are important in discrimination problems but do not appear to be particularly relevant in originality training situations of the kind described here. Likewise, the analysis of learning to learn by Morrisett and Hovland (1959) in terms of the discrimination between stimulus trace patterns does not appear applicable to originality training.

AN INTERPRETATION
OF ORIGINALITY TRAINING

Two basic problems, not unrelated, posed by the experiments on originality training by Maltzman and his associates (1958, 1960) demand an interpretation. First is the nature or source of the reinforcement for originality. In all of the experiments, successive training trials in the standard experimental conditions are accompanied by increases in the uncommonness of the responses. The originality induced in this manner transfers to different stimulus materials, and these effects tend to persist. Originality training thus produces behavioral changes that are characteristic of learning, yet they occur in the absence of differential reinforcement administered by E. Nevertheless, we believe that uncommon responses received differential reinforcement. Reinforcement was obtained, because the occurrence of any previously established intraverbal association is self-reinforcing. As Thorndike puts it: "The mere occurrence of a connection strengthens it" (1949, p. 23). Thus, where there is an initial probability greater than zero that a given verbal stimulus will evoke a verbal response in an operant situation such as word association, the occurrence of that response will increase the probability of its occurrence on a subsequent presentation of that stimulus. Different initial conditions may only increase or decrease the amount of reinforcement affecting the stimulus-response connection. In the type of experimental situation with which we are concerned here, the uncommonness of the response evoked by the stimulus is one of these conditions. In other words, the amount of reinforcement is inversely related to the initial probability of a verbal stimulus evoking a verbal response. Originality is more reinforcing than commonplace responding.

An impression gained from observing Ss in the experimental situation is that repeated evocation of different responses to the same stimuli becomes quite frustrating: Ss are disturbed by what quickly becomes a surprisingly difficult task. This disturbed behavior indicates that the procedure may not be trivial and does approximate a nonlaboratory situation involving originality or inventiveness, with its frequent concomitant frustration. This impression of frustration accompanying the task of producing repeated uncommon responses would lend support to the notion that when such responses do occur they are self-reinforcing to a considerable degree. These speculations, however, are not essential to the investigation of the initial hypothesis of the self-reinforcing character of uncommon responses. However, these as well as other considerations suggest that the distribution and scheduling of the evocation of uncommon responses may be of great importance in determining the extent to which a transfer effect will be obtained.

It should be noted, however, that the role of self-reinforcement is probably less significant in producing an increase in originality during training, the successive repetitions of the same word list, than in the test situation. Since instructions to the standard experimental group prohibits the reoccurrence of the same response to a given stimulus word, successive responses to that word will be progressively lower in the related response hierarchy. This is sufficient to account for the increase in the uncommonness of responses with successive repetitions of the same stimulus words. However, we believe that a second variable contributes to the increase in originality during the training session, generalization of the reinforcement effects from the evoked response to still more uncommon responses in the same hierarchy. However, the role of self-reinforcement becomes significant when the transfer of originality to the test situations is considered. In this case the carrying out by S of previously administered instructions to give different responses will not account for the greater originality of the standard experimental condition in the test situations.

This leads to the second problem presented by the experimental data: the fact that the evocation of uncommon responses on one list of stimulus words facilitates the occurrence of original responses on a different list of words, and even more perplexing, on the rather different Unusual Uses Test. The problem is to account for the fact that reinforcement of one instance of original behavior increases the response tendency for other instances of such behavior under different stimulus conditions. A relatively nonspecific kind of transfer of training is induced. Without it, the facilitation of originality would not be possible.

We do not have any simple rigorous explanation of this phenomenon at the present time, but offer the following tentative suggestions. The intraverbal associations possessed by a normal educated adult are enormously extensive and complex. In all likelihood, almost every verbal response is associated to some extent with every other. Furthermore, the intraverbal associations among common verbal responses are stronger than between common and uncommon responses. Likewise, the intraverbal associations among uncommon responses are relatively stronger than between uncommon and common. The evocation and reinforcement of uncommon responses will, through complex kinds of mediated generalization, therefore increase differentially the probability of occurrence of other uncommon responses even though they do not ordinarily occur to the same stimuli as the original reinforced responses. In a similar fashion, the evocation of common responses would differentially increase the probability of occurrence of other common responses even though they may be members of different response hierarchies. An additional characteristic of the standard experimental procedure used in originality training is that it provides for the inhibition of common responses as well as the facilitation of uncommon responses. Through mediated generalization the effects of inhibition will produce a decrement in the excitatory potential of other common responses. It is this characteristic which may be responsible for the more general transfer effects obtained with the standard experimental procedure than with the procedures that induce uncommon textual responses or employ uncommon stimulus situations for evoking, in turn, uncommon responses. None of these other procedures would involve the inhibition of common responses.

It should be clear that the foregoing hypotheses are speculative and their connection with the data presented is tenuous.

Considerable careful experimentation tracing the intraverbal associations present in the experimental situation is needed as well as the development of laws of verbal compounding before a completely adequate explanation of the basis for originality training can be given. Whether or not such explanations can be given, the method of training originality described in this paper seems worthy of further study in its own right, and potentially may have considerable practical application. This again is a problem requiring sustained experimental research employing different kinds of test materials.

In conclusion, it should be emphasized that little is to be gained by disputing the usage of the term "originality" as it has been employed here, or whether the current experiments described are investigating the essence of originality. The important problem is the experimental one of determining the variables influencing the occurrence of uncommon responses in relatively simple situations and the functional relationships that obtain in these situations. Finally, the extent to which these effects hold for more complex behavioral situations must be determined. Such work is now in progress in the UCLA laboratory. But to designate only highly complex behavior of a given sort as original to the exclusion of simpler better controlled behaviors seems gratuitous, as well as an obstacle to the progress of research in this vital area.

SUMMARY

The basic problem in the training of originality is to devise a means of increasing the frequency of uncommon behavior. Once it takes place it may receive reinforcement and increase the probability that other original behavior will occur. Earlier attempts to devise training methods for originality were briefly mentioned, as well as related studies of problem solving.

A series of experiments by Maltzman and his associates was reviewed, and a procedure which consistently facilitated originality was described. This procedure involves the repeated presentation of a list of stimulus words in a modified free association situation accompanied by instructions to give a different response to each stimulus. Under these conditions the responses become more uncommon. When presented with new stimulus materials, Ss receiving such training are reliably more original than Ss receiving no training. Tentative suggestions as to the behavioral bases for the training effect were given.

References

Barnett, H. G. *Innovation: The basis of cultural change.* New York: McGraw-Hill, 1953.

Barron, F. The disposition towards originality. *J. abnorm. soc. Psychol.*, 1955, **51**, 478–485.

Christensen, P. R., Guilford, J. P., & Wilson, R. C. Relations of creative responses to working time and instructions. *J. exp. Psychol.*, 1957, **53**, 82–88.

Dennis, W. The age decrement in outstanding scientific contributions: Fact or artifact? *Amer. Psychologist*, 1958, **13**, 457–460.

Drevdahl, J. E. Factors of importance for creativity. *J. clin. Psychol.*, 1956, **12**, 21–26.

Duncan, C. P. Transfer after training with single versus multiple tasks. *J. exp. Psychol.*, 1958, **55**, 63–72.

Flavell, J. H., Cooper, A., & Loiselle, R. H. Effect of the number of preutilization functions on functional fixedness in problem solving. *Psychol. Rep.*, 1958, **4**, 343–350.

Ghiselin, B. (Ed.) *The creative process.* New York: New American Library, 1955.

Guilford, J. P. Creativity. *Amer. Psychologist*, 1950, **5**, 444–454.

Guilford, J. P. Traits of creativity. In H. H. Anderson (Ed.), *Creativity and its cultivation.* New York: Harpers, 1959.

Hargreaves, H. L. The faculty of imagination. *Brit. J. Psychol., Monogr.*, 1927, No. 10.

Harlow, H. F. The formation of learning sets. *Psychol. Rev.*, 1949, **56**, 51–65.

Judson, A. J., Cofer, C. N., & Gelfand, S. Reasoning as an associative process: II. "Direction" in problem solving as a function of prior reinforcement of relevant responses. *Psychol. Rep.*, 1956, **2**, 501–507.

Lehman, H. C. *Age and achievement.* Princeton: Princeton Univer. Press, 1953.

Maier, N. R. F. Reasoning in humans: II. The solution of a

problem and its appearance in consciousness. *J. comp. Psychol.*, 1931, **12**, 181–194.

Maltzman, I. Thinking: From a behavioristic point of view. *Psychol. Rev.*, 1955, **62**, 275–286.

Maltzman, I., Bogartz, W., & Breger, L. A procedure for increasing word association originality and its transfer effects. *J. exp. Psychol.*, 1958, **56**, 392–398.

Maltzman, I., Brooks, L. O., Bogartz, W., & Summers, S. S. The facilitation of problem solving by prior exposure to uncommon responses. *J. exp. Psychol.*, 1958, **56**, 399–406.

Maltzman, I., Simon, S., Raskin, D., & Licht, L. Experimental studies in the training of originality. *Psychol. Monogr.*, 1960, **74**(6, Whole No. 493).

Meadow, A., & Parnes, S. J. Evaluation of training in creative problem solving. *J. appl. Psychol.*, 1959, **43**, 189–194.

Mearns, H. *Creative power: The education of youth in the creative arts.* New York: Dover, 1958.

Morrisett, L. Jr., & Hovland, C. I. A comparison of three varieties of training in human problem solving. *J. exp. Psychol.*, 1959, **58**, 52–55.

Osborn, A. F. *Applied imagination.* New York: Scribner's, 1957.

Royce, J. The psychology of invention. *Psychol. Rev.*, 1898, **5**, 113–144.

Saugstad, P. Problem-solving as dependent on availability of functions. *Brit. J. Psychol.*, 1955, **46**, 191–198.

Saugstad, P., & Raaheim, K. Problem-solving and availability of functions. *Acta Psychol.*, 1957, **13**, 263–278.

Slosson, E. E., & Downey, J. E. *Plots and personalities.* New York: Century, 1922.

Springbett, B. M., Dark, J. B., & Clarke, J. An approach to the measurement of creative thinking. *Canad. J. Psychol.*, 1957, **11**, 9–20.

Staats, A. W. Verbal and instrumental response hierarchies and their relationship to problem-solving. *Amer. J. Psychol.*, 1957, **70**, 442–446.

Stein, M. I. Creativity and culture. *J. Psychol.*, 1953, **36**, 311–322.

Taylor, C. W. (Ed.) *The 1955 University of Utah research conference on the identification of creative scientific talent.* Salt Lake City: Univer. of Utah Press, 1956.

Taylor, C. W. (Ed.) *The second (1957) University of Utah re-*

search conference on the identification of creative scientific talent. Salt Lake City: Univer. Utah Press, 1958.

Taylor, D. W., Berry, P. C., & Block, C. H. Does group participation when using brainstorming facilitate or inhibit creative thinking? *ONR 150–166, Tech. Rep. 1* 1957, Dept. Industr. Admin. and Dept. Psychol., Yale Univer.

Taylor, D. W., & Block, C. H. Should group or individual work come first on problems requiring creative thinking when equal time is devoted to each? *NR 150–166, Tech. Rep. 1* 1957, Dept. of Indust. Admin. and Dept. Psychol., Yale Univer.

Thorndike, E. L. *Selected writings from a connectionist's psychology.* New York: Appleton-Century-Crofts, 1949.

Thorndike, E. L., & Lorge, I. *The teacher's word book of 30,000 words.* New York: Columbia Univer. Press, 1944.

Van Zelst, R. H., & Kerr, W. A. Some correlations of technical and scientific productivity. *J. abnorm. soc. Psychol.,* 1951, **46,** 470–475.

Wilson, R. C., Guilford, J. P., & Christensen, P. R. The measurement of individual differences in originality. *Psychol. Bull.,* 1953, **50,** 362–370.

Indexes

Indices

Author Index

A

Ach, N., 51
Adamson, R. E., 630
Alberts, E., 553
Anderson, Richard C., 395–405
Anderson, Scarvia, 135 fn.
Apostel, L., 581
Archer, E. James, 454–461
Attlee, Clement, 202
Austin, G. A., 165, 467–469
Ausubel, David P., 3–17, 58–75, 87–
   102, 103–115, 217–228, 290–302

B

Bartlett, F. C., 47, 51, 52
Battersby, W. S., 632
Beebe-Center, J. G., 247, 248, 251
Bender, M. B., 632
Berko, J., 319 fn.
Berlyne, D. E., 41–57, 69, 173–193
Berry, P. C., 661
Binet, Alfred, 194, 195
Birch, H. G., 631
Birge, J. S., 553
Block, C. H., 661
Bogartz, W., 664
Bousfield, W. A., 66, 264
Braine, Martin D. S., 303–320, 328
Briggs, G. E., 553
Brooks, L. O., 664
Brouwer, L. E. J., 408
Brown, F. G., 454
Brown, Roger, 415
Bruner, Jerome S., 76–86, 136 fn., 165,
   415–434, 467–469, 606–620
Buchwald, Alexander, 521–531
Bugelski, B. R., 552
Buss, A.H., 442, 505, 529

C

Cantor, Gordon N., 476–478
Carmichael, L., 264
Caron, A. J., 613
Chapanis, A., 252
Chapman, D. W., 255

Chomsky — F

Chomsky, N., 333, 335, 337, 616
Churchill, Winston, 202
Cofer, C. N., 19, 20, 230, 546–563, 663
Cohen, B. H., 264
Coonan, T. J., 249, 558
Cooper, A., 664
Corman, B. R., 380
Crafts, L. W., 641, 642, 654, 655
Crawford, H. L., 20

D

Dallenbach, K. M., 281, 286
D'Amato, M. F., 504, 505, 529
Dashiell, J. F., 641, 642, 654
Davidon, R. S., 551
Deese, James, 66, 327
de Groot, Adrian, 136 fn., 153
Dinneen, G. P., 163
Dollard, J., 69 fn., 551, 554, 563
Doob, L. W., 563
Dostálek, C., 31
Downey, J. E., 660
Duncan, Carl P., 622, 623, 641–656, 671
Duncker, K., 550, 569 fn., 573

E

Ebbinghaus, H., 263
Eckblad, Gudrun, 601
Eckstrand, G. A., 655
Ehrenfreund, D., 553
Eisner, Jerome, 632
Eriksen, 249, 252, 253
Ewert, P. H., 381, 382, 389

F

Ficks, L., 252, 254
Fitzgerald, Donald, 290–302
Flavell, J. H., 664
Fleishman, E. A., 129
Foley, 230
Frick, F. C., 251, 256, 270 fn.
Friedberg, R. M., 163
Friedman, G. B., 505, 529

Subject Index

A

Accommodation, 174
Adaptation, 174
Adaptive flexibility, 203–205
Air Force Operational Applications Laboratory, 249
Aptitudes project, 195
Assimilation, 174
Association,
  grammatical approach to, 415
  passive principle of, 414, 415
  rules of, 417, 418
  See also Grouping stategies
Associational fluency, 203
Associationism, 151–153
Associativity, 184

B

Behavior,
  verbal control of, 557–559
Behavior theory, 563–578
Belief, 46
"Brainstorming," 661

C

Closure, 184
Cognition, psychology of,
  and cognitive theories, 8–11
  and computer models, 11–13
  and neobehaviorist theories, 5–8
  and Piaget's theory, 13, 14
  and structure of intellect, 14–16
Cognitive processes,
  controversy over, 3
  See also Cognition, psychology of
Cognitive structure, 103, 105, 106
  theoretical formulations of, 107–109
  variables, 107
Communication,
  Mowrer's conception of, 30
Complex formation, 421–424
Compromise, 49
Computer,
  advantages of, 167, 168
  difficulties of, 168–170

and human thinking, 158, 159
and information processes, 136, 137
program for (*see* Program)
simulation (*see* Simulation)
Concept, 26–33
  conjunctive, 166
  definition of, 27
  disjunctive, 166
  learning of, 164–167
  neobehaviorist view of, 72, 73
  in problem solving, 149, 150
  relational, 166
  understanding of, 32
Concept extension, 41
Concept formation, 26–33
  and behaviorism, 399–403
  and cognitive psychology, 395–399
  and mediating process, 504–515
  mediating responses in, 491–499
  models of, 435–451
  negative instances in, 435–453, 462–470
  and nonreversal shift, 492–499, 521–529
  perceptual responses in, 491–499
  positive instances in, 435–453, 462–470
  and relevant stimulus patterns, 495–499
  and reversal shift, 492–499, 521–529
  See also Concept meaning
Concept identification,
  and obviousness of information, 454–460
  and relevance of information, 454–460
Concept meaning, 70–73
Conflict, 49
Conservation,
  extinction of, 602–605
  See also Conservation of weight; Conservation of substance
Conservation principle, 411
Conservation of substance, 582, 584, 586–601
Conservation of weight, 581–601

685

M

I

C

wholly achieved) uneasily noticeable by marking it only obliquely.[94] Reprint editions of these and other books unfortunately often eliminate illustrations or reproduce them poorly.[95] Indeed, despite the fame of the period, the culture's record of keeping its art and literature available is dismal.

Even at the time, however, not all artists were equally well publicized and supported. Black women poets in particular rarely received the visibility and patronage accorded the most famous male writers of the Renaissance. A number of white women writers with better support networks and greater financial independence overcame the effects of sex discrimination to establish themselves as influential voices. But several black women poets—confronted with twofold discrimination—were not so successful. Even here, a narrative of victimization should not serve, as it does in some criticism on women writers, to obscure their real achievements, but it does seem clear that a number of women had their careers curtailed by repressive forces they had no way to resist. Angelina Weld Grimké (1880–1956), one of a number of black women poets active in the Renaissance, published in *Opportunity* and *The Crisis* and was well-known for her play *Rachel* (1919).[96] She was also well represented in *Caroling Dusk*, but her poems were never collected in a book and she never published much of the sometimes incantatory love poetry she wrote to other women. She stopped writing poetry in the 1930s, but there are unpublished poems and fragments in manuscript that are surprisingly contemporary. Here, in its entirety, is an untitled fragment in holograph:

> I am the woman with the black black skin
> I am the laughing woman with the black black face
> I am living in the cellars and in every crowded place
> > I am toiling just to eat
> > In the cold and in the heat
> > > And I laugh
> I am the laughing woman who's forgotten how to weep
> I am the laughing woman who's afraid to go to sleep[97]

Grimké has other holograph poems that invoke laughter in repeated rhythms. Another fragment offers "a laugh for the hopes that came and passed by" and "a laugh for the man that you might have been." But here she breaks into the first person and dramatically into her own voice. And in the process her own struggle turns into a representative song for her race and sex. These unpublished fragments of racial witness, frustrated love, and culturally suppressed vocation gain part of their meaning from the anguished circumstances of their composition. But they also speak to us now in witness to their virtual erasure from our history. They also record a private—and finally successful—effort to find vital, original figures for female sexuality. Grimké's early poems are taken up with Victorian conventions for describing women, but in her unpublished work a dramatic, obsessional, erotic voice achieves controlled but powerful realization. It is the changes she can ring on figures of a lover's eyes, above all, that absorb her, perhaps because her isolation became so extreme that a look of recognition becomes an ultimate value. In the end of "Your Eyes," their eyes finally kiss through "the hot languor of noon, / Sudden, through its cleft peace," "through the beautiful blue-black hair of the Dusk." Reciprocally eroticized, the body and nature together are mediated through sight—"feathered breasts and throats" and "maiden trees kissed aflame by / the mouth of the Spring."[98]

If Grimké's work has been long ignored by the profession and her unpublished work nearly lost, other Renaissance poets also had a delayed reception. Thus one singularly interesting body of work produced by a black poet prior to the Second World War did not actually have its full impact until the following decade—Sterling A. Brown's (1901–1989) *Southern Road* (1932) and the twenty-some additional poems he published in journals in the 1930s. Brown's second book, rejected by publishers at the time, did not appear until his *Collected Poems* of 1980.[99]

In Brown, many of the major strains of modernism undergo a powerful realignment. The indictment of the modern social milieu in Robinson, the regionalism and ordinary language of Frost, the empowerment of working-class lives in Sandburg, the opposition to the dominant culture in Strong, the verbal concentration and mixed forms frequent in the poetry of the 1920s, all combine in Brown's carefully nuanced dialect poems. Brown's use of dialect, drawing on but exceeding Hughes's own advance on James Weldon Johnson, is an extraordinarily compressed register for an ironic sense of cultural difference, for pride in an alternative knowledge amid racial oppression. With their enjambed lines, their hypermetrical rhythms, and their subtle blending of humor and malice, Brown's dialect poems simply do not read like anyone else's. Brown also uses dialect very differently in different poems, sometimes limiting it to a strategic line, sometimes adjusting its rhythms and effect in poem sequences. Consider the opening stanzas of "Scotty Has His Say," a kind of synecdochic fable of all hierarchical race and class relationships, in which Brown playfully decides to personalize the vulnerability of the class in power. The forms of oppression here are relatively mild, and the threats to the white master are comic, though they play on white fears of black voodoo power and witchcraft. Nonetheless, the warnings demonstrate complete black self-possession and invoke the possibility of substantive resistance. It is the humor, finally, that makes these warnings stick. And it is the intimate relations of daily life—relations available to individual intervention—that offer Scotty the opportunity for revenge:

> Whuh folks, whuh folks; don' wuk muh brown too hahd!
>
> > 'Cause Ise crazy 'bout muh woman,
> > An' ef yuh treats huh mean,
> > I gonna sprinkle goofy dus'
> > In yo' soup tureen.
> Whuh folks, whuh folks; don' wuk muh brown too hahd!
> Muh brown what's tendin' chillen in yo big backyahd.
>
> > Oh, dat gal is young an' tender,
> > So jes' don' mistreat huh please,
> > Or I'll put a sprig of pisen ivy
> > In yo' B.V.D's.[100]

During this time, Louise Bogan (1897–1970) also published her first two books, *Body of this Death* (1923) and *Dark Summer* (1929), showing immediately a talent for poetry of elegantly compressed force. "I am the chosen no hand saves," she declares in "Cassandra," "The shrieking heaven lifted over men, / Not the dumb earth,

wherein they set their graves."[101] Simultaneously, E. E. Cummings
(1894–1962) had started his career, combining typographic and grammatical experimentation with romantic humanism and occasional
social commentary (*Tulips and Chimneys*, 1923, &) and *XLI Poems*,
1925), and Wallace Stevens had started his life-long phenomenology
of discourse about the imagination in poems like "The Comedian as
the Letter C," "Sunday Morning," and "Sea Surface Full of Clouds"
from *Harmonium* (1923). "The pensive man," he would write later,
"sees that eagle float / For which the intricate Alps are a single
nest."[102] Cummings is a particularly instructive case in modern
poetry, for he demonstrates a reliance on technique alone as a way of
putting sentiment at a slight (and thereby indecisive) distance, as in
these lines about childhood:

> in Just-
> spring   when the world is mud-
> luscious the little
> lame balloonman
>
> whistles   far   and wee [103]

To recognize how constitutive sentimentality is for Cummings—
how many of his poems are structured by their formal relation to
sentimentality—is potentially disabling not only for Cummings but
also for the profession's view of other modern poets. More broadly,
Cummings can help us realize that there is more commonplace sentiment in many modern poets than English professors like to admit.

   This was also the moment when Amy Lowell's short but awe-
somely varied and productive career came to an end with her death
in 1925. Championing free verse with a fine sense of how to generate
public awareness, she also wrote poetry continually distinguished by
wit, intelligence, and passion. Her reputation has since been one of
the real oddities of modern literary history—formed, it seems, partly
by Pound's hauteur once she took control of imagism and partly
by critics' continuing obsession with her physical appearance and
health. A reevaluation of her career might begin with a love poem
like "The Weather-Cock Points South" (1919), whose reordering of

the natural world in layers around a pursuit of intimacy we can now
see as heralding the deep image poetry of the 1960s:

> I put your leaves aside,
> One by one:
> The stiff, broad outer leaves;
> The smaller ones,
> Pleasant to touch, veined with purple;
> The glazed inner leaves.
> One by one
> I parted you from your leaves,
> Until you stood up like a white flower.[104]

One might then move to some of Lowell's forgotten poems on social
and historical topics to get a sense of her range and dexterity. There
are relatively few subjects that Lowell did not experiment with and
convincingly master and her stylistic range is greater than we have
been inclined to remember, ranging from the polyphonic prose poetry
of *Con Grande's Castle* (1918) to the long narrative poems of *East
Wind* (1926). Nor are the results she achieves easily anticipated; one
expects that her "Twenty-four Hokku on a Modern Theme" from
What's O'Clock (1925) will be consistently and conventionally imag-
istic, but it is not. Some of the poems in the sequence have the
hauntingly aphoristic quality of Sappho's fragments.

Socially and politically engaged poetry would continue to diver-
sify and be intensely debated through the 1920s and 1930s and continue to be published into the 1940s—most notably in publications
that made a clear commitment to publishing poetry dealing with
social issues, including journals like *The Masses, Liberator, The
New Masses, Dynamo, The Rebel Poet, The Latin Quarterly, Challenge, Morada, Poetry, Midwest, The New Quarterly, The Anvil,
New Anvil,* and *Partisan Review,* which initially billed itself as "A
Bi-Monthly of Revolutionary Literature." It could also be found in
books by individual poets and in collections like *We Gather Strength*
(1933) and *Proletarian Literature in the United States* (1935), the
three annual volumes each of *Unrest* (1929–31) and *Calendar* (1940–
42), and *Seven Poets in Search of an Answer* (1944)—and also, after

the stock market crash of 1929, through much of the poetry of
the period, either directly or reactively. *Pagany*, for example, hardly
a politically oriented magazine, nonetheless published poetry and
prose in sympathy with the impoverished and unemployed. Other
journals found themselves involved in social critique almost despite
themselves. *American Poetry Journal*, explicitly distancing itself
from the Communist party and from the unqualified demand that
literature be political nonetheless opens its June 1934 issue with the
following statement:

> With this number we continue, in the three feature pieces, a series
> of poems critical of the present order of things, poems arising from
> perceptions of society as a whole rather than of the individuals
> comprising it. In the May number John Guenther presented the
> dilemma of the human spirit caught in the machine age. In the
> present number the triad of features, especially the powerful,
> condensed epic of Mr. Paquette, carry the arraignment farther
> and prophesy that society, as now constituted, is doomed. It is
> the intention of the editors to close the series with *Steel-flanked
> Stallion*, a poem of social affirmation, by Elsa Gidlow, in the July
> number. However, poems with a 'social bias' are always invited
> and will be printed from time to time hereafter if they qualify as
> poetry.[105]

The myth that has facilitated the elimination of much of this poetry
from our cultural memory holds that the resulting literature was
always formally conservative, thematically monochromatic, and rhetorically wooden. My argument here is that, to the contrary, this
diverse and highly interactive period of political poetry is one of the
real treasures of our literary heritage. Even at the time the sheer variety of socially engaged poetry astounded writers on the left. As the
preface to the poetry section of *Proletarian Literature in the United
States* points out, "there are orations, descriptions, exhortations,
narratives, reveries, satires, epigrams, songs. And in form the diversity is as abundant as in the moods. From the simple tap rhythms
of workers songs we go into echoing mazes of counterpoint; and
from statements as direct as outcries we go into a diction as subtle,

and at times, unfortunately as obscure, as anything to be found in contemporary poetry."[106]

Lucia Trent (1897–) may be said to initiate the decade with her 1929 *Children of Fire and Shadow*. The first three sections of the book may seem merely to record the contending rhetorics of the genteel and modern traditions. But her subject matter, such as the pain of childbirth, is hardly conventionally genteel. Thus poems like "Pregnant" ("I know my flesh to be / A pathway to eternity") and "In a Maternity Ward" ("Watching . . . the young moon saddle the gaunt, black hill") play out a rhetorical struggle within the context of an emerging cluster of social and political commitments. In the final section, titled "Banners of Rebellion," the politics breaks through decisively. There she urges women to realize what it means to "Breed . . . for the war lords who slaughter your sons" and, in another poem, castigates the culture for the economics of prostitution. In "Parade the Narrow Turrets," one of several satiric poems, she takes on academia, succinctly characterizing its elitism, its class positioning, its subservience to power and wealth, its contempt for popular culture, and its sexism and racism:

> Thumb over your well-worn classics with clammy and accurate
>   eyes,
> Teach Freshmen to scan Homer and Horace and look wise . . .
> And at official dinners kowtow to fat trustees.
> Wince at the Evening Graphic, whose bold pink pages shriek,
> Frown on the drooping shopgirl, rouging her lip and cheek . . .
> What do you care if blacks are lynched beneath a withering
>   sky?[107]

By the time Lucia Trent gathered her poems together, Mike Gold (1893–1967) was already an established figure on the left. He wrote manifestos urging a proletarian poetry, from the idealistic, mystical, and hortatory "Towards Proletarian Art," published in *Liberator* in 1921, to the very practical, numbered arguments of "Proletarian Realism," published in *New Masses* in 1930.[108] Gold also wrote poetry in several distinctly different voices. "Ode to Walt Whitman" ends with Gold invoking the New York immigrant tenements of his childhood:

> The Lenin dreams of the Kelleys and Greenbaums
> Deep in the gangrened basements
> Where Walt Whitman's America
> Aches, to be born—[109]

But his most interesting work may be the poems he crafted out of found materials for his 1930s column in the *Daily Worker*. Gold's series of "Worker's Correspondence" poems were apparently sometimes assembled from letters sent to the paper and sometimes invented out of his populist sympathies, often combining a number of letters in one poem. Here are fragments from several of his efforts:

> This is a troubled time in Alabama
> I took my boys out of school as they had no shoes or clothes
> I can hear the Klan mutter about Scottsboro
>
> I am resigning from the American legion
> It reminds me of a dog I used to have
> That picked up toads in her mouth
>
> Arrested as a picket in a recent strike
> I have found my cellmate here an Indian chief
> His name John Thunder of the Ottawas
> Once his fathers owned America[110]

Resistant as Gold was to experimental modernism ("We are not interested in the verbal acrobats—this is only another form for bourgeois idleness"),[111] these poems are themselves part of the effort, promoted by Williams and Frost and others, to bring American speech rhythms into poetry. It would not have seemed *possible* to adapt their understated rhetoric to poetry without the modernist revolution. Their open irony, on the other hand, echoes continuing traditions in political poetry; American modernism's irony, one may argue, owes itself—as a discursive option for poetry—to those socially critical poets who had been working that vein since the nineteenth century.

Gold was not, as it happens, the only poet using workers' correspondence as a basis for poetry. *The Daily Worker* in fact credits the practice of turning letters into poems or drawing on them as a resource to Harry Potamkin.[112] One of the more notable instances of the genre is Tillie Olsen's "I Want You Women Up North to Know." Published under the name T. Lerner in the West coast John Reed Club magazine *Partisan* in 1934, the poem includes a headnote identifying it as "based on a letter by Felipe Ibarro in *New Masses*, Jan. 9th, 1934." The poem is, to be sure, more lyrical than Ibarro's letter, but both its facts and a number of its phrases come from her letter. It amounts to a miniature indictment of the entire economic system that exploits women of color for the convenience of a wealthier class. Here are some lines from its opening and closing stanzas:

> I want you women up north to know
> how those dainty children's dresses you buy
>   at macy's, wannamaker's, gimbels, marshall fields
> are dyed in blood . . .
> what it means, this working from dawn to midnight . . .
> for Catalina Rodriguez comes the night sweat and the blood
>   embroidering the darkness . . .
> And for Maria Vasquez, spinster, emptiness, emptiness,
>   flaming with dresses for children she can never fondle.
> And for Ambrosia Espinoza—the skeleton body of her brother
>   on his mattress of rags, boring twin holes in the dark
>   with his eyes to the image of Christ . . .[113]

In their use of found material, such "worker correspondence" poems may be compared and contrasted with Moore's more intricate reworkings of existing prose texts. And the image of the poet here —as the recorder of history in its intimate particulars—would later find its potential neutrality fully realized in Reznikoff's *Testimony.* "Proletarian realism," Gold wrote, "deals with the *real* conflicts of men and women who work for a living. . . . No straining or melodrama or other effects."[114] These worker's correspondence poems are often true to these principles, but they are also sensitive to the uses of poetry as a special discursive terrain. Given line breaks and stanzaic form, these workers's letters gain symbolic cultural force, a literary status they would not have on their own, and potential long-term visibility. They become representative cultural texts, examples of worker's experience that have at once the conditional authenticity of confession and the generality of types. As poems, one reads them more slowly and their language becomes more studied. Turning these letters into poems considerably alters the cultural functions they can serve. Their meaning becomes more variable, their political usefulness gets a much longer potential life, and they are positioned to establish working relations with other cultural domains either overtly or implicitly connected with literary value. Thus they are in no sense merely the same texts they were as letters, for they have been reconstituted within literariness and thereby rearticulated to numerous possibilities for poetic idealization.[115]

While these poets were constructing their worker's correspondence poems, John Beecher, whose family tree included Harriet Beecher Stowe and the abolitionist Edward Beecher, was writing compressed poems about the representative disasters of workers' lives.[116] Beecher often drew on his own experience of working in a steel mill, which he did even though his family had money. Many other poets during the Depression, however, found themselves part of the working class or among the unemployed without having any choice in the matter. For many poets, therefore, it required no radical move across a class barrier to write sympathetically about the lives of ordinary people. In this stanza from Beecher's "Report to the Stockholders," the unexpected rhythm of the last line leaves the narrative (and our response) uneasily unresolvable:

> a ladle burned through
> and he got a shoeful of steel
> so they took up a collection through the mill
> and some gave two bits
> and some gave four
> because there's no telling when [117]

It is not only that all of us are made vulnerable by the uncertain "when"—since no one knows if or when they might be the victim of an accident at work—but also that a collective movement toward general change is potentially embedded in that undated future. Like many political poets of the period, Beecher experimented with a number of different styles and employed varying levels of rhetorical complexity. "A Million Days, A Million Dollars," presents a series of work songs in dialect. "Henry Matthews was a blas furnace man," Beecher writes,

> He slung a sledge an he shovel san
> Watch yo step, o watch yo step
> Henry stepped in where de hot iron ran [118]

Other poems deal economically with the bleakness of life in the Depression. "Now mills and men are down," he concludes "Ensley, Alabama, 1932." In "Appalachian Landscape" the people are observed "crawling / About their irremediable fields or plodding / Unwashed homewards from their failing mines." He also presents searing reflections on race relations. Here are the opening and concluding passages from "Beaufort Tides," in which the South's throttled present is overlaid with images of the history of slavery:

> Low tide.
> The scavenging gulls
> scour the reaches of mud.
> No slavers ride
> at anchor in the roads. Rotting hulls
> are drawn up on the shore . . .
> Time ebbs, blood flows, the fear
> shows in the master's eye while jubilee
> bursts from the bondsman's throat.
>
> Now
> no shout
> rings out.
> Neither hopes. Both fear.

What future tide will free
these captives of their history? [119]

Other strains of modernism had already begun to find their way
into explicitly political verse. Lola Ridge, in the title section of *Red
Flag* (1927), mixed intricate, radiant imagery with revolutionary fervor: "ice-fangs bristle in the cooled-off guns." [120] This is one distinctly
politicized strain of imagism—precisely in its classical mode of concise, colorful, sensuous description—that we have tended to forget;
it demonstrates that imagism not only had a longer life than we
usually conclude but also served rather different cultural functions
than we have been willing to recognize. One can even hear echoes of
this tradition in the 1930s work of Herman Spector (1895–1959), who
produced self-consciously overwritten and polemical poems with
wildly contrapuntal rhythms:

> . . . the tugs, *bloot* their egregious pride,
> and the scummy waters twinkle with light . . .
> in the brief white glare of the smart arc-lamps
> strange shadowshapes loom, and threaten, and pass.
>
> the phosphorescent worms emerge
> like vacant, jangling trolleycars . . .
> the walls are eaten with decay.
> the eliots, the ezra pounds
> play jazztunes of profound regrets . . .
> fascism yawns,
>   black pit of death. [121]

Richard Wright (1908–1960) wrote Whitmanesque catalogs and
broadsides of protest, including "I Have Seen Black Hands," "We of
the Streets," "I am a Red Slogan," and "Child of the Dead and Forgotten Gods." [122] Although he only published some twenty poems in
the 1930s, they are notable for the depth of his anger and for his
willingness to try out a number of different voices. "Hearst Headline Blues," published in *New Masses* in 1936, oscillates unstably
between wit and anger; it juxtaposes a series of newspaper headlines
that work against each other to expose the contradictions in Ameri-

can culture: " 'Charge Reds Foment Revolution' / 'Lynch Negro Who Wouldn't Say Mister' "—" '100 Educators Praise Nation' / 'Striking Miner Gets Twenty-Year Term.' " "Obsession," published in *Midland Left*, the short-lived journal of the Indianapolis John Reed Club, ends with this powerful testimony to the racial ground of his identity:

> Because I know I am black
> And because I know there is no way out
> I accept it all
> The stake
> The torch
> The noose
> I accept it all
> And make of the deaths of my brothers
> And the knowledge of my surely promised own
> The deep rock on which I stand to face the world!

Kenneth Patchen (1911–1972) mixed ordinary speech with hortatory flourishes. Horace Gregory (1898–1982) promoted the careers of poets writing political verse, edited the "Social Poets Number" of *Poetry* in 1936, and wrote numerous poems critical of American culture that gained additional social purchase by association with the more radical poetry of the time. Kenneth Fearing (1902–1961) began to write his frenetic, exuberant, Whitmanesque social satires. Strongly identified with the poor, like many political poets who wrote both before and during the Depression, Fearing is also, conversely, quite ruthless about the emptiness of the idealizations that drive self-delusion in modern culture. The mass culture of consumer capitalism is one of his frequent targets:

> But that dashing, dauntless, delphic, diehard, diabolic
>   cracker likes his fiction turned with a certain elegance
>   and wit; and that anti-anti-anti slum-congestion
>   clublady prefers romance
>
> Foolproof baby with that memorized smile,
>   burglarproof baby, fireproof baby with that rehearsed
>   appeal,

> reconditioned, standardized, synchronized, amplified,
>> best-by-test baby with those push-the-button tears,
>
> He's with you all the way from the top of the bottle to the
>> final alibi.
>
> Where everything lost, needed, each forgotten thing . . .
>> Gathers at last into a dynamite triumph, a rainbow
>> peace, a thunderbolt kiss.[123]

John Wheelwright (1897–1940), who coedited the miniature journals *Poems for 2 Bits* and *Poems for a Dime* that advertised a correspondence course in revolutionary poetry (fig. 13), combined Christianity with Marxism to produce a visionary poetry of politically grounded self-transformation; he also articulated perhaps the most rhetorically intricate negative apocalypse of the Depression. In his "Paul and Virginia" the greed underlying industrial expansion is everywhere: "Unseen / a hungered Octopus crawls under ground"; in "Plantation Drouth" the milieu of *The Waste Land* is rewritten for a particular landscape and a specific historical context:

> It has not rained.
> The fields lie powdered
> under smoke and clouds.
> The swamps are peopled
> with smoldering cedar
> reflected on black, hoarded water.
> The furrow in the field
> behind the negro's heels
> smokes, as though the plowshare stirred
> embers in the earth.[124]

Genevieve Taggard (1894–1948) wrote poems on most of the social and political issues of her day and often gave special attention to women's social conditions. In "Everyday Alchemy," first published in 1922 but reprinted during the Depression, she writes of the peace "poured by poor women / Out of their heart's poverty, for worn men." In "At Last the Women are Moving," she warns us that "these, whose

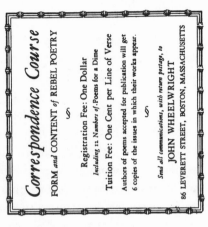

13. The back and front covers of different issues (June 7, 1935, and October 12, 1934) of John Wheelwright's little magazine Poems for a Dime (4½ × 6¼). Issues numbered from twenty to forty pages and were occasionally illustrated. Baskette Collection, UIUC.

business is keeping the body alive, / These are ready, if you talk their language, to strike."[125] Edna St. Vincent Millay (1892–1950) regularly published poems on political subjects, as well as articulate, ironic, and sometimes antiromantic sonnets:

> Gazing upon him now, severe and dead,
> It seemed a curious thing that she had lain
> Beside him many a night in that cold bed . . .[126]

Joy Davidman (1915–1960) and Muriel Rukeyser (1913–1980) produced strongly committed first books, *Letter to a Comrade* (1938) and *Theory of Flight* (1935), that were both published in the Yale Series of Younger Poets. Davidman's career followed one of the patterns now regularly invoked by critics aiming to marginalize the history of political poetry; she continued to publish poetry and fiction for a time but eventually stopped writing poetry, abandoned her left politics, and turned her commitments toward Christianity.[127] Rukeyser, however, wrote a historically and politically engaged poetry throughout her life.[128]

Among her early poems, Rukeyser's most distinctive achievement is probably "The Book of the Dead," the long poem sequence that opens her second book, *U.S. 1* (1938). The sequence creates an unstable collage of perspectives and styles that reflect on and amplify the body of facts at its core: the cynical destruction of workers' lives to maximize profit in constructing a 1930s tunnel in West Virginia. Designed to divert water to generate electricity, the tunnel happens to pass through a vein of pure silica, a valuable mineral in steel processing. Seeing a chance for a rapid double profit, the company drills without the standard precautions, the air fills with silica fibers, and the workers begin to die in large numbers as they learn to "curse the air, breathing their fear again." While her outrage is appropriately unqualified, Rukeyser also assembles about the core events a series of cultural analogues and paradoxes whose meaning is open to continuing and varied interpretation and historical action. She reaches back to the seventeenth-century setting of the area to suggest a historical imperative in America's long relation to the land but avoids working out a more coherent myth in the manner of Williams' *In The American Grain* (1923). The power plant, she allows, in lines recalling Hart Crane's rhapsodies about the Brooklyn Bridge, turns out to be a beautiful machine, even if it draws its energy from that tunnel of death. She calls on John Brown to return "to break the armored and concluded mind" of the culture as a whole but suggests that not only practical change but also mystical belief is necessary to America's redemption. She refuses, finally, to specify what conclusion we are to draw from the multiple perspectives she assembles. But nothing, she makes certain, can transcend either the brute reality of the congressional testimony she weaves through the sequence or the representative singularity of the workers' voices she recreates and lyricizes.

Davidman's *Letter to a Comrade* also helps demonstrate what should, even in this brief summary, be beginning to become apparent: the diversity of styles, topics, and vantage points at work in 1920s and 1930s political poetry. "Twentieth-Century Americanism" invokes the genocidal history that counters an idealized myth of America: "Our roots / push apart the bones of an Indian's skull." Despite her reputation as a writer committed to political change—in the 1940s she regularly reviewed books and films for *New Masses*— one of Davidman's recurrent themes is actually the human inadequacy for the task of revolution. "We have only the bodies of men" with which to make our stand, she writes of the Spanish Civil War, "the wincing flesh, the peeled white forking stick, / easily broken, easily made sick." "Snow in Madrid" views nature as a relief from war and carnage, the only vantage left in Spain; for once, instead of bombs, "the clouds send something down / that one need not fear."[129]

Edwin Rolfe (1909–1954) also writes about the Spanish Civil War in a complex range of voices. "City of Anguish," written in Madrid in August 1937 while Rolfe was serving in the Abraham Lincoln Brigade, has a passage whose surreal violence—rendered in incredibly acute images—recalls Picasso's "Guernica":

> The headless body
> stands strangely, totters for a second, falls.

The girl speeds screaming through wreckage; her
      hair is
wilder than torture.
            The solitary foot,
deep-arched, is perfect on the cobbles, naked,
strong, ridged with strong veins, upright, complete . . .
there, where the soil and stone
spilled like brains from the sandbag's head . . .
Trees became torches
lighting the avenues [130]

Later, in "First Love," and repeatedly in his poems of the 1930s
and 1940s that are collected in *First Love and Other Poems* (1951)
he would write of the war's continuing hold on him: "Again I am
summoned to the eternal field / green with the blood still fresh at
the roots of flowers." "Madrid Madrid Madrid Madrid," he writes
in "Elegia," "I call your name endlessly, savor it like a lover." He
records the death of his friends—"one bomb, shrieking / found the
thin axis of his whirling fears"—and struggles to find the meaning,
now, of a war that was decisive in his own life but is already passing
from the culture at large. His work marks the specificity of Spain
with exquisite precision, while serving at the same time as a meditation on the way the transformative violence and camaraderie of
war can shape one's life thereafter. Rolfe, it should be noted, is one
of the politically committed poets whose work largely meets New
Critical standards for producing formally coherent, metaphorically
inventive, fully realized, and self-sufficient poems. That he is almost
wholly excluded from our cultural memory demonstrates that political—not merely purportedly disinterested aesthetic—criteria have
helped determine what poets we honor in our texts and literary histories.[131] His case also suggests that careful individual evaluations
have not necessarily been the mechanism for deciding whether particular poets are canonized.[132] Nor are the vicissitudes of individual
careers—timing, advocacy, publicity—always crucial in determining a poet's reputation. Rolfe was simply swept up in the wholesale
suppression of political poetry between the two world wars.

Finally, as part of *our* legacy from the period, we need to confront

the furiously antiwar poems Robinson Jeffers (1887–1962) wrote from
1941–1945. Some were published in *The Double Axe* (1948), some
were suppressed at the request of his publishers, but a 1977 expanded
edition of *The Double Axe* means that they can all now be part of
our historical memory. "Fantasy" (written in 1941) imagines the end
of the Second World War with a sardonic bitterness that cannot be
ameliorated by the peace to follow:

> Finally in white innocence
> The fighter planes like swallows dance,
> The bombers above ruined towns
> Will drop wreaths of roses down . . .

We will "dance in the streets," he continues, and "boys will hang /
Hitler and Roosevelt in one tree" while "new men plot a new war." A
few years later (1944) he warns us, anticipating superpower relations
with an image that nuclear arms have made distinctly forbidding,
that "the next chapter of the world / Hangs between the foreheads of
two strong bulls ranging / one field." As for that future,

> . . . We are not an ignoble people, but rather
>   generous; but having been tricked
> A step at a time, cajoled, scared, sneaked into war; a
>   decent inexpert people betrayed by men
> Whom it thought it could trust: our whole attitude
> Smells of that ditch. So will the future peace.
>   No multibil-
>   lion credits, no good will, no almsgiving;
> Not even the courage of our young men, bitterly wasted,
>   forever to be honored—will be able to sweeten it.[133]

Writing with a carefully articulated rage, Jeffers is clearly able to address quite specific historical conditions from a broad philosophical
and political perspective. Moreover, the poems speak at once directly
to their moment and to ours—not, however, because they are "universal" but because we continue as a nation to become embroiled in
equally compromising military conflicts.

To begin to understand the relations between poetry and politics in this period, one needs, in fact, to make comparisons across
the whole spectrum of socially conscious poetry, including work by
poets whose efforts were mostly in other registers. Charles Henri
Ford (1910–), for example, edited *Blues* and *View* and is mostly identified with surrealism. "Song Without a Singer," its red title printed
on pale blue paper in Ford's beautifully designed *The Overturned
Lake* (1941), is a characteristic poem.[134] Infinitive phrases simultaneously form a series of injunctions to imaginative action and revelations of what we have been doing all along unawares: "Set the trunk
on a hill of water"—"watch the day die as if it were Someone"—
"To stumble on the past, without recognizing it, / and dream of the
future as though it were gone." In "Song," from the same volume, a
series of two-line stanzas is based on commodified and desacralized
body images: "the pink bee storing in your brain's / veins a gee-gaw
honey for the golden skillet." But this pattern explodes in the wild
mock-newspaper headline that forms the final line: "BABY WITH
REVOLVER HOLDS HURRICANE AT BAY." Yet Ford also published
in *New Masses* and, among other socially conscious poems, wrote
"Plaint," in which a black man speaks before a lynch mob in Kentucky ("I, Rainey Betha, 22, / from the top-branch of race-hatred look
at you."). Here surrealism is articulated to political outrage and to
subtle transformations of the tree image:

> Now I climb death's tree.
> The pruning-hooks of many mouths
> cut the black-leaved boughs.
> The robins of my eyes hover where
> sixteen leaves fall that were a prayer.[135]

Poems about black American life and about race relations were
a continuing feature of the poetry of these decades, not only for
the black poets of the Harlem Renaissance but also for white
poets. It is notable in this context that Langston Hughes and Arna
Bontemps's retrospective anthology *The Poetry of the Negro* (1949)—
repeating a pattern set at least as early as the poetry sections in Nancy
Cunard's massive *Negro: An Anthology* (1934)—includes a section

of forty-eight "Tributary Poems by Non-Negroes," from Robinson's thoughtful and sometimes quite powerful "Toussaint L'Ouverture" to Lindsay's still flamboyantly outrageous "The Congo" and Crane's conflict-ridden "Black Tambourine," from Sandburg's celebratory but stereotypical "Jazz Fantasia" to Patchen's brutally direct and accusatory "Nice Day for a Lynching" and several poems about the Scottsboro case, including Rukeysers's "The Trial."[136] Moreover, this represents only a small sample of the poems white authors wrote on racial topics. Their sometimes contradictory motives ranged from a deep outrage at injustice to ambivalent fantasies about black culture as a threatening but potentially redemptive source of a transformative primitivism associated with the unconscious. Moreover, relatively few whites understood how deeply constitutive race prejudice was for American culture and thus few really confronted racial issues in sufficient depth. Predictably, therefore, very few white poets recognized how ambivalent their poems about race often were. Yet in many cases it is nonetheless entirely possible to prefer the willingness of some whites to learn about and take pleasure in black culture, along with the sense of necessity many white poets on the left felt about writing on racial issues, to our current reluctance and uneasiness about making comparable commitments. It is difficult, from the perspective of the 1980s, to recover the innocence that made it easy for a considerable number of white poets to attempt poems in black dialect. But better the risks of those efforts than the inhibitions that make indifference to race in America a defining absence in the work of many poets in the 1980s. I would also argue that more of the poetry in dialect remains viable today than much of the fiction and drama produced by whites under similar impulses; problems of both motivation and representation severely restricted the cultural work fiction, drama, and nonfiction prose could do even at the time of their original publication.

Yet difficult, provisional distinctions must be made here between those poems in dialect that appear to be significantly compromised by racist associations and those that do not. By the 1920s dialect was already controversial among black poets, since it often seemed a mark of deficiency. With Sterling Brown, however, dialect came to be the discourse of an alternative, oppositional knowledge. Resonant with wry self-awareness, it could signify pride in the political vantage point of the margins of American society. It was also typically ruthlessly sardonic about mainstream white culture. Yet other problems arose when white poets took on dialect poems, whether in imitation of white or black speakers, since paternalistic appropriation or condescension are traps the culture makes readily available. Dialect in the end has no essential and unchanging meaning. Even the same dialect poem can have different effects in different contexts. At least from the contemporary vantage point, however, it is possible to argue that Covington Hall's dialect poems—in *Rhymes of a Rebel* (1931) and elsewhere—are hopelessly mawkish and that his poems about racial issues are often paternalistic, despite his steadfast insistence on interracial labor unions. And despite the self-consciousness introduced by staggered lines and onomatopoetic typography there seems little reason to count Cummings' "theys sO alive / (who is / ? niggers)" (1935) as anything other than despicable.[137] On the other hand, the rather modest dialect poems in Sol Funaroff's posthumous *Exile From a Future Time* (1943) represent efforts to honor the ironic realism of an oppressed race: "Yes, I'm standin on the corner, speakin my mind, / Next thing I know I'm on the chain gang line." Rather than erase the special history of racial oppression in a universalizing gesture of worker's solidarity, these poems try to mark both similarity and difference: "Ah wukked mah time and ovahtime / Ah wukked mah time and too much time."[138] What seems clear is that successful poems on racial issues by white poets required a certain amount of willed selflessness, whether in these dialect poems or in the neutral recitations of Reznikoff's *Testimony*. Poems indicting the culture's violent racism were also more manageable than poems evoking the specificities of black culture. Occasionally, however, even problematic poems erupt in moments of indictment and revelation. Sandburg's "Nigger," from his *Chicago Poems*, vacillates between clichéd characterizations ("Lazy love of the banjo thrum") and fair historical references ("sweated and driven for the harvest-wage") until its final moment, in which, as one critic writes, "it is as if the stereotype suddenly stood up on its own and gestured threateningly toward its maker":[139]

> Brooding and muttering with memories of shackles:
> I am the nigger.
> Look at me.
> I am the nigger.[140]

Overall, it was the poets writing explicit poems of political critique who were most likely to gain enough distance from a racist culture to write poems that could do useful work on racial issues. Yet that was not always the case. Stanley Kimmel's "Niggers" ("Do da white people have fun? / No, child, dey's too dignified") is really no more tolerable than the Cummings poem just mentioned, despite Kimmel's effort, throughout the book, to defamiliarize the epithets of racial and ethnic prejudice.[141] On the other hand, Lucia Trent's 1929 "Black Men" successfully calls its own metaphoricity into question retroactively with its bare evocation of a lynching:

> Tonight the earth is leper-pale and still;
> The moon lies like a tombstone in the sky.
> Three black men sway upon a lonely hill.[142]

And Genevieve Taggard, in a section of *Long View* (1942) devoted to poems "To the Negro People," imagines that a black poet might yet prove to be a unifying force against all oppression: "He comes to us with the authority of those who cried / In darkness. He, to be the poet of all rising people."[143]

Something of the special powers both poetry and the visual arts had in dealing with the conjunctions between racism, cultural critique, and Marxist analysis are apparent in the August 1932 issue of *The Rebel Poet*. On the cover of the issue (fig. 14) Olga Monus' powerful linoleum block print fills the right-hand side. In its foreground, an anonymous figure hangs from a massive tree trunk. The symbolic strength of the black man being lynched cannot be taken away even in death; his neck may be broken and thus his head bowed, but his body, taut and poised as though he were standing on the ground, retains its force and presence. Perhaps unconsciously rendered as a phallic contest, it is in any case a contest the domi-

THE REBEL POET

Official Organ of Rebel Poets,
the Internationale of Song

Number 15   August, 1932

A Call to Negro Poets and Writers   Page 3

A Negro Mother to Her Child

Quit yo' wailin' honey bo'
'Taint no use to cry
Rubber nipple, mammy's breast
Both am gone bone dry.

Daddy is a bolshevik
Locked up in de pen
Didn' rob nor didn' steal
Led de workin' men.

What's de use mah tellin' you
Silly li'l lamb
Gon'ter git it straight some day
When you is a man.

Wisht ah had a sea o' milk
Mek you strong an' soun'
Daddy's waitin' till you come
Brek dat prison down.

—V. J. Jerome

"SOUTHERN SILHOUETTE"   by Olga Monus

Poems by
Seventeen Rebel Poets

Translations by
Fred R. Miller and Philip Rahv

News Notes - - - Reviews

10c the Copy

14. The cover of the August 1932 issue of The Rebel Poet (8 × 11), edited by Jack Conroy from his home in Moberly, Missouri, and published by B. C. Hagglund at his farm in Minnesota. Baskette Collection, UIUC.

121

nant culture cannot win. In the background schematic versions of the idealized symbols of American life—a church spire below and an American flag above—stand as testimony to the culture's general complicity in his death. But the church spire is compressed to a miniature size, and the flag dissolves as its stars take flight. In an unstable metonymic effect of the man's presence, the tree trunk becomes an upraised fist of protest. Across the page V. J. Jerome's (1896–1965) poem in dialect, "A Negro Mother to Her Child," is equally inarguable.[144] First published in *The Daily Worker* in 1930 and later set to music in the first number of the *Worker's Song Book* (1934),[145] the poem's connections between the suppression of blacks and the suppression of communists—and its consequent articulation of their common interests—constitute a thing done; within the space of the poem they are irrefutable. "Quit yo' wailin' honey bo,'" the black woman calls to her hungry child, "mammy's breast . . . am gone bone dry." What's more,

> Daddy is a bolshevik
> Locked up in de pen
> Didn' rob nor didn' steal
> Led de workin' men.

On the other hand, compare these two effective elements of the cover with Leonard Spier's prose exhortation "A Call to Negro Poets and Writers" later on in the issue. There all our doubts about interested rhetorical pleading are likely to dominate our response.[146]

In this period at least, it was nearly impossible for poets to ignore the defining issues of their day. Nor were all the political poems sympathetic with the left. Cummings, again, provides a counterexample. Willing to satirize all forms of political conviction, he made a brief trip to Russia in 1931 and did not care for what he found. *Emi* (1933) described the visit in prose and *No Thanks* (1935) included his notorious poem on party loyalty:

> Kumrads die because they're told)
> Kumrads die before they're old . . .
> (all good Kumrads you can tell

by their altruistic smell
moscow pipes good Kumrads dance) . . .
every Kumrad is a bit
of quite unmitigated hate [147]

Other poets would remain partly conflicted about the political poem, though such conflicts were by no means necessarily incapacitating. Stephen Vincent Benét (1898–1943), long committed to the notion that poetry had a special capacity to reflect on the meaning of American history, chose Davidman's and Rukeyser's first books for the Yale Series of Younger Poets and published his own *Burning City* in 1936. It is a collection in which alternative versions of poetry's social function are almost schizophrenically segregated into different voices, styles, and choices of subject matter. The opening section includes his famous "Litany for Dictatorships," an honor roll of the groups and individuals chosen for twentieth-century violence ("for all those beaten, for the broken heads . . . the ghosts in the burning city of our time"), a very specific "Ode to the Austrian Socialists" who died in 1934, and "Ode to Walt Whitman," a dialogue about the state of America in the 1930s: "They burn the grain in the furnace while men go hungry . . . and the giant dust-flower blooms above five states." After these poems, to proceed to the stunningly naïve lyrics of Part II is to encounter, in effect, a wholly different poet and a wholly different notion of what poetry needs to do in the world. Here the genteel tradition and a secure world of resolved contradictions reigns. If Benét, however, could neither integrate these impulses nor choose between them, he also chose not to abandon committed writing, as his poem "This for Russia" (broadcast by several radio stations and published in *The Daily Worker* in May 1942) and his posthumous *We Stand United and other Radio Scripts* (1945) testify.[148]

Perhaps the key point here is that a continuing dialogue about political issues was being carried on in poetry. Millay's *Conversation at Midnight* (1937), indeed, was written as a book-length dialogue between a Republican stockbroker, a priest, a communist poet, and several other people. Even Wallace Stevens in *Owl's Clover* (1936) tried to negotiate between the claims of the imagination and those of politics, though this poem sequence is primarily an intricate defense of art's paradoxical double capacity for transcendence and recontextualization.[149] Art, Stevens argues, is adaptable to the circumstances that matter; a statue of leaping horses can catch the light of all the changing seasons. If, in our occasional despair, we should see the "mass of stone collapsed to marble hulk," that is a problem of our capacity, not of art's irrelevance. History, apparently, is a matter of moods, whereas natural change is essential. In the second poem of the sequence, "Mr. Burnshaw and the Statue," written in response to Stanley Burnshaw's critical review of Stevens' *Ideas of Order*, Stevens has an articulate but still vulgar Marxist complain that "these are not even Russian animals." Artificial "images / made to remember a life they never lived," they are far inferior to the real thing "hot and huge with fact." Later, the statue proves adaptable to Africa as well. For Stevens, this is apparently the ultimate test of the power of art; the statue survives in part because he believes transcendence is grounded in primitive universals.

As one reads through this stylistically and ideologically multifarious poetry—all of it politically inflected—it is clear that much more than the *subject matter* of poetry is at stake. Poetry, for a time, had the power to help people not only come to understand the material conditions of their existence but also to envision ways of changing them. Poetry offered people oppositional language they could quote and identify with—socially critical perspectives of anger and idealization they could accept as their own. In part because of its long historical links with song and with the speaking voice, and in part because we are especially aware of its formal properties, poetry offers us subject positions we can take up consciously and with a paradoxically self-conscious sense of personal identification. Compared to prose, and certainly in contrast to many forms of public rhetoric, poetry is perhaps less likely to write itself out on our tongues unawares.

Moreover, unlike the more divided and programmatic loyalties evoked by political prose, poetry provided the equivalent of manifestos to which different constituencies could give a partial but essential degree of common assent. As a result, poets sometimes (though not always) avoided becoming victims of the more vicious political disputes on the left. In effect, in one of its modes poetry could temporarily sweep aside both petty disputes and substantial conflicts and restore awareness of those core commitments to recognizing injustice and the need for change that cut across competing allegiances on the left. One might agree or disagree with various prose statements, but anyone on the left could identify with Langston Hughes's "Let America Be America Again." Hughes's poem, of course, explicitly aims for this kind of consensus. "Let it be the dream it used to be," Hughes continues after repeating the poem's title, "America never was America to me." One cannot help but want to draw that speaker into a community of voices, something Hughes himself does a few stanzas later:

> I am the poor white, fooled and pushed apart,
> I am the Negro bearing slavery's scars.
> I am the red man driven from the land,
>
> I am the farmer, bondsman to the soil.
> I am the worker sold to the machine.[150]

Whitman comes under fire for what might appear to be a similar universalizing claim to occupy an infinite range of subject positions. But Hughes is not invoking all people—or even all Americans— but rather is willing himself to understand all oppressed groups. He recognizes a specific historical imperative to cut across cultural differences and acknowledge shared interests. "We the people," he writes in the final stanza, "must redeem / The land." Poetry could thus help forge alliances and build a consensus discourse. One might argue elsewhere over tactics, policy, and leadership but in the cultural space of poetry the left might temporarily speak with a collaborative tolerance, even if never in one voice. Moreover, because of its historical links with individual voice, poetry could also offer a more idiosyncratic political vision without triggering programmatic implications and disputes.

As one begins to credit poetry's ability to serve multiple social purposes, it becomes apparent that the wide dissemination of political poetry in the 1930s substantially redefined the cultural function of poetry, the cultural space it occupied, and its relation to all the other discourses of the day. In fact, the cultural space occupied by poetry has been at issue and frequently undergone radical transformation throughout its history. Poetry's power to define and alter human relations; its influence on, recognized engagement with, dependence on, and power over other discourses; the conceptual, psychological, spiritual, and political resources people experience it as offering; its capacity to establish convincing and politically effective judgments about a variety of other cultural institutions; its changing power to relocate the discourses of politics, religion, justice, and both personal and national identity within itself: all these are sites of continual struggle and rearticulation.

As I write now, I see scattered before me a few representative material fragments of poetry's alternative social functions: a folded five-by-nine-inch 1894 broadside of E. Fitzwilliam's "People's Party Campaign Songs"; a six-by-nine-inch 1900 broadside by Samuel M. Jones, the reform mayor of Toledo, Ohio, titled "Freedom Songs" and including not only several of Jones's songs but also his statement of principles in support of women's suffrage and guaranteed employment for all; a 1911 broadside version of Lindsay's poem "To the United States Senate," distributed to all members of congress to protest the senate's validation of William Lorrimer's election; a three-by-seven-inch card with "The Internationale" and Ralph Chaplin's "May Day Song" on opposite sides, printed for distribution at a mass meeting in Detroit in 1920; two poems printed on a card as a memorial souvenir for the 1928 funeral of Frank Johns, Socialist Labor Party candidate for United States President; a 1936 seven-by-eight-inch broadside version of Covington Hall's "A Proletarian's Lament," printed by the IWW as a means of publicizing its commitments; Irene Paull's poem "Ballad of a Lumberjack," first issued as a organizing leaflet for the 1937 strike of the Minnesota Timber Workers.[151] Suffice it to say that in terms of its social meaning and semiotic effects, the poetry printed to help organize a strike or the poetry read at a large public meeting, galvanizing a wide range of social classes for political action, may at certain points in our history have relatively little in common with, say, the varieties of poetry published in a mass circulation magazine, read at a conventional religious service, or analyzed in a scholarly journal or in a classroom. Even today, when we compare the functions of poetry in different cultures across the world, we will recognize that the poetry at risk of judicial or police suppression does not occupy the same cultural space as the poetry welcomed or ignored by the state. The poetry that merely entertains us or gratifies us within our present social relations does not create the same poetic effects, or establish the same poetic relations with the other languages and institutions of our day, as the poetry that troubles and excites and urges on us different social actions and investments. When major shifts in the balance of these relationships are in process, the entire nature of "poetry" begins to change.

As the cultural space occupied by poetry changes, the discursive relations throughout the culture may be shifting as well, not, however, because poetry has decisive influence but because historical process involves "a structural rearrangement and reconfiguration of domain and hierarchy within a cultural semantics for which *all* the terms change, sometimes drastically."[152] At stake in the changes occuring in this period are the discourses privileged to negotiate political questions, the discourses which themselves are taken to be primary sites of political knowledge. Poetry in this time became one of the most dependable sources of knowledge about society and one's place and choices within it. Indeed, for some people poetic discourse was capable not merely of talking about but actually of substantially deciding basic social and political issues. The issues at stake ranged from the most general to the most specific. Thus poetry contributed to people's understanding of race relations and relations between men and women. It provided a forum where slogans about economic injustice could gain a complex semiotic resonance from their embattled rearticulation to literariness. It helped reshape the operative concept of political leadership and even served to fix attitudes toward particular political leaders, much as Whitman's poetry had helped to shape the memory of Lincoln. But the changes in the nature of poetry went deeper still. For it is one thing to decide that poetry can help illuminate a "real" political world which is, however, itself decisively (and self-evidently) *elsewhere*, an entirely separate cultural domain; it is another thing to imagine that poetry is itself a terrain of political action, that what poetry does to and for people, what people do for themselves with poetry's assistance, reshapes the political arena itself: altering the metaphors by which politics is thought, positioning people differently within political action, politicizing discourses and human relations and institutions —from the domain of sexuality to the domain of religion—previously considered "outside" politics. At least at some points in our history, certainly almost pervasively in the 1930s and again in the 1960s and for many subcultures at other times, poetry was not only a valid place to comment on such matters (itself a significant shift) but also one of the places where political consciousness was forged. Locating themselves in poems, people thereby located themselves in relation to what they would change or preserve within their lives or in society as a whole. In the process, other categories of social meaning begin to change as well, for the nature of what people take to be "political," the issues considered necessarily part of the valid domain of politics, are also continually at issue in such renegotiations of the discursive registers of social life.

These conclusions are startlingly at odds with the image of poetry that now dominates academic life. English professors tend to think that there is a literary tradition, called "poetry," whose changing textual contents are adjudicated by experts but whose social function ideally should remain unchanged. Many of us imagine that the genre has an essential and transhistorical meaning that is unaffected by the different nature of the poems it includes and the changing (and thus incorrect) nature of the social uses to which poetry is put by various subcultures. Of all the literary genres, in fact, poetry has the strongest history of being idealized as ahistorical, transcendent, nonreferential, and self-contained. This has special implications for the way we understand poetry's cultural potential.

To argue that the poetic, as such, constitutes a wholly independent cultural domain with its own exclusively internal struggles over aesthetic preferences, is often, it seems, to obliterate the complex relations between poetry and the rest of culture. In fact, poetry is a discursive formation whose meaning necessarily depends on, is constituted by, its differential relations with all the other discourses and social institutions of its day. Moreover, all these domains and discourses are deeply implicated in one another, for each of them is differentially constituted. And none of the individual relations is unidirectional or independent. Despite the professional fiction that poetry has a wholly independent history, poetry is necessarily embedded in an overdetermined network of discursive affiliations and expulsions. Thus whatever qualities are attributed to poetry so that it is admired, idealized, or hierarchically elevated in the culture's value system are necessarily differentially related to, and dependent on, all the other cultural domains that have acquired comparable attributes. Considered as a field of discourses displaying an intelligible (though shifting and contested) range of aesthetic variations, poetry's generic, internal characteristics nonetheless remain relational. Its internal characteristics are defined by their similarities to and differences from other discourses, both literary and nonliterary. Only these external relations—affirmative, negative, competitive, indifferent—enable poetry to be a genre with socially accepted internal boundaries and a degree of independent cultural meaning. Thus we cannot choose *whether* poetry will be articulated to such areas as common sense, human relations, politics, religion, education, cultural myth, philosophy, sexual difference, and a whole range of idealized and debased cultural domains. A denial of poetry's relation to politics and cultural struggle is thus itself a constitutive, structural definition of poetry; the denial in a sense establishes a version of the very relation it would deny, turning poetry into the fixed "other" of the political, the everyday, the contingent. Poetry then acquires differential relations with other cultural domains, like religion, that some like to believe are outside the rough contingencies of social life. Poetry is always a function of such articulations. At issue merely is the nature of those articulations and whether we will try to deal with them more openly, recognizing, however, that neither the discursive logic of the past nor of our own time is ever wholly available to us.

When we speak of "poetry," it is to this discursive formation that we refer. It is a formation constituted not only by the subject matter and style of poetry, by statements about poetics, and by the struggle over the changing social functions poetry serves, but also by all alternative efforts to define and co-opt the other social domains poetry addresses. Other discursive formations, then, are in explicit or implicit collaboration or competition with poetry. As the discourses of morality or religion or philosophy or economics or electoral politics, for example, vie for effective control over certain possibilities for idealization, they may not only resist or give way to poetry, but also redefine the nature of the space given over to poetry within the culture. Literary idealization is thus necessarily in dialogue with, and embedded in, all the other idealizations by which our culture sustains and justifies itself. We have often convinced ourselves that the idealizations available in literature are largely or wholly positive forces, but this disciplinary self-persuasion not only obscures the discriminatory filters for idealization built into the canon; it also ignores the complex social and political struggle over idealization that takes place continually in the culture and defines the possibilities for idealization we are able to recognize in literary texts. Idealization is a necessary and often salutary part of cultural life, but it has also proven to be a powerful aid to repression in areas like race, religion, and ethnic and sexual difference. Literary idealization is not a separate domain that is innocent of these forces. Thus one cannot fully think the concept of the poetic without asking how the culture's available forms of idealization feed into and relate to one another. These forms are the idealized subject positions offered to us (and from which, to some degree, we choose): from the subject position of one who loves literature to the subject position of one who loves his or her country, from the idealization of poetry to the idealization of national power. However marginalized literary study may be in the United States, it is nonetheless implicated in an overdetermined field of privileged social roles and admired cultural domains. Indeed, there are differential relations of mutual dependency between the various idealizations that structure and facilitate the ideologies of our moment. Negotiations between and among those differential relations make possible not only our academic specializations but also our governmental policies.[153] It is all these relations that were at stake—and were transformed for significant numbers of people—as political poetry became increasingly visible in the 1920s and exploded in a profusion of new journals in the 1930s. In the process not only poetry but also those cultural domains either traditionally or newly defined in relation to poetry found their "essential" nature changed as well.

Relations between poetry and religion exemplify this kind of transformative struggle. As modern poetry gained certain sacramental power for some audiences, it changed not only the perceived nature of "the poetic" but also the nature and credibility of sacramental functions elsewhere in the culture. For centuries, poetry had been a site both for discourse that was unambiguously devotional and for reflective and ambivalent relations with religious faith. In the modern era, ever since Matthew Arnold observed that poetry might eventually take over the functions of religion, we have been aware that the arts in an age of skepticism can become the model of an alternative sacrament. Such effects have been universally observed in Eliot's poetry, from the closing lines of *The Waste Land* to *Four Quartets*. In the canonical version of modernism, moreover, that is all we need to know about religion in modern poetry, for the contest model it promotes simply sets Eliot against the religious effusions of the genteel tradition. But more varied sacramental effects are also deeply embedded elsewhere in modern poetry, from the ritualistic and incantatory sound poems of Harry Crosby (1898–1929) and Eugene Jolas (1894–1952) to the late poetry of Vachel Lindsay. "Celestial flowers spring up in Glacier Park," Lindsay writes in a 1925 poem, "Invisible to all but faithful eyes":

> These are the flowers: The Bear's Bridal Wreath,
> The Glacier's Dance, The Summer Storm's White Teeth,
> The Frost's Temple, The Icicle's Dream,
> Going Toward the Rainbow, Sunlight on the Stream,
> The Mountain Carpet, The Red Ant's Towers,
> These are the flowers.[154]

If Lindsay wants to honor the sacred flowering of all natural phenomena, Jolas in "Mountain Words" uses frivolous play to invoke the primitive ritual power behind rhythm and sound in all poetry:

> mira ool dara frim
> oasta grala drima
> os tristomeen.[155]

Such sound poems give the illusion of putting us in touch with the sheer recombinative power of language, with a metonymic wit in-

herent in language's independent power of sliding from one signi-
fier to another. Texts like these also suggest a cultural struggle over
what discourses and what social domains would have the authority
to evoke the sacred within modern culture. In fact, the relations between poetry and religion were frequently unstable in this period,
with some poets implying their work was a more consistent and
uncompromised source of moral knowledge than organized religion.
Such convictions were embodied affirmatively in poetry's sacramental effects and negatively in poetry's frequent critiques of organized
religion. The latter category ranges from Hall's "The Curious Christians" to Viola C. White's (1890–1977) fiercely anticlerical "To Holy
Church, 1918."[156] Such poems demonstrate that the subject of religion was precisely the site of a political struggle in modern poetry.
Indeed, a wide, noncanonical gathering of modern poems on religious themes cuts across the familiar categories of literary history
and points to an important discursive formation that runs from Sara
Cleghorn's (1876–1959) "Comrade Jesus" to Countee Cullen's *The
Black Christ*, in which the resurrection of a black man who was
lynched gives a grounding to faith that nothing in the dominant
white culture could provide.[157] Thus this competition for influence
and power clearly has substantial productive effects. Poetry gains
meaning from its struggle with various discourses trying to win the
credibility to serve similar cultural functions. In the modern period,
of course, the discursive formation of poetry is increasingly hetero-
geneous. The concept, then, does not imply a uniform or consistent
discourse, merely a historically situated struggle over the nature and
potential of poetry.

The concept of a discursive formation, a concept put in circulation by Michel Foucault but since used more widely and variously
by others, allows us to credit poetry as a meaningful way of grouping
certain texts and discourses together, while realizing that the meaning of any one discursive formation is not intrinsic but differential.
This suggests there is no secure, transcendent category of the poetic
from which individual poems gain their meaning. There may in any
given period be a dominant, idealized notion of poetry which individual poems may emulate or toward which they may aspire; the
culture, indeed, may mark that notion as "transcendent," and crit-

ics may work to interpret poems in such a way as to reinforce this association. But that is quite different from an assumed, pregiven, universal, and unchanging literary category. The cultural meaning of poetry is historically constructed, and it is often quite energetically contested. Poetry's transcendent effects are culturally produced and historically specific.

Poetry actually has no immutable essence. These texts that often have irregular right margins can be *anything* that particular cultures want and need them to be. Any social function that language can serve—and this exceeds the functions that seem plausible for language in our own time—can be served by poetry in the right historical context. We need to remain open to the possibility that poetry may previously have served personal and institutional needs we no longer associate with literature at all. Even in the present it can serve widely different roles in different cultures and subcultures. Finally, there is no reason to assume that poetry might not, in the future, serve cultural functions not yet imagined for any form of literature.

Yet the perennial question asked in response to modern poetry's more radical innovations, a question still posed today, with perhaps slightly less sense of warrantable outrage, remains "Is this poetry?" The question is always a rearguard action, one taken too late. For some writers and some audiences will have already answered the question affirmatively. At least for them, the question, more properly, might be "What has poetry now become?" Or, what is this new human, social, textual terrain that shares a name—poetry —with certain very different literary pieties and practices of the past? What is now the rather established and often unquestioned complaint that political poetry has a fated and rapidly transitory topicality does not speak in the least to the nature of past political poetry. It speaks instead to our own resistance to (and fear of) a literariness that is socially engaged, politically critical, and committed to change. The insistence that the political past is *not usable* assists a resistance to politicizing the study of literature in the present and helps mask the knowledge that everything in the present is already politicized. In fact, because political poetry typically reads specific historical crises in the light of other more general discourses —morality, ethics, religion, aesthetics, social justice, human identity, epistemology, national destiny—it provides dialogic discursive models that are often capable of being adapted to, revitalized by, and reinterpreted in different historical conditions. It is the adaptability of these dialogic structures, rather than the repeatedly celebrated humanistic fiction of their universal content, that can give "topical" poetry continuing relevance in later periods. The war poetry of another time can often serve as our own war poetry as well; the poetry of sexual difference of an earlier period may negotiate issues that reappear, with different cultural registers, in our own lives; the poetry of class conflict of distant historical periods may be resemanticized to illuminate the class conflicts of our own time. Yet the idea that political poetry merely speaks narrowly to its own moment has other problematic implications as well, for it suggests that, at least for poetry and perhaps for other culturally "superior" discourses as well, having an impact on one's contemporaries is either diminishing or actually degrading, a falling away from the high, productive cultural mission of transcendent discourses. This position actually implicitly valorizes political passivity and impotence in general by articulating political ineffectuality to a decisively (and unreflectively) idealized cultural domain.[158] Indeed, the relative social marginality of literary studies for many academics purifies its cultural prestige of any contaminating vestiges of power. It is not difficult to see why those who identify with this ideology would not only resist crediting an oppositional poetry but also might imagine themselves capable of living outside history and contingency.

These arguments may help us to begin addressing what literary historians have made the most problematic body of twentieth-century political poetry: the poetry that falls, at least arguably, within the notorious category of "proletarian literature." Although the international debates over proletarian literature were primarily a feature of the 1930s, in America they were rearticulated to and grounded in a long literary and critical history. Whitman's enactment of a broadly democratic literature was, for example, celebrated by most of the political poets of the period. Others were strongly influenced by books and pamphlets of socialist poetry and song that began appearing widely in England in the 1880s, including H. S. Salt's 1893 anthology *Songs of Freedom*, William Morris's *Chants for Social-*

ists (1885), and the popular *Socialist Sunday School Hymn Book.* In America, Charler H. Kerr compiled *Socialist Songs* and published it in the Pocket Library of Socialism in 1900. An expanded version, *Socialist Songs with Music* appeared the following year. *The Comrade*, an illustrated socialist journal that was one of the models for *The Masses*, was published in this country from 1901–1905.[159] Though its poetry was formally and rhetorically quite conservative, it nonetheless promoted a class analysis of economic oppression and strengthened a thematics of concern for working-class conditions. Meanwhile, volumes of labor poetry continued to appear, as they had for several decades.[160] They include such forgotten books as George Howard Gibson's *The People's Hour* (1909) and William Francis Barnard's (1865–1947) *The Tongues of Toil*, first published in 1910, then revised and reprinted by the Worker's Art Press in 1913.[161] Finally, as the socialist party in America began to gain in membership toward the end of the first decade, it started issuing increasing numbers of inexpensive pamphlets of protest poetry. Josephine R. Cole and Grace Silver's anthology *Socialist Dialogues and Recitations* was published in 1913. By 1913 as well, Harvey Moyer's anthology *Songs of Socialism*, first published in 1905, was in its thirteenth edition, with some thirty thousand copies in print.[162]

A whole series of volumes of poetry in which genteel values often struggle with socialist or Marxist commitments begins to appear and continues on into the 1920s, including Adolf Wolff's *Songs, Sighs and Curses*, which was issued as the first number of *The Glebe* (1913), James Oppenheim's *Songs for the New Age* (1914), Henry M. Tichenor's *Rhymes of the Revolution* (1914), I. S. Tucker's *Poems of a Socialist Priest* (1915), S. A. De Witt's *Iron Monger* (1922), George Sterling's *Selected Poems* (1923), Viola C. White's *The Hour of Judgment* (1923), and Simon Felshin's *Poems for the New Age* (1924). In 1920 Ruth Le Prade edited *Debs and the Poets*, a series of poems and prose statements written in honor of Eugene Debs while he was running for president from federal prison. Several volumes by Hall, Giovannitti, Chaplin, and Strong fall into this period as well. Tichenor's (1858–1923) *Rhymes of the Revolution*, along with a folded broadside of selections from the book, was issued by *The National Rip-Saw* ("America's Greatest Socialist Monthly") in St. Louis. Tichenor

was on the magazine's staff and himself edited *The Melting Pot*,
which billed itself as "The Magazine Without a Muzzle." Tichenor's
book is a mixture of poems, prose parables, and songs. Its introduction, by Eugene Debs, calls Tichenor "above all the poet of the proletariat." Tichenor's version of "Onward Christian Soldiers," a text
repeatedly rewritten over a period of decades, is particularly irresist-
able. Its partial naïveté, in a way, enhances its relevance to industrial
markets in the 1980s:

> ONWARD, Christian soldiers,
> On across the seas—
> Christianize the Hindus
> And the heathen Japanese.
> Christianize the Chinamen
> And Christianize the Turk,
> And when you've got them Christianized
> We'll
> > Put
> > > Them
> > > > All
> > > > > To
> > > > > > Work.
>
> Big Business is behind you
> In your fight for kingdom come—
> It is sailing with its cargoes
> Of Gatling guns and rum—
> Just fill the heathen with your creeds
> To keep them out of hell—
> And tell them of the shoddy goods
> Big
> > Business
> > > Has
> > > > To
> > > > > Sell.[163]

With figures like Tichenor one begins to see some loosening of
formal and rhetorical conventions. Modernism, in short, is begin-

ning to work changes on and be shaped by the poetry of the American left. The changes are not absolute, however, since poets like Tichenor and Chaplin will continue to use older rhetorical modes as well. Sometimes these impulses are mixed in individual poems, as in Viola C. White's "Pro Patria," a powerful evocation of the First World War that anticipates the antiwar poems Jeffers would write two decades later:

> A liner submarined, the life-boat tossed
> All night on winter sea. A rotting mound
> Where grain was growing, where a woman, crazed,
> Wandering past, cries out, "A jolly war!"
> Earth's quiet folk, made venemous with hate,
> Gloating at ruined cities and maimed boys,
> Standing upon irreparable loss,
> To shout of victory.[164]

Other forms of publication and distribution continued to come into play and guarantee diverse audiences for political poetry. In 1916 the Rand School of Social Science in New York, founded as a center for socialist education in 1906, issued Giovanniti's "The Revolution," set to music, as a large illustrated song sheet. Drawing on a tradition of publishing songs in union newspapers that dates back to the 1820s in America and drawing as well on the late-nineteenth-century American mining tradition of song writers and worker poets, the IWW began publishing radical poetry in its newspapers, notably *Solidarity*, *The Industrial Democrat*, and *One Big Union Monthly*, and issuing equally large (10½ by 13½) illustrated four-page song sheets, including "We Have Fed You all A Thousand Years" ("Poem by an Unknown Proletarian") (fig. 15) and such Joe Hill songs as "The Rebel Girl" (fig. 16) and "Workers of the World Awaken!" (Pl. C).[165] In each case the cover helps set the tone for the text to follow. With its alternating bands of orange sunbeams and white background, the cover to "Workers of the World Awaken" seems almost to be in vibrant, serial motion on the page. The rising sun, figure at once for a new world and an awakened consciousness, heralds kaleidoscopic change. On the cover of "We Have Fed You All a Thousand Years,"

15. *The cover of the IWW song sheet "We Have Fed You All a Thousand Years" (10½ × 13½, 1918). Blue printing on a white background. Also issued in a red and black version. Baskette Collection, UIUC.*

16. The cover of the IWW song sheet of Joe Hill's "The Rebel Girl" (10½ × 13½, 1918). The illustration is in black and grey, except for the flag, which is dark red. Baskette Collection, UIUC.

a muscled worker breaking his chains stretches open the space of the page. The image suggests that the ecstasy of liberation empowers the whole body and alters the ground of representation as well. "The Rebel Girl" carries her dark red "One Big Union" banner with a sense of dignified commitment that demonstrates her centrality to the cause. Self-absorbed, serious, she is also more problematically an icon of the union's ideals, whereas the young boys at her side are ordinary mortals who hail us from everyday life. Finally, although the concept remained essentially undefined, calls for more working class, or proletarian, writers began appearing early in the century.

Some of these traditions, to be sure, developed within distinct subcultures, such as the miners' songs and the very active tradition of political poetry in Yiddish.[166] These vital subcultures, however, provided the base for later, much more broadly visible movements of political writing. Mike Gold and Joseph Freeman (1897–1965), for example, grew up with Yiddish poetry describing workers' lives and later became central figures in the radical literature of the 1920s and 1930s. Moreover, traditions like these sometimes reentered the culture in ways that gave them new audiences, new meanings, and new cultural functions. Miner's songs were eventually taken out of union newspapers and published in books, including George Korson's *Songs and Ballads of the Anthracite Miner* (1927) and *Minstrels of the Mine Patch* (1938). Yiddish poetry was occasionally translated into English. A selection of Morris Rosenfeld's (1862–1923) poems, *Songs of Labor and Other Poems*, was published in an English translation in 1914.[167] Joseph Leftwich's anthology of Yiddish literature, *The Golden Peacock*, appeared in 1939. During the 1930s public readings of political poetry sometimes included Yiddish poetry in English as well.

In 1917 the *Masses* published Soviet plans for the encouragement of proletarian art. Other calls for working-class art and literature appeared in the 1920s. *The Liberator* mixed love poems and poems from IWW members in prison, for a time reaching a circulation of 60,000. But already, the impulse toward proletarian literature, at best vaguely defined, was under stress. It was unclear, for example, whether proletarian literature need be written by (or even about)

members of the working class, or whether it might simply be devoted to serving their interests whatever the class focus of its subject
matter. The question of audience was equally uncertain. Need proletarian literature be written for working-class readers or might it
equally appropriately be designed to revolutionize the middle class?
In discussions of proletarian poetry the focus of controversy was
often over whether complex language not accessible to a wide audience could be counted as revolutionary. Claude McKay resigned as
coeditor of *The Liberator* in 1922 in part because he objected to
Gold's commitment to making it "a popular proletarian magazine
printing doggerels from lumberjacks and stevedores"; while McKay
felt it was good to get that sort of material, he also believed it had
to be judged by standards of quality.[168] Related complaints would be
raised about the poetry by middle-class writers that idealized the
working class. Writing about John Reed in 1914, Walter Lippmann
anticipated this reaction. Reed, Lippmann wrote, "made an effort to
believe that the working class is not composed of miners, plumbers,
and working men generally, but is a fine, statuesque giant who stands
on a high hill facing the sun."[169]

This image would be one unifying element of the diverse phenomenon of proletarian poetry, as we can see from Robert Gessner's
(1907–1968) *Upsurge* (1933) or from the opening lines of Sol Funaroff's (1911–1942) "An American Worker":

> He stands solid,—
> unbudging newengland rock;
> and his mighty head rears firm, mighty,
> a high mountain in the Rockies,
> into the red fields of sunrise.
> *His heart's the dynamo that runs this country . . .*[170]

But Funaroff's poem concludes with a modernist experiment. The
worker will sweep the land clean like a train that changes everything
as it passes by. Anger, we now can see, was behind the reactive idealization of the opening lines; the revolutionary alternative, however,
is mounted with almost whimsical flourishes:

NO STOPS FOR THE BIG BOSS, CAPITAL
          His hating heart generates the electric buffalothunder
of the 20th Century Express pounds the pistons punch hiss
squirts of steam spit niagaras salt with bitterness scorch
scald the faces of the smalltowns mainstreets cities,
roar NOSTOPSFORCAPITAL   NOSTOPSFOR

smalltownsmainstreetscitiescapital vanish past the thunder
lost in the smoke of an old world burnt behind

Lippmann's model of simple, totalized idealization of the worker
was certainly a part of the culture of the 1930s, however complexly
overdetermined—most notoriously, perhaps, in some WPA public
murals—but it does not wholly encompass either the verbal or the
visual products of the era. In some of the visual images reproduced
here, for example, one sees other currents. The tiny covers to the
Little Red Song Book, for example, often aimed for rather simplified
generic workers, but Ralph Chaplin's cover to one edition (Pl. H) adds
enough detail to suggest that the man is actually a representative
individual. The cover to the September–October 1934 issue of The
Anvil (fig. 17) gives us a stylized worker whose face is crossed with
an unstable mix of emotions; as a result, the image cannot be read
in any single way. On the other hand, the dynamic, Blakean cover to
the September–October 1933 issue of The Anvil (fig. 18) gives us the
first stage of a whole cultural allegory—the worker at a forge at the
fulcrum of historical change. Historical change is more ambiguously
at issue in Hardin D. Walsh's witty, self-conscious cover for Joseph
Hoffman's 1938 B. C. Hagglund pamphlet Contrast: A Testament to
Social Progress (fig. 19).[171] Two palpably stolid figures are contrasted:
a knight in mail with shield and pike in hand, in service to fight
for his master, and a casually dressed worker holding his sledge,
employed in industry and in service for a wage. Even the massive
worker, sledge in hand, on the cover of the first issue of The New
Force (fig. 20) is presented as the subject position of the journal's
title: the worker as a potential power (and threat) in America, a new
force in the culture, rather than as a static figure of idealization.
     No more easily can the literary texts quoted here be read as

17. The cover of the September–October 1934 issue of The Anvil *(7½ × 10½),
edited by Jack Conroy. Hagglund, Jarrboe, Kalar, Lewis, Rogers, Rolfe, Spier, Weiss,
and others were listed as coeditors. Dark red on a white background. Baskette
Collection, UIUC.*

Sept. - Oct., 1933   Price 15 Cents

18. The cover of the September–October 1933 issue of The Anvil *(7½ × 10½). The illustration is in red on a white background. A number of the issues were printed at the Newllano Cooperative Colony in Louisiana.*

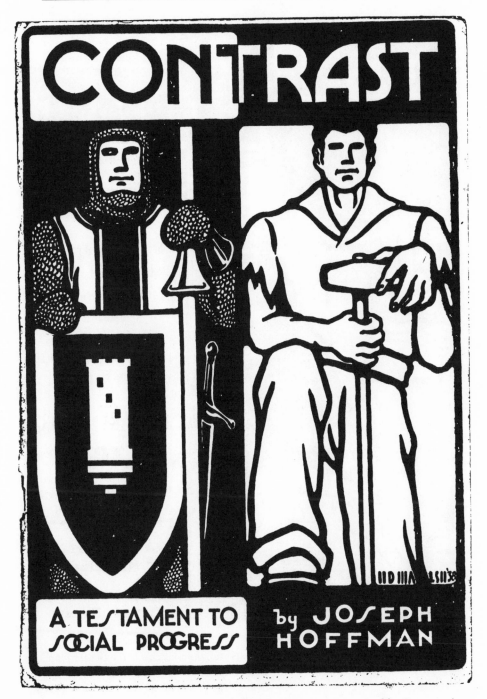

19. Hardin D. Walsh's design for the cover of Joseph Hoffman's poetry pamphlet Contrast: A Testament to Social Progress *(1938). Black against pale gray.*

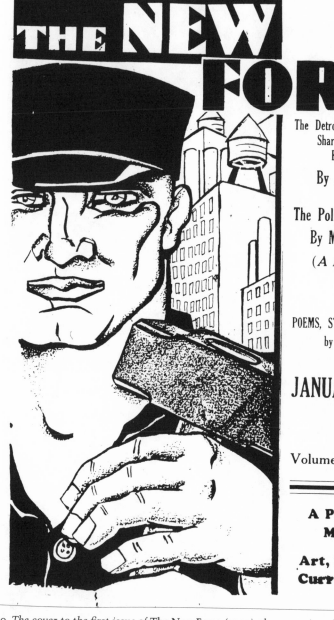

20. *The cover to the first issue of* The New Force *(1932), the magazine of the Detroit John Reed Club. New York Public Library.*

instances of mere idealization; that will certainly not be sufficient to account, say, for Gold's or Olsen's workers' correspondence or Beecher's dialect songs. Nor can idealization account for the merciless specificity of Taggard's "Up State—Depression Summer," which records the economic obliteration of a farm family. "June was sinister sweet," she writes near the opening, "can you eat wild flowers?" Apparently not, as the child, undernourished, proves vulnerable to spring fever. The family struggles, but begins to give up:

> One day no one came out to feed the cows.
> The house was like a rock stuck in mud.
> Tom's half-gone Ford
> Stopped in the barn-yard middle. There the hens
> Fluffed dust and slept beneath it.
> . . . The cows stamped on
> Inside the barn with caking heavy udders.

Their daughter dies, the couple sleeps "apart / Like grieving beasts . . . That fall the bank took over."[172] Finally, we can take note of Edwin Rolfe's "Asbestos," which ends with a chilling conceit to describe an asbestos worker's body, dying as he works:

> John's deathbed is a curious affair:
> the posts are made of bone, the spring of nerves,
> the mattress bleeding flesh. Infinite air,
> compressed from dizzy altitudes, now serves
>
> his skullface as a pillow. Overhead
> a vulture leers in solemn mockery,
> knowing what John had never known: that dead
> workers are dead before they cease to be.

Rolfe's poem, first published in *The Daily Worker* in 1928 under the title "The 100 Percenter" and then retitled to be printed in *We Gather Strength* and again in Rolfe's own *To My Contemporaries* (1936), gathers new meaning along the way so that it comes to reflect a decade of change.[173] By then a series of events had alienated many writers and intellectuals, making them at least sympathetic to socialism or Marxism.

It had not, to cite a key issue, been a very good decade for civil rights, despite supposed constitutional guarantees. In 1918 the editors of *The Masses* were twice tried (unsuccessfully) for publishing editorials and cartoons critical of the First World War. Next year Attorney General A. Mitchell Palmer conducted a series of vicious "red raids," culminating in a December mass deportation of 249 "undesirables," including Alexander Berkman and Emma Goldman. The following years saw a whole series of repressive government actions, including the continuing persecution of IWW members. In 1920 five socialists who had been elected to the New York State legislature, among them poet S. A. De Witt, were denied permission to take their seats.[174] In 1920 as well two immigrant working-class anarchists, Nicola Sacco and Bartolomeo Vanzetti, were arrested for robbery and murder in Massachusetts. Many were persuaded they had been framed, but they were nevertheless sentenced to death in 1921, and the case began to be publicized in left magazines. By the mid-1920s it had begun to attract broad national attention. A number of writers, including John Dos Passos, Mike Gold, Dorothy Parker, Katherine Anne Porter, Edna St. Vincent Millay, and Lola Ridge, were among those arrested at a Massachusetts demonstration in 1927. Innumerable articles and pamphlets of protest were issued, but Sacco and Vanzetti were executed nonetheless. It was a watershed for many American intellectuals, who ceased to believe in the possibility of reforming the culture's institutions.

We are left with "a blighted earth," Millay wrote, "to till / with a broken hoe." Her poem, "Justice Denied in Massachusetts," is from *America Arraigned*, a memorial volume of protest poetry edited by Lucia Trent and Ralph Cheney and published the year after the execution.[175] "This isn't a poem," Dos Passos begins his contribution, "This is two men in grey prison clothes." "Do you know the dreams of men in jail?" he asks the reader. "They are dead now," he continues, and cremated: "Their flesh has passed into the air of Massachusetts." But that air now carries a revolutionary message:

> Ten thousand towns have breathed them in
> and stood up beside workbenches

> dropped tools
> flung plows out of the furrow
> and shouted
> into the fierce wind from Massachusetts.

In 1933 Robert Gessner would put the line "Sacco and Vanzetti are still burning in their chairs" in boldface in his poem *Upsurge*.[176] By the time these two working men were executed, "proletarian poetry" had come to mean poetry either explicitly or implicitly urging revolutionary change. In the process, modern poetry—already steeped in a sense of the bankruptcy of Western culture and often enamored of forms that would disrupt the perception of the contemporary scene —became articulated to quite specific political goals.

Then in 1929 the stock market crashed, and capitalism seemed not merely morally corrupt but actually finished as a working economic system. Suddenly a great deal of modern poetry coalesced into a coherent vision of history. The first volume of *Unrest*, edited by Ralph Cheney and Jack Conroy, appeared in 1929, and Marcus Graham published his *Anthology of Revolutionary Poetry* the same year.[177] It opens with Sandburg's "I am the People, The Mob," and then presents sections titled "The Forerunners" and "The Moderns." The forerunners range from Blake's "London" and Shelley's "To the Men of England" through Whitman's "Song of the Open Road" and William Morris's "No Master."[178] Graham includes as well those poets who regularly published in *The Comrade*. It is clear that it is possible to see the explosion of political poetry in the 1930s as part of a long tradition; some poets, moreover, felt it important to see their own work that way. In Graham's collection, some two hundred modern poets follow, not only, as one would expect, Cullen's "The Dark Tower," Gold's "A Strange Funeral in Braddock," Taggard's "Revolution," Dreiser's "The Factory," McKay's "If We Must Die," Markham's "The Man With the Hoe," and Spector's "Billiard Academy," but also, more surprisingly, Frost's "Fire and Ice," Eliot's "The Hollow Men," and Pound's "Commission." It does not matter what intentions these poets may have had for their work. History had taken these poems up and given them new meanings.

Graham's collection, to be sure, which takes Salt's earlier collection as a partial model, is an extreme instance of rearticulation. But it helps set the stage for what has to be treated in part as a collective, dialogic moment in American poetry: the evolution of the discourse of proletarian revolution in the 1920s and 1930s. Yet, unlike proletarian fiction, poetry was rarely pressed to abandon all marks of stylistic and political idiosyncrasy. Indeed, even writers who generally had little patience with what they considered the bourgeois cult of individualism left considerable space for poetry to register individual experience, conflicts about political commitment, and linguistic effects that suggest the peculiarity of an individual language.

Gold's introduction to *We Gather Strength*, a collection of poems by Herman Spector, Joseph Kalar, Edwin Rolfe, and Sol Funaroff, is a good example of the special status granted poetry even among some of the most relentless advocates of a proletarian literature. Commenting that the contemporary revolutionary movement has so far regrettably only valued doggerel and that it needs more complex poetry to keep "alive the spirit of faith and wonder," Gold goes on to make brief remarks about the poets themselves:

> I have always felt a peculiar kinship with Herman Spector. Bitter and lonely, the "bastard in a ragged suit," this poet of youthful revolt roams our familiar New York streets at midnight. He is the raw material of New York Communism. Confused, anarchic, sensitive, "at times the timid Christ," nauseated by the day's ugly and meaningless work, he prays for quick death to fall on this monstrous capitalist city. . . .
>
> Joseph Kalar is a young lumber worker and paper mill mechanic of Minnesota. There is power in him that has not yet found words; but nobody can miss the ardor, the fierce proletarian groping for a clue to the world, the painful cheated sense of beauty . . . all, all the tangled stuff that makes up the proletarian poet's mind. . . . He is a mystic, and he works in a papermill, sweating and starving. This is the contradiction, and this is the secret of his communism.
>
> Doggerel is highly useful to the revolution, but so is reflective poetry such as Kalar's or Edwin Rolfe's. The latter has a marked sense of order and design; he has been affected by all the influences of modern bourgeois poetry, T. S. Eliot, Ezra Pound, William Carlos Williams. One watches in him a conflict between these

influences and the crude primitive material of revolution. . . .
Rolfe is a spectator; he is a critic . . . whereas in Kalar and Spector
the class war goes on in every heartbeat and vein: they are torn by
it. . . .

S. Funaroff . . . seems to me to combine abstract manifesto and
personal lyricism . . . He is eclectic, derivative, and rhetorical,
jazz and revolution mix.[179]

Each poet, Gold concludes, alternates between despair and dreams
of revolution. It is notable here that Gold admires these poets in
part because of the contradictory discursive strands in their work—
the rhetoric of revolution counterpointed with lyrical passages. Even
the influence of Eliot, Pound, and Williams is valued. Moreover, the
poetry is validated as a distinctive record of the poet's personal conflicts and ambivalences, his divided loyalties. It is clear that poetry
for Gold retains the cultural status it has had since Romanticism
as a special site for expressive subjectivity. Yet the writers are also
responding to general historical conditions—the decay of urban life,
class conflict, and the pressure for revolutionary change. Each, then,
negotiates his way through a common social and political context.
So their subjective experience is historically grounded and Gold real-
izes it is potentially politically useful to readers working their way
through similar situations.

Moreover, as Rolfe argues in "Credo," political action requires that
we "learn / the wisdom . . . of bodies phalanxed in a common cause."
If we are to "welcome multitudes" and have "the miracle of deeds /
performed in union," then "the mind / must first renounce the fiction of the self."[180] Despite the play of difference among these poets,
their work also serves as a dialogue on social conditions and as a collective invocation of the desire for change. Inevitably, as one reads
through their work, passages echo one another, marking both similarity and difference, across poems and poets to create a continuing
general conversation about 1930s culture. For such a conversation,
moreover, finished and successful poems are not always necessary.
Phrases and stanzas can contribute to the discourse collected around
the imperatives of life in the Great Depression. To deny ourselves
the possibility of taking pleasure in the way fragments of poems can
contribute to a pervasive social conversation is to reject one of the

unique benefits available in this part of our literary heritage. If there are what seem powerful lines or phrases in poems that, on the basis of our current taste, seem to be generally weak, then the discursive formation of poetry offers these lines a way of functioning effectively. Part of what is exciting about this period, part of what it offers to us as a legacy, is thus exactly what the New Critical tradition has found so repellent here—the instability and sometimes obliteration of individual difference and the reduced importance of the formal integrity of individual poems. Suffice it to say on this point that it is ideology—not transcendent criteria for excellence—that has led critics to find religious self-abnegation, as in Eliot's *Four Quartets*, so appealing, and a revolutionary commitment so unacceptably unpoetic.

The discursive formation of proletarian poetry begins by sounding the intolerable conditions of contemporary life: "The dynamos whir in the sheds of steel. / The powerhouse of steel distributes pain" (Stanley Burnshaw); an "unseen hand / Weaving a filmy rust of spiderwebs / Over . . . turbines and grinding gears" (Kalar); "Outcries of unrest in a dream" (Funaroff); "pale children bowing in beetfields" (Kalar); "In these days of marking time, / While the whole tense land marks time" (Burnshaw); "Where there is no life, no breath, no sound, no touch, no warmth, no light" (Fearing);[181]

> the earth smoked and baked;
> stones in the field
> marked the dead land:
> coins taxing the earth (Funaroff);[182]

> This is the sixth winter.
> This is the season of death
> when lungs contract and the breath of homeless men
> freezes on restaurant window-panes (Rolfe);[183]

"See the set faces hungrier than rodents. In the Ford towns / They shrivel . . . Their mouths work, supposing food" (Taggard); "Skeletons cast on a shore devoted to business" (Ettore Rella); "And no lilacs bloom, Walt Whitman" (Gold); "Our age has Caesars though

they wear silk hats" (Freeman); "men, pig-snouted, puff / and puke
at the stars" (Spector);[184]

> The friend of caesar's friend murders the friend
> who murders caesar. The juggler of knives
> slits his own throat. Tight-rope walkers
> find democracy in public urinals.
> Black-robed ministers stand with hatchet crosses;
> the headsman hacks a worker's life to bone (Funaroff).[185]

But this discursive formation also ends in demands for revolution
and warnings and expectations of change: "I am black and I have
seen black hands / Raised in fists of revolt, side by side with the
white fists of white workers" (Wright);[186]

> We've eaten tin-can stew, tin-can java, tin-can soup
> Inside the jungles of America!
> We've slept in rain-soaked gondolas, across ice-caked bars,
>   On top of wind-beaten boxes.   (Gessner)[187]

>   I'm not too starved to want food
> not too homeless to want a home not too dumb
> to answer questions come to think of it
>   it'll take a hell
> of a lot more than you've got to stop what's
> going on deep inside us when it starts out
> when it starts wheels going worlds growing
> and any man can live on earth when we're through with it.
>   (Patchen)[188]

> The million men and a million boys,
> Come out of hell and crawling back,
> maybe they don't know what they're saying,
> maybe they don't dare,
> but they know what they mean:
> Knock down the big boss . . .
> hit him again, he cut my pay check, Dempsey.   (Gregory)[189]

let the workers storm from the factories,
the peasants from the farms;
sweep the earth clean of this nightmare.   (Freeman)[190]

In the title poem of his Rebel Poets booklet, *The Unknown Soldier Speaks* (fig. 31), a poem that was also translated into Russian and published in the Soviet Union, George Jarrboe's (1898–?) unknown soldier calls to his "comrades of the muck, / of merciless iron sleet," to join "the brother on the truck, / the sister on the street" in revolution.[191] And here, finally, is Henry George Weiss (1898–1946), writing in *Lenin Lives*, another of the largely forgotten Rebel Poets booklets printed—with its characteristically inventive and ebullient John C. Rogers cover (fig. 21)—by B. C. Hagglund in Holt, Minnesota.[192] On the cover, a stylized figure of Lenin (with an oversized head) is at once oddly domesticated and emblematized. He raises his arm to show us the revolutionary workers exiting from their schematic factories and carrying placards toward the foreground. This rather surprising cover, a kind of whimsical icon, helps sensitize us to the pleasure Weiss takes in his rhetoric. In one poem Weiss borrows his rhythms from Blake's "The Tyger":

> If the dispossessed should rise,
> Burning anger in their eyes . . .
> Oh my brothers in the mire,
> Clothe with lightning, shoe with fire . . .[193]

Of the various discursive strains in proletarian poetry, such invocations of a possible or imminent proletarian revolution—the subject in proletarian poetry most regularly accompanied by expressions of solidarity with the Soviet Union and world communism—have received perhaps the most attention. This may be largely because it is now easy to dismiss predictions of either a Communist party victory or a working-class revolt in America as singularly benighted. As a result, images of a working-class uprising have been inaccurately taken as the dominant theme of political poetry in the 1930s, and this has made it easy in turn to discount a body of work that is, as

21. John C. Rogers' design for the cover of Henry George Weiss's Rebel Poets pamphlet **Lenin Lives** (1935). Lenin's name also appears in Russian in the upper-left corner of the illustration. Black on gray.

we have seen, thematically, stylistically, and politically much more varied.

Before addressing this issue directly, however, I should emphasize again that "proletarian poetry" was a discursive formation that gathered together a number of continuing traditions in American political poetry. For a period of time in the 1930s this new poetic configuration gained considerable interpretive power and influence throughout the culture. It was accompanied by an extraordinary range of politically committed publications. In addition to the books and journals noted so far, the publications of the John Reed Clubs across the country—often featuring poetry and fiction—deserve special mention, including *Cauldron* (Grand Rapids, S. D.), *Hammer* (Hartford, Conn.), *Left Front* (Chicago) (fig. 48), *Leftward* (Boston), *The New Force* (Detroit) (fig. 20), *Partisan* (Hollywood), *Partisan Review* (New York), *Red Pen* and *Left Review* (Philadelphia), and *Midland Left* (Indianapolis). The John Reed Clubs claimed writers and artists as a major part of their audience, but there were also many efforts to reach working-class audiences, from the song books published in cities across the country (fig. 22) to collections like Manuel Gomez's anthology *Poems for Workers*, with its front cover showing an idealized worker reading a book during his lunch break and its back cover showing workers wielding a hammer and a sickle (fig. 23).[194] The 92-page *Rebel Song Book*, edited by Samuel Friedman and Dorothy Bachman and published by the Rand School Press in 1935, included Giovannitti's "The Revolution," Gilman's "To Labor," Chaplin's "Solidarity Forever," Strong's "Over All the Lands," Oppenheim's "Bread and Roses," and Hill's "The Preacher and the Slave." As part of the effort to reach that audience, a number of writers abandoned some of the complexities of modernism and adopted a more accessible style. Isidor Schneider, for example, changed from the poet of *The Temptation of Anthony* (1928) to the poet of *Comrade: Mister* (1934). He ends his essay "Toward Revolutionary Poetry" with this account of what he lost and gained in the process:

> I wrote, and tore up, forty or fifty attempts at revolutionary poetry before I produced any that were acceptable to me. Of those that I considered fit for publication, I sent some to the magazines

22. Song books of the period adopted a variety of styles in aiming for different audiences. Compare this cover to the multiracial and multiethnic cover to Irene Paull's We're the People. Labor Songs was compiled by Zilphia Horton, Music Director of the Highlander Folk School in Tennessee. It was published in 1939 by the Atlanta, Georgia, office of the Textile Workers Union of America. In addition to Joe Hill's "The Preacher and the Slave"—here printed with the warning "The above song is written about so-called preachers who sell themselves to reactionary bosses, and is not intended as any reflection on religion or on honest ministers of the Gospel"—the sixty-four-page booklet includes such songs as "If the Fascists Have Their Way" and "There is Power in a Union." Baskette Collection, UIUC.

23. The front and back covers of Poems for Workers, *a 1927 collection edited by Manuel Gomez. Red type on a white background.*

that had published my verse before. In almost every instance these poems were rejected. Fortunately I could afford to do without the five dollars apiece that they would have fetched in most of these mediums, and I sent them, instead, to the new revolutionary magazines which make no money payment, but put a poet in contact with responsive readers. And the readers responded. I received letters; people came up to speak to me; workers' clubs invited me to lecture to them. Writing a poem was no longer a lonely and dead operation, but a living act.[195]

By 1940, the combative but effective configuration that made this kind of experience possible had largely come to an end. Certainly the aggressive strain of proletarian poetry identified with revolutionary world communism largely collapsed under pressure from historical events—particularly the notorious Moscow "show" treason trials of the years following 1935 and the Hitler-Stalin nonaggression pact of 1939. It collapsed, however, not only because many people on the left became disenchanted with communism but also because the Communist Party of the United States (following Comintern orders) changed its basic policy in 1935. It shifted from the strong revolutionary commitment of the Third Period to a policy of accommodation with most left and liberal constituencies and institutions as part of the struggle against fascism.[196] The contrast between the worker's culture and bourgeois culture was shifted to opposing a generalized people's culture to fascist and anti-democratic impulses. At that point the party summarily eliminated the John Reed Clubs, along with their publications.[197] Poetry suggesting the possibility of a communist revolution continued to be published in 1936, but by the end of that year *New Masses* and *The Daily Worker* would no longer publish poems like Hughes's "Advertisement for the Waldorf Astoria" (1931) (fig. 38) or "One More 'S' in the U. S. A." ("Put one more S in the U.S.A. / To make it Soviet") (1934). Independent publishing projects made more limited accommodations; thus B. C. Hagglund continued to publish explicitly revolutionary poetry pamphlets after 1936 but dropped the provocative "Rebel Poets" designation. Proletarian poetry recurred as a rallying cry through 1938, but its focus changed to fit new circumstances as it was rearticulated to the fight against fascism. In many cases, however, very similar poems could continue to be published. Thus *The Daily Worker* published poems in sympathy with sharecroppers through much of its history. It is fair to conclude, however, that the broader revolutionary cultural configuration known as proletarian poetry eventually came to an end as well. In effect, a conversation and debate about proletarian poetry, conducted amid great social and economic distress, had drawn together a number of related but partly independent strands in political poetry. When that conversation ceased, some of those traditions continued to grow and develop.

Proletarian poetry, however, was more than a rallying cry for poetry urging massive social change. It also signalled a broad cultural configuration that was significantly empowered during the 1930s. For awhile, it seemed a genuine counter-hegemonic force in American life. The Communist party provided the inescapable reference point for this sense that left interests and possibilities were coalescing across all cultural domains. Some writers tried, with great anxiety, to stand apart from the party while specifying their shared interests. Consider this passage from the introduction (by Seymour Link and Kenneth Porter) to Ralph Cheyney's little 1933 collection *Banners of Brotherhood: An Anthology of Social Vision Verse*:

> The general editors, while claiming comradeship with all who strive for world emancipation of labor, maintain that there is room in this struggle for more than one spirit, more than one set of tactics. They share with Ralph Cheyney a preference for the spirit of Gandhi rather than the spirit of Lenin, though admiring both men; they favor non-violent non-cooperation, over mass-violence, as a method of social change; they believe that in the battle against wage-serfdom, as in the fight against chattel-slavery, there is a place for the pacifism of William Lloyd Garrison as well as for the pike and rifle of Osawatomie Brown; and they feel, with the 'leaders of the new social movement,' that more good can be done by stressing social consciousness than by making consciousness of class the battle cry. Essentially, of course, there is no real conflict between the two, if only class consciousness be regarded as a spirit of looking forward to a world in which no one

class shall dominate and exploit another. . . . The sponsors of this chapbook recognize no necessary antithesis between the slogan of the Soviet Republics and that of the Gandhi adherents, but they prefer the goal of the first and the spirit of the second.[198]

By offering Lenin and Gandhi as alternatives, the authors carefully give as much as they take away, since they thereby credit the Soviet Union with both its historicity and its status as a continuing cultural option. On the other hand, note the effort to remind readers that both violent and nonviolent protest are American, not merely foreign, traditions. The authors maintain solidarity with an economic analysis of culture but rearticulate it to religious values. As this uneasy effort to articulate common ground suggests, the party was impossible to ignore. It was impossible, moreover, to publish socially committed literature without, in effect, being brought into partial relation with the party's interests and positions. Poets like Gold, Quin, and Schneider, indeed, were longterm party members. Some, like Malcolm Cowley, remained committed Stalinists until the end of the decade. Some abandoned the party for the anti-Stalinist left, a movement identified with *Partisan Review*.[199] Other poets, like thousands of Americans, no doubt joined the party briefly but soon found its tedious political meetings unappealing. More important, large numbers of writers were sympathetic fellow travellers, recognizing that the party was an extraordinarily effective promoter of left causes and beliefs. It promoted these causes far more effectively, in fact, than it promoted itself.[200] Many also sympathized with the Soviet Union, even if they were not about to advocate a similar revolution in America. In the midst of the Depression, the Soviet Union for many writers was an essential image of the possibility of cultural and political change, and it was idealized in part to keep that sense of possibility present. The Communist Party of the United States, on the other hand, was not widely idealized, but many writers strongly supported some of its initiatives.[201] The party, for example, was a major force in promoting national concern about the Scottsboro Boys.

Although the party generally distrusted intellectuals and never had a fully worked out policy in cultural matters, it did sponsor a number of left journals that published poetry. Other journals were edited by people strongly sympathetic to the party. Not all left publications, however, were party controlled. Indeed, the party reserved its worst invective for what it called the Social-Fascists, all those who mounted an alternative Marxist or socialist position. Poets committed to social change generally could not publish in all these venues. Once a poet, therefore, became identified with what the party considered a Trotskyite heresy, he or she need not seek to publish in *The Daily Worker* or *New Masses*. As party policy changed, or as people changed their allegiances, a number of writers fell precipitously in or out of favor. This resulted in a good deal of rhetorical, interpersonal, and social violence done to individual lives, a fact that played a part in the vehemence with which many intellectuals eventually rejected their 1930s politics.

The most famous case of a poet falling in and out of favor is Archibald MacLeish. During the hard line of the Third Period, MacLeish was attacked as a key example of liberal indecisiveness and lack of commitment. MacLeish himself was in conflict about the relation between art and politics. "Invocation to the Social Muse," a poem published in *The New Republic* in October 1932, argued that the poet had to remain detached from politics. Yet one of its questions—how is a poet "to embrace an army?"—was given a partial answer the same year in MacLeish's *Conquistador*. "Public speech" was a category MacLeish derided at the same time as he chose it as the title of his 1936 collection.[202] "Invocation to the Social Muse" provoked a controversy that only intensified when MacLeish published *Frescoes for Mr. Rockefeller's City* the following year. Mike Gold argued that it exhibited a "fascist unconscious," a phrase that points to a useful way of thinking about the cultural and political determination of art but that is a risky epithet to hurl at a particular writer. The key issue, in any case, was MacLeish's consistent anticommunism. For that reason Gold's phrase was invoked again in a January 1934 *New Masses* review titled "Der Schöne Archibald" and in another *New Masses* piece in July of that year in which Burnshaw assigns MacLeish "first place among the incipient Fascists of American Poetry." But the party was about to change its position, effectively reversing itself and building alliances with liberals like MacLeish who could now be considered antifascist. *The Daily Worker* reviewed MacLeish's *Panic* positively in its March 22, 1935, issue, and the following month Burnshaw decided in *New Masses* that MacLeish had some virtues after all, specifically his sympathy with workers and his awareness of the "necessity for social change." In December of that year, *New Masses* placed a display ad in *The Daily Worker* advertising its next issue; MacLeish's name was at the head of the list of contributors. That month *New Masses* published MacLeish's "The German Girls! The German Girls!" and in February 1936 they published his "Speech to those who say Comrade."[203] It is a poem that still rejects Marxism but offers implicitly to work together anyway. The poem finally is ambiguous. Two years earlier it would have been taken as an attack on the party but now, especially by being published in *New Masses*, it seemed to offer the minimum grounds for cooperation. Writing fifty years later, it is possible to say that, while MacLeish never mounted a coherent politics in the 1930s, he did continually write poetry deeply engaged with social issues. In his attacks on economic greed, in his warnings about fascism, he was part of—not apart from—the political poetry of the time.

MacLeish was not actually excoriated for his liberalism but for his anticommunism. What the party demanded of poets in fact was rather simple: clear sympathy for the working class, invocation of revolutionary passion, or concentration on topics (like Scottsboro) that the party was committed to publicizing. Beyond that, poetry was rather difficult to police. Prose statements, of course, were another matter, as was fiction, where realistic narratives could be judged on the basis of plot and character. Fiction writers could be pressed to explain economic conditions in terms of class difference, to show working-class people gradually acquiring an awareness of social and economic inequities, and to depict revolutionary social action. Even there, however, left journals often settled quite happily for revealing portrayals of working-class life, the stories Williams published in *Blast: A Magazine of Proletarian Short Stories* being good examples. But poetry never had to answer to such specific argumentative or representational demands.

The myth, set in motion by statements like Philip Rahv's polemical 1939 *Southern Review* essay "Proletarian Literature: A Political Autopsy," is that to recognize the party's influence is to recognize that nothing more need be said about much of the political poetry of the 1930s.[204] As I have shown, the poetry is too diverse to fit any simple model of party influence. Indeed, even if the CPUSA had never been founded, the Great Depression would have intensified existing American traditions of labor poetry and poetry about class conflict. The party helped to rearticulate these traditions partly to its own interests and it helped give these traditions counter-hegemonic force for a period of time. But it could not in the end control the varied poems its cultural influence helped produce. Neither then nor now do party policies even begin to exhaust the semiotic effects these poems can have.

During its heyday, "proletarian literature" came for some to include all the socially conscious poetry written from the vantage point of the left, whatever its intended audience, subject matter, style, or implied political commitments. Thus Alan Calmer's afterword to a 1938 booklet *Salud!—Poems, Stories and Sketches of Spain by American Writers* identifies the anthology as "made up almost entirely of excerpts from the writings of a single literary group—the younger, socially minded, 'proletarian' authors."[205] Calmer includes poems by Rolfe, David Wolff, Funaroff, Rexroth, Norman Rosten, Fearing, John Malcolm Brinnin, and Vincent Sheean. They are all, in different ways, rhetorically complex and, for the most part, relatively understated in their polemical moments. The afterword also recommends a number of other poems, including Rukeyser's "Mediterranean," Taggard's "Silence in Mallorca," Millay's "Say That We Saw Spain Die," and Davidman's entire *Letter to a Comrade*. Certainly passages here are accented in distinctive ways in the context of the 1930s: expressions of solidarity carry a powerful social and emotional freight they might not have for us; the interplay between physical distance from Spain and the sense of the whole world as physically proximate, politically and ethically interdependent, was stronger then than now, despite the technological changes of the last fifty years. But these are not poems grounded in convictions about the American working class. Nor do these poems represent a tradition that died in 1939.

What did *not*, therefore, come to an end, despite the virtually canonical claims to the contrary by literary academics, was the whole range of traditions of social and political poetry in America. ←
Black poets certainly continued to write political poetry in the 1940s, and other poets as well carried their sense of political commitment to the historical concerns of a new decade. Like many other poets, MacLeish continued to write poems attacking fascism. Other poets turned to the inescapable subject of the Second World War. Joy Davidman, for example, edited the international anthology *War Poems of the United Nations* in 1943.[206] The tenor and social meaning of this poetry, to be sure, changes, both because political poetry was no longer part of a credible counter-hegemonic force and because the carnage of the Second World War made affirmation impossible for many. In its place—in collections like the three volumes of *Calendar* (1940–42) that Norman MacLeod edited for the Poetry Center of the New York YMHA (all published by James Decker's press in Prairie City, Illinois) or the 1944 *Seven Poets in Search of an Answer*—one finds homages to the murdered poet Federico García Lorca, repeated depictions of fascism, anguished protests about racial injustice, poems about death in war, and a more general despair that amounts to something like a phenomenology of drowning in water. Read in anthologies, these poems too become a collaborative dialogue: "a Negro swings / from the branch of a tree; the organizer / tied and shot and thrown in a swamp"—"the butchering must be wholesale"—"normal souls write gibberish in mud"—"they will say of this age / It set a blight / on every living impulse."[207] No longer identified with a political movement, these poems become acts of witness. Their potential importance to the culture, however, is no less for that. The opportunities for publishing socially critical poetry are fewer, but they still exist. Although most of the politically oriented poetry journals of the mid-1930s were no longer publishing, *New Masses* and *The Daily Worker* continued to publish political poetry, and other new journals interested in social poetry were founded in the 1940s, including *Negro Quarterly*, *The Span*, and *Retort: An Anarchist Quarterly of Social Philosophy and the Arts*.

Imagining that radical political poetry as a whole came to an end in America in 1939—showing no evidence of vitality in the 1940s and 1950s—requires a whole series of fragmentations, repressions, and redefinitions. A number of highly interested interpretive moves, in other words, need to be installed as facts of nature. First, the general social and political challenges of black poets need to be subsumed under race and race made a matter of black self-interest rather than national concern. Then numerous individual poems and entire books by Langston Hughes, Muriel Rukeyser, Kenneth Fearing, Alfred Hayes, Don West, Genevieve Taggard, Norman Rosten, Edwin Rolfe, Thomas McGrath, Aaron Kramer, Ruth Lechlitner, Walter Lowenfels, Melvin Tolson, Olga Cabral, and others need to be forgotten.[208] Finally, when Robert Lowell and Sylvia Plath, among others, appear, they need to be contained within autobiographical confession, their interests in history and sexual difference turned back on themselves rather than outward on American culture.

The relative obscurity of some of these names suggests how successful has been the process of repression and the construction of a diminished, sanitized cultural memory. Yet all these poets at one time or another had some national following. Even now, scattered across the country, there are people who read and value poets like Don West. When West was publishing in *New Masses* and *The Daily Worker* in the 1930s thousands of people had contact with his work; thousands of people thereby recognized the existence of a radical southern literary tradition (including poets like Hall, Lewis, and West), a tradition largely forgotten now that the agrarians are taken to represent the South.

Throughout this period, however, there were other poets who had primarily local impact, either within a particular geographical area or for a specific audience. When it is still possible to find the forgotten mimeographed sheets and local pamphlets of the period, we can see people using poetry to make their historical existence intelligible, to intervene in the way other people understand contemporary events, and to structure the meaning of the totality of the social formation. Again, the last thing we need to do is to work through the surviving ephemeral pamphlets to decide which should be preserved and which forgotten. Their relative failures are as instructive as their relative successes. Let us, then, honor a few of these texts: Joe Hoffman's 1938 B. C. Hagglund Minnesota pamphlet *Let Them Eat Cake!*, which straightforwardly announces that

The word *worker* has taken on
A depth of meaning
That we never knew, before
We acted as one man;[209]

Barney Baley's 1942 antifascist *Hand Grenades*, published in Los
Angeles, which argues that "a sonnet must be whet-stone, hammer
wedge / Or trumpet"; Fred Blair's 1946 *The Ashes of Six Million
Jews* ("Settling upon the pregnant loam / Of every acre . . . Breathed
in the air we daily breathe"), published by the People's Book Shop
in Milwaukee, Wisconsin, with a cover by Joseph Eisler (fig. 24) that
links the Holocaust with the iconography of depictions of lynchings
and race hatred in the American South; and Edith Segal's 1953 New
York pamphlet *Give Us Your Hand! Poems and Songs for Ethel and
Julius Rosenberg in the Death House at Sing Sing.*[210]

In any case, our legacy from the proletarian poetry of the period is
not primarily a legacy of failed revolutionary predictions. For a time
many people did believe such radical change to be a real possibility
for America. But those convictions do not in themselves fully account for the role proletarian literature played in American culture.
We need to begin to ask very different questions about how an influential—but never decisive—body of imagery can contribute to the
social field. One might point out in this context that poetry's success at predicting the course of history is not typically a major factor
in its evaluation.[211] Ordinarily we accept and even value considerable figurative excess and improbable idealization in poetry. Obviously it is the nature of the interest in class difference and the possibility of revolutionary change—not its predictive accuracy—that
has troubled succeeding generations of academic readers. Dismissals
of proletarian poetry based on the fact that predicted revolutions did
not come to pass have, however, been effective in achieving ideological closure for us within literary history; thus they have blocked us
from asking what the poetic vision of a revolutionary working class
might still contribute to our culture.

Poetic images of working-class suffering, discontent, and resistance certainly promote more awareness of the material consequences of class difference. Abstractions about democracy and
justice are thereby articulated to specific social and economic dis-

24. *Joseph Eisler's design for the cover of Fred Blair's poetry pamphlet* The Ashes of Six Million Jews *(1946). Black and orange on a buff background.*

parities, and those disparities, in turn, are given—through poetry—a
generalized and generic status. Metaphors like those in the political
literature of the 1930s, moreover, can have a quite complex future
as they are distributed among and perhaps resemanticize a variety
of other discursive fields. That is a potential they still have today.
Finally, these poetic images, like all others, are unstable, since their
meaning is necessarily contingent and contextual; their eventual
effects are thus unpredictable—*if* we continue to encounter them.

In the 1930s, under the pressure of social life, past and present
discourses underwent a realignment to form a new field of meanings. These are meanings that must—to the extent we are able—
be read contextually and relationally, both in the light of the 1930s
and in the light of the interests and resistances of our own time. But
the left did not provide the only such configuration in the period.
Such issues are equally appropriate in considering the conservative
political poetry of this period. Indeed, as modernism in the 1920s
seemed to have become the dominant set of discourses, a conservative counter-reaction began to take form among southern poets
publishing in *The Fugitive* (1922–25), including Donald Davidson
(1893–1968), Allen Tate (1899–1979), John Crowe Ransom (1888–
1974), and the young Robert Penn Warren (1905-). These poets were
also radically disenchanted with contemporary society, but their
solutions were rather different.

Ransom was the senior member of the group that met, near Vander-
bilt University, for regular conversations about the poetry they were
writing. At first, their discussions were largely literary. Although
most argued for a return to more classically formal verse, Tate did
defend Eliot and Crane. Later, they began to recognize a shared sense
of antagonism toward modern culture in general, especially toward
the increasing authority of science and the depredations of industri-
alization. When the stock market crashed in 1929, their conservative views also seemed confirmed. Alienated from the contemporary
South, they began to urge a return to what they saw as the best of
traditional southern values.[212]

Some effort has been made since to universalize Tate's poetry, to
detach it from its social context and treat it as emblematic of a universal modern wasteland. In fact, southern despair of the time has its

roots in a very specific sense of history that deserves to be preserved
and credited. To gain a stronger grasp on southern feelings of historical defeat, alienation from the nation, and connectedness to the past,
one might read, say, Tate's famous "Ode to the Confederate Dead"
—"The headstones yield their names to the element, / The wind
whirrs without recollection"—alongside Davidson's more obviously
psychoanalytically accessible "Lee in the Mountains"—"The hurt of
all that was and cannot be . . . What I do now is only a son's devoir /
To a lost father."[213]

The special social and historical background of the group explains
some of the obsessions one finds in Ransom's poetry. Not all contemporary readers will consider Ransom's struggle to reconcile honor
and passion in "The Equilibrists" to be a timeless and universal problem. Ransom is generally credited with being preoccupied with dignified problems like mutability and the inevitability of death. More
prosaically, his difficulty was clearly with women, for they consistently represented for him the transitoriness of physical beauty and
the horror of spiritual emptiness. Sexual difference is the opposition that underlies the pervasive binarism in his work. The first
two sections of his 1974 *Selected Poems* are titled "The Innocent
Doves" and "The Manliness of Men." While some might argue that
this opposition is ironic, no attribution of ironic implications, in
the end, can explain away poems like "The Cloak Model."[214] There
a young man is described (by an older speaker) as imagining that
a woman's "broad brow meant intelligence," that "her fresh young
skin was innocence, / Instead of meat that shone." The older man
draws his attention to "God's oldest joke, forever fresh; / The fact
that in the finest flesh / There isn't any soul." "The Cloak Model"
was not reprinted in Ransom's *Selected Poems*, but there too sexual
difference is pervasively, if often less blatantly, constitutive. "Dead
Boy," for example, mourns the loss of a complex, ambiguous, individual human being; "Bells for John Whiteside's Daughter," on the
other hand, mourns an empty, unspecific feminine innocence: "We
are vexed at her brown study / Lying so primly propped." Moreover, the male child is taken as a figure for the ambivalent status of
southern history and culture; the female child is decisively other.
In the very inescapability of its obsessions, Ransom's poetry in turn

can help us to focus on the politics of sexual difference in modern poetry in general. Ransom wrote most of his poetry in the 1920s and continually revised it for the rest of his life. He also contributed to the important political and social manifestos that were published as the Fugitives evolved into the more loosely affiliated Agrarians, *I'll Take My Stand* (1930) and *Who Owns America? A Declaration of Independence* (1936).

The range of poetry marked as "political" in this period was so diverse, its style and subject matter so varied, that the nature of the "political" is, in fact, itself continually being extended and called into question. That may explain why it is so important for many literary historians to treat the political poetry of the period as a unitary phenomenon and reject it contemptuously. For in the 1920s and 1930s there simply is no obvious boundary to political subject matter. In the social environment of the time the avoidance of the political was itself constitutive of poetry. Moreover, it was constitutive not only at the level of the discursive formation available to poetry, not only at the level at which literariness was broadly conceived, but also at the level of individual choice in its network of determinations. By the time these issues are thought through, the problematics of poetry and politics have contaminated the whole of literary history.

Meanwhile, throughout this period, radically experimental forms proliferated, some with clear political aims, some without. In 1929, Bob Brown (1886–1959) published *1450–1950*, a collection of his whimsical, instinctively deconstructive picture poems in holograph (fig. 25). Paralleling such holographic and picture poems as Apollinaire's "Madeleine," "Venu de Dieuze," and "La Mandoline l'Œillet et le Bambou," gathered together in Apollinaire's *Calligrammes* (1918), Brown had published one of these drawings in the May 1917 issue of the dadaist magazine *The Blind Man*, under the name Robert Carlton Brown, and would later publish several others, including "Prohibition" and "Adam Joyce / Eve Stein" in the August 31, 1932, issue of *Contempo*, which he guest edited.[215] "Art" (fig. 25), like the other picture poems, aims for the effect of a found poem, a graffiti scribbled on a wall. In this case, that form mirrors the poem's epigrammatic argument, which proposes a series of revisionary defi-

25. "Art," from Bob Brown's collection of picture poems, 1450–1950, first published in 1929.

nitions of art: "Pictures on Toilet Walls"—"Drawings of Children"—
"An Exhibition in an Insane Asylum" and then inserts between them
the resources of nature's artfulness ("Bed-Bugs & Angle-Worms")
and a surreal, code-breaking interpretation of the phallic and vaginal doodles repeated between the lines ("Innocent Incest Guns").
The categories of high art, seriousness, representation, and literariness were all at risk in his project. Hart Crane's (1899–1932) major
work, the 1930 poem sequence *The Bridge*, welded a sometimes ex-
quisitely idiosyncratic diction ("The basalt surface drags a jungle
grace / Ochreous and lynx-barred") and references to popular culture ("singing low *My Old Kentucky Home* and *Casey Jones*") with
the broadest, mythic cultural ambitions. Aiming to counter Eliot's
impact by writing a long, visionary, and affirmative poem about
the modern world, Crane adopted the Brooklyn Bridge as symbol of
transcendence:

> Through the bound cable strands, the arching path
> Upward, veering with light, the flight of strings,—
> Taut miles of shuttling moonlight syncopate
> The whispered rush, telepathy of wires.[216]

Overtly Whitmanesque, the poem also displayed Crane's adaptations
of French symbolism and cubism.

At the same time, Eugene Jolas edited *transition* (1927–1938) from
Paris and published sound poems, surrealist experiments, and manifestos, the latter including the famous proclamation that "the revolution of the English language is an accomplished fact" (fig. 26), a
manifesto whose multiple signatures challenge the romantic ideology of individual achievement and aesthetics grounded in authorial
identity. In the opening lines of "Firedeath," one of Jolas's surrealist
poems, the human figure is literally consumed by the recombinative
powers of the language:

> crackleflame and the circle the snapop and the
> implosion the volleybang the whirtatoo in the sandring
> the man stood up and yawned his cheeks roseflickering

PROCLAMATION

TIRED OF THE SPECTACLE OF SHORT STORIES, NOVELS, POEMS AND PLAYS STILL UNDER THE HEGEMONY OF THE BANAL WORD, MONOTONOUS SYNTAX, STATIC PSYCHOLOGY, DESCRIPTIVE NATURALISM, AND DESIROUS OF CRYSTALLIZING A VIEWPOINT...

WE HEREBY DECLARE THAT :

1. THE REVOLUTION IN THE ENGLISH LANGUAGE IS AN ACCOMPLISHED FACT.

2. THE IMAGINATION IN SEARCH OF A FABULOUS WORLD IS AUTONOMOUS AND UNCONFINED.
(Prudence is a rich, ugly old maid courted by Incapacity... Blake)

3. PURE POETRY IS A LYRICAL ABSOLUTE THAT SEEKS AN A PRIORI REALITY WITHIN OURSELVES ALONE.
(Bring out number, weight and measure in a year of dearth... Blake)

4. NARRATIVE IS NOT MERE ANECDOTE, BUT THE PROJECTION OF A METAMORPHOSIS OF REALITY.
(Enough ! Or Too Much !... Blake)

5. THE EXPRESSION OF THESE CONCEPTS CAN BE ACHIEVED ONLY THROUGH THE RHYTHMIC " HALLUCINATION OF THE WORD ". (Rimbaud).

6. THE LITERARY CREATOR HAS THE RIGHT TO DISINTEGRATE THE PRIMAL MATTER OF WORDS IMPOSED ON HIM BY TEXT-BOOKS AND DICTIONARIES.
(The road of excess leads to the palace of Wisdom... Blake)

7. HE HAS THE RIGHT TO USE WORDS OF HIS OWN FASHIONING AND TO DISREGARD EXISTING GRAMMATICAL AND SYNTACTICAL LAWS.
(The tigers of wrath are wiser than the horses of instruction... Blake)

8. THE " LITANY OF WORDS " IS ADMITTED AS AN INDEPENDENT UNIT.

9. WE ARE NOT CONCERNED WITH THE PROPAGATION OF SOCIOLOGICAL IDEAS, EXCEPT TO EMANCIPATE THE CREATIVE ELEMENTS FROM THE PRESENT IDEOLOGY.

10. TIME IS A TYRANNY TO BE ABOLISHED.

11. THE WRITER EXPRESSES. HE DOES NOT COMMUNICATE

12. THE PLAIN READER BE DAMNED.
(Damn braces ! Bless relaxes !... Blake)

— *Signed* : KAY BOYLE, WHIT BURNETT, HART CRANE, CARESSE CROSBY, HARRY CROSBY, MARTHA FOLEY, STUART GILBERT, A. L. GILLESPIE, LEIGH HOFFMAN, EUGENE JOLAS, ELLIOT PAUL, DOUGLAS RIGBY, THEO RUTRA, ROBERT SAGE, HAROLD J. SALEMSON, LAURENCE VAIL.

26. Eugene Jolas's famous Revolution of the Word manifesto from transition 16/17 *(1929). UIUC.*

his hands drumrapping the atlas and
    his hair began to simounflash it bonfired Africa red
blazesheaves sweltered.[217]

A series of Harry Crosby's ecstatic, obsessional, sometimes mi-
sogynist books—with poems ranging from Whitmanesque chants to
tirades to concrete poems—were published posthumously in 1931.
Very nearly a poet of one infinitely variable figure, Crosby was driven
to record all the changes he could ring on images of the sun: "red
burning tomb," "sunflakes falling in the sea," "humanity is the forest of the sun."[218] "Photoheliograph," a concrete poem, presents his
vision at its most economical.[219] It consists of ten lines that each re-
peat the word "black" (in black ink, of course) five times. In the fifth
line, however, the word "SUN" burns in capital letters, at the heart
of the matter of language:

> black black black black black
> black black SUN black black
> black black black black black

In other poems and prose poems, the sun is not only the object of but
also the provocation for verbal transformations: " 1) Take the word
Sun which burns permanently in my brain. It has accuracy and alac-
rity. It is monomaniac in its intensity. It is a continual flash of insight.
It is the marriage of Invulnerability with Yes, of the Red Wolf with
the Gold Bumblebee, of Madness with Ra. 2) Birdileaves, Goldabbits,
Fingertoes, Auroramor, Barbarifire, Parabolaw, Lovegown, Nombrilo-
mane."[220] As with Jolas's sound poems, the power of the language to
disassemble and recombine its parts only manifests itself in each of
these local changes. One never reaches the original (and originating)
sound whose absence is marked by its haunting echo through all the
poem's substitutions.

    That same year Louis Zukofsky (1904–1978) edited a special Objec-
tivist issue of *Poetry* and in 1932 *An "Objectivists" Anthology* was
published, thereby creating a new movement (whose members had
relatively little in common stylistically). Zukofsky began to publish
portions of his major poem sequence, *"A"* (1979), a hermetic, musi-

cally counterpointed poem that juxtaposes autobiographical and historical references. Sometimes attacked at the time for being apolitical (Herman Spector, for example, satirized the Objectivists), meaning that they failed to make explicit revolutionary commitments, the Objectivists were often deeply involved in thinking through the relations between literature and politics. In fact we are only now beginning to understand how Zukofsky's work amounts to a series of specifically linguistic historical and political interventions.[221] In the first half of section 9 of "A", Zukofsky mounts an explicit critique of capitalism. Section 10 of "A", however, puts his critical aims in crisis. Written in 1940 as the Second World War was widening, the poem presents a field of precisely drawn particulars whose differential implications are left for us to decide. Zukofsky's individual moral judgments are often very clearly articulated:

>   All the people of Paris
>   Mass, massed refugees on the roads
>   Go to mass with the air
>   and the shrapnel for a church
>   A Christian civilization
>   Where Pius blesses the black-shirts . . .
>   Henri Philippe Petain and Herr Hitler
>   have made peace
>   One name is spit
>   The other is hawked from the throat . . .
>   A vicar of Christ sworn to traitors
>   His priests who thrive on silver
>   More ashamed beaten to sleep beside lashed Jews
>   Than to abet murder.[222]

Though "A" obviously shares little ideological ground with Pound's *Cantos*, it has much in common technically. Yet Zukofsky lacks an equivalent to Pound's totalizing paranoia. Thus the field of powerful local effects, like those above, coalesces neither into shimmering mystical plenitude nor into a conspiracy of implications. In many ways this makes the poem's demands on the reader even greater.

Other poets associated with Objectivism include George Oppen

(1908–1984) and Lorine Niedecker (1903–1970), both notable for their exquisite craft. Throughout this period, Pound continued to publish additions to *The Cantos*. Lola Ridge published her last book, *Dance of Fire* (1935), issued in a gleaming, metallic, copper-colored jacket. It would combine mysticism and social critique: "This is to feel the slip of the world's crust"—"When San Quentin / Prison shall be caved in"—the "body of the coast . . . made solvent in this heat."[223] Stevens published his next two books, *Ideas of Order* (1935) and *The Man With the Blue Guitar* (1937); Taggard, Cummings, Williams, and Laura Riding (1901–) issued collected poems in 1938. The following year W. H. Auden (1907–1973) came to live in the United States. Eliot published *Four Quartets* in 1943, and H. D. began her ambitious mythic narratives with *The Walls Do Not Fall* (1944) and *Tribute to the Angels* (1945).

Riding deserves special mention because her work is in some ways quite anomalous in modern poetry. The extraordinarily self-conscious pressure she places on language would seem to align her with the whole strain of modernism devoted to unstable linguistic experimentation. Yet her declared aim was to control and limit her poetry's meaning to a degree perhaps no other poet believed possible. "We must learn better," she writes in "The Why of the Wind," "what we are and what we are not." Poetry, she felt, could help us divest ourselves of sensory distractions and historical contingency and lead us to the deepest, universal human truths. She shows, indeed, a kind of implacable hostility toward the socially constructed medium in which she works. Her poems are tense, deconstructive implosions of play and aggression. Finding, however, that her readers would not cooperate in reading her work the way she intended and that she herself could not wholly bend poetry to her will, she stopped writing it. Much of her poetry requires a knowledge of her theoretical work if one is to credit her intentions. Other poems, however, draw on issues in the air at the time and are more accessible. In "The Tiger" she warns that she is not at all the kind of woman patriarchal society would have her be:

> Earlier than lust, not plain,
> Behind a darkened face of memory,

My inner animal revives.
Beware, that I am tame.
Beware philosophies
Wherein I yield.[224]

Then, in the 1940s what we have come to think of as the next generation began to publish their first books. Margaret Walker's (1915–)
For My People, the 1942 volume in the Yale Series of Younger Poets,
is worth special note. Composed of three sections in very different styles, it suggests, more than many other mixed collections,
how a plural textuality can articulate the fragmented, conflicted subcultures of the social formation. In the first section, incantatory
poems build on a historically imposed schizophrenia, alternating between enraptured affirmation and the weight of social oppression.
The second section uses jazz and ballad rhythms and dialect to give
folk heroes, workers, and outcasts opportunities for violent self-
assertion. And the third section, tries, problematically, as Claude
McKay had twenty years earlier, to adapt the sonnet for a poetry of
social conscience.[225] Finally, by 1946 Theodore Roethke (1908–1963),
Robert Hayden (1913–1980), John Berryman (1914–1972), Robert
Lowell (1917–1977), Gwendolyn Brooks (1917–), Elizabeth Bishop
(1911–1979), and Denise Levertov (1923–) had published their first
books. And other poets linked with the years since the Second World
War began publishing in journals.

In any anthology adequately representing this diversity, modern
poetry would emerge, not as a single coherent development, but
as a shifting mixture of alliances and rejections, innovations and
counterreactions, with new poets frequently discovering what had
already been anticipated in the careers of others. Indeed modern
poetry remains a contested terrain; its still-shifting image is central
to how we define *ourselves*. Contemporary analysis of modernism,
including my own analysis here, is thus part of the same process of
reterritorialization that occupied the poets of the period. New polemical positions are articulated, new groupings of poets proposed,
new anthologies edited; this competitive rearticulation of the terrain
continues unbroken to the present day. There are no disinterested,
objective maps to be drawn.

Yet the maps we do have are demonstrably inadequate. If, for example, we consider two key (but by no means universal) elements of the modernist revolution—(1) the shift to an emphasis on either the self-referentiality of poetic language or the overall coherence of language as the preeminent cultural system and (2) the increasing doubt about either the possibility or the political wisdom of identifying a single, unified speaking subject as the voice of a poem— then it is, at least arguably, clear who is the major poet of modernism. I have in a mind a poet nowhere in evidence in the hefty 1973 *Norton Anthology of Modern Poetry* (though finally granted some space in the 1988 second edition), a poet whose poetry was in fact mostly published posthumously (*Bee Time Vine and Other Pieces*, 1953, *Painted Lace and Other Pieces*, 1955, and *Stanzas in Meditation and Other Poems*, 1956). The author of these books is, of course, Gertrude Stein.

For all the pages already spent on debating and contesting the relative radicalism of the other dominant modernists, no one else so thoroughly overturns language's representational claims while exploring its signifying power. Hers is a lifelong project in cultural semiotics, in its totality quite impossible to naturalize and domesticate in the way much of the rest of modernism has been. Indeed, because her long poems depend on incremental repetition and variation, they are almost impossible to quote effectively or edit for anthologies. Her work is generically undecidable, sometimes feminist and lesbian, wholly unassignable to a humanizing persona, and more purely and powerfully devoted to an exploration of how language works than that of any other poet of the period. By 1914, her work had anticipated not only most of the linguistically experimental strain of modernism but much of postmodernism as well. These are perhaps at once the reasons why she deserves to be and the reasons why she is not yet considered to be a central figure in modernist poetry. Good work has been done on Stein, first by critics interested in experimental prose and more recently by feminist critics, but she remains unjustly marginalized in writing on modern poetry.[226]

Clearly, Stein represents only some of the key elements of the modernist revolution, but her work, like that of many of the poets of the period, simultaneously synthesizes multiple existing tendencies and provokes others. Masterpieces like "Lifting Belly" (1915–17) and "Patriarchal Poetry" (1927) can be grouped with feminist poetry,

with the most radical linguistic innovation, with the effort to intro-
duce ordinary speech rhythms into poetry, or with movements like
dadaism. That we use such taxonomies is inevitable and necessary,
but we risk serious distortion if we refuse to entertain multiple classifications for individual poets and even single texts.

Our taxonomies are unavoidably political. By grouping the poets
of the Harlem Renaissance of the 1920s together, despite their differences, we are able to emphasize their vital expression of black pride
and recognize its independent and oppositional cultural force. But in
the process we suppress certain other important aesthetic connections and political alliances that informed their work, both directly
and indirectly. Grouping black poets and regional poets separately,
for example, can blind us to the political significance of dialect
poetry and help make it seem merely quaint and harmless; alternatively, we can see it as a continuing tradition of resistance to the
dominant metropolitan culture. A taxonomy of mutually exclusive
categories will also consistently falsify the history of aesthetic innovation. Jean Toomer's (1894–1967) *Cane* (1923), with its mixture
of poetry, prose poetry, fiction, and dramatic dialogue, is one of the
triumphs of modernist mixed forms and needs to be discussed with
William Carlos Williams' *Spring & All*, which appeared the same
year.[227] At the same time, one could highlight the imagist element
in *Cane*, or discuss its jazz rhythms, its cubist dislocations, its use
of ordinary language. Because of his deeply troubled relation to his
own racial identity, Toomer himself came to resent being classed as
a black poet.

Other poets have specifically rejected the categories we habitually use to arrange literary history. Laura Riding, for example, objects to being viewed within experimental modernism. Langston
Hughes, perhaps the most versatile political poet of the period, made
a number of efforts to link the oppression of blacks with poverty
and discrimination throughout American society. One might want
to see him within the whole long populist tradition in American
writing. Not to link Hughes with other socially conscious poets
amounts to maintaining, by way of the discourse of literary history, the same racial and cultural divisions and antagonisms (some
of which Hughes himself expressed in *Fine Clothes to the Jew*, 1927)
that the capitalist class in America promoted to prevent the working

class from organizing effectively. Writing and teaching literary history that way is not a neutral activity; it is an activity that reinforces (and treats as transhistorical, even natural) some of the most divisive and discriminatory impulses in American society.

Although some who criticize this tradition are reluctant either to prescribe or to recommend how to bring about appropriate changes, I do believe specific corrective actions can be taken. The first step in reconstituting the history of the poetry of the period, I would argue, is to work to get as close as possible to the actual publications of the period—the periodicals that poets published in, the individual books in which their work (in some cases) was collected. As objects, individual books provide a stronger sense of engagement in specific cultural contexts and of the development of a poet's career. The way in which individual volumes can constitute acts of cultural intervention is sometimes even signalled by their jackets, a particularly ephemeral element of book design, since libraries typically discard them and collected works almost always obliterate the visual history of individual volumes. The jacket copy for Edna St. Vincent Millay's "1940 Notebook," *Make Bright the Arrows*, declares it to be "a collection of poems on which the ink is scarcely dry: they . . . deal with themes which vitally concern every American and the cause of democracy throughout the world." Far from backing away from the poems' wartime topicality, then, the jacket makes that the reason for the book's existence. The jacket of MacLeish's *Public Speech* (1936) achieves its impact through its pointed minimalism. Three years earlier, in "Background with Revolutionaries," he had satirized Marxist claims about class interests: "You and d'Wops and d'Chinks you are all brudders! / Havend't you got it d' same ideology?" Now, in "Speech to Those Who Say Comrade," he reiterates his earlier argument that polemics do not forge a real brotherhood but also offers the possibility of an alliance based on collaborative struggle:

> The brotherhood is not by the blood certainly;
> But neither are men brothers by speech—by saying so;
> Men are brothers by life lived and are hurt for it.[228]

The flaps and back panel of *Public Speech* are blank, but these three lines are printed on the front cover, thereby making that poem the center of the book's project. Genevieve Taggard's *Collected Poems*, to take an extreme case, prints a manifesto on the back jacket that is not included in the book itself. Its first two paragraphs, drawing on arguments from her uncollected essays, prepare the reader for the poems by defining an antiromantic view of the subject and distinguishing her feminism from conventional femininity:

> The reader will misunderstand my poems if he thinks I have been trying to write about myself (as if I were in any way unique) as a biographer might—or as a romantic poet would, to map his own individuality. Since the earliest attempts at verse I have tried to use the 'I' in a poem only as a means for transferring feeling to identification with anyone who takes the poem, momentarily for his own. 'I' is then adjusted to the voice of the reader.
>
> Many poems in this collection are about the experiences of women. I hope these express all types of candid and sturdy women (I think of friends and historical figures as I write). All those who try to live richly and intelligently. I have refused to write out of a decorative impulse because I conceive it to be the deadend of much feminine talent. A kind of literary needlework.

The book jackets, pamphlet covers, and illustrations accompanying the political poetry of the period were also often more diverse, innovative, and significant than we now tend to assume. Hugo Gellert's inventive jacket design and illustrations for Stanley Kimmel's *The Kingdom of Smoke* take the familiar themes of proletarian art and reinvent them in surprising ways.[229] On the jacket, a coal miner sketched in the heavy crayon style of the old *Masses* stands over the body of a coworker lying on a stretcher. In the final illustration to the book (fig. 27) oppression and resistance are mapped out in elegant simplicity: in the background a crowd of working-class men and women struggle forward. Near us, in exaggerated perspective at the foreground of the image, are placed a bowl of soup and a piece of bread. Between the food and the workers a line of armed soldiers is positioned behind barbed wire. One of the workers has already been shot. To traverse the image from top to bottom is to enact a narrative that negotiates the bare dichotomies of social life. Here, as in an infinite allegory, are arrayed the people and their minimal needs.

27. One of Hugo Gellert's illustrations for Stanley Kimmel's book of poems The Kingdom of Smoke *(1932).*

But between them the state and industry have imposed their power. Louis Lozowick's dramatic red and black design for the jacket of *Unrest 1930* (Pl. B), which the editors felt was important enough to reproduce as the frontispiece to the book, makes an energetic visual statement that rather belies the dour "socialist realist" reputation of

1930s political graphic art and poetry.[230] Echoing both the dynamic graphic art of the Russian revolution and the polished art deco tradition in America, the cover fuses aesthetic and political confidence. Meanwhile, its reversing arrows promise an interchange between metropolitan culture and world unrest. Indeed, taken together, a number of the illustrations reproduced here—from Aaron Douglas's cover for *Fire!!* (fig. 28) to the cover of S. A. DeWitt's *Rhapsodies in Red: Songs for the Social Revolution* (fig. 29)—suggest a coherent phenomenon that one might call "left deco" of the 1920s and 1930s. Few of these covers in fact deliver the simple and obvious message political art is often reputed to offer. Like the title to *Unrest 1930*, the title to *Rhapsodies in Red* is run together so that it needs to be decoded to be read at all. It is also explicitly dialectical, as the elegant high cultural typeface of the title is juxtaposed with the dark figure of a worker who carries both a shovel and a set of horns. His songs, we can conclude, will be the culture of the future. Similarly, Olga Monus's red and black cover for Leonard Spier's *When the Sirens Blow and Other Poems* (1933) (fig. 30), another of the Rebel Poet booklets, needs to be visually analyzed before the components of its apparent graphic force can be understood.[231] A series of schematic human figures carrying a communist banner join together and with one collective boot crush the forces of militarism. Familiar as a cubist motif, here the mechanized and serialized human figures gain a specific political meaning.

A number of other modern styles feed into the illustrations for political poetry as well. A strong expressionist component appears in John C. Rogers' deathly cover to George Jarrboe's 1932 Rebel Poet booklet *The Unknown Soldier Speaks* (fig. 31) and in the frontispiece and jacket to Robert Gessner's *Upsurge* (fig. 32).[232] In the latter image the recurrent motif of upraised revolutionary fists gains special power from its multiple semiotic effects. The background, for example, simultaneously suggests flames and the muscles of another massive upraised arm. The image thereby combines fibered strength with incendiary outrage. Finally, a single fist, the representative of all the others, rises into a beam of futurist light that bisects the image. That single fist, thrust into a beam of light, is reproduced again on the title page. It is an icon that will have to stand for every-

28. Aaron Douglas's red and black cover for the first and only issue of Fire!! (1926). It included a section of poems by Cullen, Hughes, and others titled "Flame from the Dark Tower."

29. The cover illustration to S. A. DeWitt's collection of poems Rhapsodies in Red *(1933). Black type on a red background. Baskette Collection, UIUC.*

30. *Olga Monus's design for the cover of Leonard Spier's Rebel Poets pamphlet* When the Sirens Blow *(1933). Black print on a red background.*

31. *John C. Rogers' design for the cover to George Jarrboe's Rebel Poets pamphlet* The Unknown Soldier Speaks *(1932). The background is overprinted in black. The author's name, title, and the central figure are in the bright red color of the card stock on which the cover is printed. Baskette Collection, UIUC.*

32. The frontispiece and jacket illustration to Robert Gessner's volume of poetry Upsurge *(1933). The same image was later used on the cover of* Spain, *a pamphlet about the Spanish civil war written by A. Souchy and published by Libertarian Publishers under the auspices of the Anarchist Federation of America.*

thing the book aims to do. The jacket description does no more than point toward the book itself: "A dramatic modern poem by the author of *Massacre* and *Broken Arrow*, which it is impossible for the publishers to describe. It is frankly a message and any description of it is inherent in its violent rhythms." John C. Rogers' cover for H. H. Lewis's *Thinking of Russia* (fig. 1) offers an equally powerful message with a quite straightforward design. Plowing his field under what is here unequivocally the sun rising in the east, the farmer cannot help but think of Russia. Held together by the matched diagonals of the plowed field and the rising sun—with rough block lettering that seems itself to have been plowed into the field of the page— the cover presents us with a pastoral politics that grows not out of rhetorical persuasion but out of reflection on the work an individual farmer must do. Rogers' design for Lewis's *Salvation* (fig. 2), on the other hand, gets its charm from the very schematic polemicism of its contrasting front and back covers. A soup kitchen in America on the front is juxtaposed with a Soviet scene on the back cover: new apartment construction crowding out the traditional architecture of imperial Russia.

A number of the jackets to Langston Hughes's books and pamphlets also make effective visual statements. The stunning cover of *The Weary Blues* (Pl. A), designed by the Mexican artist Miguel Covarrubias, shows a black piano player silhouetted against a red background; the image foregrounds the simultaneity of music and poetry and suggests not only the interrelations but also the common interests that can link different elements of black culture.[233] Here too the stylized hands and the vibrant piano light that is as bright as the sun partly suggest an exuberant, confident cultural mission. Hughes's *Jim Crow's Last Stand* (1943), on the other hand, a pamphlet issued by the Negro Publication Society of America, effects a very different intervention. Its bold, unambiguous block lettering announces an imperative project: poems to be used by ordinary people in bringing about social change. Joe Jones's cover to *A New Song* (fig. 33) carefully articulates its political message to a more traditional humanism—specifically to a black heterosexual couple, suggesting that the emphatic social critique of Hughes's "Ballads of Lenin" and "Lynching Song" is now the proper outgrowth of the values associated with

33. *Joe Jones's cover to Langston Hughes's poetry pamphlet* A New Song *(1938). The figures are printed in black and gray. The background is blue.*

the traditional family. Notably, in Jones's drawing of the man's right arm the militant fist of the 1930s is quietly incorporated into underlying determination. Even though such design elements are often not under an author's control, they can have a significant role in giving a book coherent meaning in its own time.

Most of these visual elements of individual volumes are, unfortunately, typically abandoned when collected volumes are assembled. But that is not the only reason to return to individual books of poetry. Collected volumes are obviously often valuable and sometimes they are indispensible—both H. D.'s *Collected Poems 1912–1944* (1983) and *The Collected Poems of Jean Toomer* (1988), for example, contain a considerable amount of previously unpublished work; the two volumes of *The Collected Poems of William Carlos Williams* (1986–88) restore the integrity of Williams' individual books and recover a substantial number of poems not included in the collected volumes Williams edited himself—but in many other cases collected works are deceptive. Until the very fine three-volume Spoon River Poetry Press edition of Lindsay's work (1984–86), the only "collected" Lindsay remained the 1925 Macmillan edition that omitted his last four books and reproduced his drawings poorly. From Robinson to Sandburg to Stevens to Millay to Moore, volumes of collected poems are not complete. Moreover, there is a regrettable tendency for people to feel a volume of collected poems eliminates the need to go back and look at individual volumes. In part, because of the profession's irrational commitment to poets' final wishes, when poets themselves compile their collected poems we tend to accept unquestioningly the announcement that these are "all the work the poet wished to preserve." It is as if we assume the poet has infallible judgment in selecting the canon of his or her own work, as if we should have the courtesy not to read uncollected poems. Uncollected poems may point to historical realities that seem irrelevant or counter-productive only at the particular moment the poet is assembling a collected volume; at a later historical moment, however, those may be just the poems that can help readers understand their own situation. Uncollected poems can also often define the outer edges of a poet's enterprise, directions a poet may have pursued for a time then rejected. In editing his *Collected Poems* (1968), for example, Patchen eliminated the more obviously pro-Soviet poems from his first book, *Before the Brave* (1936). Moore's collected volumes eliminate the history of her notoriously elaborate revisions. Sandburg's collected poems may block us from realizing that some of the writing in his *Abraham Lincoln: The War Years* should count as poetry. The editor of Marsden Hartley's posthumous *Selected Poems* (1945) silently eliminates the poems from Hartley's dadaist period, presumably because he does not care for that sort of thing. Hartley's *Collected Poems* (1987) restores those poems but remains selective in its printing of his unpublished work. John Beecher tells us his *Collected Poems* (1974) excludes "a body of highly personal poetry" because he deems it more appropriate for an autobiography. It also excludes all the illustrations Barbara Beecher did for his individual books.

Important illustrations and design elements that helped shape the cultural work a book did in its own time are almost always eliminated from collected volumes edited by others, in part because the textual bias of most literary critics makes such visual features seem either trivial, irrelevant, or virtually invisible. Thus the striking prints E. Simms Campbell did for the 1931 edition of Sterling Brown's *Southern Road* are predictably eliminated from his collected poems. In an extreme case, like that of Paul Laurence Dunbar (1872–1906), the individual books and the collected poems seem wholly different cultural artifacts. Dunbar's individual books are often heavily illustrated with photographs of blacks in different settings, and the poems are printed on elaborately decorated pages. Like other books of the period, including Lindsay's first books, the bindings may be intricately embossed. All of this disappears from his 1913 collected poems. One looks forward to the forthcoming collected poems of Langston Hughes, since many poems now out of print or forgotten in newspapers and journals will thereby become visible again. A collected Hughes could also reprint the illustrations from Hughes's individual books and all the illustrated poems that appeared in journals and newspapers, even if that meant printing some poems twice. Once the collected poems appears, people will be far less likely to seek out those poems in their original settings.

Similarly, when Pound published *A Draft of XXX Cantos* in 1930 he substantially reduced the chance that people would seek out the heavily decorated *A Draft of XVI Cantos* (1925) and *A Draft of the Cantos XVII–XXVII* (1928), with their illuminated letters and ornamented borders. Gladys Hynes's elaborate illuminated letters for the 1928 collection, each five or more inches high and printed in red and black on a ten-by-fifteen-inch page, play out part of the dichotomous system of Pound's text.[234] Hynes's illustrations thus help focus the reading the *Cantos* offer of their own historical moment and make that reading accessible to Pound's audience. The illustrations within and around the letters are generally devoted either to an idealized world of medieval romance or to a modern world of oppression and death. The style is equally contrastive: the letters evoking Pound's nostalgia for the earlier period provide architectural support and formal resolution for the fantasy images; the letters depicting modern scenes impose an iron law of social control. In those letters men are ground up into skulls by the war industry (fig. 34), an industrial behemoth turns men into exhausted slaves (fig. 35), and financiers manipulate kings, soldiers, and statesmen like puppets. The letters themselves are often structured as a binary system. The letter for "Canto xx," devoted to the world of medieval romance Pound wanted to revive, divides into an image of formal courtship rituals above and sexuality below. The two letters reproduced here, both based on the letter A, also separate roughly into a visible upper world and a lower world that may be hidden from view. The illustration for "Canto XVIII" (fig. 34) shows us battlefield dead above and what we now call the military-industrial complex below and to the side. The illustration for "Canto XXII" (fig. 35) displays monolithic industrial power above and its human cost below. The bar in the "A" thus serves partly as a figure for the repression of cultural knowledge. All these productive components are eliminated from the collected *Cantos*.

Collected volumes can also draw our attention away from extremely important versions of poems published in journals. Pound's "Salutation The Third," published in the 1914 volume of *Blast*, includes the lines "Let us be done with Jews and Jobbery, / Let us SPIT upon those who fawn on the JEWS for their money."[235] *Personae* (1926) changes the lines to read "Let us be done with pandars and

THE XVIII CANTO

AND OF KUBLAI:
"I have told you of that
                emperor's city in detail
And will tell you of the coining in Cambaluc
        that hyght the secret of alchemy:
They take bast of the mulberry-tree,
That is a skin between the wood and the bark,
And of this they make paper, and mark it
Half a tornesel, a tornesel, or a half-groat of silver,
Or two groats, or five groats, or ten groats,
Or, for a great sheet, a gold bezant, 3 bezants,
                Ten Bezants;
And they are written on by officials,
And smeared with the great kahn's seal in vermilion;
And the forgers are punished with death.
And all this costs the Khan nothing,
And so he is rich in this world.

34. Gladys Hynes's illuminated letter for Ezra Pound's "Canto XVIII," from A Draft of the Cantos XVII–XXVII *(1928). The large letter and the title of the Canto are printed in red. UIUC.*

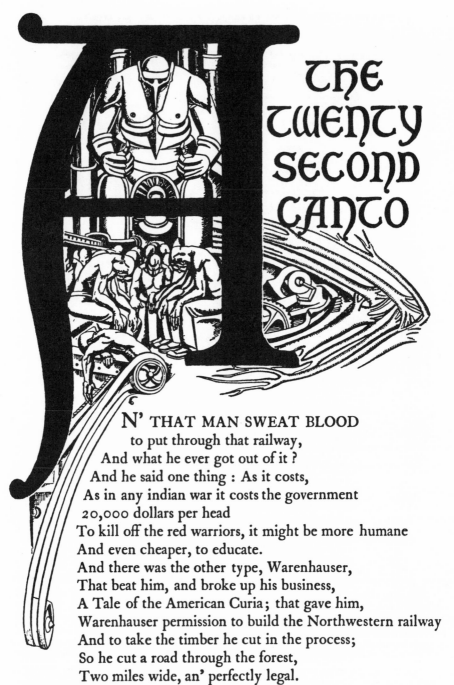

THE TWENTY SECOND CANTO

'N' THAT MAN SWEAT BLOOD
to put through that railway,
And what he ever got out of it ?
And he said one thing : As it costs,
As in any indian war it costs the government
20,000 dollars per head
To kill off the red warriors, it might be more humane
And even cheaper, to educate.
And there was the other type, Warenhauser,
That beat him, and broke up his business,
A Tale of the American Curia; that gave him,
Warenhauser permission to build the Northwestern railway
And to take the timber he cut in the process;
So he cut a road through the forest,
Two miles wide, an' perfectly legal.
Who wuz agoin' to stop him !

35. Gladys Hynes's illuminated letter for Ezra Pound's "Canto XXII" (1928). The edition was limited to 101 copies. UIUC.

jobbery, / Let us spit upon those who pat the big-bellies for profit." Since the rest of Pound's career rules out the possibility of a change of heart here, we can assume he thought the change merely politic. Certainly no argument that Pound was simply articulating a persona here can explain away his attraction for such a persona or its deeper relation to his character or career. The *Blast* version not only establishes how early anti-Semitism was central in Pound's thought; it also suggests Pound's anti-Semitism may be hidden behind a series of substitutions and code words elsewhere in his work.

In other cases, there either were no collected poems published or the collected poems distort the record. In the introduction to his 1986 *Collected Poems*, Carl Rakosi argues that he rejected a chronological arrangement "because the presumption underlying chronological sequence is that a literary development and some kind of psychological progression or evolving take place in this way. They may or may not" (p. 17).[236] There is, of course, nothing wrong with Rakosi reorganizing his poems thematically, and his *Collected Poems* thereby becomes an important statement about his work, but it cannot under these conditions actually replace his earlier books and journal publications or, when necessary, manuscript evidence of dates of composition. The value of the chronological arrangement is not merely biographical but rather historical; it enables us to test the poems against the pressures of their historical moment. Moreover, a nonchronological (and essentially spatialized) collected poems may give the impression of an even more wondrously unified human subject by obliterating both biography and historical context. For other poets, however, the deletions from the work are too severe for the volume to count as a collected poems at all. John Crowe Ransom's *Selected Poems*, repeatedly refined and reprinted in revised editions, simply does not give us sufficient access to the full range of his ideological commitments. Langston Hughes's *Selected Poems* (1959), to cite an extreme case, is both incomplete and misleading, in part because it is arranged thematically rather than chronologically but primarily because it was assembled after a convulsively reactionary period of American history and excludes most of his more radical poems.[237] Some of these poems were never even gathered in his books and pamphlets; they remain in the journals of the time.[238] Just before his death, Hughes attempted to counter the politics of the *Selected Poems* by assembling *The Panther and the Lash* (1967), which printed new poems and reached back into the 1930s and 1940s to rescue texts like the Scottsboro poem "Justice" ("Her bandage hides two festering sores / That once perhaps were eyes") and "Ku Klux." But the *Selected Poems* continues to do its damage, remaining the text of choice in most literature courses, since it provides many faculty members with the timeless, decontextualized humanism they want in poetry.

Even collected poems that appear to be complete, however, often raise problems that are not apparent unless one looks at the original publications. The 1929 edition of Crane's *The Bridge* produced by Caresse and Harry Crosby's Paris-based Black Sun Press presents the poem in a spacious format that suggests the scale of its cultural ambitions in a way none of the editions of Crane's collected poems have been able to do. Similarly, Nancy Cunard's Hours Press, also based in Paris, published Riding's *Twenty Poems Less* (1930) and Lowenfels' *Apollinaire* (1930) in a large format of seven and a half by eleven inches that gives the texts a material coherence and integrity one never feels in cramped collected volumes. One is led to dwell on the poems at length, to move through them slowly. At the other end of the spectrum, Amy Lowell's *Collected Poems* (1955), assembled posthumously, were published in an unattractive two-column edition that gives almost no white space around the texts. The effect is almost archival, as if we are not really meant to read the book. That much, any reader can see. But readers will not necessarily be aware that the important prefaces to her individual books have been omitted. The preface to *Legends* (1921) gives the sources of the narratives she retells. The preface to *Con Grande's Castle* (1920) summarizes her theory of polyphonic prose and makes a claim that substantially enriches and complicates the text to follow. The poems in the book, she argues, "all owe their existence to the war . . . they are the result of a vision thrown suddenly back upon remote events to explain a strange and terrible reality."[239] Until Mina Loy's 1982 *The Last Lunar Baedeker*, editions of her selected poems essentially obliterated her long, uncollected poem sequence, "Anglo-Mongrels and the Rose," a remarkable synthesis of personal and public myth that remained in *The Little Review* and the *Contact Collection of Contemporary Writers*, just as others of her poems were scattered for years in journals like *Others*, *Trend*, *The Dial*, *Contact*, *Broom*, and *Rogue*. The editor of Loy's collected poems, however, regrettably decided to normalize her spacing and punctuation; these are not, therefore, always precisely the disruptive, witty poems Loy wrote and published.[240]

In addition to having the opportunity to see uncollected poems and poems in earlier versions, there are other reasons why it is essential to follow the journals of the period, ranging from *Fire!!* (1926), which only published one issue—its revolutionary cultural criticism staged with art deco elegance (fig. 28)[241]—to *Hound and Horn* (1927–1934), whose commitments varied from southern regionalism to humanism to Marxism. In the highly interactive culture they helped to create, little magazines defined their enterprises not only in manifestos but also in commenting on one another. Especially in the 1920s and 1930s, running from *The Daily Worker*, *The Modern Quarterly*, and *Hound and Horn* through *Blues*, *The Rebel Poet*, *Contact*, *Fantasy*, *1933—A Year Magazine*, *Partisan Review*, and *Monthly Review*, newspapers and magazines praised each other's accomplishments and critiqued each other's weaknesses. Even *International Literature*, published in Moscow but with assistance from American writers (and distributed here in an English language edition), covered American little magazines in great detail; like *Broom*, the *Liberator*, and *Kosmos*, it also published an extensive letters column that fostered further interaction and debate.

In reading journals one can begin to recognize the strategic, dialectical, and exclusionary relations between poetry and the other discourses of the time.[242] To do so one needs to read not only journals devoted largely to poetry but also journals and newspapers in which poetry plays a small but culturally specific role. It is actually impossible to judge what kind of discursive terrain poetry occupied, what social, political, and aesthetic functions it served, if one only reads it in anthologies and books of poems. Charlotte Perkins Gilman (1860–1935) authored a monthly journal, *Forerunner*, from 1909 to 1916, publishing her own essays, editorials, serialized books, and poetry. Reading only her poetry, one misses the way she uses poetry in relation to her other work—the topics she addresses there, the stances she takes, the metaphors and levels of generality possible in the poetry as opposed to the prose. Similarly, to read Langston Hughes's "Christ in Alabama" in context—in the December 1931 issue of *Contempo* devoted largely to the Scottsboro case, in which eight black men were sentenced to death for rapes they did not commit—is a different cultural experience from reading the poem in isolation. Hughes's poem is placed in the center of the page, under a stylized silhouette of a black man bearing three stigmata (fig. 36), an image that effectively fuses the two panels of Charles Cullen's jacket for *The Black Christ* (fig. 11). Essays on Scottsboro by Lincoln Steffens, by a defense attorney, and by Hughes himself frame the poem. The central wound in the illustration also figures as a pair of lips; the poem and the essays serve partly to give this emblematic Black Christ the kinds of varied speech his suffering warrants. "Christ is a nigger," Hughes writes in the poem, "Mary is his mother":

> Most holy bastard
> Of the bleeding mouth;
> *Nigger Christ*
> *On the cross of the South.*

Clearly, the poem can aim for a condensed but multiple indictment —religious, humane, and mythic—that the essays cannot achieve. In one sense it says all that needs saying. But the essays in turn root the poem in an unyielding, pressing set of historical facts that cannot be transcended even by myth. Similarly, to read the new black poetry in journals like *The Crisis* and *Opportunity* is to see the poetry as part of a whole critical and transformative social project. In the case of these black journals, then, one encounters coherent relations of similarity and difference when reading the poetry in context.

The project in fact begins with the covers, though the covers of *Opportunity* and *The Crisis* are too diverse to be easily characterized. They range from sentimental portraits of children to abstract invocations of cultural aspiration to decorative adaptations of motifs from African masks. Christmas covers often insist on significant black roles in Biblical stories. But one continuing feature of this key mechanism for a magazine's self-presentation and the definition of its mission persists in *Opportunity* and *The Crisis* through the 1920s and 1930s: the repeated presence of women on the covers. The effects, to be sure, are sometimes contradictory. Many will now find Alan Freelon's June 1928 *Crisis* portrait of a nude "jungle nymph" naively sexist. And there is arguably a problematic idealization in Aaron Douglas's September 1927 *Crisis* cover "The Burden of Black Womanhood." But the overall effect is that of a rich diversity that quite overturns any essentialist notion of black female identity. Many of the covers indeed are significantly empowering. Douglas's May 1927 *Crisis* cover (fig. 37) is dedicated to the Women's Auxiliary of the NAACP, but it suggests not selfless dedication but pride, dignity, strength, and self-possession. A stylized silhouette, it plays productively off against the whole range of styles *Opportunity* and *The Crisis* adopted for their covers, from elaborate illustrations echoing the arts and crafts and art nouveau styles to explicitly modernist experiments. Women were depicted by both female and male artists and by both blacks and whites, just as both magazines published poems on racial issues by both black and white poets. Some covers used abstract images of types, others intricately realist portraits of individuals. The magazines as a result offered women a variety of subject positions they might choose to identify with or resist. In this *Opportunity* and *The Crisis* were nearly unique. Certainly on the left in the 1920s and 1930s, as the illustrations for this book demonstrate, the revolutionary worker was almost always male. Here, however, as Roscoe Wright's January 1928 *Crisis* cover "Negro Womanhood" shows, the figure reaching past her chains toward the sun is as likely to be female. Finally, along with other illustrations in the magazines, these covers establish a rich field of visual analogues to the many poems on black women published here. Thus Gwendolyn Bennett's (1902–1981) witty, self-conscious July 1926 *Opportunity* cover (fig. 38) can be taken as partly anticipating her poems "Song" and "To a Dark Girl" ("Something of old forgotten queens / Lurks in the lithe abandon of your walk) in the magazine's October 1926 and 1927 issues. Both the cover and the poems demonstrate, moreover,

CONTEMPO

A Review of Books and Personalities

Volume 1. Number 13   Dec. 1, 1931, Chapel Hill, N. C.   Ten Cents a Copy

To Lynch by Law is as Bad as to Lynch by Obscene Hands of a Lustful Mob

By LINCOLN STEFFENS

The first time I heard of the now famous Scottsboro case, the narrator told how those colored boys under sentence saw it. And they saw what they saw of it from a rear car. There was some sort of a row—a scrap—or a fight going on in a car so far ahead that they could get glimpses of it only as the train bent around the curves till, by and by, the train stopped. Then they saw a lot of the fighters jump off of that front car and run away. They went up forward to hear more about it.

It was later, when the train arrived at its destination, that those witnesses of the incident, were arrested as the scrappers and—rapists. They were so dazed that they never quite recovered from their frightful astonishment.

But you don't have to go by this casual alibi. Take the record of the trials, the speed of them, the ages of the convicted and the circumstances, and one can realize for himself that there was no justice in these cases. There was the opposite. There was righteousness in it.

Southern Gentlemen, White Prostitutes, Mill-Owners, and Negroes

By LANGSTON HUGHES

If the 9 Scottsboro boys die, the South ought to be ashamed of itself—but the 12 million Negroes in America ought to be more ashamed than the South. Maybe it's against the law to print the transcripts of trials from a State court. I don't know. If not, every Negro paper in this country ought to immediately publish the official records of the Scottsboro cases so that both whites and blacks might see at a glance to what absurd farces an Alabama court can descend. (Or should I say an American court?) . . . The 9 boys in Kilbee Prison are Americans. 12 million Negroes are Americans, too. (And many of them far too light in color to be called Negroes, except by liars.) The judge and the jury at Scottsboro, and the governor of Alabama, are Americans. Therefore, for the sake of American justice, (if there is any) and for the honor of Southern gentlemen, (if there ever were any) let the South rise up in press and pulpit, home and school, Senate Chambers and Rotary Clubs, and petition the freedom of the dumb young blacks—so indis-

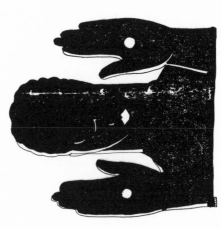

Christ in Alabama

By LANGSTON HUGHES

Christ is a Nigger,
Beaten and black—
O, bare your back.

In Alabama and some parts of the South the more respectable people are yielding to the Northern clamor against lynching. There is lynching in the North, too, but it is not against blacks. It is against the Reds. And it is not by mobs. It is by the police, the courts and juries; and therefore legal, regular, righteous. The righteous people of the South have been gradually waking up to the idea that they can save their face by taking justice out of the rude hands of the mob and putting it in the delicate hands of the lawyers, and judges and a few representatives of the better people in a jury. That is to say, they can lynch their blacks the way the superior North, West and East get their Reds.

Well, now, you can see that the Alabama righteous must feel the Scottsboro case was a perfect example of the new ideal of justice modelled on the great (anti-) Red North. They had some blacks in a jam where the whites might have wreaked their fear of the colored folk by a deeply satisfying lynching. And they did not

(Continued on page four)

Revolts and Rackets
By Louis Adamic

In a sense *The Populist Revolt* is a timely book. Its subject is—remotely—of current interest. It deals with the expansion, overproduction, underconsumption, unemployment, misery, falling prices, agricultural and bank failures—the familiar cycle of boom, deflation, depression—which produced or accompanied the so-called Populist

---

Mary is His Mother—
Mammy of the South,
Silence your mouth.

God's His Father—
White Master above,
Grant us your love.

Most holy bastard
Of the bleeding mouth:
Nigger Christ
On the cross of the South.

Notes from Nowhere

Langston Hughes, prominent poet and novelist, is soon to be the guest of the editors of Contempo *** Phillips Russell, of historical and literary biography fame, recently married Cara Mae Green, sister of Paul Green of *The House of Connelly* *** William Faulkner while guest of Contempo was surprised to learn that the University of North Carolina library cannot afford a copy of any of his novels *** And while we are local, a John Reed Club has come, and the Carolina Playmakers are sponsoring a Theatre Guild production of *Elizabeth the Queen* *** When the first version of Archibald Henderson's *Shaw* appeared, Max Beerbohm made cartoons and caricatures out of the illustrations and by changing words cleverly mutilated the text to create idiotic meanings. This copy of the book is now in the

---

creet as to travel, unwittingly, on the same freight train with two white prostitutes . . . And, incidently, let the mill-owners of Huntsville begin to pay their women decent wages so they won't need to be prostitutes. And let the sensible citizens of Alabama (if there are any) supply schools for the black populace of their state, (and for the half-black, too—the mulatto children of the Southern gentlemen. [I reckon they're gentlemen.]) so the Negroes won't be so dumb again . . . But back to the dark millions—black and half-black, brown and yellow, with a gang of white fore-parents—like me. If these 12 million Negro Americans don't raise such a howl that the doors of Kilbee Prison shake until the 9 youngsters come out, (and I don't mean a polite howl, either) then let Dixie justice (blind and syphilitic as it may be) take its course, and let Alabama's Southern gentlemen amuse themselves burning 9 young black boys till they're dead in the State's electric chair. And let the mill-owners of Huntsville continue to pay women workers too little for them to afford the price of a train ticket to Chattanooga . . . Dear Lord, I never knew until now that white ladies (the same color as Southern gentlemen) travelled in freight trains . . . Did you, world? . . . And who ever heard of raping a prostitute?

Facts About Scottsboro
By Carol Weiss King
(Attorney for Defense)

On March 25, 1931, two white girls, seven

36. The upper two-thirds (11 × 14) of the front page of the December 1931 issue of Contempo, published in Chapel Hill, North Carolina. The entire page is 19 inches high. Baskette Collection, UIUC.

37. *Aaron Douglas's design for the May 1929 issue of* The Crisis. *Red on white.*
UIUC.

38. Gwendolyn Bennett's design for the July 1926 issue of Opportunity. *University of Wisconsin.*

that a cultural struggle was taking place over who would have the power to make analogies between contemporary life and an African heritage.

In other cases, however, the relations are more problematic. *The Masses* (1911–1917), for example, despite its varied radical and liberal commitments, often published love poetry and descriptive poetry that was not overtly political. The point there was to demonstrate, by way of a lyrical, universalizing, and sometimes sentimental human-ism—a humanism permissible specifically in poetry—that a radical political commitment did not preclude experiencing other kinds of human emotions. Indeed, these other human engagements might be-come morally acceptable from the vantage point of the magazine's more political prose. In other cases, *The Masses* published poetry that may seem excessively romantic or sentimental to us but that had specific uses for readers at the time. Thus Louise Bryant's poetry, which contemporary readers are likely to find merely weak and romantic, was in a sense socially charged and politicized when it appeared in *The Masses*, since it spoke for the contested emotions surrounding the issue of free love. Part of what is interesting in all of this is that the "meaning" of such poetry is not intrinsic but histori-cally and discursively contextual. In general, *The Masses* was taking the poetry of the genteel tradition and trying to give it altogether dif-ferent cultural significance, to dislodge that poetry from its earlier conservative social connections and articulate it to the magazine's own radical project. At least in a limited way, the genteel tradition thereby becomes modern.

The publication on the left where the poetry is most intricately contextualized may well be *The Daily Worker*, the official news-paper of the Communist party. This may also appear, from the van-tage point of the dominant postwar ideologies, to be the publication where the use of poetry is most instrumental. About that I have some doubts: first, because poetry in conservative, mass circulation magazines and newspapers is equally obviously instrumental; sec-ond, because effective instrumental uses of poetry typically adapt long-established cultural roles for literariness in general and poetry in particular. *The Daily Worker* does, however, give us the opportu-nity to see how a political party used poetry in the major medium it had for communicating with its members. Since the newspaper was a daily publication, its editors had the opportunity to solicit and rapidly publish poetry that was closely tied to particular events and interests. Publishing topical poetry in a party newspaper required careful monitoring of both the occasional poem that aimed to mount detailed polemical positions on key issues and poems with intensely explicit loyalties. Writing to H. H. Lewis in July 1942, Edith Anderson of *The Daily Worker* suggested in effect that the Third Period fervor of his poems did not match the party's current stand: "I like your poem 'Mass Movement March,' but the editor of the page, Milton, does not agree. However, I too feel that the end of it is too aggressively red for right now when we have an immediate goal which absorbs most of our energy. It simply is not wise, not correct, not helpful to the war effort or to the opening of a second front, to talk of red marches." After revision, the poem was published.[243]

Poetry had a strong presence in *The Daily Worker* in the late 1920s. Through the first years of the Depression, however, the paper's financial difficulties combined with the militant party's doubts about the centrality of cultural work to keep the paper short and relatively free of poetry. They only published 31 poems in 1930 and fewer still in 1931, 1932, and the first half of 1933. As the paper became longer and the party was persuaded of the value of cultural work, the number more than doubled, rising to a peak of over 100 poems and songs in 1934. Drawing on practices set by IWW newspapers in the second decade, *The Daily Worker* published poems about union organizing and workers suffering throughout its history. It also regularly renewed the IWW tradition of using poetry as an effective medium for satire. In the 1940s readers were encouraged to send in short poems for a special column.

The most distinctive thing about *Daily Worker* poetry overall is its frequent topicality. The major causes the paper took up were regularly reinforced in poems, from the Sacco and Vanzetti and Scottsboro cases through to the efforts to get the allies to open up a second front in 1942. Countee Cullen's "Scottsboro, Too, is Worth Its Song," which the paper first published in October 1933 and then reprinted in November 1934, suggests the special role poetry played.[244] "Now," Cullen anticipates, "will the poets sing" about the Scottsboro Boys.

"Remembering their sharp and pretty / Tunes for Sacco and Vanzetti," surely this new "cause divinely spun / For those whose eyes
are on the sun"—a cause offering "in epitome . . . all disgrace / And
epic wrong"—will produce its own body of poetry. But the poets
"have raised no cry," he concludes, "And I know why." The reason,
of course, is that the boys are black. But also at issue here is the
clear notion that poetry is securely established as a special site for
idealization. Scottsboro is an appropriate topic for poetry because it
exemplifies transcendent values. Its injustice is thus of epic scale.

It is a link with idealization, overall, that poetry regularly offers
the causes the party espouses in *The Daily Worker*. More often than
one might expect, the editors are able to publish poems making that
connection and thus demonstrating that the party's interests reflect
the highest human motives. But not always. When the writer and
communist leader Ernst Thaelman is arrested by the Nazis more
than half a dozen poems are published in his behalf. When Earl
Browder is convicted on a passport violation and sentenced with
unusual severity because he had been head of the party, reader after
reader sends in poems urging his release, and Walter Lowenfels writes
a poem on his behalf. Yet when the Soviet Union signs a nonaggression pact with Germany, it is another matter. Either the poets will
not do the work or the pact—however pragmatic and reasonable the
recently antifascist party deems it to be—proves no subject for idealization. Poems are published in the hope that, in context, they can
offer indirect support for the decision, but they are either generic
antiwar poems or poems reminding readers of the pointless slaughter
of the First World War. In November 1939 Carl Sandburg's antiwar
"Buttons" is reprinted from Upton Sinclair's 1915 anthology *The Cry
for Justice*, Mike Quin writes "March of the Cheated Millions," and
Joseph Freeman publishes "A Million White Stones," reminding us
that headstones are the major legacy that ordinary people had from
the First World War. The poems in all these cases are published in the
same time frame as related news stories or feature articles. In addition, photographs and editorial cartoons add differential support and
contextualization. Particularly in its coverage of the Spanish Civil
War, *The Daily Worker* is able to mount a strikingly wide range of
discourses and images.

Overall, however, the newspaper rarely matches the visual power of the old *Masses*, which was a stunning journal graphically; there the poetry and the prose gain from a powerful visual environment.[245] In other journals, even typeface and type size become important. Toward the end of its brief life, *The Rebel Poet*, which published seventeen issues from 1931 to 1932, used varying typefaces and inventive, modernist layout on its title pages to add an element of self-conscious style and semiotic diversity to its polemical mission (fig. 39). *Blast*, edited by Wyndham Lewis in England, issued manifestos in an extraordinarily large, bold typeface that lends each statement an aggressive, architectural presence. *New Masses* regularly devoted one of its large pages to a single long poem or five or six short poems by one author, thereby simultaneously drawing on the long history of the broadside in England and America and making an early magazine version of the large poetry broadsides that would become especially popular in the 1960s. Thus its first six oversize 1926 issues (10⅞ by 13⅞ inches) included full pages devoted to poetry by Fearing and Jeffers. Thereafter the page size was reduced by two inches, but the practice of occasionally giving full pages to poems continued, with Hughes and Ridge soon represented. *The Daily Worker* also occasionally devoted all or part (fig. 43) of one of its large pages to one or more illustrated works by one author, including works by Quin, Hughes, and Rukeyser.[246] At times *New Masses* would devote a full two-page illustrated spread to a single major poem. Hughes's sardonic anticapitalist "Advertisement for the Waldorf-Astoria," written in angry response to a *Vanity Fair* ad for the refurbished hotel, appeared in the December 1931 issue (fig. 40).[247] Hughes invites all the homeless to take up residence at the hotel and closes with his own "Christmas Card": "The new Christ child of the Revolution's about to be born / (Kick hard, red baby, in the bitter womb of the mob.)" An early illustrated version of Funaroff's "What the Thunder Said: A Fire Sermon" is printed across two pages in the August 1932 issue (fig. 41). Herbert Kruckman's framing illustrations reinforce the structural analogy between both the oppressive ruling classes and the mass revolutionary impulse in America and Russia. In Funaroff's *The Spider and the Clock* (1938) it is announced as "a cinematic poem," its version of political montage designed to answer

EL POET

September, 1932

10c copy

AGAINST IMPERIALIST WAR!

FOR THE COOPERATIVE SOCIETY!

210

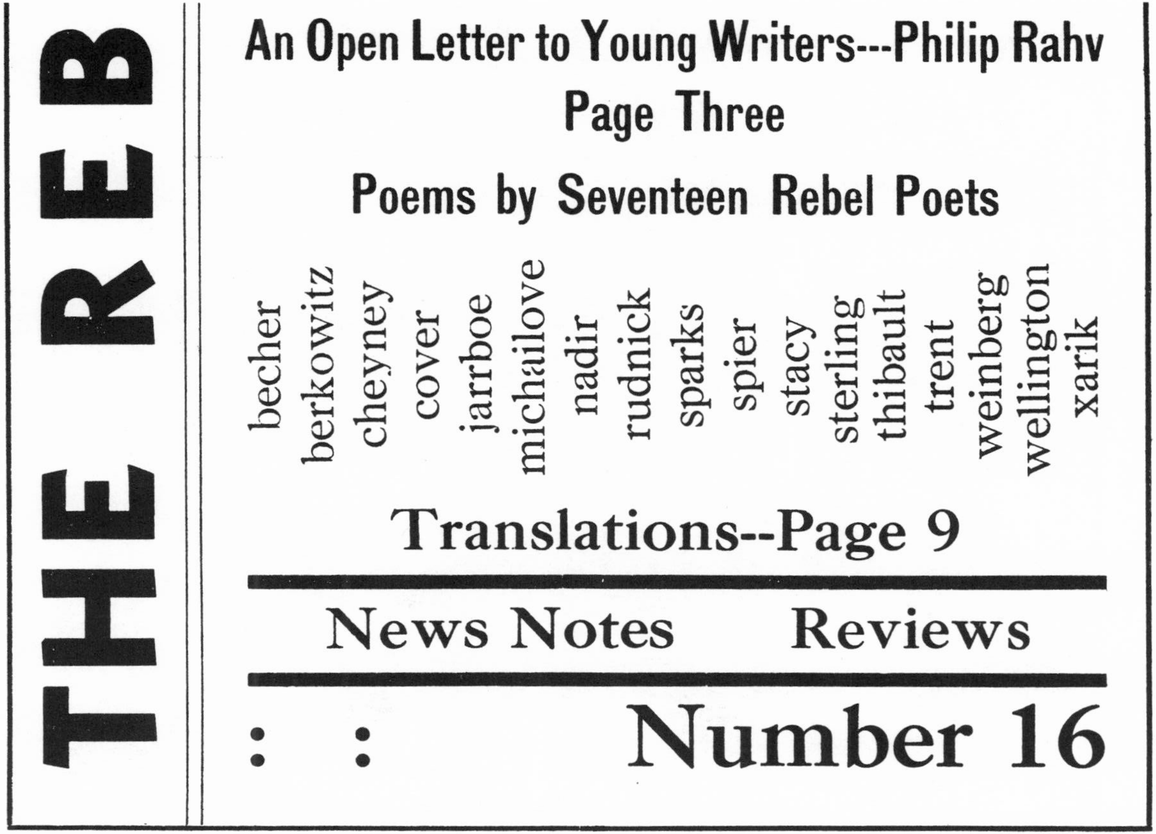

THE REB

An Open Letter to Young Writers---Philip Rahv

Page Three

Poems by Seventeen Rebel Poets

becher
berkowitz
cheyney
cover
jarboe
michailove
nadir
rudnick
sparks
spier
stacy
sterling
thibault
trent
weinberg
wellington
xarik

Translations--Page 9

News Notes   Reviews

: :   **Number 16**

39. *The cover of the September 1932 issue of The Rebel Poet (8 × 11). Baskette Collection, UIUC.*

FINE LIVING ... *a la carte ??*

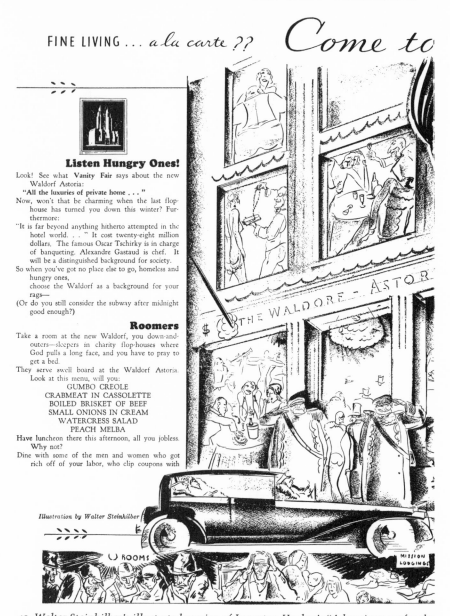

Listen Hungry Ones!

Look! See what **Vanity Fair** says about the new
  Waldorf Astoria:
"All the luxuries of private home . . . "
Now, won't that be charming when the last flop-
  house has turned you down this winter? Furthermore:
"It is far beyond anything hitherto attempted in the
  hotel world. . . " It cost twenty-eight million
  dollars. The famous Oscar Tschirky is in charge
  of banqueting. Alexandre Gastaud is chef. It
  will be a distinguished background for society.
So when you've got no place else to go, homeless and
  hungry ones,
  choose the Waldorf as a background for your
  rags—
(Or do you still consider the subway after midnight
  good enough?)

Roomers

Take a room at the new Waldorf, you down-and-
  outers—sleepers in charity flop-houses where
  God pulls a long face, and you have to pray to
  get a bed.
They serve swell board at the Waldorf Astoria.
  Look at this menu, will you:
       GUMBO CREOLE
    CRABMEAT IN CASSOLETTE
    BOILED BRISKET OF BEEF
    SMALL ONIONS IN CREAM
       WATERCRESS SALAD
          PEACH MELBA
Have luncheon there this afternoon, all you jobless.
  Why not?
Dine with some of the men and women who got
  rich off of your labor, who clip coupons with

Illustration by Walter Steinhilber

40. *Walter Steinhilber's illustrated version of Langston Hughes's "Advertisement for the Waldorf Astoria" (17 × 11).* **New Masses** *(December 1931). Sukov collection, UWM.*

the Waldorf-Astoria!

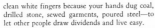

clean white fingers because your hands dug coal, drilled stone, sewed garments, poured steel—to let other people draw dividends and live easy.

(Or haven't you had enough yet of the soup-lines and the bitter bread of charity?)

Walk through Peacock Alley tonight before dinner, and get warm, anyway. You've got nothing else to do.

Evicted Families

All you families put out in the street: Apartments in the Towers are only $10,000 a year. (Three rooms and two baths.) Move in there until times get good, and you can do better. $10,000 and $1.00 are about the same to you, aren't they? Who cares about money with a wife and kids home-less, and nobody in the family working? Would-n't a duplex high above the street be grand, with a view of the richest city in the world at your nose?

"A lease, if you prefer; or an arrangement terminable at will."

Negroes

O, Lawd, I done forgot Harlem!

Say, you colored folks, hungry a long time in 135th Street—they got swell music at the Waldorf-As-toria. It sure is a mighty nice place to shake hips in, too. There's dancing after supper in a big warm room. It's cold as hell on Lenox Avenue. All you've had all day is a cup of coffee. Your pawnshop overcoat's a ragged banner on your hungry frame. . . . You know, down-town folks are just crazy about Paul Robeson. Maybe they'd like you, too, black mob from Harlem. Drop in at the Waldorf this afternoon for tea. Stay to dinner. Give Park Avenue a lot of darkie color —free—for nothing! Ask the Junior Leaguers to sing a spiritual for you. They probably know 'em better than you do—and their lips won't be so chapped with cold after they step out of their closed cars in the undercover driveways.

Hallelujah! under-cover driveways!

Ma soul's a witness for de Waldorf-Astoria!

(A thousand nigger section-hands keep the road-beds smooth, so investments in railroads pay

ladies with diamond necklaces staring at Cert murals.)

Thank God A-Mighty!

(And a million niggers bend their backs on rubber plantations, for rich behinds to ride on thick tires to the Theatre Guild tonight.)

Ma soul's a witness!

(And here we stand, shivering in the cold, in Har-lem.)

Glory be to God—
De Waldorf-Astoria's open!

Everybody

So get proud and rare back, everybody! The new Waldorf-Astoria's open!

(Special siding for private cars from the railroad yards.)

You ain't been there yet?

(A thousand miles of carpet and a million bath rooms.)

What's the matter? You haven't seen the ads in the papers? Didn't you get a card? Don't you know they specialize in American cooking?

Ankle on down to 49th Street at Park Avenue. Get up off that subway bench tonight with the eve-ning POST for cover! Come on out o' that flop-house! Stop shivering your guts out all day on street corners under the L.

Jesus, ain't you tired yet?

Christmas Card

Hail Mary, Mother of God!

The new Christ child of the Revolution's about to be born.

(Kick hard, red baby, in the bitter womb of the mob.)

Somebody, put an ad in Vanity Fair quick!

Call Oscar of the Waldorf—for Christ's sake!

It's almost Christmas, and that little girl—turned whore because her belly was too hungry to stand it any more—wants a nice clean bed for the Im-maculate Conception.

Listen, Mary, Mother of God, wrap your new born babe in the red flag of Revolution:

The Waldorf-Astoria's the best manger we've got.

For reservations: Telephone

ELdorado 5-3000.

by Langston Hughes

U. S. A. — 1932

S. FUNAROFF

FIRE SERMON

A worker whose dusty clothes smelled wet and gassy like an excavation, whose clodboots were caked with drymud, shook his fist furiously. A sudden shot of voice like a sledgehammer banged against cobblestones.

"Cah-pit-ah-leests! . . . They bloodsucker-rs!
Wor-rker-r or-rganize! . . . We fight!"

He began sputtering, his mouth boiling full with words. His words full with grievance. His greenswollen neckveins purpled. Dark eyes raged in his reddened face. His excited body trembled.

Slowly, he simmered into a tense, nervous silence.

An uneasy silence, a high humidity of emotion was felt amid the crowd of workers,—the barometer of a storm.

No happy, no contented faces here.

Only laborers with grim faces, feeling anger, feeling sorrow like rain packed into stormclouds, packed to the explosive bitter point, dangerously packed like dynamite eager for the first dangerous spark or lightning blow to—
Power!

Down with Capitalism!

The Communards, they are storming heaven!

A damp gust of March wind
Whirls and scatters papers.

And the hot, critical July days!—
tense wireless bristling with flashes,
stammering, stuttering,
awaiting what code,
what code to translate
Capital, Famine, Predatory War,
into what dialectic odyssey
the machine guns' riveting shall inscribe—
the Leatherjacket fatally indite?

And when the thunderheads hammer,
the palaces reverberate,
the napoleonic columns fall;
the cracked plaster of paris Narcissus
drowns in his fragments.

The Thorthunder speaks:
Workers! Soldiers! Sailors!
We are the riders of steel storms!
We are the fire-bearers!
Ours the heritage of the first flame-runner
racing up the steep dark slopes
a flambeau in the night!
Created and creator of fire!
We are the riders—
Budenni-men!—
riders of steel stallions,
the kinetic synergy of factories
snorting flambent plumes,
charging,
rushing up the tracks beacon-eyed!

And the scarlet ships of space
wing time's fires
cataclysmic bear
earth's heirs
the communists with battle shouts
rumble over the skyways,
scatter cannonades of stars,—
flowers of life and death,
flowers of revolution
rocket amid acrid clouds!

The Thorthunder says:
(rumblin crumblin)
Da!
Da Da!

All Power to the Soviets!

The spring rain blows over the steppes.

41. Herbert Kruckman's illustrated version of Sol Funaroff's "What the Thunder Said: A Fire Sermon" (17 × 11), in an early version published in New Masses *(August 1932). Illustration no. 49 reproduces the cover to the same issue.*

RUSSIA — 1914

In October
lightning ripples in the windwaved wheat—
great streak of silver whistling scythe!
And tractors bloom in the wheatfields!
They rumble,
they crumble the earth to their powerful wills.
They speak:
Gigant!

Overhead—
the soft sunsetwinds blow rosegold odors
twilightly descend with their first young star.
Over the bridge strong hands on wheels and levers skim.
Over the bridge trains sew and bead red stars
weld through fire and iron
five years!
detonate electric songs of speeding lights!
A blow torch simmers sparkles
and the Leatherjacket welds
weaves from the silken cloth of golden sun
the workers spun
red stars over the bloody waters below.

Red coals foam and toss in torrents
in galvanic waterfalls of the Dnieprostroi,
and the Dnieper sows her banks with rubies.
There spring up the socialized cities of red giants!
Workers of Magnitogorsk with her huge blast furnaces
write in flame,
through fire and iron,
steel statements of steel deeds:
armored trains of revolution
electrodynamic steel drilling through black rock
dynamiting tunnels
mining blackgold ores!
Subways without christbeggars
whose blind eyes beseech piaculatives!
While the bursting sun flings from chaotic flame-pits
the synthesis of new worlds . . .
Far into the night, far into the ages,
the burning worlds whirl and shine . . .
. . . Citytowns . . . worker palaces of art and culture . . .
. . . Workers! Across transition belts of time and space,
tools in hand,
we mould the human race,
we lay the base,
assemble and rivet bolts and parts
of marxist machinery,
and build mighty structures,
higher bonds of social union . . .
. . . classless society . . . Gigant!
We are at once the makers and the made,
the mechanic and the mechanism of marx-leninism!

Here are the blazing windows of iron mountains
in an electromagnetic sunset.
These are the heights men reach.
Still higher—
the Communard soars like a propelled comet,
until the earth is small tinder for such a blaze of space!

Yes the world is burning and the stormwind's big bellows fan
the flames and the hammer pounds stronger and stronger the fist
voices the bolshevist and the bitter heart leaps in answer Thalatta!
Thalatta! and her all-conquering legions of horsemarines shout
and clash and clang their armor and the scarlet seas surge exult-
ant upon new shores flowers of revolution red and gold bursting
the magniloquent red battlehorses of plunging plumes in the
thundering wind paced with the lightning *roar* a song of flame
and the world in the embrace of the flaming flood and the hammer
heard clanging clanging upon an anvil clanging and shaping world
october and the cry and call of Defend the Soviet Union! Onward
to the Dictatorship of the World Proletariat! and they march and
demonstrate and bright banners of faces cheer thorthunderclap-
plause! and they shout through the streets of the universe yes
and the sun like an executed head falls and the whole sky bleeds
dripping over church and skyscraper and bloodied arms like ham-
bers strike stars forge new worlds shoot upwards yes!

Herbert Kruckman

Eliot's images of the decline of civilization. What is dying, Funaroff argues, is capitalism; the thunder's "Da," rearticulated from *The Waste Land*, now announces the revolution.

Funaroff's poem is often cited as a signal example of the excesses of revolutionary enthusiasm in the poetry of the 1930s, but such poems announcing the imminent revolt of the proletariat can promote other issues of value. "Out of this stony rubbish," Funaroff predicts, will come "the synthesis of new worlds." The worlds Funaroff imagined never came to pass, but poetry is not so easily invalidated. Part of its use is to keep alive utopian visions that history may otherwise seem to have extinguished. Many of the poets on the left clung to the initial vision of the Russian revolution long after its promise had been substantially betrayed. That vision, however, can continue to do vital cultural work—both here and in the Soviet Union—despite its subsequent tyrannical or bureaucratic distortion and suppression.

These dramatic two-page poster poems confirm again the social power of political poetry. But the formal impulse at least was taken in other directions as well. Thus *View* in the next decade followed the example of *291* by mixing typefaces on individual pages, making each page into a striking poster, and making poems into structural elements of the page. By the second volume, the issues were quite elegantly printed, often with some pages of poems printed on colored paper. These techniques alter the roles language and poetry are expected to play in the culture, giving them a strongly material existence and suggesting they can be part of the physical and visual environment. *View* was concerned to put forward a distinct sensibility, one that crossed poetry, prose, and the visual arts and broke down their divisions. Under the journal's motto, "through the eyes of poets," Max Ernst's cover for the April 1942 issue of *View* (fig. 42) gives us a figure part human, part animal, that leaves unanswered the question of whether this is an image of what poets and artists are or what they see. Embellished with five legs, no visible torso, a leonine head, and an expression that may be leering or angry, it invokes eruptive, transgressive presence without judgment. Equally ambiguous, Kurt Seligmann's witty cover for *View* (Pl. F), reversibly vaginal and phallic, serves as a universal meditation on form that collapses human production and natural process together and gives both the

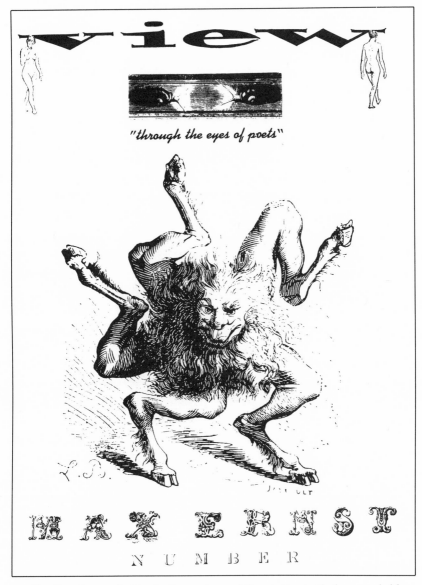

42. *Max Ernst's cover for the April 1942 issue of* View *(7 × 10). Black on a pale blue background. Sukov collection, UWM.*

character of eerie, involuntary organicity. Like a surrealist poem, its subject matter is at once wholly indeterminate and infinitely suggestive.[248] Many other literary journals also printed photographs of paintings and sculpture, thereby invoking a general revolution in the arts and urging us to mark similarities and differences between the literary and visual avant-garde. It is, however, very difficult for academics to read this way, since it works against the way they are trained in traditional disciplines. The counter-reaction is also apparent. *The Fugitive* aimed to have almost no physical presence; anticipating the aesthetic that would dominate conservative magazines in the 1950s, its neutral typography and layout was designed to project the poetry it printed directly into the imagination. Poetry, for *The Fugitive*, was a spiritual not a material phenomenon.

The cumulative evidence of the illustrations in this book should demonstrate that the material presentation of texts can significantly increase the kinds of meaning they can be used to produce. Printed, designed, and illustrated in a particular way, a poem can be sent out to do certain kinds of cultural work it might otherwise be unable to do. Malcolm Cowley's (1898–1989) "The Last International," published under different titles almost simultaneously in *The New Republic* and *The Daily Worker* in the spring of 1936, demonstrates how a text can be urged in a particular direction with an illustration. Unillustrated in *The New Republic*, in *The Daily Worker* the poem is given the more celebratory title "A Poem for May Day" and accompanied by a dramatic illustration (fig. 43). Throughout most of the poem the maimed and martyred political victims of the century gather together to march against their enemies. Nothing can stop these people "with mummified limbs that bullets could not tear." Yet the text is not confidently revolutionary until the end, for its grisly effects—"some had snapped-off bayonets / in their ribs"—also make it a poem of horror from which we may recoil. The illustration, to be sure, includes wounded figures struggling on the ground on the lower left and a few figures carrying their severed heads in their hands. But it is dominated overall by the massive, determined fist that rises up through the two columns of the poem.[249] Partly wrapped in a flag, it thrusts up past the toppling Capitol and breaks into the

sunlight above. It thus prefigures the poem's concluding revolutionary optimism and underwrites all its other connotations with that
confident effect.

Hughes's 1931 "Advertisement for the Waldorf-Astoria" is an even
more complex example of interaction between text and illustration.
Making pointed use of the hotel's own advertising slogan ("Fine
Living . . . a la carte"), the wonderful layout by New York painter
and graphic artist Walter Steinhilber (fig. 40) is designed to imitate
a fancy hotel menu.[250] The poem's section divisions—from "Listen Hungry Ones" to "Evicted Families"—replace the conventional
menu divisions into appetizers, main courses, and desserts. The division between the two pages replicates the fold in a typical restaurant
menu. Like a number of the illustrations discussed above, the typefaces, graphic design, and even the central illustration play off and
reappropriate art deco design features characteristic of the period.
Hotel menus are usually designed to create a fantasy world in which
external reality is forgotten; here, however, the realities of Depression social life are instead served up for our consideration. The visual
presentation thus gives the poem's satire more pointed social impact. And the quickly sketched wealthy celebrants above, the faces
of the poor beneath, do not so much restrict as encourage our further
associations. In the process, Hughes's poem also has its stylish wit
intensified, so that it gains some of the mixed anger and play one can
find in Sterling Brown's poetry of the same era. Yet the deco style
had such a rich and contradictory cultural and political history in
the 1920s and 1930s that its appropriation is never fully controllable.
More distinctly perhaps than with any of the other illustrations I
discuss, those contesting forces are evident in the design for "Advertisement for the Waldorf Astoria," for the image uses the deco style
not only to critique the excesses of wealth but also to shape its own
revolutionary bravado.

These interpretive possibilities become even richer when one reads
poems in the context of entire journals. The challenge, at least in
some cases, is to read journals as if they were themselves coherent
mixed genres, as if they were books like *Cane* or *Spring & All* that
meld and juxtapose traditional genres. Not all journals, of course, are

A Poem for May

I saw them, yes, I saw their unbreathing armies
Marching against the Capitol in ranks
That filled the boulevard from curb to curb;
They were a river high between its banks

In the March gales. I saw their featureless faces
Wax-pallid, saw their tight-clenched bony fists,
Saw their right forearms skyward raised, and saw
Among them stumps of arms, hacked off at the wrists,

And some I saw that walked in a frozen circle
Of flame, and some had snapped-off bayonets
In their ribs, and some a wound between the shoulders
From which the blood congealed in two black jets.

And some there were and some I saw that carried
In their left hands each his own dissevered head,
And others with a hangman's noose down-dangling
From twisted neck, and all their host was dead—

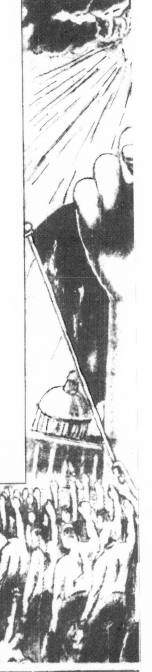

For comrades, dead, for having loved tomorrow,
Betrayed and bastinadoed, burned at the stake,
Slow-starved in prison or exile, buried alive,
Beaten insensible, roused at the day's break,

Then hurried through the snow to execution,
Shot down in Florisdorf, in Chapei Road,
And now reprieved from prison graveyards, piled
So high with sorrows that they overflowed,

Yes, poured their victims out, a long parade
Of spectres high upborne on rivers of air
And silence. Not a banner flapped in the wind.
There was only the dry whisper everywhere

Of feet like dead leaves over asphalt scudding
Under a cold sky heavy as a vault
And the slit eyes of iron-shuttered windows;
And suddenly were voices crying, Halt!

I heard them, human voices that were more
Unhuman than the silence of the dead;
In terror, in a dream, I turned and saw them
Waiting, the gas-masked, shrapnel-helmeted,

Day By MALCOLM COWLEY

Identical brown frozen bodies, heard
The click of rifle bolts behind barbed wire,
And turning back I pleaded,
                    "Comrades, not
Weaponless, not to crumple under fire,

"Comrades, no farther—"
                    Would they hear me ever?
"Comrades—"
                    They still moved on to the attack,
Until the enemy ordnance volleyed out
Against them, an enormous thundercrack.

The rivet-hammering of Lewis guns,
The spit and crackle of Springfields in the ranks.
Gases that spread in miasmatic fogs.
Planes zooming low. The grumble of the tanks.

And still and still the mutineers marched on
With mummified limbs that bullets could not tear,
Nor gases poison them, who did not breathe,
Nor tanks crush out their bodies that were air.

I saw them sweeping forward, saw the soldiers
That cast their rifles down and blindly fled;
Barons I saw and bankers and archbishops
Driven before the whirlwind of the dead;

Stone walls that crumbled, barracks and asylums
Fast emptied, penitentiaries ablaze;
A half-unconscious sigh of liberation
Rose from mean streets and moonless areaways,

From factory gates and convict camps and cabins
Unpainted, windowless, deep in the Cotton Belt—
Tensed muscles loosening, a first free breath
A hundred million times repeated, felt

Then slowly heard, tornado of the mind
Driving the mist and terror from the head.
The vault of cloud was split by a sharp wind.
The sky was suddenly blue and the sun shone red.

(From the New Republic)

43. Malcolm Cowley, "A Poem for May Day," The Daily Worker (April 30, 1936).

such coherent enterprises, but some are, and they offer perspectives on the American culture that are simply unavailable in volumes by individual authors.

The Soil: A Magazine of Art, a New York magazine that published five issues from December 1916 to July 1917, printed a statement of aesthetic principles by the art editor, R. J. Coady, near the opening of its first issue. Opposite two photographs of locomotives, Coady announces "There is an American Art" and then lists two pages of instances, from the Panama Canal to the steam shovel, from Charlie Chaplin to ragtime, from Walt Whitman to Ty Cobb. It is art, he adds, as an expression of American life, and "it has grown out of the soil." With prose by Gertrude Stein and Arthur Cravan to articles on "The Dime Novel as Literature" and "The Woolworth Building" the journal maintains its plural cultural project.[251] A "moving sculpture" series reproduces photographs of machinery. Poems by Wallace Stevens and Maxwell Bodenheim (1893–1954), among others, are printed. Here is the end of Bodenheim's "Transfiguration":

> Her eyes are flames, bent, just before leaping up,
> And her lips arch away from each other.
> You wait to hear her cry out, thin-blown and straight . . .
> She sweeps up the buttons and thread upon her table,
> And with the broken face of an angered Madonna
> Drags herself away.[252]

The physical appearance of the magazine, one must note, is deceptively composed and traditional. Each cover reproduces a work of classical art, as if to suggest at once a continuity with the history of civilization and an aggressive claim for the artistic status of *Soil's* photographs of machine hammers and cowboys. Moreover, many of the reproductions are unexpected, since they are not listed in the contents, though reproductions of paintings by Cézanne and Picasso are. The cumulative effect, despite the classical equanimity of the magazine's layout, is one of surprising juxtaposition and displacement, rather than holistic synthesis. Indeed, occasional playful and surreal questions are printed in the wide margins above and below the page's text: "Who will paint New York? Who?" or "Who

has seen the Battery? Who?" or "Why no photos of Tugs? Why?" In
The Soil the severity of our epistemological and cultural categories
is already under assault.

As the color reproductions in this book should demonstrate most
succinctly, there is no substitute for holding the actual journals in
your hands and working through them. This remains true whether
one wants to reflect on what it might have been like to encounter
these journals when they first appeared or to ask what impact the
journals might have in the present. Unfortunately, many journals
as recent as the 1930s and 1940s are now exceedingly rare. Reprint
editions provide a real service, but they can be immensely deceptive. Many substantially transform the appearance and import of the
journal. Some reprint publishers, for example, routinely eliminate
covers, which can be a significant part of how the journal aims to
intervene in the culture. Initially issued with the motto "An International Magazine of the Arts Published by Americans in Italy,"
Broom's elegant color covers, designed by a variety of artists, constitute an anthology of modernist styles (Pls. D–E) designed collectively to sweep away the past.[253] The catholicity of the magazine's visual taste—from the cool phenomenological intimacy of
Alice Halicka's domestic scene (Pl. D) to the warm tones of Edward
Nagle's cubist collage (Pl. E), which simultaneously deconstructs
and reassembles the magazine's title, to the austere but playful abstraction of the three-dimensional numbers and letters arrayed in
space in El Lissitsky's constructivist-influenced cover (fig. 44)—suggests an editorial policy open to any new initiative.[254] The covers also
prepare us for the ambiguities of reading modern texts. El Lissitsky's
cover does so through ambiguities of scale, since the letters can be
read either as massive architectural forms or as a child's small alpha-
bet blocks. On the most famous cover of *Broom* (fig. 45) a sexually
ambiguous figure, stylistically evoking both contemporary taste and
primitive myth, sits on its haunches and thumbs its nose at tradition and bourgeois values. In 1943 *View* adopted an enlarged format,
nine-by-twelve-inch pages, with stunning color covers (Pl. F). An
even more extreme case is the surrealist magazine *VVV*, published
in New York.[255] The back cover of nos. 2–3 (1943) includes a piece
of chicken wire bound into the cover. The reader is invited to run

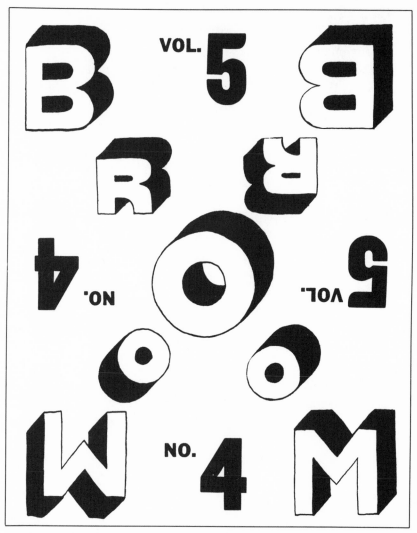

44. *El Lissitsky's elegant design for the November 1923 cover of* Broom *(7½ × 11), drawing on the constructivist use of type as a design element. This cover was printed with black type on a white background, but the design was revised for the next issue, where red type was used. Sukov collection, UWM.*

45. *Perhaps the most famous cover of* Broom, *for the February 1922 issue (8½ × 13), in which the figure thumbs its nose at tradition. The type at the top and the bottom is in red, while the figure is printed in black. The background is white. Sukov collection, UWM.*

his or her hands over it, write up the experience, and send it to the editors.

The quite diverse styles of the covers of *The Crisis, Opportunity,* and *New Masses* (figs. 46, 48–49) present, in succinct form, the range of visual discourses the magazines aim to appropriate for their purposes. They point as well to the different audiences the magazines hope to reach, as well as the needs those audiences are likely to bring to the magazine. *The Crisis* uses romantic photographs and paintings of blacks to demonstrate that they are appropriate sources of pride. Yet the magazine is equally likely to use the most stylish art deco designs, both to invoke black involvement in contemporary art and fashion and to rearticulate images of an African heritage to contemporary style. *New Masses* also adapts a surprising range of modern styles both to promote and to complicate its polemical purposes. Louis Lozowick, serving as the art editor of the magazine, designed the August 1928 cover (fig. 46) to resemble a fanciful machine constructed of words. Comparable in many ways to the Spring-Summer 1924 cover of *The Little Review* (fig. 47), it suggests that to read is to traverse a labyrinth of multiple connections. It is up to us, finally, to decide how the "poems of brutal beauty" the cover promises are to be related to the commemoration of Sacco and Vanzetti. Theodore Scheel's striking January 1930 *New Masses* cover (fig. 48) is even more ambiguous. It places the worker decisively at the center of industrial production but also shows machine and body as so interdependent that the potential for human control is altogether in doubt. On the other hand, the editorial cartoon by Jacob Burck that fills the August 1932 cover (fig. 49) issues a specific warning—linking the rise of Nazism with earlier German militarism.[256] Finally, some covers have a specific literary function. The October 1926 cover of *Opportunity* celebrates the Langston Hughes and Aaron Douglas collaboration in that issue. Statements of editorial principles, sometimes embedded in advertisements and subscriptions forms, can also be lost when covers are eliminated. Reprint services also quite commonly eliminate advertising pages, which are helpful in establishing the range of readers the magazine appealed to and in helping us to recognize the related magazines publishing at the same time. These ad pages, as in the case of the 1934 page from *Left Front* reproduced

46. *Louis Lozowick's design for the August 1928 cover to* New Masses *(8½ × 11). Princeton University Library.*

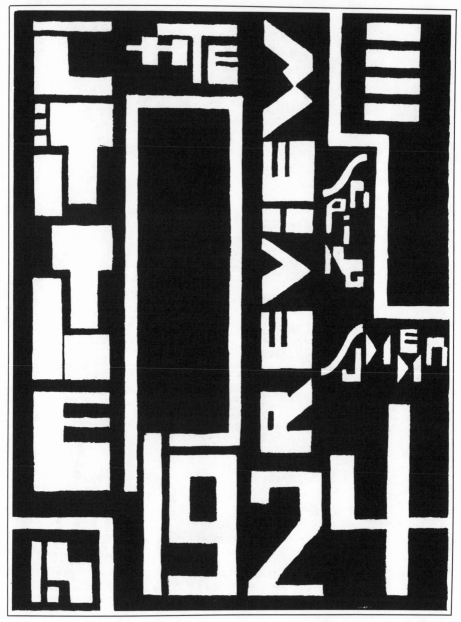

47. *The Spring–Summer 1924 cover of* The Little Review *(7 × 9½). The cover is bright mauve on a tan background. UIUC.*

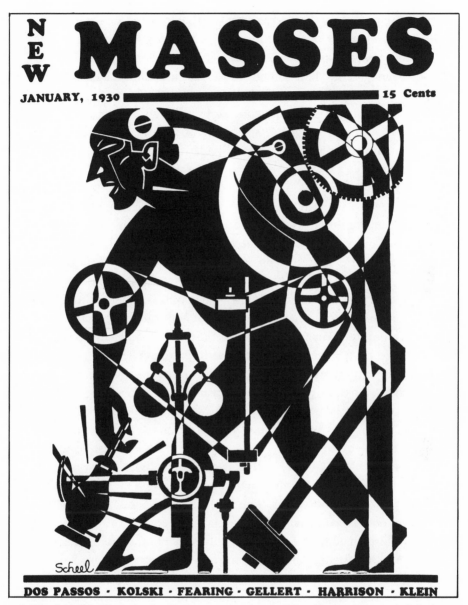

48. *Theodore Scheel's design for the January 1930 cover of* New Masses *(8½ × 11). Sukov collection, UWM.*

here (fig. 50), in fact establish networks of shared commitments. Billing itself as an organ for "Revolutionary Art of the Midwest," the Chicago-based magazine includes pages that print notices for other radical magazines, lists of books received (including Lewis's *Salvation*), and an ad for an antiwar ball. The inside back cover of the first issue of *Front* makes the network explicit, listing seventeen "magazines of our contributors." The contents listed on *Front's* back flap —also eliminated in the reprint—divide the names of its contributors into three geographic and political groups: America, the Soviet Union, and Europe.

If we read widely in the journals of the period, some of the competing and reinforcing styles of the time, invisible in the collected works of individual poets or the canon-reinforcing anthologies and literary histories, become apparent. To return to the little magazines of 1914–1930 is to feel the established groupings and hierarchies of modern poetry disappear. Imagism, political poetry, linguistic fragmentation, and other tendencies are continually reshuffled and counterpointed. The major names in the current canon are set beside poets we have since marginalized or forgotten. The modernism of the little magazines is undecided, unfixed, still exploring its potential and its possible alliances. In Margaret Anderson's *The Little Review* (1914–29), first edited from Chicago, the magazine celebrated for serializing *Ulysses*, one finds juxtapositions of what are now, for us, it seems quite separate discourses. In 1916, feminist editorials coexist with John Gould Fletcher's essays on imagist poets and Amy Lowell's dialect poetry and imagist prose; Emma Goldman writes from prison; Pound writes from London; Carl Sandburg publishes several poems; editorials appear on labor issues. In 1917 Pound becomes foreign editor for a year and publishes Eliot, Wyndham Lewis, Ford Madox Hueffer (later Ford); the following year, Wallace Stevens and William Carlos Williams appear, along with Marsden Hartley and Freytag-Loringhoven. This was the moment, at the height of modernism, when a revolution in poetry seemed naturally to entail commitment to social change, when all the arts were in ferment and aesthetic innovations were politically inflected. In a few years, allegiances would begin to coalesce differently, and one would have to turn to more explicitly political magazines to find a similar mix of

49. Jacob Burck's design for the August 1932 cover of New Masses *(8½ × 11).*

page twenty-four

PARTISAN REVIEW

A Bi-monthly Magazine of Revolutionary Literature and Criticism

Published by the John Reed Club of New York at 430 6th Ave.

"The appearance of *Partisan Review* is a cause for celebration." — Isidor Schneider.

The February-March issue contains:

Two Sketches Grace Lumpkin
In a Coffee Pot Alfred Hayes
Studs Lonigan James T. Farrell
The Sheep Dip Ben Field
Death of a Shop Arthur Pense
Four Poems Joseph Freeman

Books: Granville Hicks on Jack Conroy
Obed Brooks on Archibald MacLeish
Philip Rahv on Ernest Hemingway

20c per copy

What they say about

THE ANVIL-

"No American magazine I have seen has printed so much good fiction in one issue."

GRANVILLE HICKS.

"Those two poems by Hughes in ANVIL make the best poetry I've read. The format is splen-

Do YOU READ

New Theatre

● Leaders in every field of the theater, dance and cinema contribute to your information and technical knowledge within the covers of this new revolutionary monthly.

Contributors: Paul Green, George Sklar, Lee Simonson, John Howard Lawson, J. Edward Bromberg, Joseph Freeman, Alfred Harding, Emjo Basshe, Irving Lerner, Samuel Brody, Oakley Johnson.

10c per copy One Dollar per year

New Theatre
5 E. 19th St., N. Y. C.

BOOKS RECEIVED

THE BLACK WORKER. By Abraham Spero and Sterling D. Harris. Columbia University Press, New York. $4.50.

UPSURGE. By Robert Gessner. Farrar and Rinehart, New York. $1.

THE FIRE. By Joel Rustam. Tomorrow, Publishers, New York. 25c.

CASTAWAYS OF PLENTY. By Willard Hawkins. Continental Committee on Technocracy, Denver. 50c.

SALVATION. By H. H. Lewis. B. C. Hagglund, Holt, Minn. 25c.

ANTI-WAR BALL

Snappy Orchestra
Entertainment by Headliners
Prizes for Costumes

Exhibit of Anti-War Posters by Leading Chicago Artists

Tickets $1; at door $1.25

Auspices: American League Against War and Fascism

Room 405, 160 North LaSalle
Phone State 6785

DYNAMO

For a Complete, Authoritative Statement of the Marxian Interpretation of American Revolutionary Literature, Read

«Revolutionary Literature In United States Today»

in the Spring Issue of
WINDSOR QUARTERLY

"did you are right and tell the kickers—with my compliments —to go to hell."

ERSKINE CALDWELL.

Editor: JACK CONROY

Subscribe Now! Eight Issues $1

15c a copy

THE ANVIL

Route Four   Moberly, Mo.

A Journal of Revolutionary Poetry

Editors: S. Funaroff, Herman Spector
Joseph Vogel, Nicholas Wirth

15c a copy $1 for 8 issues

Second number includes poems by William Pillin, C. D. Lewis, Muriel Rukeyser, Hector Rella, Edwin Rolfe.

DYNAMO For samples send 10c

34 Horatio St, New York City

Regular contributors of Essays, Short Stories, and Poetry include: Alvah C. Bessie, Moe Bragin, Edward J. O'Brien, Samuel Putnam, Louis Zukofsky, Norman Macleod, W. D. Trowbridge, Alexander Godin, Meridel Le-Sueur, Lowry Charles Wimberly, Louis Mamet, Benjamin Appel, Karlton Kelm, Carl Rakosi.

$2.00 a year—or send 50c for a sample copy.

The Windsor Quarterly

Hartland Four Corners, Vermont

A New Way of Writing and Seeing

Tired of the fairy-tales of some magazines and the sophisticated half-truths of others, thousands upon thousands of readers are turning to the growing revolutionary press. Strikes, demonstrations, and the day-by-day struggles of the workingclass are no longer "propaganda"; they are the stuff of literature and art, the working material for young revolutionary writers and artists.

You will find much of their vigorous work on the pages of Left Front. Published by the midwestern section of the John Reed Clubs, an organization close to the militant workingclass, Left Front is the expression of world revolutionary theory in concrete regional terms.
In the past year, this midwestern magazine has shown indubitable evidence of the strength of its background. Each issue has grown in size and in the quality of its material. New writers such as J. S. Balch, Tom Butler, Mark Marvin, William Pillin; and artists such as Groth, Rocke, and Breinin, appear in its pages. If you are interested in this new way of writing and seeing, you will want to receive Left Front regularly. The coupon below is for your convenience.

LEFT FRONT
1475 S. Michigan Ave.
Chicago, Ill.

Enter my subscription at once for Left Front.
I enclose $1 for twelve bi-monthly issues.

Name............ Address............
City............ State............

LEFT FRONT

REVOLUTIONARY ART
OF THE MIDWEST

50. *The back page of the May–June 1934 issue of Left Front (9 × 12), published in Chicago. Sukov collection, UWM.*

aesthetic and social commitments. One lesson we may learn is this: that an aesthetic revolution need not necessarily be tied to radical politics. Pound and Eliot would, in time, turn more overtly toward racism and anti-Semitism; Eliot would commit himself to religion; Pound would become entangled in the greatest fascist evils of the century. But a second lesson is this: that an aesthetic revolution can be articulated to a social conscience—and, for a time, was. Furthermore, although political poetry is widely regarded as unimaginatively polemical, in fact many journals continued to publish political poetry that was experimental, rhetorically complex, and explicitly modernist.

What was operating, at moments throughout the modern period, in the margins of the disciplinary history now fixed in our textbooks, was exactly what we cannot now recognize without the expectation of compromise and betrayal: an emergent alliance politics of resistance. From the most fleeting publications of the age to a celebrated journal like *The Masses*, the passion of educated liberalism, the rough outlines of social configurations that now seem beyond our reach, are apparent. In many of these journals the poetry of the feminist movement coexists with the poetry of the unemployed, the poetry of desperation on the farm, the poetry of the industrial workplace, and the poetry of black pride. Even when the organized feminist movement collapsed after suffrage was won, radical journals continued, through the 1920s and 1930s, to give special attention to women's issues.[257] Although many men on the left regarded feminism as less important than the need for a general social revolution, radical journals still helped to keep feminist issues alive, empowering a number of women poets. An ability to devote special issues to women poets and black poets, while integrating their poetry into general numbers, is something we still find difficult to achieve in many domains. Yet, in the ordinary, individual literary practices of the period, such alliances were frequently reaffirmed. The *Suffragist* reprinted a poem from *The Masses*. Max Eastman, editor of *The Masses*, wrote the introduction to Claude McKay's *Harlem Shadows* (1922). The International Workers Order published Langston Hughes's *A New Song* (1938), with an introduction by Mike Gold, in a first edition of 10,000 copies (fig. 33).

In such examples as these, we can discover why it is not enough to seek redress for the individual disenfranchisements of the existing canon, severe and inexcusable though these may be. It is easy, but unsatisfactory, merely to search for a past that mirrors our own fractured image. For, despite frequent conflict and deluded expectations, something more cohesive and broadly revolutionary was at work in the diverse conflation of the popular and the elite that characterized the left publications of the first few decades of the century.

In some ways, it is less surprising that poetry was widely revitalized this way than that it took so long. There were precedents, of course, more indeed than I have cited so far. Through the second half of the nineteenth century, Whitman created a publically committed and democratic poetry. During the 1890s, the rural populist presses published hundreds of poems as part of an effort to create an alternative culture. Poets like Edwin Markham (1852–1940) and William Vaughn Moody wrote poetry that was socially engaged and critical, as did many other poets, some of them cited here, whose names we have forgotten. Edgar Lee Masters and Carl Sandburg grew up on the edges of radical currents that clearly entered their poetry. In short, evidence of the need for cultural change had been felt even before the broad revolution in poetic style began.

Standard histories of the late nineteenth and early twentieth centuries note, quite accurately, that the era was one of enormous change —featuring a new wave of mass immigration, increasing urbanization, a shift toward consumer-oriented production, the rise of mass advertising, the spread of a communications network, the coming of the second industrial revolution, the appearance of radio, film, and the automobile. Literary historians tend to be quite comfortable with the claim that the rate and degree of cultural transformation left people baffled and troubled. But, as historians have shown, the negative consequences of rapid change were not just existential; they were material, and we need to inform our sense of the period with an understanding of that material reality.[258]

The first decades of the twentieth century saw the age of reform come to an end. The corruption exposed in books like Upton Sinclair's *The Jungle* (1906) led to new laws. But reforms in law are not necessarily reforms enforced. The century in fact began with another in a sequence of imperialist projects, in this case the genocidal suppression of a popular rebellion in the Philippines, events protested in William Vaughn Moody's "An Ode in Time of Hesitation" and in many of the poems in Morrison I. Swift's (1856–1946) *Advent of Empire* (1900).[259] At home, a similar enterprise was taking place in the West: by 1910, the U.S. Army's slaughter and suppression of the Indians of the Great Plains was largely complete. In the South, laws were in place disenfranchising black citizens. In the East and across the Midwest, farming was becoming more mechanized and a major population shift to the cities was under way, thereby concentrating people in conditions of more volatile discontent. From 1860 to 1914, New York City's population grew from 850,000 to 4,000,000 people, perhaps half of whom lived in tenements, some of which were rat-infested. Hundreds of thousands of children aged ten to fifteen worked a sixty-hour week in mines and factories. In 1914, 35,000 workers were killed in industrial accidents and more than 100,000 permanently disabled. In the steel mills in Pennsylvania in 1919, an adult worked twelve-hour days six days a week in extreme heat, earning barely enough to survive. At times, wages were cut below survival level. When workers struck, police or troops suppressed them with force. That same year, in Ludlow, Colorado, the National Guard set fire to a tent city set up during a coal strike; men had been killed in strikes often enough before, but this time eleven children and two women were incinerated, provoking a public outcry. Meanwhile, in 1911, Frederick W. Taylor proposed a division of labor in factories so that no worker would make an entire product. Production would be divided into simple tasks and workers would be interchangeable. It seemed an ideal system for the new immigrant population, and work was rapidly commodified and dehumanized. In the First World War, an economically motivated competition among the European powers, we encounter the first full expression of the modern social formation; ten million people died on the battlefield; twenty million died of starvation and disease.

The limited improvements of the 1920s were motivated in part by the realization that some sharing of the nation's wealth would promote social stability and thus ensure long-term profits. But the jazz age did not set everyone dancing. During the 1920s an average of 20,000 workers were killed each year in industrial accidents. The Harlem Renaissance coincided with the revival of the Ku Klux Klan, which had over four million members by 1924. There were also some important social achievements, most notably the conclusion of a century of struggle when women won the right to vote in 1920. But poverty was widespread, particularly in the South, even before the onslaught of the Great Depression.

When Edwin Arlington Robinson began, at the turn of the century, to write poems about the emptiness of American life, he was not, therefore, articulating a merely private sense of despair. He was inaugurating a major strain of modernism, responsive to actual social conditions, that not only diverged into a literature of protest and a literature of hopelessness but also underwent problematic totalization in the work of two very different poets. In a paradoxical consummation, Robinson's vision found both its most visible exposition and its most definitive abstraction in Eliot's "The Love Song of J. Alfred Prufrock" (1915), *The Waste Land* (1922), and "The Hollow Men" (1925). But Robinson's vision also found expression in an uncompromising poetry of human emptiness, a poetry without underlying restorative myth or ultimate affirmation, written by Robinson Jeffers, in a series of books throughout the 1920s, 1930s, and 1940s. In both long, allegorical narratives and short, historically specific lyrics, Jeffers evokes a fierce natural world that would best flourish if the earth were to be rid of all human presence. As a first step, he urged that the human mind be uncentered from itself. In solutions that are deeply radical, Jeffers both anticipates and preempts the post-apocalyptic and ecological concerns of contemporary writing.

Jeffers worked within the unresolvable paradox of trying to capture the pure otherness of nature in a language itself wholly a product of human culture, of "a rich and vulgar and / bewildered civilization dying at the core."[260] The strain of trying to depict nature in and of itself, when combined with his relentless misanthropy, gives his poetry a special force. He is often drawn to read the natural world by way of its difference from human life. "The heights glimmer in the sliding cloud," he writes, "the great bronze gorge-cut sides of the mountain tower up invincibly." Only a human witness can record the shining relation between the mountain and the sky, but it is with "invincibly" that the mountains are described by way of the challenge they offer us. Indeed, he goes on to write, they are "not the least hurt by this ribbon of road carved on their sea-foot." As for us, he would come to write in the mid-1940s, "we need a new dark-age, five hundred / years of winter and the tombs for dwellings."[261]

The standard explanations of the disillusionment that dominates much modern literature tend to emphasize both the loss of secure, shared values—including religious beliefs—and the loss of confidence in the power of human reason. Whatever managed to survive Nietzschean skepticism, so the argument goes, was more or less done in by the mounting influence of Darwin, Freud, and Marx, combined with the experience of World War One: the massive hypocrisy of governments and the mindless, apocalyptic slaughter of trench warfare. For many intellectuals Freud was a source of tremendous excitement, but the increasingly oppressive social fabric, dominated by the unsafe work place and the squalid city environment, was more than disillusioning. Everyday life, admittedly, is more polymorphous and contradictory than intellectual history, but it almost certainly created many of the most intense pressures toward change that poets felt.

Why then, despite a countertradition in specific subcultures, such as the tradition of labor poetry, was much poetry relatively slower than fiction and nonfiction prose in evoking the texture of everyday life and employing the language of ordinary speech? The answer, it seems, lies in the social functions of poetry: the places it occupied (and the ways it occupied them) in the dominant, though not universal, discursive formations preceding modernism. In promoting an elevated style of vague idealism, in reinforcing belief in the spiritual superiority and political irrelevance of high culture, the genteel poetry sometimes published in the mass circulation magazines (from *American Magazine, The Century, Collier's,* and the *Saturday Evening Post* to *Harper's* and the *Atlantic*) gave a specific message to its readers: that whatever the vicissitudes of history a certain transcendent realm of atemporal values was always available to those deserving access to it. This suggests that poetry was articulated precisely in terms of the roles it served in the dominant social formation, which means that a socially disengaged history of modern poetry merely repeats the ideological status that genteel poetry occupied before the modernist revolution.

We err, then, in imagining that modernism permanently and utterly altered the structural place of poetry within society. Modern literary history, as practiced within the discipline of academic literary studies, often proves the contrary, reinforcing the idea that poetry can retain its privileged social status as an atemporal reserve of idealization only if it refuses to engage aggressively in cultural critique. This occasionally produces such wondrous contortions as arguments that, say, poetry by Langston Hughes or Robinson Jeffers deals only with universal human truths, not with issues that have immediate bearing on contemporary political life. The conservative arguments are always carried out in terms of what poetry essentially *is* and what practices would violate that essence. The real issue is fear, the anxiety that poetry (and those who analyze it) cannot survive the vicissitudes of political life. It seems clear that poetry critics feel their status—fragile, harmless, but relatively privileged —has been purchased with their political silence.

To begin to understand the modern history of an idealized view of the poetic, we need to draw a conclusion, uniquely available now, some sixty years after *The Waste Land* first scandalized the bourgeois reading public. It is now a fact of the history of interpretation and debate surrounding this and other major modern texts that readings of modern poetry are not only widely variable but also, in certain key respects, literally reversible. For many readers *The Waste Land* seemed merely a scattered dumping ground for literary allusions and images of urban dislocation and dissolution; others recognized a partly cubist collage, or a musical counterpointing of themes.[262] In fact, readings that stress formlessness and readings that stress form both have ample textual support. If we tend now to emphasize the poem's quest for a new mythic synthesis, that is partly a result of how our awareness of Eliot's subsequent work and its religious dimensions inevitably foreground those elements of the earlier poem. In any case, the poem is now available to us in two distinctly different ways: as a revolutionary, code-shattering text, the poem primarily responsible for making disjunctive collage central to the modern literary sensibility, or as a conservative, even reactionary, text, one that evokes the multiplicity of modern life only to condemn it and urge on us some reformulation of an earlier faith.

If we step back from the history of readings of modern poetry, we realize that virtually every "major" poet—every poet, that is, who has been repeatedly reread—has been subjected to similarly contradictory analyses. Eliot, in this respect is simply one of what we might call the "reversible poets" of modern American literature. We have encountered a number of them here, and there are others I have not mentioned. There is the rhapsodic, swooning Edna St. Vincent Millay who burns her candle at both ends; there is the politically committed Millay of a carefully constructed antiromantic rhetoric. There is the Claude McKay whose poems succumb to a stilted formalism he cannot master; there is the McKay whose anger shakes those same forms loose from their connections to the dominant culture. There is the restrained, cautious Marianne Moore whose achievements are confined to a very narrow range; there is the Moore, recently described as a "subversive modernist,"[263] who leaves us with no secure notions of authorial creativity or stable textuality. There is the Gertrude Stein whose uncontrolled, seemingly bodiless linguistic experimentation exceeds what any reader may reasonably be expected to tolerate; there is the Gertrude Stein whose specific strategies articulate the psychological and discursive positioning of the lesbian body. There is the John Crowe Ransom who struggles elegantly with the philosophical burdens of mutability and death; there is the John Crowe Ransom who projects his revulsion at mortality onto the bodies of women. There is the Langston Hughes whose poems on racial injustice are always reassuringly subsumed within a universalizing humanism; and there is the Hughes whose poetry about American racism mounts an uncompromising and pervasive cultural indictment. At times, the debates about these and other poets are conducted as if such matters can be settled, as if it were simply a question of deciding the immanent, essential nature of the poems themselves. What seems clear instead is that these questions are not decidable, that once discursive practices are in circulation they become available to be rearticulated to suit the historical needs of different generations, different social groups.[264] Thus it is time to stop expressing something like astonished gratitude when we credit a critic with, say, "showing us a Wallace Stevens we have never seen before." We should begin instead to anticipate such radical reversals and reinterpretations and try to read and write accordingly. And when we cannot anticipate such new readings, which will often be the case, we need to reflect on what has prevented us from doing so. Although it is perfectly true to say that modern American poetry is intrinsically contradictory, that is a less pertinent observation than to recognize what *use* we make of the poetry of our past.

Modernism, then, has been continually reconstituted, with new movements rearticulating already existing writing practices. Thus the *Fugitive* group, consolidated in *Fugitives: An Anthology of Verse* (1928) and in *I'll Take My Stand* (1930), a collection of essays, mixed traditional tastes in poetic form with an anti-industrial agrarianism that drew on a history of rural organizing and social advocacy but rearticulated it to positions that were largely conservative. Some of the members of this group, including Ransom, Tate, and Warren, gave the New Criticism, with its emphasis on ahistorical literary analysis, its initial impetus. In doing so, they drew on some of Eliot's critical essays and thereby reinforced a disciplinary inclination to view the fragmented modernist text as a purely aesthetic object, its linguistic fragmentation purified of social influence and critique. In a remarkable reversal of the revolutionary strain in modernism, a reversal that is still empowered today, literary theory thereby covertly fused the disjunctive modernist poem with the idealized view of poetry in the genteel tradition.

Both the local and the systemic results of this complex rearrangement and reconsolidation of discourses are often invisible to us. Let us take one poignant, ironic, and improbable result: Ezra Pound's survival. From 1941 to 1943 Pound broadcast several hundred pages of original talks over Italian radio. The full text of these talks was not published until 1978 (*"Ezra Pound Speaking": Radio Speeches of World War II*), though a number of them had been widely available before then.[265] Suffice it to say that these profascist, vitriolic, and anti-Semitic talks are often utterly despicable; if discourse alone (when it is produced for the enemy during wartime) can constitute treason, these texts would appear to meet most relevant criteria. In the absence of full public disclosure of the talks at the time, though in full knowledge of the main outlines of Pound's activities, a number of poets and critics came to Pound's defense after the Second World War, arguing that Pound was primarily a poet and should not be brought to trial. Ironically, they relied for their persuasiveness on the still potent assumptions about poetry that dominated the genteel tradition at the turn of the century, assumptions Pound himself had been at work to overthrow: that poetry is a harmless and impotent realm, unrelated to history and incapable of provoking real change.

Tracing the complex and multiple relations among these speeches, Pound's other political writings, and *The Cantos*, relations long suppressed by academic critics, will probably be the center of Pound scholarship for the next decade. One of the problems, however, that has so far blocked a more open and reflective inquiry into the relation between Pound's politics and his poetry is the general repression of considerations of the mixed relationships of determination and displacement between personality and writing. Consider, for example, the shocked reaction to the view of Frost mounted in the three-volume biography that appeared in the 1970s.[266] The cherished image of Frost as the wry New England sage was, it seemed, quite shattered by the picture of him as a rather petty, malicious, and competitive man. What the reaction suggests is that, hidden behind New Criticism's traditional rejection of authorial psychology as irrelevant to literary analysis, was a wholly naïve view of the psychology of writing, one assuming a relation of complete identity. That relation of identity, furthermore, is founded on mutually reinforcing views of human personality and the literary text as unitary and coherent—with an unchanging and retrievable essential core of meaning. None of this need be the case. These assumptions are largely ideological, reinforcing a whole set of social relations. If one becomes aware of these beliefs, however, and seeks to abandon them, one does not thereby solve the problem of the relationship between personality and writing but rather enters into an overdetermined arena whose constituents cannot be decisively sorted out and interpreted. Between Frost's personality and his writing, then, between Pound's political beliefs and his poetry, there will be partial and mixed relations of compensation and identity. Bound up with diverse other cultural influences, poetry and personality become an intractable but necessary arena of thought. Just as one cannot simply set aside Pound's politics so as to indulge oneself in the supposed lyrical and idealized literariness of the poetry, so too the politics of the *Cantos* may not be consistent or finally determinable. Their major discursive strains, however, include fascism and sexism of the worst sort.

The history of academic commentary on these issues, at least until the 1980s, has not been impressive.[267] Otherwise intelligent critics, either ignorant of or choosing to forget Pound's long history of fascist and anti-Semitic commentary in both his poetry and prose, have held to the fiction that Pound's fascist period dates from the 1930s. Their ways of accounting for Pound's politics are so unsound as to be almost unbelievable. One suggests his fascism was merely a "straightforward enthusiasm for all things Italian."[268] But the most indicative observation—indicative, that is, of how the profession of English studies is in some ways intellectually bankrupt—is the frequent statement that the *real* issue, the issue available on the high ground above history occupied by English studies, is how Pound's political beliefs do or do not influence his poetry. The political texts themselves are merely collateral information, data disposable on the way to an understanding of the poetry, itself, on the other hand, a form of discourse generically guaranteed luminous transcendence.

There would seem, to the contrary, to be a host of other essential questions that need to be formulated and reformulated, their elements rearticulated in new combinations, until they gain some purchase on our lives. Of what value is an elegant literary sensibility that is contaminated by exhortations to genocide and murder? Is it a social or disciplinary virtue to work to separate poetry from its historical entanglements? What does it mean for us, in our own time, to try to suppress discussion of Pound's politics? Do we really do so in service of the poetry's higher truth? Are there grounds for despising some elements of the man and his work and admiring others? How are such distinctions to be maintained once we recognize the poetry is itself, at least at moments, clearly fascist? Are the temptations of arrogance in poetics wholly separate from those in politics? Is Pound's service to the State altogether exceptional? Or does it compel us to look more deeply at the general relations between poetry and power? Once we identify the clearly racist, sexist, anti-Semitic, and fascist passages in the poems, once we recognize how Pound's economic and social theories and his gestures of historical recovery are tied up in these prejudices, what is left of the "radiant gist" that one of Pound's major critics finds at the core of his enterprise?[269]

Yet Pound is not the only modern poet whose writing is internally contextualized and compromised in this way. Indeed, the institutional practices that make it possible to contain Pound's more deplorable beliefs and idealize his lyricism are precisely the institutional practices that make it possible generally to idealize poetry and ignore its relations with the rest of culture. It should not be news to anyone that national cultures generally suppress recognition of poverty, inequality, prejudice, injustice, and oppression in order to promote an idealized self-image. The dynamic mechanisms that enable us to suppress awareness of sexism and racism across the discursive field of modern poetry operate in much the same way. In the case of Pound this means, ironically, that his poem containing history has been read, represented, and idealized in somewhat the same way American history is selectively idealized in popular memory and political rhetoric. Forgetting much and white-washing what it remembers, the profession of English studies behaves in this regard rather like the general culture. The hierarchical division between literature and history or politics, one eternal and idealized, one temporary and debased, is entirely a disciplinary fiction, one, however, also entirely in the service of the real world power the discipline considers unseemly and tries to believe it has surpassed.

The lesson (hidden for some time) to be learned from the poetry of 1910–1945 is that *none* of this is necessarily true, that poetry is by no means given in its essence to be apolitical and historically irrelevant. The social function of poetry is a contested domain and its political meaning is open to disputation, as any writing of its history must show. Poetry is continually articulated and rearticulated in terms of power. Indeed, poetry is a cultural domain that is constantly being reformed and repositioned. Despite academic efforts to prove otherwise, poetry will not stay still. The gradual broadening of the canon that has overtaken the academy in the past two decades is precisely that kind of struggle: over who wrote the poetry worth remembering, over which audiences count, over whose views of history will continue to be available to us and remain persuasive, over what aesthetic and social criteria underlie the canon, over what kinds of discourse and what subject matter would count as poetic, over what kinds of competitive and mutually stimulating connections would be recognized between different groups of poets, over what moral and political claims the poets of the past may make on us now—in short, over the social meaning and political significance not only of poetry but also of our interpretation of it.[270] All readings of the period, including those that claim to transcend politics, necessarily enter into this struggle and take stands on these issues. By virtue of this argument it should now be clear—if it was not already so—that any resemblence between this book and a normative literary history, any suggestion that such a project is achievable, amounts to a wager that reason and the discourses of mastery are intended to lose. The received notion of literary history is here the object of a deliberate deconstruction; it is the false promise of an objectivity I have done what I can to disallow.

I think it should now be apparent that what is at stake in the varied poetic discourses of modern American poetry is not only the aesthetics of an individual cultural domain but also the network of relations that define the nature and boundaries of that domain and grant it influence or irrelevance elsewhere in social life. In the competition to define and dominate our sense of what poetry is and can be, quite different notions of what poetry can do within the culture are validated and rejected. In the dominant mode of literary history, such issues are suppressed in favor of a narrowly aesthetic history of the conflicts between different kinds of poetry. We need to recognize that poetry throughout the twentieth century is the site of a much broader cultural struggle. It is a struggle over whether poetry can be an effective and distinctive site for cultural critique, over whether poetry will offer readers subject positions that are reflective and self-critical, over whether poetry can be a force for social change, over what discourses poetry can plausibly integrate or juxtapose, over what groups of readers will be considered valid audiences for poetry, over what role poetry and the interpretation of poetry can play in stabilizing or destabilizing the dominant values and existing power relations in the culture as a whole. Since poetry is the literary genre that is most consistently, thoroughly, and unreflectively idealized, these differences over its meaning are crucial to the whole definition of the institution of English studies. As a discipline, English gets a good part of its self-image and its ideology from an idealized notion of the poetic. The struggle over the meaning of poetry may in the end determine whether people whose self-image is strongly identified with literature see themselves as centrally engaged with cultural struggles or as structurally guaranteed a place that transcends them. These are not merely questions, therefore, about the appropriate subject matter of poetry or about its aesthetics. They are questions about what cultural territory poetry will claim for itself, questions about what power poetry can have in our lives, questions finally about the social meaning of a life lived on poetry's behalf.

NOTES

INDEX

NOTES

1. Although literary historiography has tended for some time not to reflect on its own historical positioning, that particular blindness is becoming increasingly difficult to sustain. At issue, to put the question baldly, is whether one can (or should) either read widely or write a literary history without thinking and talking about how and why one is reading and writing. In a period in which the canon of American literature has been undergoing massive pressure for change, in which a variety of interpretive languages compete for our attention, and in which we are beginning to become increasingly sensitive to the politics of literary historiography, it is difficult to avoid polemical and theoretical reflection and argument and difficult as well to avoid at least some awareness of how one's own project is historically situated. If I wanted a practice relatively free of theoretical reflection, I would have to try to edit that element out of my writing in the process of revision. That, in fact—edit at least those more extended overtly theoretical passages out in the course of revision—is what I did for an essay on modern poetry that I wrote for the *Columbia Literary History of the United States* (1988), an essay that was the inspiration for this book. The editors of that volume did write a theoretical introduction to the book, but they felt that thereafter theoretical issues should be implicit, not explicit. Yet it was impossible either for me or for many other contributors altogether to eliminate theoretical passages from our essays; in the contemporary environment, such reflections are often the glue that holds a discourse together and marks its necessities.

In thinking through the question of how literary history has been written in the past and might be written in the future it is important to remember that the discourse of literary history can have a somewhat different audience than the now frequently more restricted, professional audience for academic literary criticism. In the case of both the Columbia volume and of another recent multi-author project, *The History of Southern Literature* (1985), markedly different social and economic forces and ambitions operated on these books than typically operate on critical books for a largely academic audience. The books were designed to be marketed to large audiences who were more likely to want the illusion of certainty in history than the problematics of doubt. But it is, in any case, often true that literary histories and anthologies are among the ways the profession of academic literary studies represents itself to the larger social formation. There is an uneasiness among some in the profession about representing ourselves as undecided about or in disagreement over the facts of our field. And the society tends to expect an orderly, properly located discipline to offer confident knowledge, not grounds for productive but unresolvable reflection.

These two large volumes are worth comparing somewhat further because they raise a number of other points about the process of doing literary history. Although the editors of the *Columbia Literary History* did not perhaps go as far as I might have liked in problematizing historical writing, they did do a number of things the editors of the *History of Southern Literature* chose not to do. Unlike the southern history, the Columbia project did not impose a relatively uniform style on its contributors. The Columbia history also allowed considerably more overlapping among its chapters, so that it includes alternate readings of the same periods and sometimes multiple readings of the same writers. It therefore presents somewhat more of an opportunity to think about American literary history than a new normative synthesis of that history. To the extent that one writer can do so, that is also the effect I am aiming for here.

2. *Rearticulation* is one of the key terms in this book, and it is used in a way that may be unfamiliar to many readers. I draw the concept from Stuart Hall's work and from Ernesto Laclau, *Politics and Ideology in Marxist Theory: Capitalism—Fascism—Populism* (London: New Left Books, 1977) and Ernesto Laclau and Chantal Mouffe, *Hegemony and Socialist Strategy: Towards a Radical Democratic Politics* (London: Verso, 1985). For a list of Hall's publications, in which articulation and rearticulation are both directly and implicitly at issue, see "A Working Bibliography: Writings of Stuart Hall," *Journal of Communication Inquiry* 10:1 (Summer 1986), 125–29. His analyses of Thatcherism are a good place to begin. See Hall's "The Toad in the Garden: Thatcherism among the Theorists," in Cary Nelson and Lawrence Grossberg, eds. *Marxism and the Interpretation of Culture* (Urbana: University of Illinois Press, 1988) and his *The Hard Road to Renewal: Thatcherism and the Crisis of the Left* (New York: Verso, 1988).

Hall, Laclau, and Mouffe employ *rearticulation* as part of a cluster of concepts they develop from Antonio Gramsci. It enables them to describe how political discourses either become dominant or organize for resistance by rearticulating existing terms, concepts, arguments, beliefs, and metaphors into new configurations that are persuasive to people in a particular historical context. The apparent unity and consistency of a particular discursive domain is always an effect of its success, in a given historical context, at disguising the seams between the different (and sometimes contradictory) vocabularies and beliefs it assembles. The struggle to gain control over the production of meaning in social life is thus dependent on this competition to articulate and rearticulate relations between the valued and devalued con-

cepts and languages in circulation in the culture. Hall lays out the issues
rather clearly in a 1985 interview in which I and others asked him about his
use of the term and his relation to Laclau:

> An articulation is thus the form of the connection that *can* make a unity
> of two different elements, under certain conditions. It is a linkage which
> is not necessary, determined, absolute and essential for all time. You have
> to ask, under what circumstances *can* a connection be forged or made? So
> the so-called 'unity' of a discourse is really the articulation of different,
> distinct elements which can be rearticulated in different ways because
> they have no necessary 'belongingness.' The 'unity' which matters is a
> linkage between that articulated discourse and the social forces with
> which it can, under certain historical conditions, be connected. Thus,
> a theory of articulation is both a way of understanding how ideological
> elements come, under certain conditions, to cohere together within a
> discourse, and a way of asking how they do or do not become articulated,
> at specific conjunctures, to certain political subjects. . . . It is not the
> individual elements of a discourse that have political or ideological
> connotations, it is the way those elements are organized together in
> a new discursive formation. "On Postmodernism and Articulation:
> An Interview with Stuart Hall," ed. Lawrence Grossberg, *Journal of
> Communication Inquiry* 10:2 (Summer 1986), 45–60.

When a given discursive formation begins to lose its hold on a particular
population or subculture, the individual verbal components it had managed to hold together may become recognizable again. These discursive elements then potentially become available for rearticulation to other discursive formations. In public life, we continually witness struggles over what
discourses will be able to take effective possession of, rearticulate to themselves, such concepts as "patriotism," "justice," or "the nation." In the period
this book covers, "poetry" was such a contested concept.

3. The claim that all structuralisms were ahistorical was largely a polemical and adversarial collapsing of differences, since, say, a synchronic reading
of a specific historical period—a recurrent project of both phenomenological criticism and structuralism, from Georges Poulet to Michel Foucault—
was not the same as a Lévi-Straussian reading of the universal structures
of the human mind. The views of history here are quite different. The synchronic analysis of a historical period—that is, an analysis which treats a
certain period of time *as though* it were a single historical moment defined
by a relatively consistent epistemology—arguably eliminates a significant
amount of difference, simplifies cultural conflicts, and ignores the local dynamics of change but certainly does not necessarily assert the existence
of universal, transhistorical cultural or mental structures. Indeed, totalized
versions of historical periods have been a major feature of both traditional

literary history and the study of the history of ideas for some time. Like it or not, on this issue there is a certain epistemological continuity that runs from Tillyard's *Elizabethan World Picture* through Poulet's *Metamorphoses of the Circle* to Foucault's *The Order of Things*. Spatialized models of history in the 1960s were thus more imitative than innovative; despite claims to the contrary, they threatened less a break with scholarly tradition than a stark revelation of the grounds of that tradition through an intensification of its totalizing tendencies. Nevertheless, by allowing itself to become an object of attack on these grounds, and by often treating itself as a kind of superior discourse that need not respond to criticism, structuralism did help place history on the table, making it a subject of discussion rather than an assumed given.

4. Margaret Dickie, *On the Modernist Long Poem* (Iowa City: University of Iowa Press, 1986), p. 162.

5. A number of feminist readings, including those cited later in this book, will be central to any effort to rethink modern poetry from the vantage point of sexual difference. Special mention must, however, be given to Sandra M. Gilbert and Susan Gubar's *No Man's Land: The Place of the Woman Writer in the Twentieth Century* (New Haven: Yale University Press, 1987), the first volume of a three-volume work that not only reevaluates a number of men and women writers but also presents a general argument about the differences between men and women writers in the twentieth century. Although their position on male and female writers is far too dichotomous and essentialist, they do mount an important challenge to the traditional suppression of gender issues in academic scholarship on modern poetry. A fair evaluation of this book may have to wait to see what kind of cultural work it does over the next few years. If their rigid claims about the difference between men's and women's writings are accepted, then their impact will be distorting and reductive. On the other hand, the book may prove to be primarily an important stimulus to debate on these issues. The second volume of this work, *Sexchanges*, was published in 1989.

6. Just how interested such narratives are is apparent from the restricted list of poets considered in Dickie's *On the Modernist Long Poem*. It deals only with four white male poets: Eliot, Crane, Williams, and Pound. Even poem sequences—as opposed to texts that are arguably one long poem divided into parts—are given no consideration. James Weldon Johnson, Jean Toomer, Mina Loy, Gertrude Stein, H. D., Melvin Tolson, and Langston Hughes, among others, are never mentioned. For a more generous but still restrictively privileged category, see M. L. Rosenthal and Sally M. Gall, *The Modern Poetic Sequence: The Genesis of Modern Poetry* (New York: Oxford University Press, 1983). This book also generally excludes minority poets who did work with long poems or poem sequences. Langston Hughes and Melvin Tolson are not mentioned.

Of course a great number of alternative readings of modern poetry exist alongside these two. And critics are sometimes implicitly aware of competing historical claims even when they never acknowledge them within their own writing. Since no individual version of American modernism is now likely to become wholly canonical—despite, say, repeated efforts to define modern poetry in terms of the aesthetic of one or another of the poets who dominate the canon—there is in effect a general professional corrective to the inherent social pathology, forgetfulness, and exclusivity of individual critical books, books whose narrow theses reinforce unacknowledged cultural prejudices or translate implicitly into repressive social practices. Critics, to be sure, often anticipate a reception that will amount to a general cultural correction of their overstated claims. They deliberately exaggerate, hoping thereby to win at least partial agreement with their thesis, and they expect no more than that from their readers. Nonetheless, the blind, relentless pursuit of narrow and sometimes repressive historical theses—simultaneously unreflective about their own enterprise and intolerant of difference —does not seem the most productive way to proceed. And when a whole community of critics works together to erase large portions of our literary past, as the historians and critics of modernism did for several decades, then the chief damage done by unreflective argument remains unchecked.

For an instructive report on one struggle to establish the paternity of the modern era, see Marjorie Perloff, "Pound/Stevens: Whose Era?" in her *The Dance of the Intellect: Studies in the Poetry of the Pound Tradition* (New York: Cambridge University Press, 1985), pp. 1–32. In this case, the evidence is weighted toward Pound, so the competing quotes from those advocating Stevens as the emblematic poet of modernism are particularly vague and fatuous. Although a broad view of Stevens' work is likely to establish him as a partly anomalous figure, a case could be made for his representative character by emphasizing the phenomenological elements of his poetry. The main point from my perspective, however, would be to argue that modernism belongs to no one.

7. For a review of Williams' reception see Paul L. Mariani, *William Carlos Williams: The Poet and His Critics* (Chicago: American Library Association, 1975).

8. Mary Douglas, *How Institutions Think* (Syracuse, N.Y.: Syracuse University Press, 1986), pp. 69–70.

9. The politically aggressive, socially critical literature of the period was the major focus of the culture's forgetfulness during the late 1940s and 1950s. A few scholars, however, worked against the grain of these tendencies. Any account of critical interest in politics and cultural production in America has to begin with the massive two-volume *Socialism and American Life*, edited by Donald Drew Egbert and Stow Persons (Princeton: Princeton University Press, 1952). Its essays and extensive critical bibliographies

remain important resources. Two additional books of particular importance, both of which retain their usefulness today, are Walter B. Rideout, *The Radical Novel in the United States, 1900–1954: Some Interrelations of Literature and Society* (Cambridge: Harvard University Press, 1956) and Daniel Aaron, *Writers on the Left* (New York: Oxford University Press, 1961). Although neither deals extensively with poetry, each provides indispensable background for any understanding of the poetry of the period.

10. In certain ways, however, this project has built in checks and balances. For example, my readings of individual poets are all brief enough to remain somewhat tentative (*not* persuading oneself that one is in possession of the truth may be more difficult in writing, say, a full book or essay on a single poet), and the rival poetries of the period can remain in contest with one another in this kind of overview.

11. Yet, as Fredric Jameson writes in *The Political Unconscious: Narrative as a Socially Symbolic Act* (Ithaca: Cornell University Press, 1981), "only a genuine philosophy of history is capable of respecting the specificity and radical difference of the social and political past while disclosing the solidarity of its polemics and passions, its forms, structures, experiences, and struggles, with those of the present day" (p. 18). There is much here I would affirm, including the attempt to inform the politics of the present with exemplary images from the past. Yet I am less willing to privilege the explanatory powers of one philosophy of history, and no philosophy of history—whatever its persuasiveness—can put us in an unmediated relation with the past, though the valences of terms like "specificity" suggest that sort of literary goal. This impossible dilemma is a pervasive one today, not only for literary studies but also throughout the humanities and interpretive social sciences.

12. Roland Barthes, *S/Z*, trans. Richard Miller (New York: Farrar, Straus & Giroux, 1974), p. 4.

13. Jane Tompkins, *Sensational Designs: The Cultural Work of American Fiction, 1790–1860* (New York: Oxford University Press, 1985), p. xiii.

14. This problem is intensified by two general conditions of contemporary textual analysis: First, that the discursive moment or element of theory almost always outdistances its application, even though the two tendencies are never wholly separable. As one can conclude from Paul de Man's analysis of constitutive rhetorical gaps and self-deception in critical prose in *Blindness and Insight: Essays in the Rhetoric of Contemporary Criticism* (New York: Oxford University Press, 1971), analytic practices are rarely true to or wholly consistent with their formal theoretical claims, though knowledge of such discrepancies is often repressed by both writers and readers of critical prose. Second, that it is only our own continuing cultural history of illusions about the possibility of achieving objective knowledge that makes the recognition of the historically bounded character of interpretation seem exclusively disabling, an arena of intellectual doubt and possible risk to the

status of humanities and social science interpretation. Indeed, the language I use above—"sort out and deal with"—reflects the contemporary anxieties and the need for mastery surrounding this problematic. In other cultural contexts, the mutual determination of past and present could be a source of interpretive pleasure. Moreover, whatever its frustrations at this moment of intellectual history, the very historicality of interpretation remains, at least potentially, at once enabling and disabling. This paradox is an inescapable feature of the semiotics of culture. From a semiotic perspective, the restrictions built into the historical specificity of interpretation are necessarily generative and productive inhibitions, since those inhibitions both structure and facilitate our writing. Thus these restrictions are less likely to be experienced as prohibitions than as inducements to produce meaning of a certain sort, followed by rewards for doing so. Yet this does not reduce the difficulty we feel in taking on the specific contemporary burden of trying to reflect on how our practices are historically situated and determined.

15. It was Saussure's 1916 posthumous *Course in General Linguistics*, trans. Wade Baskin (New York: McGraw-Hill, 1966), that suggested language is not made up of a series of autonomous entities—each possessing an inherent and essential meaning—but rather of a system of terms whose meaning is established by their differential relations to one another. Interest in Saussure revived with structuralism and semiotics in the 1960s, but it became clear that the structuralist notion of a system of differences often proved far too stable and schematic to account for either the diverse production of meaning or the processes of historical change. My use of the term *differential* is designed to invoke what I would describe as a politicized, poststructuralist Saussurianism, a notion recognizing both the unstable nature of any field of differences and the social and political struggle that determines how those differences are articulated to one another. In my use of the term "differential" I thus draw both on Jacques Derrida's notion of différance and on the British cultural studies tradition, in which Stuart Hall and others see discursive practices as shaped by a Gramscian war of position. Derrida's radical reading of difference begins with his 1967 *Of Grammatology*, trans. Gayatri Chakravorty Spivak (Baltimore: Johns Hopkins University Press, 1976) and his 1968 essay "Différance," trans. David B. Allison in Derrida, *Speech and Phenomena And Other Essays on Husserl's Theory of Signs* (Evanston: Northwestern University Press, 1975).

16. Marguerite Wilkinson's *New Voices: An Introduction to Contemporary Poetry* (New York: Macmillan, 1919) is partly an anthology with extended critical introductions to its individual sections. Part 1, "The Technique of Contemporary Poetry," includes essays on "The Pattern of a Poem," "Organic Rhythm," "Images and Symbols," "Diction," "Certain Conservative Poets," and "Certain Radical Poets." Part 2 is thematic, with essays on love, religion, nature, "Democracy and the New Themes," and "Patriotism and the Great War" preceding selections of poems on these topics.

17. Llewellyn Jones's *First Impressions: Essays on Poetry, Criticism, and Prosody* (New York: Knopf, 1925) gives other examples of perspectives we have repressed for many years and only now rediscovered and rearticulated to our own interests. His chapter on "Four Younger Women Poets" (Edna St. Vincent Millay, Genevieve Taggard, Louise Bogan, and Elinor Wylie) opens with the observation that "poetry does not have to be major to be enjoyable and important" (p. 111). He goes on to point out that, though Millay is mostly known for her romantic or ecstatic poetry, her sonnets are as likely to show women's "scorn of the sort of half-love which is too often offered them by men who are unworthy of their mettle" (p. 113). He begins his remarks on Bogan with these lines: "Her first volume, 'Body of This Death,' is a small one but one of concentrated poetry. As the title implies, it is the poetry of struggle against—shall we say, circumstance? Not circumstance in the gross sense of the word, but against all that stifles, diverts, and disarms life in its original intention; against the pettiness that haunts the footsteps of love, especially against the limitations, imposed and self-imposed, on women; and at the same time a cry for something positive, for something compelling" (p. 118). He goes on to show that "for this mood of protest and of assertion of an austere and uncompromising scale of values, Miss Bogan has an appropriately austere style" (pp. 119–20). In general, these poets "unite in presenting a picture . . . of the young, sensitive, self-conscious woman . . . in a civilization which has theoretically made room for her as a person but practically has not quite caught up to her—which does not understand her, and is often aghast at her actions, and often, too, callous to her sufferings" (p. 112).

18. While working on this study I had occasion to evaluate a proposal for a multi-author history of American poetry that simply omitted the first decade of the century. For a commentary on and sample of some of the political poetry such a historical model erases, see Dan Tannacito, "Poetry of the Colorado Miners: 1903–1906," *Radical Teacher* 15 (March 1980), 1–15.

19. See Pound's *Patria Mia* (Chicago: Ralph Fletcher Seymour, 1950), first submitted for publication in 1913, for a good indication of the sense of constraint some writers felt: "It is well known that in the year of grace 1870 Jehovah appeared to Messrs. Harper and Co. and to the editors of 'The Century,' 'The Atlantic,' and certain others, and spake thus: 'The style of 1870 is the final and divine revelation. Keep things always just as they are now,' And they, being earnest, God-fearing men, did abide by the words of the Almighty, and great credit and honor accrued unto them, for had they not divine warrant!" (p. 42).

20. Paul Lauter, "Race and Gender in the Shaping of the American Literary Canon: A Case Study from the Twenties," *Feminist Studies* 9:3 (Fall 1983), 456. An influential general collection on the challenge to the prevailing canon is Leslie A. Fiedler and Houston A. Baker, Jr., eds., *English Literature: Opening Up the Canon*, Selected Papers from the English Institute,

1979, new series, no. 4 (Baltimore: Johns Hopkins University Press, 1981). Also see Lillian S. Robinson, "Treason Our Text: Feminist Challenges to the Literary Canon," *Tulsa Studies in Women's Literature* 2:1 (1983), 105–21; Cornell West, "Minority Discourse and the Pitfalls of Canon Formation," *The Yale Journal of Criticism* 1:1 (1987), 193–217; and Paul Lauter, "Working Class Women's Literature—An Introduction to Study," *Radical Teacher* 15 (March 1980) 16–26, for both Lauter's essay and his bibliography.

21. These are the last two (of three) stanzas of "Incident," which was first published in Cullen's *Color* (New York: Harper and Brothers, 1925), p. 15.

22. Mike Quin (and sometimes Michael Quin) was the name that Paul William Ryan adopted for his political work. Born in San Francisco, he left school at age 15 and worked in shops and offices until becoming a sailor (1925–1929). Upon his return he worked in a bookstore, joined the John Reed Club, and contributed to *Partisan*. He became a labor activist and wrote for *The Waterfront Worker, Western Worker,* and *The Daily Worker.* In the 1940s he had a radio program and a column in the *Daily People's World.* His unpublished radio scripts are in the Baskette collection at the University of Illinois. Two important collections of his poems and columns are *Dangerous Thoughts* (San Francisco: People's World, 1940) and *More Dangerous Thoughts* (San Francisco: People's World, 1941). These may be supplemented by *On the Drumhead: A Selection from the Writings of Mike Quin,* ed. Henry Carlisle (San Francisco: Pacific Publishing Foundation, 1948), which includes a biographical sketch by Carlisle and reprints a good selection of the poems and columns published under the Quin pseudonym, along with some of the pieces he published under his own name. Quin also wrote several political pamphlets: *The C.S. Case Against Labor* (San Francisco: International Labor Defense, 1936), *Ashcan the M-Plan* (San Francisco: Yanks are Not Coming Committee, 1938), *The Yanks Are Not Coming* (San Francisco: Maritime Federation of the Pacific, 1940), and *The Enemy Within* (San Francisco: People's World, 1941), as well as the full-length *The Big Strike* (Olema, Calif.: Olema Publishing, 1949), which was translated into Russian in 1951. Toward the end of his life he wrote three mystery novels, *The Lying Ladies* (1946), *The Bandaged Nude* (1946), and *Many a Monster* (1948), all of them featuring his detective Dan Bannion and all of them published by Simon and Schuster under the pseudonym Robert Finnegan. No discussion of Quin's poetry would be adequate without a sample of the satiric poetry that remains as pertinent today as it was when first written. Here are four (of eight) stanzas from Quin's "The Glorious Fourth" (*More Dangerous Thoughts,* pp. 91–92):

> Senator Screwball would nearly die
> If he couldn't make a speech on the Fourth of July;
> If he couldn't stand up there beside Old Glory
> And blow off his mouth like a damned old tory.

When Senator Screwball rises to rave,
Thomas Jefferson rolls in his grave
And our country's flag, as it flaps and flutters,
Blushes at every word he utters.

What kind of an annual celebration
Is this for the birth of a free-born nation?
Rubber stamp stooges yelling like Neroes
To honor a revolution's heroes!

He howls for war and beats the drums
And thinks the unemployed are bums.
He voted for a free speech gag,
But God, how the Senator loves the flag!

23. See Paul Lauter, ed., *Reconstructing American Literature: Courses, Syllabi, Issues* (Old Westbury, N.Y.: Feminist Press, 1983). The relative conservatism of many of these syllabi is evident not only in the exclusion of all except a very few of the noncanonical modern poets but also in the poems selected and in the very traditional notion of literariness that constrains the kinds of texts chosen for study. Langston Hughes, for example, is generally represented only by the more acceptable humanistic texts in his *Selected Poems;* the more aggressive political poems are ignored. One exception to these general observations, however, is offered by the final syllabus in the book, Jean Fagan Yellin's very innovative course "Criticisms of American Culture."

24. These efforts have resulted in a number of excellent compensatory alternative anthologies, including Jerome Rothenberg, ed., *Revolution of the Word: A New Gathering of American Avant Garde Poetry, 1914–1945* (New York: Seabury, 1974); Jack Salzman and Leo Zanderer, eds., *Social Poetry of the 1930s: A Selection* (New York: Burt Franklin, 1978); Dexter Fisher, ed., *The Third Woman: Minority Woman Writers of the United States* (Boston: Houghton Mifflin, 1980); Erlene Stetson, ed., *Black Sister: Poetry by Black American Women, 1746–1980* (Bloomington: Indiana University Press, 1981); Louise Bernikow, ed., *The World Split Open: Four Centuries of Women Poets in England and America, 1552–1950* (New York: Vintage Books, 1974); Sandra M. Gilbert and Susan Gubar, eds., *The Norton Anthology of Literature by Women: The Tradition in English* (New York: Norton, 1985). It may also be said, however, that no one anthology exists that gives adequate treatment to the whole range of modern American poetry. Something of the power of the traditional canon, moreover, can be seen by comparing the excellent Salzman and Zanderer anthology with a reference book that Salzman himself edited, *The Cambridge Handbook of*

American Literature (New York: Cambridge University Press, 1986). Of the twenty-four poets included in *Social Poets of the 1930s* only seven receive entries in *The Cambridge Handbook of American Literature*. No doubt the usual arguments about space requiring the exclusion of "minor" poets would be offered in defense, but there is no real excuse for the damage done by such reference works to our cultural memory. In the context of this project, the anthologies above should help remind the reader that there are other minority traditions, including the Native American, that I have not dealt with here.

25. Yet new alliances often come at the expense of actually fracturing—or at least threatening, destabilizing, and resemanticizing—existing political and discursive relations. Consider the current productive, but contentious, interactions between black literature and contemporary theory or between feminism and men. These basic cultural and territorial struggles involve stressful processes of renegotiating interests, differences, and mutual benefits that are only made more painful by trying to deny their reality. Such shifting allegiances are a continuous, unavoidable feature of the social formation. All alliances are contingent, partial, and conflicted. Constructed with an effort to recognize differences, however, they can be effective without being self-deceiving. Thus the issue is whether one wishes to be part of the process that shapes cultural domains and gives them influence. Certainly it is quite different to proceed in your work with an anticipation of seeking out opportunities for new alliances. Positions that block potential alliances thereby may become less desirable. Most important, one begins to think realistically about the social meaning of the interpretive commitments one makes.

26. See Lauter's "Race and Gender in the Shaping of the American Literary Canon" for further discussion of this process.

27. See, for example, Isidor Schneider, "Poetry: Red-baiting Victim," *New Masses*, January 18, 1944, 24–26.

28. I am borrowing these quotes from "The End of the Line," the excellent opening chapter of James E. B. Breslin's *From Modern to Contemporary: American Poetry, 1945–1965* (Chicago: University of Chicago Press, 1984). The original sources are: Hayden Carruth, "Foreword," *The Voice That is Great Within Us: American Poetry of the Twentieth Century* (New York, 1970), p. xix; Paul Carroll, *The Poem in Its Skin* (Chicago: 1968), p. 204; W. D. Snodgrass, *In Radical Pursuit* (New York, 1975), p. 47; Robert Lowell in *The New York Review of Books*, March 6, 1972, 3; Richard Howard, "Made Things: An Interview with Richard Howard," *Ohio Review* 16 (Fall 1974), 44.

29. On the status of minor literature see Louis A. Renza's extended introduction to his very fine *"A White Heron" and the Question of Minor Literature* (Madison: University of Wisconsin Press, 1984) and T. S. Eliot's famous

1944 essay "What is Minor Poetry," reprinted in T. S. Eliot, *On Poetry and Poets* (New York: Farrar, Straus & Giroux, 1957).

30. Charles Altieri, "An Idea and Ideal of a Literary Canon," in Robert von Hallberg, ed., *Canons* (Chicago: University of Chicago Press, 1984), pp. 41–64. Altieri's powerful essay is the only defense of the existing canon that I am inclined to take seriously, in part because he doesn't descend to the usual fatuous stance of defending civilization against barbarians without taste. Instead, he has the courage to make a strong claim for the social function of the canon: "I want to argue that the past that canons preserve is best understood as a permanent theater helping us shape and judge personal and social values." I would largely agree with him here, but I have less faith than he does that the canon preserves a sufficiently diverse and representative range of "contrastive frameworks." As a result, I find its theater partly coercive and restrictive rather than generously broadening. But I would strongly agree with him, as I will argue below, that "the roles we can imagine for the canon require us to consider seriously the place of idealization in social life." Again, I am less confident that idealization always has positive effects; I see it rather as a social and psychological mechanism with no inherent content, one that can therefore be articulated to both liberating and repressive projects. Ironically, those on the left have sometimes attacked the mechanism of idealization at the same time as they have depended on unexamined idealization to maintain their own commitments. On this issue, see, for example, Etienne Balibar's analysis of the contradictory idealization of the proletariat in Marxist theory in his "The Vacillation of Ideology," in Cary Nelson and Lawrence Grossberg, eds., *Marxism and the Interpretation of Culture*. My own position is that idealization is most beneficial if it is reflective and self-aware.

31. The way that poems are packaged for publication can have a good deal to do with their cultural meaning. In 1942, as a gesture of support for the Soviet Union, which was then under attack by Hitler's armies, Genevieve Taggard selected ten poems from her two most recent books and reprinted them as a separate pamphlet under the title *Falcon: Poems on Soviet Themes*. That special edition was dedicated to Liudmilla Pavlichenko, a Soviet war hero.

32. Edna St. Vincent Millay, *The Murder of Lidice* (New York: Harper & Row, 1942).

33. All these H. H. (Harold Harwell) Lewis pamphlets were published by B. C. Hagglund of Holt, Minnesota, as part of his "Rebel Poet Booklets" series. None has ever been reprinted. *Midfield Sediments* was scheduled for publication by Hagglund in 1936. Quotations are identified internally as *RR = Red Renaissance, TR = Thinking of Russia, S = Salvation,* and *RU = Road to Utterly.*

For Lewis's prose, see "Memoirs of a Dishwasher," *New Masses* (February 1929), 7; "School Days in the Gumbo," *The American Mercury* (January 1931), 50–58; "Adverse Publicity," *The Left*, no. 2 (1931), 37–44; "Home Guards," *New Masses* (June 1932), 24; "Some of a Sort," in *Folk-Say*, 4 (Norman: University of Oklahoma Press, 1932), pp. 189–93; "Down the Skidway," *The Anvil* (May 1933), 9–10; "Kicked Along," *Blast* (October–November, 1934), 9–17; "The Great Corn-Husking Derby," *Hinterland* (November–December, 1934); "Frez for Frezno," *The Anvil* (March-April 1936).

34. Proofs of several pamphlet covers are included in the H. H. Lewis papers in Kent Library at Southeast Missouri State University, Cape Girardeau, Missouri: *I Speak to the World: Poems*, and *We March Toward The Sun* in two versions, one subtitled *Poems* and one subtitled *A New World Songbook*. Another of Lewis's unfinished projects was tentatively titled *Lexicon of the Trade Jargon*. A section of entries in dictionary format survives as a typed manuscript titled "Migratory Agricultural Farm and Ranch Workers' Slang and Jargon." An application for a Guggenheim fellowship lists several other prospective projects. A television station, KFVS-TV, taped a 28-minute interview with Lewis in 1981; a copy is included in the Lewis archive. At the end of his life, Lewis was working on a manuscript dealing with the relations between Marxism and Christianity.

Included in H. H. Lewis's papers are about fifty of the letters Lewis received ordering copies of his pamphlets. A number of the letters are from people living in large metropolitan areas, including Boston, Chicago, Cleveland, Detroit, Harrisburg, Madison, Milwaukee, Minneapolis, New York, Oklahoma City, Philadelphia, Seattle, and Washington. But there are also numerous letters from small towns and cities and rural areas: Annadale, N.J.; Bloomington, Ill.; Billings, Montana; Dixon, Ill.; Elroy, Wis.; Hudson, N.Y.; Knoxville, Tenn.; Legion, Texas; Montgomery, Ala.; Milton Junction, Wis.; Newman Grove, Neb.; Norway, Maine; Oakwood, Oklahoma; Parsons, Kansas; Satus, Wash.; Sausalito, Calif.; Sea Cliff, N.Y.; Tonkhannock, Pa.

35. See Alfred Kreymborg, *New Masses*, April 28, 1942. Of the very few essays on Lewis, Jack Conroy's are of special note. Conroy wrote a three-page introduction to Lewis's *Red Renaissance* and followed it up with two essays: "Poet and Peasant," *Fantasy* (Autumn 1933) and, some thirty-six years later, "H. H. Lewis: Plowboy Poet of the Gumbo," *December* 11 (1969) 203–6. V. F. Calverton mentioned Lewis as one of the emerging major figures of proletarian literature in his 1932 *The Liberation of American Literature*. More recently, Harold L. Dellinger visited Lewis and wrote "Pegasus and the Plow," *Foolkiller* 3 (Fall 1976), 6–7, reporting him at the time living "in a one room farmhouse within a mile of where he was born and about three miles out of town." At that time, Lewis was still able to work occasionally. According to the librarian at Southeast Missouri State University, Lewis died in considerable poverty.

36. For an interesting defense of Auden's *Spain* see Frank Kermode's essay

"Eros, Builder of Cities," in his *History and Value* (Oxford: Oxford University Press, 1988).

37. See William Carlos Williams, "A Twentieth-Century American," *Poetry* (January 1936), 227–29. In addition to this review of Lewis's four pamphlets and the longer essay in *New Masses* (Nov. 23, 1937), 17–18, Williams also wrote "An Outcry from the Dirt," an advance review of Lewis's *Midfield Sediments*. Williams' review of *Midfield Sediments* was published for the first time (and the *New Masses* essay "An American Poet" reprinted) in James Breslin, ed., *Something to Say: William Carlos Williams on Younger Poets* (New York: New Directions, 1985). Williams and Lewis corresponded regularly from 1936–1938 and occasionally thereafter; the last letter from Williams in the Lewis papers is dated 1947. Williams had hoped that Lewis's collected poems would eventually be published and that it might include all of Williams' reviews of Lewis's work; to date that book has yet to appear. In *William Carlos Williams: A New World Naked* (New York: McGraw-Hill, 1981), Paul Mariani devotes some pages to Williams's reviews of Lewis's poetry.

38. William Vaughn Moody, "On a Soldier Fallen in the Philippines," *The Poems and Plays of William Vaughn Moody*, vol. 1 (Boston and New York: Houghton Mifflin, 1912), pp. 29–30.

39. On poetry about the Vietnam war see my *Our Last First Poets: Vision and History in Contemporary American Poetry* (Urbana: University of Illinois Press, 1981).

40. On the concept of the potential canon, see Alastair Fowler, *Kinds of Literature: An Introduction to the Theory of Genres and Modes* (Cambridge: Harvard University Press, 1982).

41. To fulfill its proper dialogic cultural function, a literary history of modern poetry would not, for example, offer the following condescending paragraph as its only observation on Muriel Rukeyser's poetry: "For Muriel Rukeyser (1913–80) writing a poem was a process of collecting 'surfacings' from the unconscious. When 'collected' these were criticized and revised, but these activities did not essentially modify her product. Her poems are difficult if one seeks intelligibility, but not at all for readers satisfied with vague, intense, idealistic emotion. Her themes were frequently political—the Depression, the Second World War, the war in Vietnam, feminism. She combined an imprecise idiom with committed emotions. A Chinese proverb warns against whipping an ox that is already running, but this is what Rukeyser does. Her poems move persons who share her emotion before they read the poems," David Perkins, *A History of Modern Poetry: Modernism and After* (Cambridge: Harvard University Press, 1987), p. 367. Perkins' last sentences would presumably serve to summarize his view of much other political poetry in this period, though his complete silence on almost all of this work is more notable in what purports to be a comprehensive literary

history. The most appropriate observation on these comments on Rukeyser may be drawn out of Perkins' own writing. Elsewhere in the same book, he observes that Archibald MacLeish in the 1930s "was trying to create new forms, forms that would address social and political issues and appeal to a very large audience." He complains that "to this day no influential critic has considered MacLeish's work of the 1930s with a general approach to literature that would be favorable to the attempt MacLeish was making" (pp. 48–49).

42. In such an intellectual environment, one might add, reference works that are supposedly the product of literary historiography would make an effort to avoid giving little reactionary ideological lessons in the guise of presenting the facts of literary history. Consider, for example, the decidedly racist message and elitist value system disguised as self-evident progressive humanism in the entry on Robert Hayden (1913–1980) in the 1983 edition of the *Oxford Companion to American Literature*: "His first volume of poems, *Heart-Shape in the Dust* (1940), shows him as a spokesman for his fellow blacks, but though he continued to use racial subjects, e.g., 'The Ballad of Nat Turner,' his fine craftsmanship and broader view of human experience rise to a more universal level in the poems of later volumes," James D. Hart, ed., *The Oxford Companion to American Literature*, 5th ed. (New York: Oxford University Press), p. 321. If it weren't for the deep racial divisions in this country, we might be able to recognize that a poet who is an eloquent spokesperson for black people is necessarily of value to all of us. But it is particularly intolerable to see it argued that a poetry devoted to black interests is inherently a poetry of lesser importance and accomplishment. And the final indignity is the assumption that the abstract humanism of the dominant culture is obviously a higher value. If the writing of literary history were more self-critical and self-aware, such politically impacted statements could not pass unnoticed.

43. If a canon, it seems, is always a way of suppressing questions of evaluation, the motives for that function can vary considerably. There are, for example, specific socioeconomic benefits to be gained from suppressing evaluative uncertainty when one is competing for funds within contemporary institutions that favor the sciences. If the quality of the major works of literature, those most frequently taught and interpreted, is taken to be an established fact of nature, then interpretation stands to lose some of its inherent instability and to gain in cultural prestige. Interpretation ceases to be mere "unscientific opinion"; it becomes an effort to spell out (and amplify) an excellence we can imagine to be grounded in facticity.

44. One might argue, I suppose, for a renegotiation of the dialectical relation between canon formation and the writing of literary history, a renegotiation with the aim of producing a new, more inclusive master discourse of literariness in which these divergent impulses were peacefully synthesized.

Those recommending such a project, I think, would have to be recognized not only as operating within an unrealistic and idealized notion of the dynamics of cultural change but also as having exclusively conservative local motives: the fixing of the inherited textual corpus. It is impossible in any case that the social tensions reflected in this discursive competition are soon to be eliminated, so any wish for a successfully hegemonic new master discourse of literariness will remain phantasmatic.

45. A dialectical relationship between canon formation and the process of reflecting on literary history has been at least implicitly at work at other points in our history. Alan C. Golding, in his "A History of American Poetry Anthologies," in von Hallberg, *Canons*, tracks two opposing impulses in anthologies: the historian's goal of preserving as much of the past as possible and the evaluator's goal of assembling a narrow, exclusive canon of the best literature of the past. As Golding very persuasively points out, however, in a review of past anthologies that remains altogether pertinent today, these opposing models—even when consciously articulated—are often contradicted by anthologists' actual practices. Thus those who seek to preserve the past may actually have quite restrictive (and unexamined) moral, political, and aesthetic criteria for what is worth preserving. Golding works this argument out through a detailed analysis of key American poetry anthologies since the 1790s. Also see Jane Tomkins' *Sensational Designs* for an analysis of how anthologies have shaped our view of American literature.

46. On the interested and largely unavoidable human activity of evaluation, see Barbara Herrnstein Smith's excellent "Contingencies of Value," in von Hallberg, *Canons*. "What produces evaluative consensus, such as it is," she argues persuasively, "is not the healthy functioning of universal organs but the playing out of the *same* dynamics and variable contingencies that produce evaluative divergences. . . . validation commonly takes the form of privileging absolutely—that is 'standard'-izing—the particular contingencies that govern the preferences of the members of the group and discounting or, as suggested above, pathologizing all other contingencies. Thus it will be assumed or maintained: (a) that the particular *functions* they expect and desire the class of objects in question (for example, 'works of art' or 'literature') to perform are their intrinsic or proper functions, all other expected, desired, or emergent functions being inappropriate, irrelevent, extrinsic, abuses of the true nature of those objects," pp. 20, 22. Smith expands these arguments in her *Contingencies of Value: Alternative Perspectives for Critical Theory* (Cambridge: Harvard University Press, 1988).

In " 'But Is It Any Good?': The Institutionalization of Literary Value," the final chapter of her *Sensational Designs*, Tompkins carries Smith's arguments further by showing how Hawthorne has been radically reconceived by different critical readings. This leads her to argue, as I also argue here, that literary works become, for all practical purposes, different texts under different cultural conditions.

47. See John Reed, *Collected Poems*, ed. Corliss Lamont (Westport, Conn.: Lawrence Hill, 1985). Reed's most famous book is, of course, his eyewitness account of the Russian revolution, *Ten Days That Shook the World* (1919). A convenient summary of Eastman's attitudes toward poetry is his essay "American Ideals of Poetry," the preface to his *Colors of Life: Poems and Songs and Sonnets* (New York: Alfred A. Knopf, 1918). Also see his *Poems of Five Decades* (1954).

48. In a less hierarchical literary environment we might all compile our own individual textbooks, a practice already common in women's studies and theory courses.

49. Gerald L. Bruns, "Canon and Power in the Hebrew Scriptures," in von Hallberg, *Canons*, p. 81. My own view of power here is obviously dependent on Foucault's work, especially the essays in *Power/Knowledge: Selected Interviews and Other Writings, 1972–1977*, ed. Colin Gordon (New York: Pantheon, 1980).

50. Readers interested in Joe Hill might begin with the chapter "Joe Hill: Wobbly Bard" in Joyce L. Kornbluh's excellent annotated and illustrated collection *Rebel Voices: An IWW Anthology* (1964; 2d ed., Chicago: Charles H. Kerr Publishing, 1988), which draws on the invaluable Archives of Labor History and Urban Affairs at Wayne State University and the Labadie Collection of Labor Materials at the University of Michigan. Kornbluh provides a biographical summary and reprints a number of Hill's songs, letters, and brief articles. For the rest of Hill's work see Barrie Stavis and Frank Harmon, eds., *The Songs of Joe Hill* (New York: Oak Publishers, 1960) and Philip Foner, ed. *The Letters of Joe Hill* (New York: Oak Publications, 1965). A collection of his cartoons is forthcoming. The bibliographies in *Rebel Voices* list a number of other books about Hill.

The standard history of the IWW, Melvyn Dubofsky's *We Shall Be All: A History of the Industrial Workers of the World* (1969; 2d ed., rpt. Urbana: University of Illinois Press, 1988) is also useful, as is Dione Miles's extensive *Something in Common—An IWW Bibliography* (Detroit: Wayne State University Press, 1986). A visit to an appropriate archive is also recommended, since the IWW's large colored posters, broadsides, and song sheets, along with their newspapers and innumerable small pamphlets, have never been adequately reproduced.

Hill himself—the subject of poems, fiction, songs, films, and essays—is now as much a legend as he is the author of some of the most famous labor songs in American history. He came here from Sweden in 1902, changed his name from Joel Hagglund to Joseph Hillstrom and finally to Joe Hill, and was involved in IWW activities by 1910. It was soon after this that he began to write his songs. In 1914 he was arrested in Utah for the murder of a shop keeper and his son, based only on the evidence that a physician treated Hill for a gunshot wound the night the grocery store was robbed. Tried in the press for his IWW connections, his case eventually became an international cause. Despite thousands of letters of protest and an attempt to intervene in the case by Woodrow Wilson, Hill was executed in November 1915. He had continued to write letters and songs while in prison, including his famous telegram to IWW organizer Bill Haywood on the eve of his execution: "Good-bye, Bill. I will die like a true blue rebel. Don't waste any time in mourning. *Organize.*"

51. The songs in the *Little Red Songbook* were typically first published in the IWW newspapers. The songbook itself was continually reedited and reprinted with a new cover. The current edition is still available from the IWW office in Chicago. Hill's "The Preacher and the Slave" was first published in the third edition of the songbook (1911) and reprinted as well in numerous other collections, including Carl Sandburg's *The American Songbag* (1927). As Henry F. May writes in *The End of American Innocence* (1961), "Here, if anywhere, was a clear breach with timidity, moralism, and the whole manner and content of the standard American culture."

52. Ralph Chaplin's first poems and songs were signed "By a Paint Creek Miner." See Charles Patterson, ed., *Paint Creek Miner: Famous Labor Songs from Appalachia* (Huntington, W.V.: n. pub., 1970s). For his poetry, see especially *When The Leaves Come Out and Other Rebel Verses* (Cleveland: published by the author, 1917), *Bars and Shadows: The Prison Poems of Ralph Chaplin* (New York: Leonard Press, 1922), *Somewhat Barbaric: A Selection of Poems, Lyrics and Sonnets* (Seattle: Dogwood Press, 1944), and *Only The Drums Remembered: A Memento for Leschi* (Tacoma, Wash.: Dammeier Printing, 1960). A number of his cartoons and illustrations, frequently signed "Bingo," are reproduced in Joyce Kornbluh's *Rebel Voices: An IWW Anthology*. His autobiography, *Wobbly: The Rough and Tumble Story of an American Radical*, was published in 1948.

The Collected Poems of Arturo Giovannitti (1962; rpt. New York: Arno Press, 1975) includes all of Giovannitti's poems in English, though he also wrote in Italian and French. The collection does include a useful introduction by Norman Thomas and it reprints Giovannitti's *Arrows in the Gale* (1914) intact, along with Helen Keller's original introduction.

Only a very tiny percentage of Covington Hall's poems—often originally published under his pen names Covington Ami and Covami—are collected in his books. The largest collection is *Battle Hymns of Toil* (Oklahoma City, Okla.: General Welfare Reporter, 1946). Also see his *Songs of Rebellion* (New Orleans: John Weihing, 1915); *Rhymes of a Rebel* (Newllano, La.: Llano Cooperative Printery, 1931); and *Quivara or The Quest of Alvarez* (Rogers, Ark.: Avalon Press, 1946). A small recent collection *Dreams and Dynamite: Selected Poems* (Chicago: Charles H. Kerr Publishing, 1985) includes a very thoughtful introduction by Dave Roediger. A convenient source for some of his uncollected poetry and prose is the reprint of the IWW publication *One Big Union Monthly* (New York: Greenwood Reprint, 1968).

53. See Melvin Dubovsky's *We Shall Be All* for an informative discussion of the trial.

54. Ralph Chaplin, "The Red Feast," *When the Leaves Come Out*, pp. 8–9.

55. *The Rebel Poets* includes, among other works, Carl Sandburg's "Jaws" and several poems by Ralph Chaplin. My dates for this and other Chaplin pamphlets are highly speculative. Chaplin was publishing such pamphlets himself, mostly undated, as late as the 1930s.

56. Covington Hall, "The Curious Christians," *Battle Hymns of Toil*, p. 35, and *Dreams and Dynamite*, p. 28.

57. Arturo Giovannitti, "One Against the World," *The Collected Poems of Arturo Giovannitti*, pp. 34–35.

58. Ibid., pp. 147–52.

59. See Steven Tracy, *Langston Hughes and the Blues* (Urbana: University of Illinois Press, 1988) for the first detailed treatment of this important topic. For a list of appropriate recordings, see the discography appended to Tracy's book. For a wide range of blues texts see Michael Taft, ed., *Blues Lyric Poetry: An Anthology* (New York: Garland, 1983).

60. Hugh Kenner's comments about the effect of collapsing Williams' famous "The Red Wheelbarrow" into prose remain, despite their sexism, the definitive observation on the uneasy formal distantiation of sentiment in modern poetry: "Try to imagine an occasion for this sentence to be said: 'So much depends upon a red wheelbarrow glazed with rainwater beside the white chickens.' Try it over, in any voice you like: it is impossible. It could only be the gush of an arty female on a tour of Farmer Brown's barnyard." *A Homemade World: The American Modernist Writers* (New York: Alfred A. Knopf, 1975), p. 60.

61. *The Complete Poems of Carl Sandburg*, rev. and exp. ed. (New York: Harcourt Brace Jovanovich, 1970), pp. 16, 11, 9. These passages are all from his *Chicago Poems*.

62. Among Lindsay's prose pieces in *The Village Magazine* see especially "An Editorial for the Art Student who has returned to the village." Even when illustrations from *The Village Magazine* are available elsewhere, it is important to see them here since Lindsay sometimes makes use of this large page size that exceeds that used in any of his books.

63. The Baroness Elsa von Freytag-Loringhoven arrived in the United States just before the First World War and stayed here until 1923, when she returned to Europe. She was murdered by a boyfriend in Paris in 1927. In her

life style and dress, she was considered at the time the living embodiment of Dada. Only a small portion of the poetry she wrote was published during her life, but it was enough to help make her a notable center of controversy. Sun Press in New York has for some time been working on an edition of her collected poems that would include translations of her extensive body of poetry in German. Sun and Moon Press in California meanwhile has been trying to edit her autobiography for publication. In the meantime one may read a number of her poems in *The Little Review* as follows:

"Love—Chemical Relationship," 5:2 (June 1918), 58–59;
"Mefk Maru Mustir Daas," 5:8 (December 1918), 41;
"Moving Picture and Prayer," "Metaphysical speculation—logic—consolation concerning love to flame-flagged man," "King Adam," 6:1 (May 1919), 71–73;
"Myself—Minesoul—and—Mine—Cast-Iron Lover," 6:5 (September 1919), 3–11;
"Buddha," "Father," 6:9 (January 1920), 18–21;
"Irrender Konig," "Klink—Hratzvenga (Deathwail): Narin—Tzarissamanili (He is dead!)" 6:10 (March 1920), 10–12;
"Holy Skirts," "Marie Ida Sequence," 7:2 (July–August 1920), 28–30;
"Appalling Heart," "Blast," "Moonstone," "Heart (Dance of Shiva)," "Cathedral," "Is It?," "Gihirda's Dance," "Das Finstere Meer," 7:3 (September–December 1920), 47–52;
"Affectionate," 9:2 (Winter 1922), 40;
"Guttrigse," "Walkuren," (both in holograph) 11:1 (Spring 1925) 13–14.

Her other published poems are "Yours with Devotion," *New York Dada* (April 1921), 4; "Circle," *Broom* (January 1923), 128; "Cafe de Dome" and "X-Ray," *transition* 7 (October 1927), 134–35. Eleven poems were recently published in *Sulfur* 6 (1983): "A Dozen Cocktails—Please," "Skin of Faith," "History. Dim.," "Jigg," "Sunsong," "Fluency," "(Untitled)," "In the Midst," "Ultramundanity," "Enchantment," and "Game (Legend)." Her prose poetry includes "The Modest Woman" *The Little Review* 7:2 (July–August 1920), 37–40, and the two-part "Thee I Call 'Hamlet of Wedding-Ring': Criticism of William Carlos William's 'Kora in Hell' and Why," *The Little Review* 7:4 (January–March 1921), 48–60, and 8:1 (Autumn 1921), 108–11. See also the posthumous "Selections from the Letters of Elsa Baroness von Freytag-Loringhoven," with foreword by Djuna Barnes, *transition* 11 (February 1928), 19–30. Her sculpture "Portrait of Marcel Duchamp" is reproduced in the Winter 1922 issue of *The Little Review*. Two photographs of her appear in *New York Dada* (1921), p. 4, and Man Ray's striking photograph of her is in *The Little Review* 7:3 (1920), 4. A photograph of her death mask was published in *transition* 11, p. 91.

64. A running debate on the baroness was carried on in the pages of *The*

Little Review from 1919 to 1920. Participants included Maxwell Boden-heim, Lola Ridge, John Rodker, and Evelyn Scott, as well as the editors, Margaret Anderson and Jane Heap. Her reputation extended to her relation-ships and her public performances. Williams devotes part of a chapter to her in his *Autobiography* and Paul Mariani comments at length on the re-lationship from Williams' perspective in *William Carlos Williams: A New World Naked*. A good recent essay is Robert Reiss, " 'My Baroness': Elsa von Freytag-Loringhoven," in Rudolf E. Kuenzli, ed., *New York Dada* (New York: Willis Locker & Owens, 1986), pp. 81–101. As Reiss writes, "the Bar-oness audaciously sought a simultaneous victory for Dada and dress reform through the Dada strategy of her own invention: she shellacked her shaven skull, colored it vermillion, wore an inverted coal scuttle for a cap, and ap-plied to her body as decorative elements mechanistic implements such as metal teaballs" (p. 86). The artist Louis Bouche reports her wearing a "black dress with a bustle on which rested an electric battery tail light" (Reiss, p. 87). George Biddle reports the following encounter: "Having asked me in her high pitched German stridency, whether I required a model, I told her I should like to see her in the nude. With a royal gesture she swept apart the folds of a scarlet raincoat. She stood before me quite naked—or nearly so. Over the nipples of her breast were two tin tomato cans, fastened with a green string around her back. Between the tomato cans hung a very small bird-cage and within it a crestfallen canary. One arm was covered from wrist to shoulder with celluloid curtain rings, pilfered from a furniture display in Wannamaker's. She removed her hat, trimmed with gilded carrots, beets, and other vegetables" (Reiss, p. 87).

One of the few contemporary critics to recognize that the Baroness was doing interesting and innovative cultural work is Dickran Tashjian in his *Skyscraper Primitives: Dada and the American Avant-Garde, 1910–1925* (Middletown, Conn.: Wesleyan University Press, 1975). As he points out, Freytag-Loringhoven was "one person who understood *Kora in Hell* at the time of its publication." In her two-part piece on the book, "Williams comes to embody the aesthetic problems which the Baroness senses are endemic to American culture," pp. 99–100.

65. Freytag-Loringhoven, "Metaphysical speculation—logic—consolation concerning love to flame-flagged man."

66. Basic information on Mina Loy's life and career may be found in Carolyn Burke, "Mina Loy," in *American Writers in Paris, 1920–1939: Dic-tionary of Literary Biography*, vol. 4 (Detroit: Gale, 1979), in Virginia M. Kouidis's very helpful *Mina Loy: American Modernist Poet* (Baton Rouge: Louisiana State University Press, 1980), and in the introduction to Mina Loy, *The Last Lunar Baedeker*, ed., Roger L. Conover (Highlands, N.C.: The Jargon Society, 1982). Born in London, Loy spent time both in Europe and in the Americas until moving permanently to the United States in 1936. It

should be noted that, although the Jargon volume is a beautiful example of fine bookmaking, and although it includes black and white reproductions of some of Loy's paintings and sculpture, it is—as Carolyn Burke points out in "The Last Lunar Baedeker," *San Francisco Review of Books* (November–December 1982), 28–29—not always an accurate text. One is better off, when possible, reading Loy in the journals in which she first published. She should also be read aloud, so that the particularities of her diction and spacing are given full weight. The bold, heavily inked typeface in *The Little Review* in the 1920s I find particularly suited to reading her poetry that way. Loy's "Love Songs" were first published in their entirety in the April 1917 issue of *Others*; they are reprinted accurately in Kouidis's book and inaccurately in Connover's edition of her collected poems.

Carolyn Burke is writing a critical biography of Loy, and her published essays on Loy—including "Becoming Mina Loy," *Women's Studies* 7 (1980), 151–58, "Without Commas: Gertrude Stein and Mina Loy," *Poetics Journal* 4 (May 1984), 43–52, and "Supposed Persons: Modernist Poetry and the Female Subject," *Feminist Studies* 11:1 (Spring 1985), 131–48—offer the most sophisticated suggestions about the issues raised in reading her poetry now: "Whether from self-protectiveness, a playful evasiveness, or a Dickinsonian sense of the self as a supposed person, Loy's own poetry is marked by a number of disappearances, falsifications, disavowals, and deliberate disguises. . . . Even 'Parturition,' one of Loy's best-known poems and perhaps the first in English on the taboo subject of childbirth, cannot be read as a direct transposition of experience. Rather it recreates analytically in the manner of Cubist perspective the recollection of childbirth's rhythms and the subsequent modifications of the 'I' who experiences these extremes of thought and sensation," "Supposed Persons," 136, 138.

67. Mina Loy, "Anglo-Mongrels and the Rose," *The Little Review* (Autumn–Winter, 1923–24), p. 41. The Connover version is again inaccurate.

68. Abraham Lincoln Gillespie's collected works have been ably gathered together in Gillespie, *The Syntactic Revolution*, ed. Richard Milazzo (New York: Out of London Press, 1980). That book includes a very useful biographical essay by Sol J. Leon and an essay by Milazzo, "Theo-Syncopation," that imitates Gillespie's own style. Also see Thomas A. Zaniello, "The Thirteenth Disciple of James Joyce: Abraham Lincoln Gillespie," *Journal of Modern Literature* 7:1 (February 1979), 51–61. George Antheil includes an anecdotal chapter on Gillespie in his *Bad Boy of Music* (Garden City, N.Y.: Doubleday, 1945), pp. 156–64, that includes some interesting material about Gillespie's expatriate period in France. This is Antheil's description of Gillespie's house at Cagnes-sur-Mer: "Outside, nothing, but inside accumulated into the maddest atmosphere into which a human being has ever stepped. The artists who from time to time Linkey had housed had decorated it, their imagination exceeding the limits of any surrealist or non-surrealist;

for instance, in one room they had attached the furniture to the ceiling, it was the 'dance hall.' Another room's otherwise white plaster was decorated al fresco with pictures no cabaret of my acquaintance could ever boast without police interference" (p. 158).

69. Gillespie, "Textighter Eye-Ploy or Hothouse Bromdick?" was first published in the March 1928 issue of *transition*. It is reprinted in *The Syntactic Revolution*, pp. 7–10. Gillespie's poetry can offer persuasive evidence in support of Jean-Francois Lyotard's argument that postmodernism was an impulse within modernism itself. See Lyotard's *The Postmodern Condition: A Report on Knowledge*, trans. Geoff Bennington and Brian Massumi (Minneapolis: University of Minnesota Press, 1984).

70. Gillespie, "Reading Modern Poetry," *The Syntactic Revolution*, pp. 69–72.

71. Walter Conrad Arensberg's experimental poetry is most readily available in Jerome Rothenberg, ed., *Revolution of the Word*.

The passage by Walter Lowenfels is from his *Elegy in the Manner of a Requiem: In Memory of D. H. Lawrence* (Paris and London: Carrefour, 1932): "Though complete in itself, this elegy is part of an unfinished work in several volumes, *Reality Prime*. Such a work, where any page is a note to another, sets up its own system of reference" (p. 31). This book, published in a limited edition of 150 copies, has unfortunately never been reprinted. It represents some of Lowenfels' best surrealist poetry and includes several pages of notes that help explain not only this poem but also some of Lowenfels' other work during this period. A good selection of Lowenfels' other poetry, including his political poems, is his *Some Deaths: Selected Poems and Communications*, 1925–1962 (Highlands, N.C.: Jonathan Williams / The Nantahala Foundation, 1964). Also see Allen Guttmann, "The Poetic Politics of Walter Lowenfels," *The Massachusetts Review* 6 (Autumn 1965), 843–50.

For Marsden Hartley, see *The Collected Poems of Marsden Hartley, 1904–1943*, ed. Gail R. Scott (Santa Rosa, Calif.: Black Sparrow, 1987). Readers interested in Hartley's brief dadaist period should also see his "The Importance of Being Dada" in his *Adventures in the Arts: Informal Chapters on Painters, Vaudeville and Poets* (New York: Boni and Liveright, 1921). Also see Elizabeth McCausland, *Marsden Hartley* (Minneapolis: University of Minnesota Press, 1952) and Barbara Haskell, *Marsden Hartley* (New York: Whitney Museum of American Art, 1980). On Hartley's poetry see especially Robert K. Martin, "Marsden Hartley," *Dictionary of Literary Biography*, vol. 54, *American Poets, 1880–1945*, 3d ser., ed. Peter Quartermain (Detroit: Gale Research, 1987), pp. 147–53, and Robert Burlingame, "Marsden Hartley's *Androscoggin*: Return to Place," *New England Quarterly* 21 (December 1958), 447–62.

Kenneth Rexroth's *The Art of Worldly Wisdom* is reprinted in *The Col-*

lected Shorter Poems of Kenneth Rexroth (New York: New Directions, 1966). For a bibliography of Rexroth's poems appearing in journals and anthologies see James Hartzell and Richard Zumwinkle, *Kenneth Rexroth: A Checklist of His Published Writings* (Los Angeles: Friends of the UCLA Library, 1967). Anyone interested in modern poetry should also read his opinionated, irreverent, and anticanonical *American Poetry in the Twentieth Century* (1971).

72. See Gertrude Stein, *Three Lives* (1909); Carl Sandburg, *In Reckless Ecstasy* (1904); Ezra Pound, *A Lume Spento* (1908) and other early collected and uncollected poems in *Collected Early Poems of Ezra Pound*, ed. Michael John King (New York: New Directions, 1976); Vachel Lindsay, *The Tree of Laughing Bells* (1905); and William Carlos Williams, *Poems* (1909).

73. See "A Few Don'ts by an Imagiste" in *Poetry* 1:6 (March 1913), 200–206 and "A Retrospect" in *Literary Essays of Ezra Pound*, ed. T. S. Eliot (New York: New Directions, 1954).

74. *Tender Buttons* is reprinted in *Selected Writings of Gertrude Stein*, ed. Carl Van Vechten (New York: Random House, 1962).

75. In *The New York Little Renaissance: Iconoclasm, Modernism, and Nationalism in American Culture, 1908–1917* (New York: New York University Press, 1976), which includes a photograph of one scene from the pageant, Arthur Frank Wertheim quotes from "Pageantry and Social Art," an unpublished essay by Randolph Bourne in the Bourne Collection at Columbia University: "Who that saw the Paterson Strike Pageant in 1913 can ever forget that thrilling evening when an entire labor community dramatized its wrongs in one supreme outburst of group-emotion? Crude and rather terrifying, it stamped into one's mind the idea that a new social art was in the American world, something genuinely and excitingly new." In her chapter on the Paterson strike in *Rebel Voices*, Joyce L. Kornbluh reproduces the program cover and reprints the text of the program with descriptions of its six episodes. She also reprints two contemporary reviews of the pageant. The New York *Tribune* noted that "there was a startling touch of ultra modernity—or rather of futurism. . . . The first episode of the pageant, entitled 'The Mills Alive—the Workers Dead' represented 6 o'clock one February morning. A great painted drop, two hundred feet wide, stretching across the hippodrome-like stage built for the show, represented a Paterson silk mill, the windows aglow with the artificial light in which the workers began their daily tasks." The *Times*, on the other hand, considered the pageant dangerous and subversive. Others thought it artless. Certainly it heralds a number of theatrical innovations, including the large scale agit-prop performances mounted by Soviet avant-garde directors the following decade. Union leaders Elizabeth Gurley Flynn and William D. Haywood recreated speeches they had actually given earlier in the strike. Audience participation was invited during mass songs. For a detailed analysis of the organization and financing of the pageant, along with summaries of other contemporary reactions

and a thorough discussion of the strike as a whole, see Anne Huber Tripp, *The I.W.W. and the Paterson Silk Strike of 1913* (Urbana: University of Illinois Press, 1987). Also see Linda Nochlin, "The Paterson Strike Pageant of 1913," *Art in America* 62 (May–June 1974), 64–68. Also see Martin Green, *New York 1913: The Armory Show and the Paterson Strike Pageant* (New York: Scribners, 1988).

76. See Loy's "Aphorisms on Futurism" and her other manifestos in *The Last Lunar Baedeker*.

77. For a convenient collection of futurist manifestos and some representative paintings see Umbro Apollonio, ed., *Futurist Manifestos* (New York: Viking, 1970). For an analysis of futurism's past and present meaning see Marjorie Perloff's innovative *The Futurist Moment: Avant-Garde, Avant Guerre, and the Language of Rupture* (Chicago: University of Chicago Press, 1986).

78. Ileana B. Leavens in *From "291" to Zurich: The Birth of Dada* (Ann Arbor, Mich.: UMI Research Press, 1983) describes the Meyer-De Zayas collaboration "Mental Reactions" as a "union of two heretofore parallel trends: pictorial simultaneism and literary simultaneism." In her autobiographical *Out of These Roots* (Boston: Little Brown, 1953), Agnes E. Meyer refers to "the crazy experiments Marius de Zayas and I made in illustrated 'stream of consciousness' writing, which was supposed to weld together the plastic and literary arts in a depiction of various levels of a total state of mind. We were on the track of something only dimly understood before the crucial analysis of Freud and the works of such successful explorers of the unconscious as Virginia Woolf and Joyce became popular" (pp. 102–3). Dickran Tashjian in *Skyscraper Primitives: Dada and the American Avant-Garde, 1910–1925* also offers a detailed reading of "Mental Reactions":

[It demonstated] that the desired nonlinear and nonlogical effects could be achieved on paper . . . thereby anticipating the simultaneous poetry of Zurich Dada. As the first of several poems in *291* that would center on womanhood or be written from a feminine point of view, 'Mental Reactions' ultimately pointed to the myth of the female machine, expressed in the November issue by Picabia's drawing *Voila Elle* printed beside De Zayas' exploding poem "Femme."

'Mental Reactions' is set in the boudoir of a New York apartment. . . . A woman takes in the view from her bedroom window . . . she responds to the interior decoration of her apartment with an anti-art loathing that is hardly coincidental . . . throughout the woman's reactions and impressions runs a scattered and elliptical meditation upon her identity, particularly in relation to her husband. In fact, she is revealed to be a female Prufrock who has difficulty affirming her own life . . . the nervous thrusts of the visual lines add another dimension of motion, suggesting thought processes in action. (pp. 33–34)

I would argue that the speaker, if there is a single speaker and I see no reason to insist on that, is at once far more reflective and far more ironic about sexual difference than Tashjian acknowledges. Tashjian also finds that the visual image divides securely into two halves, but I would argue that is only one of several competing visual effects.

Agnes Ernst Meyer's career went in a quite different direction after *291* came to an end. She wrote *Chinese Painting as Reflected in the Thought and Art of Li-Lung-Mien* (1923), translated Thomas Mann's *The Coming Victory of Democracy*, and became involved in a series of social and political issues. When her financier husband purchased the Washington *Post* in 1933, she became part-owner of the newspaper. A number of years of reporting on social issues followed.

On Katherine Rhoades, whose poems and art appear in *291*, see the illustrated catalog to the 1939 memorial exhibition of her paintings at the Richmond, Virginia, Museum of Fine Arts.

79. *291* was edited by a collective at Alfred Stieglitz's "291" galleries, which took their name from their Fifth Avenue address. In addition to Stieglitz, the collective consisted of Marius De Zayas, Agnes Ernst Meyer, Paul Haviland, and Katharine Rhoades. Francis Picabia also participated while he was in the United States. Copies of the original are extremely rare, since, despite the magazine's subsequent fame and influence, barely more than a hundred subscriptions were sold at the time of its publication, and Stieglitz later sold the remaining sets to a rag picker. In 1972, however, Arno Press brought out a quite credible reprint edition with an introduction by Dorothy Norman. Although Norman suggests the group was altogether harmonious, Ileana B. Leavens in *From "291" to Zurich: The Birth of Dada* cites surviving letters by Stieglitz and Meyer to prove otherwise. Leavens argues that De Zayas was the moving force behind *291*. Stieglitz and De Zayas were beginning to become estranged because De Zayas was in the midst of establishing the Modern Gallery as a more commercial alternative to "291" but also because the sometimes machinist aesthetics of *291* were foreign to Stieglitz's humanism. For further information on De Zayas see the excellent "New York Dada: Bibliography" in Rudolf E. Kuenzli, ed., *New York Dada*. For analytic essays and issue-by-issue summaries of *291* and other related periodicals see Dawn Ades, *Dada and Surrealism Reviewed* (London: Arts Council of Great Britain, 1978).

80. John Gould Fletcher, *Preludes and Symphonies* (Boston: Houghton Mifflin, 1922). This volume reprints *Irradiations—Sand and Spray* and *Goblins and Pagodas*.

81. See H. D., *Collected Poems, 1912–1944*, ed. Louis L. Martz (New York: New Directions, 1983).

82. In "H.D. and the Origins of Modernism," *Sagetrieb* 4 (Spring 1985), Cyrena Pondrom argues persuasively that H. D.'s poetry not only overturned the static notion of imagism at the virtual origin of the movement but actu-

ally provided Pound with the model of vorticist imagery that he adopted when he abandoned imagism. As Shari Benstock argues in an excellent chapter on H. D. in her *Women of the Left Bank: Paris, 1900–1940* (Austin: University of Texas Press, 1986), a chapter that synthesizes and extends much of the recent work on H. D., "whereas Pound argued for a 'fusion' through the image . . . or juxtaposed images that 'instantaneously' rendered certain effects (as in 'In a Station of the Metro'), H. D. used images to deny the possibility of such a 'fusion': her images simultaneously concentrate and diffuse the mysterious energies they invoke" (p. 328). In "Freud and H. D. —Bisexuality and a Feminine Discourse," *m/f* 8 (1983), 53–66, Claire Buck suggests that these tendencies are grounded in "the uncertainty of sexual division itself." After years of rather narrow readings, a genuine renaissance in H. D. scholarship has substantially revised her place in literary history. See Rachel Blau DuPlessis, *H. D.: The Career of That Struggle* (Bloomington: Indiana University Press, 1986), Susan Stanford Friedman, *Psyche Reborn: The Emergence of H. D.* (Bloomington, Indiana University Press, 1981), Barbara Guest, *Herself Defined: The Poet H. D. and Her World* (New York: Doubleday, 1984), and Janice S. Robinson, *H. D.: The Life and Work of an American Poet* (Boston: Houghton Mifflin, 1982).

83. Charles Reznikoff, *Poems 1918–1936: Volume I of the Complete Poems of Charles Reznikoff*, ed. Seamus Cooney (Santa Barbara: Black Sparrow, 1976). Along with *Poems 1937–1975: Volume II of the Complete Poems of Charles Reznikoff*, ed. Seamus Cooney (Santa Barbara: Black Sparrow, 1978), the multivolume *Testimony: The United States* and *Holocaust*, this constitutes the final versions of Reznikoff's poetry. Earlier versions, however, also merit our attention. Also see *Charles Reznikoff: Man and Poet*, ed. Milton Hindus (Orono, Maine: National Poetry Foundation, 1984).

84. Reznikoff's imagist poems were first gathered together in *Five Groups of Verse* (New York: published by the author, 1927), pp. 7, 28.

85. Carl Sandburg, *Collected Poems*, p. 3.

86. Sherwood Anderson, *Mid-American Chants* (New York: B. W. Huebsch, 1923), p. 11. On *Mid-American Chants* see especially Walter B. Rideout, "Sherwood Anderson's *Mid-American Chants*," in Richard M. Ludwig, ed., *Aspects of American Poetry* (Columbus: Ohio State University Press, 1962).

87. Stanley Kimmel, *The Kingdom of Smoke: Sketches of My People* (New York: Nicholas L. Brown, 1932), p. 11.

88. For information on "Anise," or Anna Louise Strong, see Tracy B. Strong and Helene Keyssar, *Right in Her Soul: The Life of Anna Louise Strong* (New York: Random House, 1983). The first two paragraphs of their foreword at least merit quoting here:

Anna Louise Strong was born in 1885 in a two-room parsonage in Friend, Nebraska. She died in 1970 in Peking, China, where she was buried with

full honors in the Revolutionary Martyrs Cemetery. During the years
between, she bore witness to most of the upheavals of our century. From
1919 until her death she followed the revolutionary uprisings in Russia,
Mexico, Spain and China, writing millions of words to try to persuade
her fellow Americans that the social transformations occurring in these
lands were to be celebrated rather than feared.

No one who met Anna Louise Strong ever forgot her. She traveled on
a journalist's visa, but she was determined to shape the news as well
as to report it. She organized labor, marched with revolutionary armies
and participated in the events she described in her writings. . . . She
knew Trotsky well, dined in the White House with Eleanor and Franklin
Roosevelt, and with Stalin's blessing edited the first English-language
newspaper in the Soviet Union. In the years before 1949 she carried news
from Chou En-lai and Mao Tse-tung to the West. . . .

Kornbluh reprints Strong's "Centralia Pictures" on pp. 271–74 of her *Rebel
Voices: An IWW Anthology*. The weekly edition of the *Seattle Union Record*, from which "The Property Man" and "Damned by a Name" are reproduced, is available on microfilm, so one may readily consult the poems she
published there (in her capacity as features editor) almost every week from
1918 through 1920. Some of Strong's poems found their way into other IWW
publications, such as the *Defense News Bulletin*, as well.

Strong's *Ragged Verse* appeared in two quite different editions, with different formats and a different selection of poems. The first, undated, but
published in Seattle by the Seattle Union Record Publishing Company in
either 1919 or 1920, includes the note "As Published in the Seattle Daily
Union Record May 6 to November 18, 1919" and reproduces the poems with
their original distinctive interlinear punctuation. A 1937 edition, also published in Seattle, has the same title but eliminates the punctuation between
lines. It includes the note "Published as a greeting to the author on her
return to Seattle, March, 1937, on a lecture tour on behalf of Spanish democracy. Selections made by a group of friends from the Washington Common-
wealth Federation, Church of the People and Washington Alpine Club, from
an album of more than five hundred similar verses in the possession of her
father, Dr. Sydney Strong."

Prior to moving to Seattle, Strong had earned a Ph.D. at the University of
Chicago. After the collapse of the *Record* she was sent to Poland and Russia
by the American Friends Service Committee to investigate famine condi-
tions. Then she became Moscow correspondent for Hearst's International
News Service. Her experiences in the Soviet Union resulted in the first of
her many nonfiction books, *Children of the Revolution* (1925). Travels to
China resulted in *China's Millions* (1928), later revised as *China's Millions:
The Revolutionary Struggles from 1927 to 1935* (1935). Her autobiography, *I*

Change the World: The Remaking of an American appeared the same year. Several more books on the Soviet Union, *Spain in Arms* (1937), and two more books on China, based on travels there in the 1940s then followed. Some seventy numbers of her *Letters from China* appeared in the 1960s. For bibliographic information see the Strong and Keyssar biography; other published lists of Strong's work tend to be rather incomplete.

89. The most readable general book on the Harlem Renaissance is David Levering Lewis's *When Harlem Was in Vogue* (New York: Knopf, 1981). This may be supplemented by Nathan Irvin Huggins' earlier but still informative *Harlem Renaissance* (New York: Oxford University Press, 1971). In his short but immensely provocative *Modernism and the Harlem Renaissance* (Chicago: University of Chicago Press, 1987), Houston A. Baker, Jr., however, quite justly takes issue with the long-standing conviction in these and other books that the Renaissance somehow "failed," either because it did not utterly transform the world or because most of its writers did not emulate Eliot and Pound. In his famous 1926 essay "The Negro Artist and the Racial Mountain," Hughes argued against emulating white culture and pointed out that black writers were creating a legacy for the future. This should have settled these issues, but apparently it did not. Among books concerned with the poetry of the period, special mention must be given to Jean Wagner's very fine *Black Poets of the United States: From Paul Laurence Dunbar to Langston Hughes* trans. Kenneth Douglas (Urbana: University of Illinois Press, 1973). Arna Bontemps, ed. *The Harlem Renaissance Remembered* (New York: Dodd, Mead, 1972), includes several informative essays, among them Ronald Primeau's "Frank Horne and the Second Echelon Poets of the Harlem Renaissance." Any effort to think about Renaissance poetry as a discursive formation will need to draw all of these poets into the discussion. Also immensely useful as an efficient reference guide is *The Harlem Renaissance: A Historical Dictionary for the Era*, ed. Bruce Kellner (Westport, Conn.: Greenwood Press, 1984). Finally, *Harlem Renaissance: Art of Black America* (New York: Harry N. Abrams & The Studio Museum in Harlem, 1987) provides essays, color reproductions, and bibliographic information on Renaissance painting, sculpture, photography, and book illustration. Aaron Douglas, perhaps the most prolific book illustrator of the Renaissance, is well represented.

90. Claude McKay's first two volumes of poetry, *Songs of Jamaica* and *Constab Ballads*—a historic use of the local dialect by a black West Indian with a British education—were both published in 1912. They inaugurated his continuing influence on West Indian literature, a story that has a life somewhat separate from the story of his influence on black American writing. A detailed discussion of McKay's whole career can be found in Wayne F. Cooper's excellent biography, *Claude McKay: Rebel Sojourner in the Harlem Renaissance* (Baton Rouge: Louisiana State University Press, 1987). Cooper

is also the editor of the indispensable collection *The Passion of Claude McKay: Selected Prose and Poetry, 1912–1948* (New York: Schocken, 1973), which reprints "Mulatto" and includes a helpful bibliography. Most of McKay's poetry is now, inexcusably, out of print.

91. Weinold Reiss (1887–1953) was a white artist who became known for his careful portraits of black men and women. Born in Germany, he painted folk groups in several European countries before coming to the United States. Later he travelled through the Americas doing portraits of Native Americans. Some of his other work on black culture may be seen in the Harlem number of *Survey Graphic* (March 1925). Reiss was Aaron Douglas's teacher.

92. Aaron Douglas (1898–1979), perhaps the most famous painter of the Harlem Renaissance, did jacket and book illustrations for a number of black writers, including the jacket for Hughes's *Fine Clothes to the Jew* (1927). His work also appeared in a number of periodicals, including *Opportunity, The Crisis, Vanity Fair,* and *Theatre Arts.* His series of murals for the Harlem Branch of the New York Public Library is particularly well-known. Douglas later became a faculty member at Fisk University. A chronology of his career and a fairly complete bibliography of the books and magazines he illustrated is included in *Harlem Renaissance: Art of Black America.* For a striking book jacket by Douglas not included in that bibliography, however, see Ina Corinne Brown, *The Story of the American Negro* (New York: Friendship Press, 1936).

93. Charles Cullen (1889–?) is one of the more fugitive among the visible book illustrators of the period. Because he has the same last name as Countee Cullen and illustrated his books, one occasionally encounters claims that they were related. Countee Cullen was born Countee Porter and later adopted by Frederick Cullen, a minister in Harlem who also became head of the Harlem Branch of the NAACP. Despite the fact that Charles Cullen is listed in several dictionaries of Afro-American artists, the evidence, including surviving census data, suggests that he was white. The following passage, from an undated letter that Charles Cullen wrote to Countee Cullen, one of several Charles Cullen letters at the Amistad Research Center at Tulane University, may at least help still the rumors that the two men were related:

Dear Countee,
   I rec'd your kind letter and the check for which I thank you very much. I have a copy of my book on hand which I'll autograph and send to you. You said you'd like to have it autographed to your father. If you want his name inscribed in it drop me a card telling me his exact name. I have forgotten. Let me hear right away and I'll send the book immediately. I hope your father is in better health.

Given Charles Cullen's obscurity and the misinformation about him available in recent publications, it may be useful to draw together what little accurate information about him does exist. Except for comments on his illustrations in book reviews, the only published information about him in the 1920s or 1930s appears to be on the jacket of his beautifully illustrated edition of Whitman's *Leaves of Grass* (New York: Thomas Crowell, 1933). There it is noted that he was born in Leroy, New York, in 1889, and that he attended the Academy of Fine Arts in Philadelphia and then studied abroad for a year. Upon his return, he found some magazine work for *Scribner's*, *Century*, and *Collier's*, including five illustrations for Amy Lowell's story "The Paper Windmill" in the December 1915 issue of *Century*. Other than the illustrations for Countee Cullen's books, his most successful work is clearly the illustrated *Leaves of Grass*, which includes an introduction by Sherwood Anderson that praises Cullen's work and says the illustrations "furnish a new breadth and meaning to the poems, and should take their place in the forefront of Whitman interpretations." Charles Cullen's other work during the period includes the green and yellow cover and four illustrations for Charles S. Johnson's *Ebony and Topaz: A Collectanea* (1927), but it is clear from his letters to Countee Cullen that his work as an illustrator did not earn him enough money to survive. He did not in fact illustrate the first printing of *Color* but rather added illustrations to a subsequent printing, after suggesting the project in a letter to Countee Cullen. His other illustrated books are Lucian's *The Mimes of the Courtesans* (1928), *American College Verse*, ed. Henry Harrison (1932), *Contemporary American Men Poets*, ed. Thomas Del Vecchio (1937), and *Jesus the Christ* (1944).

94. Prentiss Taylor (1907-) is a white painter and graphic artist who illustrated two of Hughes's works published by Golden Stair Press: *The Negro Mother and Other Dramatic Recitations* (1931) and *Scottsboro Limited* (1932). Taylor's work also appeared in *The Crisis* in 1934. Four of the poems from *The Negro Mother* were also issued as illustrated broadsides. In the 1940s Taylor became interested in art as a form of therapy; he worked as an art therapist at St. Elizabeth's hospital in Washington.

95. Reprint editions, and even editions that use the term facsimile too loosely, often compromise on quality and sometimes make significant changes in the impact a book can have. When Harper and Row reprinted *Caroling Dusk* they dropped Aaron Douglas's colored endpapers. Later editions of *God's Trombones* used a less expensive (and less dramatic) binding; eventually, Aaron Douglas's jacket, which reproduced the final illustration in the book and thus added an element of circular reoccurence to the illustrations, was replaced with a modern illustration; finally, the current edition provides only cheap, muddy vestiges of Douglas's original illustrations. The Atheneum reprint of *The New Negro* silently drops the dramatic colored endpapers and reproduces Reiss's fine color portraits in dull black and white

versions. At the minimum, the effect of changes like this is to reduce our sense of the interrelationships between writing and the visual arts in this period. At the other extreme, the cultural power a book can wield can be reduced when its illustrations are eliminated or badly reproduced. As Houston A. Baker writes of *The New Negro*, "the work of Reiss and Douglas serves in fact as a kind of graphic, African presence qualifying and surrounding all prose, poetry, and drama in the volume. . . . Locke quickly concedes that the *outer* objectives of the life of Afro-Americana are coextensive with general American ideals. But he also forcefully notes that the *inner* objectives of the Afro-American nation—located in 'the very heart of the folk-spirit' (p. xv) —are still in the process of uneasy formation. What these inner objectives constitute is represented by the drive and force implied by the graphics of the collection . . . to found a nation of Afro-Americans on the basis of RACE" (*Modernism and the Harlem Renaissance*, pp. 73, 79).

96. After several decades of near complete obscurity, Angelina Weld Grimké is finally beginning to receive serious critical attention. See Gloria T. Hull, *Color, Sex, and Poetry: Three Women Writers of the Harlem Renaissance* (Bloomington: Indiana University Press, 1987), and William Drake, *The First Wave: Women Poets in America, 1915–1945* (New York: Macmillan, 1987). Grimké's unpublished poetry is at the Moorland-Spingarn Research Center of Howard University. Her play *Rachel* (1919) was reprinted in *Black Theater, U.S.A.: Forty-Five Plays by Black Americans*, ed. James V. Hatch (New York: Free Press, 1974).

Among other black women poets of the period, one might mention Gwendolyn Bennett, who published twenty-two poems in *Opportunity*, *The Crisis*, and *Palms*, and in the anthologies *Caroling Dusk* and *The Book of American Negro Poetry*. She also published short stories and wrote a column, "The Ebony Flute," for *Opportunity* from 1926 to 1928. An accomplished graphic artist as well, she did two covers for *The Crisis* and three covers for *Opportunity*. For basic information on her life and work see Walter C. Daniel and Sandra Y. Govan, "Gwendolyn Bennett," in Trudier Harris, ed. *Afro-American Writers from the Harlem Renaissance to 1940: Dictionary of Literary Biography*, vol. 51 (Detroit: Gale, 1987).

97. Grimké, unpublished *ms*, Grimké Papers, Box 38–10, Howard University.

98. Ibid.

99. The major source for Sterling Brown's poetry is now *The Collected Poems of Sterling A. Brown*, selected by Michael Harper (New York: Harper and Row, 1980). There are, however, a few (presumably inadvertent) omissions from this book. The last two poems in the "Slim Greer" sequence, "Slim Hears 'The Call'" and "Slim in Hell" are missing. They were most recently published in Sterling A. Brown, *The Last Ride of Wild Bill* (Detroit: Broadside Press, 1975). "Bitter Fruit of the Tree," originally published

in the *Nation* 149 (August 1939), p. 223, and "Cloteel," included in "Sixteen Poems by Sterling Brown," Folkways Recording, 1973, are both incomplete. Joanne V. Gabbin's biographical and critical *Sterling A. Brown: Building the Black Aesthetic Tradition* (Westport, Conn.: Greenwood Press, 1985) includes a detailed bibliography listing Brown's extensive essays and reviews and lists other bibliographic sources as well. Brown's first book was widely reviewed at the time of its publication and his great talent immediately recognized, but, except for sporadic comments, his work did not receive anywhere near the attention it deserved for nearly the next forty years, though Jean Wagner devoted a chapter to him in *Black Poets of the United States* and other histories of black writing certainly took note of his work. The publication of his *Collected Poems*, however, has helped spark a Brown revival. See, for example, Baker's *Modernism and the Harlem Renaissance* and Henry Louis Gates's "Songs of a Racial Self: On Sterling A. Brown" in his *Figures in Black: Words, Signs, and the 'Racial' Self* (New York: Oxford University Press, 1987).

100. Sterling Brown, "Scotty Has His Say," first published in *Southern Road*, is reprinted in *Collected Poems*, p. 35.

101. Louise Bogan's *The Blue Estuaries: Poems 1923–1968* is highly selective. For a broader view of her work see *Body of This Death* (New York: McBride, 1923), *The Sleeping Fury* (New York: Scribner's, 1937), *Poems and New Poems* (New York: Scribner's 1941), and *Collected Poems, 1923–1953* (New York: Noonday, 1954). See also Elizabeth Frank's biography *Louise Bogan: A Portrait* (New York: Knopf, 1985), *Critical Essays on Louise Bogan*, ed. Martha Collins (Boston: G. K. Hall, 1984), and Gloria Bowles, *Louise Bogan's Aesthetic of Limitation* (Bloomington: Indiana University Press, 1987).

102. Wallace Stevens, "Connoisseur of Chaos," *The Collected Poems of Wallace Stevens* (New York: Knopf, 1972), pp. 215–16.

103. E. E. Cummings, "Chansons Innocentes," *Complete Poems 1913–1962* (New York: Harcourt Brace Jovanovich, 1972), p. 24.

104. Amy Lowell, "The Weather-Cock Points South," *Pictures of the Floating World* (New York: Macmillan, 1919), pp. 51–52.

105. *American Poetry Journal* (June 1934), p. 2. This journal, which was edited in New York, attempted to maintain a fairly conservative aesthetic stance but found itself drawn to comment both positively and negatively on the political poetry of the period. The journal is notable for its willingness to publish long poems and for its detailed editorial introductions to the featured poems in each issue. The December 1933 issue notes that "In the recent controversy in the *New Republic* concerning the necessity of a poet's identification with social and economic conditions and trends, it was assumed that the definitive trend today was that of industrial radicalism, and that over against this movement there stood nothing but capitalistic

reaction. . . . it seems to me that the force of our agricultural civilization is more significant than either of them" (p. 2). A review of Robert Gessner's *Upsurge* in the May 1934 issue argues that "achievement has seldom followed the doctrinaire approach," a position confirmed by the "overpublicized trend toward a proletarian literature." "Unquestionably," the reviewer argues, Gessner's book "fails as a poem because of the determined propaganda with which it is invested." At the same time its generic status is uncertain: "it is something powerful and immediately provocative, a great deal less than poetry, a great deal more than a speech in Union Square. Some of the lines have inestimable force. . . . They almost become poetry" (p. 38). The series of poems that includes Donald Paquette's "The Journey of the Flesh" and is to end with Elsa Gidlow's "Steel-flanked Stallion" is interesting in part because it represents an editorial effort to place the more socially critical poems in a larger sequence that will conclude in a mode of transcendent reaffirmation.

106. *Proletarian Literature in the United States*, eds. Granville Hicks, Michael Gold, Isidor Schneider, Joseph North, Paul Peters, and Alan Calmer, introduction by Joseph Freeman (New York: International Publishers, 1935), p. 146. Also see Henry Hart, ed. *American Writers' Congress* (New York: International Publishers, 1935).

107. Lucia Trent, *Children of Fire and Shadow* (Chicago: Robert Packard, 1929), pp. 38, 39, 79, 85. Trent's first books of poetry were *The Frigate of My Fancy* (New York: Hudson Press, 1922) and *Dawn Stars* (New York: Henry Harrison, 1926). She is also known for a number of editing projects, including the magazine *Contemporary Verse* and some ten books, on many of which she collaborated with her husband, Ralph Cheyney.

108. Mike Gold was born Itshok Isaac Granich in New York. For a time he published as Irwin Granich, but the name Michael Gold, which he assumed for self-protection during the notorious "red raids" of 1919–1920, seemed to take and he stayed with it thereafter. He served as an assistant editor of *The Masses*, edited *Liberator* from 1920 to 1922, and helped to found *New Masses*. His most famous work is the loosely autobiographical novel *Jews Without Money* (1930), which chronicles lower East Side life at the turn of the century. In 1930 Gold published an attack on Thornton Wilder in the *New Republic* ("Wilder: Prophet of the Genteel Christ"), which provoked wide antagonistic response. In 1932 Edmund Wilson, writing again for the *New Republic*, observed that "there is no question that the Gold-Wilder row marked definitely the eruption of the Marxist issues out of the literary circles of the radicals into the field of general criticism. After that, it became very plain that the economic crisis was to be accompanied by a literary one." Gold's poetry has not all been gathered together, but the best collection of his work is *Mike Gold: A Literary Anthology*, ed. Michael Folsom (New York: International Publishers, 1972). Folsom provides a good intro-

duction and useful headnotes to his selections. Also see Gold's collection
120 Million (1929) and the selection of his poetry in Salzman, ed., *Social
Poetry of the 1930s*. It should be noted that Gold sometimes toned down his
Daily Worker columns when collecting them in his books. Critical work
on Gold includes Paul Berman, "East Side Story: Mike Gold, the Commu-
nists, and the Jews," *Village Voice Literary Supplement*, 15 (March 1983),
1, 9; John Pyros, *Mike Gold: Dean of American Proletarian Writers* (New
York: Dramatika Press, 1979); Utz Riese, "Neither High Nor Low: Michael
Gold's Concept of a Proletarian Literature," in Heinz Ickstadt et al., eds.,
The Thirties: Politics and Culture in a Time of Broken Dreams (Amster-
dam: Free University Press, 1987), and Art Shields, "Mike Gold, Our Joy and
Pride," *Political Affairs*, 51 (July 1972), 41–51.

109. Mike Gold, "Ode to Walt Whitman," *New Masses*, November 5,
1935, p. 21.

110. Mike Gold, "Workers' Correspondence," *The Daily Worker*, January
20, 1934, p. 9, and *Dynamo: A Journal of Revolutionary Poetry* 1:1 (January
1934), pp. 5–6.

111. Mike Gold, "Proletarian Realism," reprinted in *Mike Gold: A Literary Anthology*, p. 207.

112. On August 22, 1934, *The Daily Worker* published "Merchant Marine"
by Harry Alan Potamkin (1900–1933), identifying it as based on correspondence to *The Daily Worker* and the *Marine Workers' Voice*, and reminding
us that Potamkin was the first to use workers' correspondence as a theme
for poetry. Potamkin had published "Mecklenburg County," identifying it as
"a poem based on worker correspondence to the *Daily Worker*," in the June
24, 1933, issue of the newspaper, p. 5.

113. T. Lerner, "I Want You Women Up North to Know," *Partisan* 1:4
(March 1934), 4. Tillie Olsen used her family name, Lerner, until she was
married. For a commentary on and bibliography of Olsen's work in the 1930s
see Selma Burkom and Margaret Williams, "De-Riddling Tillie Olsen's Writing," *San Jose Studies* 2 (1976), 65–83, and Deborah Rosenfelt, "From the
thirties: Tillie Olsen and the radical tradition," in Judith Newton and Deborah Rosenfelt, eds. *Feminist Criticism and Social Change* (New York:
Methuen, 1985), 216–48. Olsen's poem "There Is A Lesson," listed by Burkom and Williams as first published in *Partisan* in April 1934, was actually
first published in *The Daily Worker*, March 5, 1934, p. 7.

A few passages from Felipe Ibarro's letter in *New Masses* demonstrate how
Olsen reworked her source:

> I want the women of New York, Chicago and Boston who buy at
> Macy's, Wannamaker's, Gimbel's and Marshall Field to know that when
> they buy embroidered children's dresses labeled 'hand made' they are
> getting dresses made in San Antonio, Texas, by women and girls with

trembling fingers and broken backs. . . . Ambrosa Espinoza . . . tells me about her brother . . . who lies on his iron cot like a skeleton. He uses rags for a mattress, and lies motionless, gazing on the Virgin of Guadalupe and the image of the young Jew of Galilee. . . . I want you women up North to know.

114. Mike Gold, "Proletarian Realism," pp. 206, 208.

115. For other examples of workers' correspondence poems see Mike Gold, "A Report from the Dakotas," *The Daily Worker*, September 2, 1933, p. 6, and Joseph Freeman, "Peasant Correspondence," *The Daily Worker*, June 30, 1934, p. 7.

116. The major source for John Beecher's poetry is now his *Collected Poems 1924–1974* (New York: Macmillan, 1974). This somewhat selective gathering of his work should be supplemented by his earlier books and pamphlets. See also Beecher's comments on the marketing and reception of his *Collected Poems*: "On Suppression," *Southern Exposure* (1981), 91–92, reprinted from *Phantasm* (1979). An informative biographical essay is Frank Adams, "John Beecher: A Political Poet," *Southern Exposure* (1981), 104–7, from which I take a few facts to give some sense of Beecher's remarkable life. Although his father was prosperous, Beecher nonetheless spent some years working twelve-hour days at the open hearth furnaces in the Birmingham steel mills. He continued to work in the mills while attending college until he was seriously injured. All the while he wrote poems about the reality of working-class life. A series of brief teaching and research jobs followed, one of which resulted in a study of sharecroppers' organizations being published in *Social Forces*. He then ran a series of New Deal agencies and subsequently served in the Merchant Marine during the Second World War. *All Brave Sailors* (1945) chronicled his experiences. After the war he took a teaching position at San Francisco State College, but was fired for refusing to sign a loyalty oath in 1950. After a stint of raising chickens and fruit at a ranch in California, he was able to begin teaching again. His book *Tomorrow Is a Day* (1980) reports his research on late-nineteenth-century populism.

117. Beecher, "Report to the Stockholders," *Collected Poems*, p. 3.

118. Beecher, "A Million Days, A Million Dollars," *Collected Poems*, p. 6.

119. Beecher, "Ensley, Alabama, 1932," "Appalachian Landscape," "Beaufort Tides," *Collected Poems*, pp. 18, 22, 20.

120. Lola Ridge, "Red Flag," *Red Flag* (New York: Viking, 1927), pp. 39–40. Her other books include *The Ghetto and Other Poems* (New York: Huebsch, 1918), *Sun-Up and Other Poems* (New York: Huebsch, 1920), and *Dance of Fire* (New York: Smith, 1935). Her book-length poem *Firehead* (New York: Payson, 1929) retells the Christ story in the light of the executions of Sacco and Vanzetti. Elaine Sproat, author of a forthcoming biography of Ridge, has also edited Ridge's essay "Woman and the Creative Will,"

published as *Michigan Occasional Paper* 18 (Spring 1981). Ridge was born
in Ireland in 1873, emigrated to Australia and New Zealand while a child,
and came to the United States in 1908. William Drake, in *The First Wave:
Women Poets in America 1915–1945*, writes of the strong feminist component in her work: "Ridge's poetry is marked both by rage at injustice and
by a fiercely maternal urgency, as if the disorder of the world arose out of
a separation from the spiritual center that the mother represents. . . . Few
poets of Ridge's generation shared her intuitive grasp of the distinction between power as oppressive in men and liberating in women, with radical
political implications" (pp. 4, 5).

121. Herman Spector, *Bastard in the Ragged Suit*, ed. Bud Johns and
Judith Clancy (San Francisco: Synergistic Press, 1977), pp. 95, 102–3. *Bastard in the Ragged Suit*, which draws its title from the self-description in the
opening line of a 1929 poem "Outcast," ably gathers together both Spector's
published poetry and prose and selections from the writing and drawing he
continued to work on but never submitted for publication in the last years of
his life. Spector was a regular contributor to *New Masses* for several years,
the key figure in the founding of the short-lived radical poetry journal *Dynamo*, and a contributor to many of the proletarian literature collections of
the 1930s. Toward the end of the 1930s he worked for a year on the WPA
Writers' Project. Thereafter, he withdrew from his literary and political con-
tacts, worked as a welder during the war, and finally survived in a series of
marginal odd jobs before becoming a cab driver until his death.

122. Richard Wright's poetry is conveniently gathered together as "Appendix B" to Michael Fabre, *The World of Richard Wright* (Jackson: University Press of Mississippi, 1985). Also see Fabre's essay "From Revolutionary
Poetry to Haiku" in the same collection. For a thorough and accurate list of
these and Wright's other publications see Charles T. Davis, *Richard Wright:
A Primary Bibliography* (Boston: G. K. Hall, 1982).

123. Kenneth Fearing, "2.50," "Dear Beatrice Fairfax," "Denouement,"
Poems (New York, Dynamo: 1935), pp. 49, 33, 57. Fearing's other volumes of
poetry include *Angel Arms* (New York: Coward McCann, 1929), *Dead Reck-
oning* (New York: Random House, 1938), *Collected Poems* (New York: Random House, 1940), *Afternoon of a Pawnbroker* (New York: Harcourt, Brace,
1943), *Stranger at Coney Island* (New York: Harcourt, Brace, 1948), and *New
and Selected Poems* (Bloomington: Indiana University Press, 1956). The last
volume eliminates many poems of value but includes Fearing's interesting
preface "Reading, Writing, and the Rackets." The political context of Fearing's 1935 *Poems* is underlined by Edward Dahlberg's introduction. Fearing
also wrote fiction, his most famous novel being *The Big Clock* (1946). The
Fearing Papers at the University of Wisconsin suggest the limits of how
much it was realistic for a young poet to contemplate earning by publishing
a fairly visible book of poetry during the Depression. *Poems* (1935) was pub-

lished in an edition of 1,000 copies. Of those, Fearing purchased 21, 79 were given away or sent out for review, and 900 were sold to the public at $1.00 per copy. Fearing's royalties came to $90.00, from which was subtracted the cost of the books he purchased. Some books of radical poetry, however, sold substantially more copies. Sol Funaroff's publishers report, for example, that *The Spider and the Clock* sold 5,000 copies. It is worth noting that many university press volumes of poetry now sell fewer than 1,000 copies.

124. John Wheelwright, "Paul and Virginia," "Plantation Drouth," *Collected Poems*, ed. Alvin H. Rosenfeld (New York: New Directions, 1971), pp. 38, 39. See also Alan M. Wald's thoroughly researched *The Revolutionary Imagination: The Poetry and Politics of John Wheelwright and Sherry Mangan* (Chapel Hill: University of North Carolina Press, 1983). Writing against the grain of our received professional beliefs, Wald documents Wheelwright's modernist commitment to political poetry.

125. Genevieve Taggard, *Calling Western Union* (New York: Harper, 1936), pp. 23, 6. "Everyday Alchemy" is reprinted from *For Eager Lovers* (New York: Seltzer, 1922). Taggard's other books of poetry include *Hawaiian Hilltop* (San Francisco: Wyckoff, 1923), *Travelling Standing Still: Poems 1918–1928* (New York: Knopf, 1928) *Not Mine to Finish: Poems 1928–34* (New York: Harper, 1934), *Collected Poems, 1918–1938* (New York: Harper, 1938), *Long View* (New York: Harper, 1942), *Slow Music* (New York: Harper, 1946), and *To the Natural World* (Boise, Idaho: Ahsahta Press, Boise State University, 1980). She is also the author of *The Life and Mind of Emily Dickinson* (New York: Knopf, 1930). For information about her life see her preface to *Calling Western Union* and her autobiographical essay "Poet out of Pioneer" in *These Modern Women*, ed. Elaine Showalter (Old Westbury, N.Y.: Feminist Press, 1978), as well as William Drake's *The First Wave: Women Poets in America, 1915–1945*. A substantial microfilm edition of Taggard's collected and uncollected works is the most complete guide to her publications.

126. Edna St. Vincent Millay, *Collected Poems* (New York: Harper, 1956), p. 622.

127. Joy Davidman's first publications appeared while she was still an undergraduate at Hunter College. *The Hunter College Echo* published an essay on George Moore, several poems and translations, and two short stories: "Reveal the Titan" and "Apostate." *Poetry* began to publish her poems in 1936 and, within a year or two, she had joined the Communist party. *Letter to a Comrade*, the only collection of her own poems, was published in the Yale Series of Younger Poets in 1938, with an introduction by Stephen Vincent Benét. It received the Russel Loines Award from the National Institute of Arts and Letters the following year. She spent the latter half of 1939 in Hollywood as an assistant screen writer for M-G-M, an experience that led to her writing a number of detailed film reviews for *New Masses*

through the early 1940s. She did publish some poetry thereafter, including several poems in *Seven Poets in Search of an Answer* (1942) and in her large anthology *War Poems of the United Nations* (1943), a collection for which she also did numerous translations. In 1944 she edited and wrote the preface for Alexander F. Bergman's posthumous collection of political poetry *They Look Like Men*. She also wrote two novels—*Anya* (New York: Macmillan, 1940) and *Weeping Bay* (New York: Macmillan, 1950)—and it is between their publication, in 1946, that she had a religious experience that reshaped the rest of her life. The story of her conversion appears as her essay "The Longest Way Around" in *These Found The Way: Thirteen Converts to Protestant Christianity*, ed. David Wesley Soper (Philadelphia: Westminster, 1951). Her *Smoke on the Mountain* (1954) is a collection of essays on the Ten Commandments, with a preface by C. S. Lewis, whom she met in 1950 and secretly married in 1956. The marriage was announced nine months later. Biographical information on her can be found in Paul Leopold's two-part essay "The Writings of Joy Davidman Lewis," *The Bulletin of the New York C. S. Lewis Society* 14:4 (February 1983), 1–10 and 14:5 (March 1983), 1–9, and in Lyle Dorsett's biography of Davidman, *And God Came In* (New York: Macmillan, 1983). See also Dorsett's lecture "The Search for Joy Davidman, *The Bulletin of the New York C. S, Lewis Society* 14:12 (October 1983), 1–7. Leopold's and Dorsett's work is heavily invested in her later commitment to Christianity.

128. See Rukeyser's *Collected Poems* (New York: McGraw Hill, 1979), as well as her *The Life of Poetry* (1949). Louise Kertesz's well-informed *The Poetic Vision of Muriel Rukeyser* (Baton Rouge: Louisiana State University Press, 1979) is also recommended.

129. Davidman, *Letter to a Comrade*, pp. 25, 67, 40.

130. Edwin Rolfe, "City of Anguish," *First Love and Other Poems*, pp. 13–19.

131. Edwin Rolfe's most famous book is no doubt his historical *The Lincoln Battalion* (New York: Random House, 1939). As Allen Guttman points out in "The Brief Embattled Course of Proletarian Poetry" in *Proletarian Writers of the Thirties*, ed. David Madden (Carbondale: Southern Illinois University Press, 1968), Rolfe had gone to Spain to be an editor of the newspaper *Volunteer for Liberty*, but "he 'deserted' and joined the battalion in the crossing of the Ebro River, the last major offensive before the withdrawal of the Internationals." Rolfe's three books of poetry are *To My Contemporaries* (New York: Dynamo, 1936), *First Love and Other Poems* (Los Angeles: Larry Edmunds Book Shop, 1951), and *Permit Me Refuge* (Los Angeles: California Quarterly, 1955). Jacket commentary on *To My Contemporaries* was provided by Horace Gregory, who also selected Rolfe as the opening poet of the Social Poets Number he guest edited for *Poetry* (May 1936). The contributors' notes to that issue of *Poetry* observe that Rolfe "was reared in the

labor movement and has long been associated with the labor press. He has served on the staffs of *The Daily Worker, Dynamo, The New Masses,* and of the recently combined *Partisan Review and Anvil.* . . . His occupations have ranged from clothing cutter, furniture worker, machine tender and filer to waiter and 'pearl diver.' " A few months later, Harriet Monroe in *Poetry* (July 1936) described him as "the best among those inflammatory young men and women." Rolfe also wrote book reviews for *New Masses* and an essay on political poetry for the April–May 1935 issue of *Partisan Review.* As Guttman reports, "after a brief stint in the U. S. Army (1942–43), Rolfe moved to California and made documentary films, the best of which is *Muscle Beach* (with music by Earl Robinson). He also wrote a mystery novel, *The Glass Room* (1946), with Lester Fuller. He died in 1954, of the heart condition which had led to his discharge from the army" (p. 274). Rolfe's *First Love and other poems,* illustrated with drawings by Lia Nickson, was, it might be noted, a limited edition of 375 copies. *Permit Me Refuge,* with a preface by Thomas McGrath, was published posthumously; it includes Rolfe's photograph on the back jacket. Something of the risks of Rolfe's virtual elimination from literary history are perhaps apparent in the fact that, though he may have written the most accomplished American poems on the Spanish Civil War, he receives no mention in Marilyn Rosenthal's *Poetry of the Spanish Civil War* (New York: New York University Press, 1975). Stanley Weintraub, however, provides some useful comments on Rolfe in his *The Last Great Cause: The Intellectuals and the Spanish Civil War* (New York: Weybright and Talley, 1968). Eric Homberger finds fault with Rolfe's early poems in his *American Writers and Radical Politics, 1900–39* (London: Macmillan, 1986).

132. For an impressive study of the specific vicissitudes of canonization and noncanonization see Michael Bérubé's 1989 University of Virginia dissertation "Marginal Authorities and Cultural Centers: Melvin Tolson, Thomas Pynchon, and the Rhetoric of Critical Response."

133. Robinson Jeffers, "Fantasy," "What Odd Expedients," "An Ordinary Newscaster," *The Double Axe and Other Poems,* with a foreword by William Everson and an afterword by Bill Hotchkiss (New York: Liveright, 1977), pp. 156, 163, 160. This edition, which includes eleven previously suppressed poems, is one of a series of newly revised editions of Robinson Jeffers' poems. They have culminated in a complete collected poems, edited by Tim Hunt, that is in the process of being published by Stanford University Press. Full details about the publishing history of *The Double Axe,* along with comments on the suppressed poems, may be found in James Shebl, *In This Wild Water: The Suppressed Poems of Robinson Jeffers* (Pasadena, Calif.: Ward Ritchie Press, 1976).

In showing equal contempt for both Roosevelt and Hitler Jeffers might seem at least to be being even-handed in his rejection of all political commitments as compromised and dishonorable. His stance here in any case is consistent with his comments in *Writers Take Sides: Letters about the war in Spain from 418 American authors* (New York: League of American Writers, 1938): "You ask what I am for and what against in Spain. I would give my right hand, of course, to prevent the agony; I would not give a flick of my little finger to help either side win" (p. 73). Of course, for those who feel there is a real moral difference in the two sides of these conflicts, Jeffers' position is untenable. As Robert Haas has written in "Robinson Jeffers: The Poems and the Life," *American Poetry Review* 16:6 (1987), 33–41:

> Jeffers seemed to have been, politically and sentimentally, an old-fashioned Jeffersonian republican. He believed in the American republic as a commonwealth of independent and self-reliant households, and saw himself—educated at a time when small boys knew the history of Rome and had been taught the parallels between the Roman and American republics—as a defender of the spartan and honest American commonweal against the thickening of the empire. He seems to have wanted his country to be, as he wanted his poems to be, as cool and aloof as a hawk from what was going forward, the inevitable and horrifying collapse of European civilization.
>
> Though this may have been philosophical conviction, it did not in practice appear to differ very much from the view of any wealthy, Republican, Roosevelt-hating citizen of Carmel, living on private income and insulated from the effects of the Depression. . . ."(p. 39).

There is one further text, however, that puts all these issues in a very different light indeed: Jeffers' appalling June 1943 "Tragedy Has Obligations," which was not included in the original *Double Axe* manuscript but rather found in the Tor House papers at the University of Texas. Here Jeffers addresses Hitler only: "If you had thrown a little more boldly in the flood of fortune / You'd have had England." So too if "you'd not have sunk your hand in Russia." "This is the essence of tragedy," Jeffers concludes the first stanza, "To have meant well and made woe, and watch Fate, / All stone, approach." Perhaps the advice that follows is sardonic, but there is also the real possibility that Jeffers admired Hitler:

> You should be Samson, blind Samson, crushing
> All his foes, that's Europe, America, half Asia, in his
>   fall.
> But you are not able; and the tale is Hebrew.

Jeffers then recommends a death like a "wing-broken hawk" showing "eternal defiance"; you should die "like a wolf, war-loser"—"The head lifts, the great fangs grin." Without the animal references one could read this as a poem about Hitler's delusions about his own heroism, but Jeffers himself was too heavily invested in images of wild defiance.

134. Charles Henri Ford's long and varied career began with his publishing

poems in magazines before his twentieth year. He edited *Blues: A Maga-zine of New Rhythms* from 1929–1931. His collections of poetry include *The Garden of Disorder* (London: Europa Press, 1938), with an introduction by William Carlos Williams; *The Overturned Lake* (Cincinnati: Little Man Press, 1941), *Sleep in a Nest of Flames* (New York: New Directions, 1949), with a foreword by Edith Sitwell; *Spare Parts* (New York: Horizon Press, 1966); *Silver Flower Coo* (New York: Kulchur Press, 1968); *Flag of Ecstasy: Selected Poems*, ed. Edward B. Germain (Los Angeles: Black Sparrow, 1972); *7 Poems* (Kathmandu, Nepal: Bardo Matrix, 1974); *Om Krishna I: Special Effects* (Cherry Valley, N.Y.: Cherry Valley Editions, 1979); *Om Krishna II: From the Sickroom of the Walking Eagles* (Cherry Valley, N. Y.: Cherry Valley Editions, 1981); *Om Krishna III: Secret Haiku*; and *Emblems of Arachne* (New York: Catchword Papers, 1986). He is also the coauthor, with Parker Tyler, of a novel, *The Young and Evil* (Paris: Obelisk Press, 1933). An exhibition of his photographs was held in London in 1955 and a show of his paintings and drawings was held in Paris in 1956; the catalog for the Paris show included a foreword by Jean Cocteau. His feature film *Johnny Mino-taur*, produced on Crete, premiered in 1971. An exhibition of sculptures and prints done in Nepal was held in New York in 1974. For further information on Ford, see his interview with Ira Cohen in *Gay Sunshine Interviews*, ed. Winston Leyland (San Francisco: Gay Sunshine Press, 1978), 35–65, and Eva B. Mills and Elizabeth Davidson, "Charles Henri Ford," in Karen Lane Rood, ed., *American Writers in Paris, 1920–1939, Dictionary of Literary Biography*, vol. 4, pp. 164–66.

135. Charles Henri Ford, "Song Without a Singer," "Song," *The Over-turned Lake*, pp. 51, 38. "Plaint," published in Ford's *The Garden of Dis-order*, is reprinted in *Flag of Ecstasy*, p. 30.

136. Nancy Cunard's anthology *Negro* is now very rare. An abridged re-print, which includes all the poems from the original edition, was edited by Hugh Ford and published by Frederick Ungar in 1970. The section by white poets includes, among others, Cunard's "Southern Sheriff," Kreym-borg's "Miss Sal's Monologue," Carl Rakosi's "The Black Crow," and Louis Zukofsky's "Poem." The comparable section in the Hughes-Bontemps' *The Poetry of the Negro* includes, among others, Whitman's "The Runaway Slave," Blake's "The Little Black Boy," Whittier's "The Farewell," Stephen Vincent Benét's "John Brown's Prayer," Bodenheim's "Negroes," Rukeyser's "The Trial," and Don West's "My South."

137. Cummings, *Collected Poems*, p. 622.

138. Funaroff, "Mean Man Blues," "Workin So Long," *Exile From a Future Time*, pp. 1, 7.

139. Aldon Lynn Nielsen, *Reading Race: White American Poets and the Racial Discourse in the Twentieth Century* (Athens: University of Georgia Press, 1988), p. 36. Nielsen's book is one of the most important books on

modern poetry to appear in many years. It will be interesting to see whether the profession views its topic as central or peripheral.

140. Sandburg, *Collected Poems*, p. 24.

141. Kimmell, *The Kingdom of Smoke*, p. 16. Also see "Dagos," pp. 45–46.

142. Trent, *Children of Fire and Shadow*, p. 87.

143. Taggard, *Long View*, p. 55.

144. Victor Jeremy Jerome's "A Negro Mother to Her Child" was first published in the November 15, 1930, issue of *The Daily Worker*, p. 4. His interest in race in America would continue through his life, as exemplified in his poems "To a Black Man," *The Daily Worker*, December 3, 1932, p. 3, and "Caliban Speaks" (inspired by the death of the black actor Canada Lee), *Masses and Mainstream*, 1953, and his pamphlet *The Negro in Hollywood Films* (New York: Masses and Mainstream, 1950). His other pamphlets included *Social Democracy and the War* (1940), *Intellectuals and the War* (1940), *The Treatment of Defeated Germany* (1945), and *Culture in a Changing World* (1947).

Born in a Polish ghetto, he subsequently moved to London and from there came to New York. Jerome joined the Communist party in 1927 and in 1937 he became chairman of the Communist party's Cultural Commission and also began editing *The Communist*, which later became *Political Affairs*. Arrested under the Smith Act in 1951 he was convicted—on the inappropriate basis of his critical writings—of conspiracy to advocate the violent overthrow of the U.S. government; he served three years in prison. *A Lantern for Jeremy* (1952) is a fictional account of his childhood in Poland.

145. Two numbers of *The Worker's Song Book* would appear, one in 1934 and another in 1935, both published by the Workers Music League in New York. Other songs in the first volume include Freeman's "Red Soldiers Singing," and Hughes's "God to the Hungry Child." The collection opens with the following motto: "Music penetrates everywhere. It carries words with it. It fixes them in the mind. It graves them in the Heart. Music is a weapon in the class struggle." The second volume included, among other songs, Alfred Hayes's "Into the Streets May First!," Jerome's "Comintern," Quin's "Stop in Your Tracks," West's "Look Here Georgia," and Gold's "John Reed Our Captain." Music is provided for all the songs. An earlier collection, the *Red Song Book* (New York: Workers Library Publishers, 1932), prepared in collaboration with the Workers Music League, set Joe Hill's "The Preacher and the Slave" to music and included, among others, Leonard Spier's "Red Marching Song," and Jerome's "Stand Guard," "Comintern," and "Red Brigadier." Some songs were also available as sheet music.

146. Spier's "A Call to Negro Poets and Writers," *The Rebel Poet* 15 (August 1932), 3, begins by accurately citing the principle of "Divide and Rule" as the key to the promulgation of racial antagonism in the United States. He goes on to summarize some of the specifics of discrimination and mur-

der here and elsewhere. But he is rather less persuasive when he declares "the tyrants of the United States" to be "the most vicious, insatiable, and blood-thirsty of the profit worshippers." When at the end he proclaims that "It is only under socialism, as in the Soviet Union of Russia, for example, where the disintegration and race-cleavage of the masses is no longer necessary, where the negro can enjoy social and economic equality" and asks that blacks rise up against those "whose cold-blooded savagery is unparalled in all the gory centuries of human history," the overblown rhetoric undercuts its own supposed concerns with racial injustice.

147. E. E. Cummings, "kumrads die because they're told," *Collected Poems*, p. 413. Ironically, Cummings did make one notable contribution to left poetry of the 1930s: his translation of Louis Aragon's long poem "The Red Front." See Cummings' translation (and Jay de Von's essay "L'Affair Aragon") in *Contempo* 3:5 (February 1, 1933). *Contempo* also issued *The Red Front* as a separate pamphlet. The year before, just after the French version of the poem was first published, Aragon was charged with "inciting to murder" and "provoking insubordination in the army" for lines like "Fire on the trained bears of the social democracy." After large protests, the charges were dropped.

148. See Stephen Vincent Benét, *We Stand United and Other Radio Scripts* (New York: Farrar and Rinehart, 1945).

149. *Owl's Clover* is reprinted in Wallace Stevens, *Opus Posthumous*, ed. Samuel French Morse (New York: Knopf, 1957). Stanley Burnshaw's review of Stevens' *Ideas of Order*, "Turmoil in the Middle Ground," *New Masses* (October 1, 1935), is reprinted along with Burnshaw's later reflections on the matter in Stanley Burnshaw, "Wallace Stevens and the Statue," *Sewanee Review* 69 (1961), 355–66.

Milton J. Bates in *Wallace Stevens: A Mythology of Self* (Berkeley: University of California Press, 1985) provides a helpful chapter ("Restatement of Romance") on Stevens' relations to the contemporary pressure to deal with political issues in poetry. Bates sees *Owl's Clover* as the central text in which Stevens works out these issues for himself and thus as a key clarifying moment in Stevens' career. An interesting and important contrast is provided by Frank Lentricchia's *Ariel and the Police: Michel Foucault, William James, Wallace Stevens* (Madison: University of Wisconsin Press, 1988), in which Stevens' politics is read by way of the issues of sexual difference, commodity fetishism, and the politics of idealization. To set these two commentaries beside one another, each addressing Stevens' "politics" and each displaying virtually no points of similarity with the other—they focus on different texts and on quite different issues—is to realize how unstable, contested, and potentially open is our whole notion of what constitutes *the political* either within poetry or in the culture at large.

150. Langston Hughes, "Let America Be America Again," *A New Song* (New York: International Workers Order, 1938), pp. 9–11.

151. Irene Paull's "Ballad of a Lumberjack" is reprinted in her *We're the People* (Duluth, Minn.: Midwest Labor, c. 1941). Here is a characteristic stanza:

> We told 'em we wanted a pillow
> And a mattress and maybe a sheet.
> And they said where's your guts? goin soft? Are you nuts?
> That hay on your bunks is a treat.   (p. 49)

We're the People is a rather unusual book in that it is divided into two parts. The first ninety-nine pages reprint Paull's poems and articles from *Midwest Labor*, where they were published under the pen name "Calamity Jane." The next thirty pages are devoted to an anthology titled "Ballads by the Workers." Paull published poems under her own name in *The Daily Worker*.

152. Peter Stallybrass and Allon White, *The Politics and Poetics of Transgression* (Ithaca: Cornell University Press, 1986), p. 195.

153. Cf. my "Against English: Theory and the Limits of the Profession," *Profession '87*, from which several of the sentences above are borrowed.

154. *The Poetry of Vachel Lindsay: Complete and with Lindsay's Drawings*, vol. 2, ed. Dennis Camp (Peoria, Ill.: Spoon River Poetry Press, 1985), p. 593. "Celestial Flowers of Glacier Park" is from Lindsay's *Going-to-the-Stars* (1926).

155. Eugene Jolas, *I Have Seen Monsters and Angels* (Paris: Transition Press, 1938), p. 164. "Mountain Words" is one of nine sound poems in a section of the book titled "Incantations." The front jacket flap includes the following paragraph: " 'I Have Seen Monsters and Angels' is a multilingual autobiography of the night-mind, containing prose poetry in new forms, such as: paramyth, grotesque, poem without words, incantation, hypnologue, fantasia, fairy tale. The author calls his efforts 'verticalist', or 'vertigralist', to mark his search for a 'language of night' with a cosmic and transcendental direction."

Jolas's other books include *Cinema* (New York: Adelphi, 1926); *Secession in Astropolis* (Paris: Black Sun Press, 1929); *The Language of Night* (The Hague: Service, 1932); *Mots-deluge: Hypnologues* (Paris: Editions des Cahiers Libres, 1933); *Vertigralist Pamphlet* (Paris: Transition Press, 1938); *Words from the Deluge* (New York: Gotham Bookmart, 1941); and *Wanderpoem: or Angelic Mythamorphosis of the City of London* (Paris: Transition Press, 1946). See Thomas E. Dasher, "Eugene Jolas," in Karen Lane Rood, ed. *American Writers in Paris, 1920–1939, Dictionary of Literary Biography*, vol. 4, for further information.

156. Viola C. White's "To Holy Church, 1918" is included in her *The Hour of Judgment* (Boston: B. J. Brimmer, 1923), pp. 37–39. It is prefaced by the following note: "This is retained as a specimen of wartime animosity. Its condemnation of the Church is as bitter as the Church's condemnation of its enemies." She describes the Church during war as a "grave-digger for ten

millions of young men" and sees its general cultural role as that of giving its blessing to oppression:

> The Negro fixed in fetters at thy word,
> The children out of factory and mine
> Who cried until thy ministers were stirred
> To seal their servitude with speech divine,
> The silent women rendered by thy sign
> Subservient forever to man's lust (p. 37).

White's first book of poems, *Horizons* was published in the Yale Series of Younger Poets in 1921. Little in it, however, anticipates the explicit socialist and Marxist commitments of *The Hour of Judgment*. White eventually drifted away from her politics, becoming a librarian at Middlebury College. *Partridge in a Swamp: The Journals of Viola C. White*, ed. William Storrs Lee (Taftsville, Vt.: Country Man, 1977) includes a helpful biographical essay.

157. Sara N. Cleghorn began her career in the genteel tradition, but by 1912 her commitments to socialism and pacifism had begun to simplify her rhetoric and take over her subject matter:

> The golf links lie so near the mill
> That almost every day
> The laboring children can look out
> And see the men at play.

Robert Frost, who wrote the introduction to her 1936 autobiography *Threescore*, found these lines particularly telling. Her two volumes of poetry are *Portraits and Protests* (New York: Henry Holt, 1917) and *Poems of Peace and Freedom* (Fulton, N.Y.: New York State Branch of the Women's International League for Peace & Freedom, 1945). The copyright page to the latter book includes the following statement: "Miss Cleghorn hopes these poems, which she says are 'probably the best sheaf from life's harvest of effort,' will be copied, quoted and used wherever they may be, suitably." She also wrote two novels, *A Turnpike Lady* (1907) and *The Spinster* (1916). Her poem "The Poltroon," published in *The New York Tribune* during the First World War, provoked wide protest. "Comrade Jesus" presents Jesus as a Marxist union member; "The Poltroon" presents him as a pacifist:

> —I will say for him, milksop as he was,
> He was consistent, for he let himself
> Be knocked about the streets, and spit upon,
> And never had the manhood to spit back.
> Of course, he had no sense at all of honor,
> Either his country's honor, or his own,
> Contemptible poltroon! His name was Jesus.

The large outpouring of anger the poem provoked suggests how charged not only religious subjects but especially religious *poetry* could be for readers of the time. The idealization of the poetic, in effect, gave special moral authority—and consequent outrage—to poems that linked politics and religion. In the 1930s some of the same anger would circulate around Langston Hughes's "Christ in Alabama"; later it would focus on his "Goodbye Christ." For Hughes's difficulties over "Goodbye Christ," see Arnold Rampersad, *The Life of Langston Hughes, vol. 2: 1941–1967, I Dream a World* (New York: Oxford University Press, 1988).

158. For a critique of the ideology of a politics of passivity in academia, see Frank Lentricchia, *Criticism and Social Change* (Chicago: University of Chicago Press, 1983).

159. *The Comrade* was reprinted by Greenwood Press in 1970 in an edition that has a useful index and does a good job with the black and white illustrations.

160. For late nineteenth-century labor, socialist, or anarchist poetry see George Marshall Sloan, *The Telephone of Labor* (1880); George P. McIntyre, *The Light of Persia or the Death of Mammon and Other Poems of Prophecy, Profit, and Peace* (1890); George Howard Gibson, *Armageddon: The Songs of the World's Workers Who Go Forth to Battle with the Kings, and Captains and Mighty Men* (1894); John William Lloyd, *Wind-Harp Songs* (1895); Charlotte Perkins Gilman, *In This Our World* (1895); James Allman, *Carmina Noctis* (1898), and Frank Everett Plummer, *Gracia: A Social Tragedy* (1899). Chicago, with the Charles Kerr publishing company, was a particularly active site for socialist and labor poetry around the turn of the century. Other cities, however, also played a role. Gibson's volume was published in Lincoln, Nebraska; Lloyd's was published in Buffalo; Gilman's was published in San Francisco; Allman's was published in New York City. For an immensely useful selection of poems and songs from labor newspapers and magazines see Philip S. Foner, *American Labor Songs of the Nineteenth Century* (Urbana: University of Illinois Press, 1975).

161. Gibson's *The People's Hour* is a particularly interesting book because of its detailed annotations and prose manifestos. Gibson often cites specific historical events as inspiration for particular poems.

162. Moyer's *Songs of Socialism* includes a number of songs by Moyer himself. Indeed, even when reprinting songs by others he feels comfortable in adding a chorus or another verse of his own. Other authors represented include William Morris and Edwin Markham.

163. Tichenor, *Rhymes of the Revolution*, n.p. "Onward Christian Soldiers" is included both in the book and on the simultaneous broadside. Tichenor was the author of a considerable number of books and pamphlets, including *Woman under Capitalism* (1912), *The Evils of Capitalism* (1912), *Mythologies: A Materialistic Interpretation, Analyzing the Class Character of Religion* (1919), and *The Life of Jack London* (1923).

164. White, *The Hour of Judgment*, p. 36. Also see her long, remarkable poetic dialogue "The Russian Revolution," pp. 77–109.

165. As Joyce Kornbluh reports in *Rebel Voices*, pp. 27–28, "We Have Fed You All a Thousand Years" first appeared in the IWW press in the *Industrial Union Bulletin* in 1908, under the title "The Cry of Toil." The poem partly parodies the last stanza of Rudyard Kipling's "The Song of the Dead": "We have fed our sea [with 'English dead'] for a thousand years. . . . If blood be the price of admiralty, / Lord God, we ha' paid in full!" Here, in order, is the last stanza of "We Have Fed You All a Thousand Years," the first stanza of "Workers of the World Awaken," and the last stanza of "The Rebel Girl":

> We have fed you all for a thousand years—
> For that was our doom, you know,
> From the days when you chained us in your fields
> To the strike of a week ago.
> You have taken our lives, and our babies and wives,
> And we're told it's your legal share;
> But if blood be the price of your lawful wealth
> Good God! We have bought it fair.
>
> Workers of the world, awaken!
> Break your chains, demand your rights.
> All the wealth you make is taken
> By exploiting parasites
> Shall you kneel in deep submission
> From your cradles to your graves?
> Is the height of your ambition
> To be good and willing slaves?
>
> Yes, her hands may be harden'd from labor
> And her dress may not be very fine;
> But a heart in her bosom is beating
> That is true to her class and kind.
> And the grafters in terror are trembling
> When her spite and defiance she'll hurl.
> For the only and Thoroughbred Lady
> Is the Rebel Girl.

All three songs are included in the current edition of the *Little Red Song Book*. Hill wrote "The Rebel Girl" from prison in 1915. On the issue of women's roles in the IWW see Ann Schofield's "Rebel Girls and Union Maids: The Woman Question in the Journals of the AFL and IWW, 1905–1920," *Feminist Studies* 9:2 (Summer 1983), 335–58. Schofield's last paragraph merits quoting here: "The IWW, too, exhibited sexist and paternalistic behavior, and Wobbly journals, like those of the AFL and its affiliates, mirrored predominant cultural attitudes toward women. Yet, the Wobblies, at least theoretically, did go one step further than any other labor organization in their view of women. The Rebel Girl, whether worker or wife of worker, was an activist in, rather than an auxiliary to, the One Big Union. In the words of Joe Hill, 'For it's great to fight for freedom with a Rebel Girl.' "

Nonetheless, the juxtaposition of the covers to two IWW song sheets, "We Have Fed You All a Thousand Years" (fig. 15) and "The Rebel Girl" (fig. 16), does suggest how sexual difference plays itself out in much of the political art of the period and certainly in a number of the illustrations in *Repression and Recovery*. Where conventional physical force or the physical power of the revolutionary worker is at issue, it is usually imaged in a male. Thus it is a male worker who breaks his chains in the cover to "We Have Fed You All a Thousand Years." On the other hand, the woman on the cover of "The Rebel Girl" does suggest an alternative kind of power: power as determined presence, as example, as witness. Some political illustrations, such as Hugo Gellert's final drawing for Stanley Kimmel's *The Kingdom of Smoke* (fig. 27) and Joe Jones's cover for Langston Hughes's *A New Song* (fig. 33), treat men and women more or less even-handedly.

166. See Benjamin Harshaw and Barbara Harshaw, eds., *American Yiddish Poetry: A Bilingual Anthology* (Berkeley: University of California Press, 1986) and Irving Howe and Eliezer Greenberg, eds., *A Treasury of Yiddish Poetry* (New York: Holt, Rinehart and Winston, 1969). Both books have valuable introductions.

167. A prose translation of some of Rosenfeld's poems, *Songs From the Ghetto*, appeared in 1898. For a more recent collection and a useful introductory essay see Itche Goldberg and Max Rosenfeld, eds., *Morris Rosenfeld: Selections from His Poetry and Prose* (New York: Yiddisher Kultur Farband, 1964).

168. In his 1937 *A Long Way from Home* McKay characterized his resignation from the *Liberator* primarily in aesthetic terms, suggesting that Gold wanted to turn the magazine into "a popular proletarian magazine, printing doggerel from lumberjacks and stevedores and true revelations from chambermaids." He approved of getting work from "the forgotten members of the working class," but not indiscriminately (pp. 139–40). Wayne F. Cooper's very fine chapter "With the *Liberator*, 1921–1922" in his biography of McKay, however, establishes that the problems went deeper. As Cooper writes, "McKay's position as a black man vitally concerned with pushing forward a black radical perspective on a predominantly white journal created for him problems that figured prominently as an unspoken though underlying reason for his willingness to leave the *Liberator* in June, 1922," *Claude McKay: Rebel Sojourner in the Harlem Renaissance*, p. 162.

169. See Lippmann's comments on Reed in the December 26, 1914, issue of *The New Republic*, p. 15.

170. Sol Funaroff, "An American Worker," in *We Gather Strength* (Liberal Press, 1933), pp. 49–50. Funaroff's two volumes of poetry are *The Spider and the Clock* (New York: International Publishers, 1938) and *Exile From a Future Time: Posthumous Poems of Sol Funaroff* (New York: Dynamo, 1943). The first section of *Exile From a Future Time* includes several songs from Funaroff's musical in black dialect, *Tough Scufflin'*. A section of prose poems was assembled by the editor from unfinished poetry manuscripts. Several brief reminiscences about Funaroff open the book. Funaroff was the editor of *Dynamo* and of the Dynamo Poets series. He served as poetry editor for *New Masses* in 1933 and *Partisan Review* in 1934. Always ill, he died when he was thirty-one; the title of his posthumous collection is taken from these lines in "The Bellbuoy," the opening poem of *The Spider and the Clock*:

> I am that exile
> from a future time,
> from shores of freedom
> I may never know

For comments on Funaroff's poetry see Estelle Gershgoren Novak, "The Dynamo School of Poets," *Contemporary Literature* 21:4 (1970), 526–39, and Dave Murray, "Poetry and Power," in Ickstadt et al., *The Thirties*.

171. Joseph Hoffman's first Hagglund pamphlet, *Let Them Eat Cake!*, was also published in 1938, though he used "Joe" as his first name on that booklet. Also see his *As the Thunder and Lightning* (1944), published in Albany, Wisconsin, with a preface by Lucia Trent and an introduction by Don West, and his *New Psalms for Old Wounds, and Selected Poems* (Boston: B. Humphries, 1948).

172. Taggard, *Calling Western Union*, pp. 50–53. Cf. the conclusion of Taggard's preface to the book, after her description of living on a farm in Vermont:

> Two years later. 1936. Now as my book goes to press I must say in the clearest and simplest manner possible that I was wrong about Vermont. At first it looked to me the way it looks to the summer visitor who goes up there to get a rest. And then the facts contradicted my hope. I saw canned wood-chuck in the farmers' cellars. I saw slums in Brattleboro and Burlington. I knew children who picked ferns for a few cents a day. I knew a man who worked in a furniture factory for ten cents an hour! I saw his starved wife and children. Slow starvation gives children starry eyes and delicate faces. I saw five men who were a few weeks ago sentenced to jail for their activity in the Vermont Marble Strike. I saw a voucher for two cents one worker got for a week's wages, all that was left after the company deducted for rent and light. I saw a pile of such vouchers. When

they eat, the quarry workers eat potatoes and turnips. . . . In Rutland County the Overseer of the Poor is a Marble Company official.

And so I say I was wrong about Vermont. The poems in this book were written after I began to see why. (pp xxxi-ii)

173. Rolfe, "The 100 Percenter," *The Daily Worker*, September 22, 1928, p. 6. Retitled "Asbestos" as the opening poem in Rolfe's section of *We Gather Strength* (New York: Liberal Press, 1933), p. 28, but nonetheless dated as 1928 in that volume.

174. Samuel Aaron De Witt was among five socialists elected to the New York State legislature in 1919. When they tried to take their seats in January of the next year, the assembly erupted in protest and the five were barred. *New York Times* headlines ranged from "Legislators Move to Bar Socialist Ballots Until They Stand for Americanism" to "Sweet Tells Them They Were Elected on Platform Inimical to State and Country." A special election was eventually held in September 1920, but all five won again, this time with even larger margins. This time De Witt and one other were seated, but the other three were expelled. "De Witt and Orr Declare Assembly Majority is Un-American and Refuse Seats," the headline then read. The following month De Witt was arrested for accepting campaign funds at a large rally without recording the names of each of the contributors.

175. Lucia Trent and Ralph Cheyney, eds., *America Arraigned* (New York: Dean & Company, 1928).

176. Robert Gessner, *Upsurge* (New York: Farrar & Rinehart, 1933), p. 40. Cf. Allen Ginsberg's line "America Sacco & Vanzetti must not die" in his 1956 poem "America," *Collected Poems: 1947–1980* (New York: Harper & Row, 1984), p. 147.

177. See Marcus Graham, ed., *An Anthology of Revolutionary Poetry*, introduction by Ralph Cheyney and Lucia Trent (New York: Active Press, 1929). Marcus Graham was the pseudonym of Shmuel Marcus. For related collections see Thomas Curtis Clark, *Poems of Justice* (Chicago and New York: Willett, Clark & Colby, 1929) and William Rose Benét and Norman Cousins, *The Poetry of Freedom* (New York: Random House, 1945).

178. Some publications on the left regularly devoted space to placing themselves in a tradition of American political writing. The claim was typically that they were the true inheritors of these traditions, but such essays also had the effect of acquainting readers with earlier political writing of which they were often wholly unfamiliar. Alan Calmer wrote in *New Masses* of the American traditions of labor poetry and of the political poetry published by the Wobblies. *The Daily Worker* carried feature articles on a number of earlier American writers who wrote on political subjects: from Philip Freneau and John Greenleaf Whittier to Walt Whitman and Joe Hill.

179. Michael Gold, "Introduction," *We Gather Strength*, pp. 7–9.

180. Edwin Rolfe, "Credo," *We Gather Strength*, p. 40, where it is dated 1931. Reprinted in Rolfe, *To My Contemporaries*, p. 11.

181. Stanley Burnshaw, "Dilemma of a Dead Man About to Wake Up," *The Iron Land* (Philadelphia: Centaur Press, 1936), p. 76; Joseph Kalar, "Papermill," *We Gather Strength*, p. 31; Sol Funaroff, "Unemployed: 2 A. M.," *The Spider and the Clock*, p. 15; Kalar, "Invocation to the Wind," *We Gather Strength*, p. 30; Burnshaw, "I, Jim Rogers" (line repeated in a poem identified as based on a case history and "retold for reciting before mass audiences"), *The Iron Land*, p. 100; Fearing, "Denouement," *Poems*, p. 62.

Stanley Burnshaw was an editor of *New Masses* and from 1939–1958 was in charge of the Dryden Press. For the next ten years he was a vice president at Holt, Rinehart and Winston. *The Iron Land* is his most famous book of political poetry, but he is also widely known for several volumes of criticism.

Joseph Kalar worked in the lumber and papermill industries and then became active in union activities and the political efforts of the Farm Labor Party of Minnesota. From 1928–1930 he travelled across the country taking odd jobs and reporting to *New Masses* on conditions everywhere he went. In addition to poetry, he published fiction and a particularly savage brand of cultural satire.

182. Sol Funaroff, "Dusk of the Gods," *The Spider and the Clock*, p. 48.

183. Edwin Rolfe, "Season of Death," *To My Contemporaries*, p. 54.

184. Genevieve Taggard, "A Middle-aged Middle-class Woman at Midnight," *Collected Poems 1918–1938*, p. 69; Ettore Rella, "Hieroglyphs," in Salzman, *Social Writings of the 1930s*, p. 213; Joseph Freeman, from "Six Poems," *Dynamo: A Journal of Revolutionary Poetry*, 1:1 (January 1934), 8–12; Herman Spector, "Outcast," *We Gather Strength*, p. 20.

Ettore Rella published poetry in *This Quarter, Fifth Story Window, Contempo*, and *Partisan Review and Anvil* during the 1930s. *Here and Now*, a collection of his poems, was brought out by his friends while he was serving in the Pacific during the Second World War. Later collections include *Spring Song on an Old Theme* (Trident Press, 1966) and *The Scenery for a Play and Other Poems* (New York: George Braziller, 1981). He is also the author of several plays in verse. The first of these, *Please Communicate*, was produced by the San Francisco Theatre Union in 1939. *Sign of Winter* and *The Place Where We Were Born* were produced off-Broadway in New York.

Joseph Freeman, born in the Ukraine in 1897 and a resident of the United States from 1904 until his death in 1961, was one of the more visible figures of the left in the 1920s and 1930s. An editor of the *Liberator*, he also helped to found *New Masses*. His poetry regularly appeared in journals, but it was never collected in a book. Freeman's most famous book is his political autobiography *An American Testament: A Narrative of Rebels and Romantics* (New York: Farrar and Rinehart, 1936).

185. Sol Funaroff, "The Spider and the Clock," *The Spider and the Clock*, p. 59.

186. Richard Wright, "I Have Seen Black Hands." First published in the June 26, 1934, issue of *New Masses*.

187. Gessner, *Upsurge*, p. 1.

188. Kenneth Patchen, "A Letter to a Policeman in Kansas City," *Before the Brave* (New York: Random House, 1936), p. 35.

189. Gregory, "Dempsey, Dempsey," *Poems 1930–1940* (New York: Harcourt, 1941), p. 21. Included in his 1930 collection *Chelsea Rooming House*, Gregory's "Dempsey, Dempsey" was also reprinted in *Proletarian Literature in the United States*.

190. Joseph Freeman, "Beat, Drums of the World," *The Daily Worker*, February 10, 1934, p. 9.

191. Jarrboe, *The Unknown Soldier Speaks* (Holt, Minn.: B. C. Hagglund, 1932), p. 12.

192. In his foreword to *Lenin Lives*, Jack Conroy writes "So many of Weiss' poems have appeared in obscure and long dead periodicals that it has been impossible to present more than a sketchy representation of his work; and this compilation is one that extends over a number of years." Weiss's first pamphlet was *The Shame of California and Other Poems* (Chicago: General Defense Committee, n.d.); it includes poems about IWW prisoners, the California Syndicalist trials, and the San Pedro strike of 1924. The February 1934 issue of *The Partisan* includes Weiss's review of another of the Rebel Poet booklets, *When the Sirens Blow* by Leonard Spier: "Here is the authentic discharge of a poetic cannoner arousing courage and enthusiasm in the ranks of toil, hurling broadsides of militant defiance at the entrenched camp of reaction and greed. Spier knows how to shoot. . . . Don't look for approbation of the poems of Leonard Spier in the enemy's camp: you won't find it there. Poems written for workers have only one audience, the Working class" (p. 7). Describing him as "a migratory worker poet," *New Masses* published Weiss's autobiographical anecdote, "A Lousy Job," in its November 1928 issue, and his manifesto, "Poetry and Revolution," in its October 1929 issue. In that statement, and in a follow-up letter to the editor in the May 1930 issue, he argues against publishing political poetry too obscure to be read by working-class people. Sandburg, he notes, demonstrated that free verse could be adapted to political subjects and to a wide audience. Like the other Rebel Poets, Weiss's life is now difficult to flesh out in much detail. He did, however, continue to publish poetry in the 1940s in *The Daily Worker* and *The Span*. The only essay I have seen on Weiss is Tim Hall's "Henry George Weiss, Rebel Poet," *Struggle* 1:1 (June 1985), 21–25.

John C. Rogers published poetry and short stories regularly in the 1930s. His block prints illustrate a number of politically oriented journals and pamphlets and were occasionally exhibited. See, for example, his cover design for the first issue of *Hinterland* and his repeated appearances in *The Rebel Poet*. The contributor's notes to *Folk-Say IV* (1932) and *Hinterland* read as follows: "John C. Rogers was born in Alexandria, Virginia, February 11, 1907. He has been railway clerk, telephone installer, brick factory clerk, tree surgeon, art gallery guard, commercial art student, amateur photographer, and free-lance artist and writer." "John C. Rogers plans to go back soon to his native Blue Ridge mountains where he feels at home. There he will continue his block-cutting, painting, and writing."

193. Henry George Weiss, "If," *Lenin Lives* (Holt, Minn.: B. C. Hagglund, 1935), p. 10.

194. Manuel Gomez's little anthology *Poems for Workers* (Chicago: Daily Worker Publishing, n.d.) includes: "The Song of the Classes" by Ernest Jones, "We Have Fed You All For a Thousand Years" (also issued as a song sheet by the IWW), "A Woman's Execution" by Edward King, "The Legacy" by James Connolly, " 'Gunmen' in West Virginia" by a Paint Creek miner, "God to Hungry Child" by Langston Hughes, "Pittsburgh" and "Bread and Roses" by James Oppenheim, "Bellies," "Statistics," "Canned," and "An Administration Delegate Reports" by Jim Waters, "When the Cock Crows" by Arturo Giovannitti, "Caliban in the Coal Mines" by Louis Untermeyer, "Spring in New Hampshire" by Claude McKay, "I.W.W." by Donald M. Crocker, "Wheatland—A Memory" by Miriam Allen Ford, "Mourn Not the Dead," "To France," and "The Red Guard" by Ralph Chaplin, "John Reed's Body" by Michael Gold, "Nobody Knows" by Edward Connor, "Muckers," "Graceland," "Anna Imroth," and "I am the People, the Mob" by Carl Sandburg, "In Trafalgar Square" by Francis W. L. Adams, "Slaves" by Joseph Freeman, "Night on the Convoy" and "Swear You'll Never Forget" by Sigfried Sassoon, "Cry of the People" by John G. Neihardt, "Out from Siberia" by Alice Corbin, and "The Five-Point Star" by J. S. Wallace. The illustrations on the front and back covers were also used separately on either the front or back of several (but not all) of the other booklets in the *Little Red Library*. Other titles in the series include *Principles of Communism* by Frederick Engels, *The Damned Agitator and Other Stories* by Michael Gold, and *Worker Correspondence* by Wm. F. Dunne.

195. Isidor Schneider, *Comrade: Mister* (New York: Equinox Cooperative Press, 1934), with two pen drawings by Gyula Zilner. The book is unpaginated, but Schneider's essay "Toward Revolutionary Poetry" occurs about midway through the book. Schneider's earlier collection was *The Temptation of Anthony and Other Poems* (New York: Boni and Liveright, 1928). Born in the Ukraine, Schneider arrived in the United States in 1901. He is well-known in particular for his essay "Proletarian Poetry" in Henry Hart, ed., *American Writers' Congress* (New York: International Publishers, 1935) and for his numerous reviews and essays in *New Masses*. His novels include

Dr. Transit (1926), *From the Kingdom of Necessity* (1935), and *The Judas Time* (1947).

196. All books on the Communist Party have fairly clear points of view. Irving Howe and Lewis Coser's *The American Communist Party: A Critical History, 1919–1957* (Cambridge: Harvard University Press, 1957) was for a long time the only standard book to cover the 1930s. It may now be supplemented by Harvey Klehr's well-documented but rather cynical *The Heyday of American Communism: The Depression Decade* (New York: Basic Books, 1984). Lawrence H. Schwartz's *Marxism and Culture: The CPUSA and Aesthetics in the 1930s* (Port Washington, N.Y.: Kennikat Press, 1980) is particularly important in this context because he argues—more strongly than anyone has before—that the CPUSA often failed to follow the Soviet line accurately in the 1930s, frequently despite their intentions to follow Comintern orders. Most informed writers acknowledge that CPUSA spokespeople often gave an American populist slant to Comintern directives, but Schwartz takes this argument much further, thereby making it necessary to abandon the assumption that Communist Party cultural initiatives here matched Moscow's aims in all respects.

197. For accounts of the John Reed Clubs see especially Richard Wright's essay in Richard Crossman, ed., *The God That Failed; Six Studies in Communism* (1950), Daniel Aaron's *Writers on the Left*, and Eric Homberger's *American Writers and Radical Politics*. The Clubs were no doubt eliminated in part because they had been contaminated by their association with a more antagonistic class politics. Moreover, as support and discussion groups for new writers, they were of little value in pursuing the party's new priority of reaching out to left-leaning writers with high visibility.

198. Seymour G. Link and Kenneth W. Porter, "Introduction," *Banners of Brotherhood*, ed. Ralph Cheyney (North Montpelier, Vt.: Driftwind Press, 1933), pp. 4–5. Link and Porter were the general editors of the Driftwind Chapbooks, of which this is no. 2.

199. On the anti-Stalinist left, see Alan M. Wald, *The New York Intellectuals: The Rise and Decline of the Anti-Stalinist Left from the 1930s to the 1980s* (Chapel Hill: University of North Carolina Press, 1987). *Partisan Review* is the most thoroughly discussed of all the political journals of the period. See James B. Gilbert, *Writers and Partisans: A History of Literary Radicalism in America* (New York: Wiley, 1968) and Terry A. Cooney, *The Rise of the New York Intellectuals*: Partisan Review *and Its Circle, 1934–1945* (Madison: University of Wisconsin Press, 1986).

200. On this point see Klehr, *The Heyday of American Communism*.

201. The high point of intellectuals' period of support for the party was perhaps the publication of the 1932 pamphlet *Culture and the Crisis*. Subtitled "An open letter to the writers, artists, teachers, physicians, engineers,

scientists, and other professional workers of America," it analyzed the economy, attacked the Democratic, Republican, and Socialist parties, and urged
people to vote Communist in the 1932 elections. It was signed by fifty-two
people, including Sherwood Anderson, Malcolm Cowley, Countee Cullen,
John Dos Passos, Langston Hughes, and Edmund Wilson.

202. In "Poetry and Power" in Ickstadt et al., *The Thirties*, Dave Murray
observes that MacLeish's "volumes of poetry in the 30s constantly tried
to forge a Popular Front all of its own." He adds that in MacLeish's work
"we find an uncertain vacillation between a holding-out against the mass,
the keeping of individual volition, and an almost voluptuous surrender to
movement and power" (pp. 211–12).

203. Mike Gold's "fascist unconscious" piece on MacLeish appeared in
the July 26, 1933, issue of the *New Republic*. Burnshaw's negative review of
MacLeish appeared in the July 31, 1934, issue of *New Masses*, his positive
commentary in the April 30, 1935, issue. "Der Schone Archibald," a review
by Margaret Wright, was published in the January 16, 1934, *New Masses*.
Isidor Schneider's review of *Public Speech* appeared in the March 24, 1936,
issue of *New Masses*. MacLeish's "The German Girls! The German Girls!"
and "Speech to Those Who Say Comrade" were published, respectively, in
the December 17, 1935, and February 11, 1936, issues of *New Masses*.

204. Philip Rahv's "Proletarian Literature: A Political Autopsy" is reprinted in his *Literature and the Sixth Sense* (Boston: Houghton Mifflin,
1970). "Within the brief space of a few years," Rahv writes, "the term 'proletarian literature' was transformed into a euphemism for a Communist party
literature which tenaciously upheld a fanatical faith identifying the party
with the working class, Stalinism with Marxism, and the Soviet Union with
socialism." The declared program, he points out appeared to be straightforward: "*the writer should ally himself with the working class and recognize
the class struggle as the central fact of modern life.* Beyond that he was
promised the freedom to choose his own subjects, deal with any characters,
and work in any style he pleased." The reality was rather different: "The
principle mystification involved in this transaction consisted of the fact that
while the writer thought he was allying himself with the working class,
in reality he was surrendering his independence to the Communist party,"
which thereby "succeeded in stuffing the creativity of the Left into the sack
of political orthodoxy . . . an international literature was created whose main
service was the carrying out of party assignments" (pp. 9–11).

The virulence of Rahv's anticommunism here, it should be noted, perfectly matches the uncompromising rhetoric of his earlier communism. See
especially his "An Open Letter to Young Writers," *The Rebel Poet* No. 16
(September 1932), 3–4, in which he argues that "we must sever all ideological ties with this lunatic civilization known as capitalism." Writers have no
real choice: "If a writer wants to retain his hold on reality . . . he must align

himself with the forces of revolution." The "world proletariat is preparing to rise and seize the political power from the infirm hands of the tottering money-grubbers." If a writer resists this commitment, "he is certain to evolve into an innocuous little libido-teaser, a producer of aphrodisiacs for the nearly impotent and soporifics for the wholly impotent."

Both positions, I would argue, are grotesquely overstated. The diverse literature of the period could never become a mere tool for party policy. To demand unqualified or universal commitment to one political vision is to misrepresent and misunderstand the varied social functions that literature can and did serve.

205. See Alan Calmer, ed., *Salud!—Poems, Stories and Sketches of Spain by American Writers* (New York: International Publishers, 1938).

206. Joy Davidman, ed., *War Poems of the United Nations* (New York: Dial Press, 1943). Sponsored by the League of American Writers. The title page describes the collection as "Three hundred poems—one hundred and fifty poets from twenty countries."

207. These passages are quoted from Thomas Yoseloff, ed., *Seven Poets in Search of an Answer: A Poetic Symposium* (New York: Bernard Ackerman, 1944). The seven poets are Maxwell Bodenheim, Joy Davidman, Langston Hughes, Aaron Kramer, Alfred Kreymborg, Martha Millet, and Norman Rosten.

208. See, for example, Olga Cabral, *Cities and Deserts* (1959); Alfred Hayes, *The Big Time* (1944); Aaron Kramer, *Till the Grass Is Ripe for Dancing* (1943), *The Glass Mountain* (1946), *The Thunder of the Grass* (1948), *Denmark Vesey* (1952), *Roll the Forbidden Drums!* (1954), and *The Tune of the Calliope* (1958); Ruth Lechlitner, *Only The Years: Selected Poems 1938–1944* (1944); Thomas McGrath, *First Manifesto* (1940), *The Dialectics of Love* (1944), *To Walk a Crooked Mile* (1947), *Longshot O'Leary's Garland of Practical Posie* (1949), *Witness to the Times* (1954), and *Figures from a Double World* (1955); Norman Rosten, *Return Again, Traveler* (1940), *The Fourth Decade* (1943), *The Big Road* (1946), *Songs for Patricia* (1951), and *The Plane and the Shadow* (1953); Melvin B. Tolson, *Rendezvous with America* (1944) and *Libretto for the Republic of Liberia* (1953).

209. Hoffman, "Sit Down," *Let Them Eat Cake!* (Holt, Minn.: B. C. Hagglund), p. 4.

210. Baley, "For All Who Hate Hitler," *Hand Grenades* (Los Angeles: Mercury, 1942), p. 3; Blair, *The Ashes of Six Million Jews* (Milwaukee, 1946), pp. 8–9. Blair, born in 1906, was Chairman of the Communist Party of Wisconsin at the time *The Ashes of Six Million Jews* was published. Blair was a labor organizer in the 1930s when mimeographed copies of his poems and songs were distributed in labor circles.

211. It may be useful to push my analysis of the illogical nature of the established ways of rejecting proletarian literature somewhat further. If a

particular perspective has no realistic possibility of achieving hegemony in the social formation—or if, on the other hand, we are dealing with the past and can see that a perspective did not in the end win out over (or incorporate) all others and become the dominant vision of reality—then it makes little sense to limit our engagement with it to the following strategies: continuing merely to advocate or contest its truth claims; persisting in a partisan celebration of its cultural failure; or judging its entire cultural meaning in terms of its success or failure at establishing its permanent influence.

212. The standard history of the fugitives is Louise Cowan, *The Fugitive Group* (Baton Rouge: Louisiana State University Press, 1959). Although Cowan's book remains useful and informative, it needs to be supplemented with more sophisticated readings of the political and ideological issues at stake. I have found Daniel Joseph Singal's *The War Within: From Victorian to Modernist Thought in the South, 1919–1945* (Chapel Hill: University of North Carolina Press, 1982) to be particularly helpful and convincing. Our current reconstruction of this period also shows little awareness either of the level of controversy that surrounded the Fugitive group at the time or of the other alternative political configurations available in the South in the 1930s. For the contemporary controversies see, for example, William Knickerbocker, "The Dilemma of the Fugitives," *Contempo* 2:2 (May 25, 1932), 1–2. Under the same title, "The Dilemma of the Fugitives," Knickerbocker and Maristan Chapman then write opposing articles in *Contempo* 2:7 (September 25, 1932). Also see R. P. Blackmur's important attack on the fugitives, "The Psyche of the South." Originally published by Tryon Pamphlets, North Carolina, in 1934, it is reprinted in James T. Jones, ed., *Outsider at the Heart of Things: The Uncollected Essays of R. P. Blackmur* (Urbana: University of Illinois Press, 1988). Neither the Knickerbocker nor the Blackmur pieces are cited in Cowan's book. Nor, more predictably, is notice taken of Don West's poem "They Take Their Stand (For some professional Agrarians)" from his *Clods of Southern Earth* (New York: Boni and Gaer, 1946). "Some poets live in Dixie Land," West writes,

> Turning the wheels of history back
> For murder, lynch, and iron hand
>   To drive the Negro from his shack.

> They never delve in politics,
>   That's all too commonplace, they say.
> Their thoughts must go to subtle tricks
> Befitting noble gents like they.   (p. 29)

West was a preacher and activist in the largely forgotten Marxist (or Marxist-influenced) south of the 1930s. His first collection of poems was *Crab-grass* (Nashville, Tenn.: Art Print Shop, 1931), followed by a pamphlet titled *Be-*

tween the Plow Handles (Monteagle, Tenn.: Highlander Folk School, 1932).
Also see his *Broadside to the Sun* (New York: W. W. Norton, 1946); *Toil and Hunger* (San Benito, Texas: Hagglund, 1940); *The Road is Rocky* (New York: New Christian, 1951); and *O Mountaineers!* (Huntington, W.Va.: Appalachian, 1974).

213. Allen Tate, "Ode to the Confederate Dead," *Collected Poems 1919–1976* (New York: Farrar, Straus & Giroux, 1977), pp. 20–23; Donald Davidson, "Lee in the Mountains," *Lee in the Mountains and Other Poems* (New York: Charles Scribner's Sons, 1949), pp. 3–7. John Gould Fletcher's statement in praise of Davidson fills the back jacket of the book.

214. "The Cloak Model" appears in Ransom's *Poems About God* (New York: Henry Holt, 1919) and in his *Grace After Meat* (London: Hogarth Press, 1924). See Thomas Daniel Young, *John Crowe Ransom: An Annotated Bibliography* (New York: Garland Publishing, 1982) for a detailed list of primary and secondary materials.

In *The Burden of Time: The Fugitives and Agrarians* (Princeton: Princeton University Press, 1965) John L. Stewart quotes a previously unpublished letter to Tate in which Ransom notes that Poe succeeds well at applying the principle of "the lovely woman seen dead" (p. 224). Ransom's most notorious comments on women, however, are in his essay on Edna St. Vincent Millay, "The Poet as Woman." Originally published in *The Southern Review* in 1937, Ransom felt sufficiently committed to the piece to reprint it the next year in *The World's Body* (New York: Charles Scribner's Sons). Here is the opening of his third paragraph:

> She is also a woman. No poet ever registered herself more deliberately in that light. She therefore fascinates the male reviewer but at the same time horrifies him a little too. He will probably swing between attachment and antipathy, which may be the very attitudes provoked in him by generic woman in the flesh, as well as by the literary remains of Emily Dickinson, Elizabeth Barrett, Christina Rossetti, and doubtless, if we only had enough of her, Sappho herself. . . . A woman lives for love, if we will but project that term to cover all her tender fixations upon natural objects of sense. . . . Her devotion to them is more than gallant, it is fierce and importunate, and cannot but be exemplary to the hardened male observer. He understands it, from his 'recollections of early childhood,' or at least of youth, but he has lapsed from it; or rather, in the best case, he has pursued another line of development. The minds of man and woman grow apart. . . . man, at best, is an intellectualized woman.

So, there is something to be learned from these creatures, but they are finally inferior beings. Their poetry, he goes on to say, suffers from the same limitations. Ransom's own poetry, I would argue, needs to be reread in the context of his struggle with sexual difference. One of the best readings of Ransom's sometimes tortured language is in Albert Gelpi, *A Coherent Splendor: The American Poetic Renaissance, 1910–1950* (Cambridge: Cambridge University Press, 1987). Gelpi recognizes the prevalance of sexual tension in Ransom's work but is inhibited by his naturalizing of these tensions as Jungian archetypes and by his own unquestioning commitment to the virtue of transcendence.

215. Bob Brown's career is in many ways as diverse and open-ended as his picture poems might lead us to expect. In addition to *1450–1950*, first published by Black Sun Press in 1929 and later reprinted in a slightly enlarged edition by Jargon Books in 1959—the title celebrates five hundred years of moveable type—his poetry includes *My Marjonary* (Boston: Luce, 1916), *The Readies* (Bad-Ems: Roving Eye Press, 1930), *Globe-Gliding* (Diessen: Roving Eye Press, 1930), *Words* (Paris: Hours Press, 1931), *Demonics* (Cagnes-sur-Mer: Roving Eye Press, 1931), and *Nomadness* (New York: Dodd, Mead, 1931). Also essential is his anthology *Readies for Bob Brown's Machine* (Cagnes-sur-Mer: Roving Eye Press, 1931), which is one of the most remarkable collaborative projects in the history of modernism. It is a collection of texts for Brown's hypothetical Reading Machine, a device that would pass words in sequence before the reader's eye at whatever rate one chooses. Punctuation would be minimal. Brown's appendix to *Readies for Bob Brown's Machine* presents his ideas in detail. Alternatively, the following passage, excerpted from a 300-word statement reduced to fit into a 1¼ by 1⅝ inch space at the beginning of *1450–1950*, gives a condensed version:

> Without any whir or splutter writing will be readable at the speed of the day—1929—not 1450; it will run on forever before the eye without having to be cut up into columns, pars & etc.; not risking the wetting of a single finger to turn a clumsy page—on forever in-a-single-line-I-see-1450 -invention-movable-type-Gutenberg-Wynkyn-de-Worde-Jimmy-the-Ink-Caxton-through-Chinese-centuries- . . . Shakespeare -bending-over-a-work-bench-making-my-language-laboriously- like-a-bellowing-blacksmith . . . Print-in-action-at-last -moveable-type-at-full-gallop . . .

In addition to his experimental work, however, Brown had some notable early successes as a writer of popular fiction: *What Happened to Mary* (1913) and *The Remarkable Adventures of Christopher Poe* (1913). He also wrote popular nonfiction, including *Let There Be Beer!* (1932) and *The Complete Book of Cheese* (1955). For further information, see Joseph M. Flora, "Bob Brown," in Karen Lane Rood, ed. *American Writers in Paris, 1920–1939, Dictionary of Literary Biography*, vol. 4. See also Guillaume Apollinaire, *Calligrammes* (Berkeley: University of California Press, 1980). This bilingual edition includes extensive notes by Anne Hyde Greet and S. I. Lockerbie.

216. Crane, *The Complete Poems and Selected Letters and Prose*, ed. Brom Weber (Garden City, N.Y.: Doubleday, 1966), pp. 69, 64, and 114.

217. Eugene Jolas, "Firedeath," *I Have Seen Monsters and Angels*, pp. 124–25. For a history of *transition*, see Dougald McMillan, *transition: The History of a Literary Era, 1927–1938* (New York: Braziller, 1976).

218. Crosby, "Sun Rhapsody," "Neant," "Q.E.D.," *Chariot of the Sun* (Paris: Black Sun, 1931), pp. 12, 25, 38.

219. Crosby, "Photoheliograph," *Chariot of the Sun*, p. 26.

220. Harry Crosby's volumes of poetry remain both rare and out of print. The four volumes published posthumously by Black Sun Press in 1931 are: *Chariot of the Sun, Transit of Venus, Sleeping Together*, and *Torchbearer*, with introductions, respectively, by D. H. Lawrence, T. S. Eliot, Stuart Gilbert, and Ezra Pound. The several small volumes of his diaries remain even rarer, but they have been reprinted as *Shadows of the Sun: The Diaries of Harry Crosby*, ed. Edward Germain (Santa Barbara, Calif.: Black Sparrow Press, 1977). For further information see Sy M. Kahn and Karen L. Rood, "Harry Crosby and Caresse Crosby," in Rood, ed., *American Writers in Paris, 1920–1939* and Geoffrey Wolf, *Black Sun: The Brief Transit and Violent Eclipse of Harry Crosby* (New York: Random House, 1976). Although Crosby is now almost exclusively identified with an apolitical experimental modernism, his identity was more contested during his life. His radical rejection of conventional American values, for example, gave his work definite appeal on the left. See those of his poems anthologized in Ralph Cheyney and Jack Conroy, eds., *Unrest: The Rebel Poets' Anthology for 1929* (London: Arthur H. Stockwell, 1929) and *Unrest: The Rebel Poets' Anthology for 1930* (London: Braithwaite and Miller, 1930).

221. On the political meaning of Zukofsky's work, see Burton Hatlen, "Art and/as Labor: Some Dialectical Patterns in 'A'-1 through 'A'-10," *Contemporary Literature* 25 (Summer 1984), 205–34, Eric Homberger, *American Writers and Radical Politics, 1900–39*, and Eric Mottram, "1924–1951: Politics and Form in Zukofsky," *Maps*, No. 5 (1973).

222. Zukofsky, *"A"* (Berkeley: University of California Press, 1978), pp. 112–16.

223. Ridge, "Via Ignis XXVII," "Stone Face," "Crucible," *Dance of Fire* (New York: Harrison Smith and Robert Haas, 1935), pp. 44, 58, 56.

224. Laura Riding, "The Tiger," *The Poems of Laura Riding: A New Edition of the 1938 Collection* (New York: Persea Books, 1980), pp. 64–67. Although this is the most complete collection of Riding's poems, one must read more widely in her work to get a full sense of her career and her ambitions; her conscious intentions, for example, are difficult to recover without reading her criticism and manifestos. Joyce Piell Wexler's *Laura Riding: A Bibliography* (New York: Garland, 1981) is a very thorough guide to primary

and secondary materials. Wexler has also written *Laura Riding's Pursuit of Truth* (Athens: Ohio University Press, 1979), a valuable book that struggles to stay reasonably close to Riding's intentions but does not, therefore, exhaust the semiotic effects of Riding's poetry.

225. See Margaret Walker, *For My People* (New Haven: Yale University Press, 1942). Walker's more recent poetry includes three pamphlets published by Broadside Press in Detroit: *Ballad of the Free* (1966), *Prophets for a New Day* (1970), and *October Journey* (1973). She is also the author of two novels, *Come Down from Yonder Mountain* (1962) and *Jubilee* (1966), as well as a critical book, *The Daemonic Genius of Richard Wright* (1982). Of special interest is *A Poetic Equation: Conversations Between Margaret Walker and Nikki Giovanni* (Washington, D.C.: Howard University Press, 1974).

226. The single best introduction to the problematics of reading Stein's poetry that I know is Karen Ford's 1989 University of Illinois dissertation, "Moments of Brocade: The Aesthetics of Excess in American Women's Poetry." Two recent collections of Stein criticism are also particularly useful: Shirley Neuman and Ira Nadel, eds., *Gertrude Stein and the Making of Literature* (Boston: Northeastern University Press, 1988); and Michael Hoffman, ed., *Critical Essays on Gertrude Stein* (Boston: G. K. Hall, 1986). In the Hoffman collection, two essays are notable for their success at looking closely at Stein's poetry: Catherine Stimpson's "The Somograms of Gertrude Stein" and Lisa Ruddick's "A Rosy Charm: Gertrude Stein and the Repressed Feminine."

227. See Jean Toomer, *Cane* (New York: Boni & Liveright, 1923). The current reprint, *Cane* (New York: Liveright, 1975), includes an introduction by Darwin T. Turner. For those of Toomer's other writings of greatest relevance see Darwin T. Turner, ed., *The Wayward and the Seeking: A Collection of Writings by Jean Toomer* (Washington, D.C.: Howard University Press, 1982) and Robert B. Jones and Margery Toomer Latimer, eds., *The Collected Poems of Jean Toomer* (Chapel Hill: University of North Carolina Press, 1988). Also see Nellie Y. McKay, *Jean Toomer, Artist: A Study of His Literary Life and Work, 1894–1936* (Chapel Hill: University of North Carolina Press, 1984).

228. MacLeish, "Background with Revolutionaries," *Frescoes For Mr. Rockefeller's City* (New York: John Day, 1933), p. 27; "Speech to Those Who Say Comrade," *Public Speech* (New York: Farrar & Rinehart, 1936), n.p.

229. Hugo Gellert (1892–1985) was one of the most famous political artists of the period. Born in Hungary, he came to New York at the turn of the century. He studied at the National Academy of Design and contributed his first drawings to *The Masses* in 1916. He drew the cover for the first issue of *Liberator* and was on its editorial board. Later, he helped to found *New Masses* and contributed drawings to *The Daily Worker*, the *New Yorker*, and

several New York newspapers. He designed murals for a number of buildings in the 1930s, including Rockefeller Center, and in the following decade was active in Artists for Victory. See Zoltan Deak, et al. *Hugo Gellert, 1892–1985: People's Artist* (New York: Hugo Gellert Memorial Committee, 1986).

230. See the jacket to Edna St. Vincent Millay, *Make Bright the Arrows: 1940 Notebook* (New York, Harper & Brothers, 1940).

Louis Lozowick (1892–1973) was a well-known American graphic artist. Born in Russia, he made his way to the United States as a child of fourteen. After training in art schools both in Russia and here, he spent several influential years in Europe where he was attracted to cubism, futurism, dadaism, and Russian constructivism. His essays on modern art appeared regularly in *Broom, The Little Review, Nation,* and *Menorah Journal* throughout the 1920s. In 1926 he joined the editorial board of *New Masses* and in 1930 collaborated with Joseph Freeman and Joshua Kunitz in publishing *Voices of October: Art and Literature in Soviet Russia* (New York: Vanguard Press). His essays of the 1930s include "Art in the Service of the Proletariat," *Literature of the World Revolution* 4 (1931), 126–27 and "Towards a Revolutionary Art," *Art Front* (July–August 1936), 12–14. For further information on his career see Janet Flint, *The Prints of Louis Lozowick: A Catalogue Raisonné* (New York: Hudson Hills Press, 1982). The full reference for Lozowick's book jacket and frontispiece is Ralph Cheyney and Jack Conroy, eds., *Unrest: The Rebel Poet's Anthology for 1930* (London: Braithwaite and Miller, 1930).

231. See S. A. De Witt, *Rhapsodies in Red: Songs for the Social Revolution* (New York: Rand School Press, 1933). Samuel Aaron De Witt's other books include *Riding the Storm* (New York: Academy Press, c.1920); *Iron Monger* (New York: Frank Shay, 1922); *Idylls of the Ghetto* (New York: Rand Book Store, 1927); *The Shoemaker of the Stars and Other Poems* (New York: Parnassus Press, 1940); and *More Sonnets to a Dark Lady* (New York: Parnassus Press, 1942). He also published several volumes of plays. Two of the stanzas from De Witt's "Nursery Rhymes of the Five-Year Plan" in *Rhapsodies in Red* suggest what he was able to do when he was most effective:

> The ladies drive tractors
> And combines and plows . . .
> Without rings on their fingers
> Or bells on their toes. . . .
>
> Little Boy Blue, don't blow your horn,
> Until we have cows and plenty of corn,
> When we have butter and muffins and bread,
> Then little Boy Blue will be Little Boy Red.

Olga Monus's cover to Leonard Spier's second pamphlet, *You Own the Hills and Other Poems* (Philadelphia: Alpress Publishers, 1935) is even more abstract in its use of the deco style for political art. Under a seam of coal that curls up over the top of the cover like a chiseled image of a fern, two miners huddle together. Their bodies are sketched in fragments; only a lighted helmet and a pick axe are clearly defined.

232. George Jarrboe, who published in *The Rebel Poet* and *The Daily Worker*, was the pen name of a young lawyer, John Thaddeus Ackerson.

233. As Arnold Rampersad reports in *The Life of Langston Hughes, Vol. I: 1902–1941—I,Too, Sing America* (New York: Oxford University Press, 1986), it was Carl Van Vechten who arranged for Miguel Covarrubias (1904–1957) to design the jacket for *The Weary Blues*. Covarrubias was a Mexican artist who had arrived in New York in 1923. He rapidly became one of the most popular illustrators and caricaturists of the period, and his work was regularly reproduced in such magazines as *Vanity Fair* and *The New Yorker*. He did a dozen illustrations for W. C. Handy's collection *Blues: An Anthology* (New York: Boni and Liveright, 1926) and then published his own volume *Negro Drawings* (New York: Knopf, 1927). The potential cultural power of his bold, caricature-like style can also be seen in the jacket and ten illustrations he did for Taylor Gordon's autobiography *Born to Be* (New York: Covici-Friede, 1929). In the 1930s Covarrubias returned to Mexico to begin a second career as an anthropologist. For an extensive list of Covarrubias' publications in American magazines see *Index to Art Periodicals: Compiled in Ryerson Library, The Art Institute of Chicago* (Boston: G. K. Hall, 1962). For further biographical information see Virginia Stewart, *45 Contemporary Mexican Artists* (Stanford: Stanford University Press, 1951).

234. Gladys Hynes (1888–1958), who illustrated Pound's *A Draft of the Cantos XVII-XXVII* (London: John Rodker, 1928), was a British painter and sculptor. She exhibited in both London and Paris. Only 101 copies of this edition of the *Cantos* were printed.

235. *Blast* was reprinted in a facsimile edition by Black Sparrow Press in 1981. "Salutation the Third" is on page 45 of volume 1.

236. Carl Rakosi, "Foreword," *The Collected Poems of Carl Rakosi* (Orono, Maine: National Poetry Foundation, 1986), p. 17.

237. Hughes had been attacked periodically throughout his career, but the McCarthy era proved uniquely painful. As Faith Berry reports in the epilogue to *Langston Hughes: Before and Beyond Harlem* (Westport, Conn.: Lawrence Hill, 1983), Hughes had begun to be harassed at his lectures in the late 1940s. By 1950 the House Un-American Activities Committee was referring to Hughes in its documents. Hughes himself finally appeared in public before Joseph McCarthy's Subcommittee on Investigations in 1953, after testifying in closed session. Having seen the careers of many of his friends destroyed and feeling that his first responsibility was to remain a visible spokesperson for black culture, Hughes agreed to recant his earlier communism on condition that he not be forced to name names. But the

attacks did not stop. As late as 1959, an essentially obscene piece, "Langston Hughes: Malevolent Force" by Elizabeth Staples, appeared in the January issue of *American Mercury*. All this is behind the politically sanitized *Selected Poems*.

238. Most of Langston Hughes's more aggressive protest poems can be found in a number of books and pamphlets. In addition to *A New Song*, see *Scottsboro Limited* (New York: Golden Stair Press, 1932), *Shakespeare in Harlem* (New York: Alfred A. Knopf, 1942), *Jim Crow's Last Stand* (Atlanta: Negro Publication Society of America, 1943), *Montage of a Dream Deferred* (New York: Henry Holt, 1951), and *The Panther and the Lash* (New York: Alfred A. Knopf, 1967). Many of Hughes's other political poems remained uncollected until Faith Berry edited Langston Hughes, *Good Morning Revolution: Uncollected Writings of Social Protest* (New York: Lawrence Hill, 1973). Some of Hughes's poems, however, are still available only in journals or newspapers. See, for example, "Our Spring," *International Literature* 5 (1933), p. 35; "Wait," *Partisan* 1:1 (December 1933), p. 3; "Ballad of Roosevelt," *New Republic* (November 14, 1934), p. 9; "One More 'S' in the U.S.A.," *Daily Worker* (April 2, 1934); "August 19th . . . A Poem for Clarence Norris," (*Daily Worker*, 1938), reprinted in Faith Berry, *Langston Hughes: Before and Beyond Harlem*, pp. 143–46. Only some of these poems, one must add, are listed in Donald C. Dickinson's immensely useful but incomplete and occasionally inaccurate *A Bio-bibliography of Langston Hughes*, 2d ed., rev. (Hamden, Conn.: Archon Books, 1972). Furthermore, with Hughes it is especially important to see how the poems were first printed. Note the startling format of "Wait" as it appears in *Partisan*, the publication of the John Reed Club of California (fig. 51). The poem is surrounded by a circle of contextualizing names of countries, issues, historical incidents, and oppressed groups. It affirms the poem's infinite power to specify social injustices and grounds for revolution.

239. Lowell, "Preface," *Con Grande's Castle* (New York: Macmillan, 1920), p. vii.

240. See note no. 66 for details on Mina Loy's *The Last Lunar Baedeker*.

241. *FIRE!!* has been reprinted more than once, but the edition to consult—given the extreme rarity of copies of the original—is the beautiful facsimile edition (Metuchen, N.J.: The FIRE!! Press, 1982). It includes a separate pamphlet with two new essays: "Lighting FIRE!!" by Richard Bruce Nugent and "FIRE!! in Retrospect" by Thomas H. Wirth. Wirth describes Aaron Douglas's cover (fig. 28) as follows:

His magnificent cover is the opening statement of FIRE!!s themes: strength, sensitivity, and pride in heritage. One's eye first sees the lion / sphinx—ancient Africa. Circles. Chains. Anger! Then, around the edges, the profile of a young Black man appears. The circles are his earrings.

CALIFORNIA STRIKING FISHERMEN KOREA BONUS MARCHERS OXNARD
SUGAR BEET WORKERS FRESNO GRAPE PICKERS FRICK'S MINERS
PATTERSON NEW JERSEY MANCHURIA SCOTTSBORO COTTON PICKERS
INDIAN MASSES POOR FARMERS CUBA ALABAMA NEGROES CHAPEI FORD

WAIT

by Langston Hughes

PICKERS	I am the Silent One,	MEERUT
CHAPEI	Saying nothing,	HAITI
FORD	Knowing no words to write,	KOREA
STRIKERS	Feeling only the bullets	CHILD
ALABAMA	And the hunger	LABOR
NEGROES	and the stench of gas,	SUGAR
	Dying,	
CUBA	And nobody knows my name.	HAITI
UNEMPLOYED	But someday,	BONUS
	I shall raise my hand	
	And break the bonds of you	
MILLIONS	Who starve me.	KOREA
	I shall raise my heel	
MEERUT	And smash the spines of you	MEERUT
	Who shoot me.	
CHILD		CHILD
	I shall take your own guns	
LABOR	And turn them on you.	LABOR

314

SCOTTSBORO   Starting with the bankers and the bosses.   BONUS

GERMAN   Traders and missionaries   HAITI

COMMUNISTS   Who pay the militarists   KOREA

   Who pay the soldiers   SUGAR

POOR   Who back the police

   Who kill me—   CHILD

FARMERS   And break my strikes

   And crush my rising—   LABOR

BLACK   I, silently,

   And without a single learned word,   HAITI

AFRICA   Shall begin the slaughter

   That will end my hunger   BONUS

GRAPE   And your bullets

PICKERS   And the gas of capitalism   KOREA

   And make the world

JAPANESE   My own.   BLACK

CONSCRIPTS   When that is done,   HAITI

JOHANNESBURG   I will find words to speak.   SUGAR

MINERS   Wait!   MEERUT

HAITI UNEMPLOYED MILLIONS CALIFORNIA CHERRY PICKERS STRIKING MINERS ALABAMA SUGAR BEET WORKERS INDIAN MASSES SCOTTSBORO SHANGHAI COOLIES PATTERSON SUGAR BEET WORKERS COLONIAL ASIA FRICK'S MINERS CUBA POOR FARMERS JAPANESE CONSCRIPTS WORKERS JOHANNESBURG MINES CHAPEI ALABAMA NEGROES OXNARD SUGAR BEET WORKERS INDIAN MASSES BONUS MRACHERS FORD STRIKERS HAITI

51. Langston Hughes, "Wait," as published in the first issue of Partisan (December 1933), the Los Angeles magazine of the west coast John Reed Club. Hoover Institution Library, Stanford University.

315

The abstract designs on the left are his eyes, nose, and lips. These features, which in the Twenties were frequently the subject of vicious racist caricature, coalesce into a new standard of beauty. The forms are elemental and strong, but not closed. So, too, is this young Black man— symbol of his people.

For additional detailed information on *Fire!!* and on Wallace Thurman's subsequent magazine, *Harlem* (1928), see Abby Arthur Johnson and Ronald Maberry Johnson, *Propaganda and Aesthetics: The Literary Politics of Afro-American Magazines in the Twentieth Century* (Amherst: University of Massachusetts Press, 1979).

242. *The Little Magazine: A History and Bibliography* (2d ed., Princeton: Princeton University Press, 1947) by Frederick J. Hoffman, Charles Allen, and Carolyn F. Ulrich remains the single most useful source for the study of modern literary magazines. Like all reference works, however, it is not complete. It should be supplemented by Joseph Conlin, ed. *The American Radical Press, 1880–1960*, 2 vols. (Westport, Conn.: Greenwood Press, 1974), and Abby Arthur Johnson and Ronald Maberry Johnson, *Propaganda and Aesthetics: The Literary Politics of Afro-American Magazines in the Twentieth Century*. These two books provide detailed information on a number of journals omitted from *The Little Magazine* as well as more full treatment of political magazines that are covered in the earlier book. Among the numerous other publications on little magazines, special mention must be made of Elliot Anderson and Mary Kinzie, eds., *The Little Magazine in America: A Modern Documentary History* (Yonkers, N.Y.: Pushcart Press, 1978), which includes Jack Conroy writing on *The Anvil* and *The Rebel Poet* and William Phillips writing on *Partisan Review*. The study of little magazines has regrettably often aimed for an illusory factual neutrality, though there are finally signs that more critical examination of their cultural role is coming to prominence.

243. H. H. Lewis's correspondence with Edith Anderson of *The Daily Worker* is in Series 2, file 8, of the H. H. Lewis Papers at Southeast Missouri State University. This correspondence followed a long period when Lewis felt himself quite cut off from major left publications. He conducted a massive letter-writing campaign to gain access to print again, sometimes composing hundred-page letters detailing Trotskyite plots against him. His sense of isolation in Missouri combined with his failure to win support from the Guggenheim Foundation to compound his sense of being victimized. It must also be said that Lewis was an insensitive correspondent, unable to realize that people would take offense at his violent polemics when they were directed against them personally. In the October 8, 1934, issue of *The Daily Worker* Mike Gold wrote that he had received a rather nasty letter from Lewis in response to what Gold had felt was a mild, friendly criticism. The pattern was set, and it continued, as the opening paragraphs of

Anderson's September 4, 1942, letter demonstrate. She expresses regret at his "bi-weekly insults" and writes that "no matter how unpleasant you may be personally, you are still a damn good poet, and a poet our people should know."

Anderson was often quite specific in her critiques of Lewis's politics:

Just changing 'capitalism' to 'imperialism' won't do the trick. All your poems suffer from one thing—your yearning towards the Soviet Union. (June 26, 1942)

In 'Mass Movement March' you have a line, 'Your country still Muniched there.' The *country* is not Muniched. There are appeasement forces in our government, but it is not the whole government nor the whole country. . . . In your poem 'U.S.-S.R.' you cry 'Let's save her! Let's save her!" Is the point of a second front to save Russia? No. It is to save the whole of civilization. At this time we cannot rally the people to fight just to save Russia. We can only rally them to save themselves. (Aug. 1, 1942)

'Song of the Black Doll' is a lovely poem, but it does not jibe very well with the type of unity we are attempting to establish between Negroes and whites. It would appear, if we published such a poem, that we sympathized with the idea of an all-black community from which whites and white ideas would be excluded, whereas what we really want is to abolish the color line from our culture. . . . (Nov. 10, 1942)

244. Margaret Perry's generally very useful *A Bio-Bibliography of Countee P. Cullen, 1903–1946* (Westport, Conn.: Greenwood Publishing, 1971) credits the *Los Angeles Post Dispatch* of December 7, 1934, with the first publication of "Scottsboro, Too, Is Worth Its Song." Actually, the poem had by then already been published twice in *The Daily Worker*.

245. There are two excellent books on *The Masses*, which complement rather than duplicate one another: Leslie Fishbein, *Rebels in Bohemia: The Radicals of The Masses, 1911–1917* (Chapel Hill: University of North Carolina Press, 1982), and Rebecca Zurier, *Art for the Masses (1911–1917): A Radical Magazine and Its Graphics* (Philadelphia: Temple University Press, 1988).

246. Illustrated poems in *The Daily Worker* include, among others: Martin Russak, "Song of Battle," November 15, 1936, p. 7; Muriel Rukeyser, "Gauley Bridge—Silicosis Town," December 12, 1937, sec. 2, p. 5; Langston Hughes, "Addressed to Alabama," January 23, 1938, sec. 2, p. 8; and a series of Mike Quin's "Barnacle Bill" poems in the following 1937 issues: January 31, February 14, and March 7.

247. Hughes reprinted part (but not all) of "Advertisement for the Waldorf-Astoria" in *The Big Sea: An Autobiography* (1940; rpt. New York: Thunder's Mouth Press, 1986), pp. 321–23. The entire text (though not the illustration)

was finally reprinted by Faith Berry in Langston Hughes, *Good Morning Revolution: Uncollected Writings of Social Protest*. For additional comments on the poem see Faith Berry, *Langston Hughes: Before and Beyond Harlem* and Arnold Rampersad, *The Life of Langston Hughes, Vol. I: 1902–1941—I, Too, Sing America*.

248. Kurt Seligmann (1900–1962) was born in Switzerland and settled in the United States in 1939. He was known as a painter, set designer, and student of magic. Several of his paintings in the 1940s, including "Memnon and the Butterflies" (1942) and "Melusine and the Great Transparents" (1943), employ forms like those in his cover for *View*. These forms then gradually acquire limbs, so that the wrapped, tuber-like shapes become explicit human torsos. His art and prose appear in other issues of *View* as well. Also see Seligmann's illustrations for Wallace Stevens, *A Primitive Like an Orb* (New York: Gotham Book Mart, 1948).

For an analysis of *View* that sets it in the context of surrealism, see Marcel Jean, *The History of Surrealist Painting*, trans. Simon Watson Taylor (New York: Grove Press, 1960).

249. Cf. the image of workers surrounding a massive upraised fist on the front page of the June 30, 1917, issue of *Solidarity*. The clenched fist was a regular image in Soviet art in the 1930s, but its history in America predates the 1917 revolution and the 1919 founding of the CPUSA. For other related images see Philip S. Foner and Reinhard Schultz, *The Other America: Art and the Labour Movement in the United States* (West Nyack, N.Y.: Journeyman, 1985).

Cowley's "The Last International" appeared in the May 6, 1936, issue of *The New Republic*. Almost predictably, its appearance as an illustrated poem under the title "A Poem for May Day" in *The Daily Worker* is not noted in Diane U. Eisenberg's extensive *Malcolm Cowley: A Checklist of His Writings, 1916–1973* (Carbondale: Southern Illinois University Press, 1975).

250. Walter Steinhilber (1897–1983) was a New York graphic artist who for many years did editorial cartoons for the *Weekly People* and other Socialist Labor Party publications. He earned his living in the 1920s as a commercial artist, specializing in hand lettering, and later taught design at Pratt Institute. He also painted hundreds of water colors during his life. Steinhilber was several times a candidate for state and city offices on the Socialist Labor Party ticket.

251. For information about and commentary on *The Soil* see Judith Zilczer, "Robert J. Coady, Man of *The Soil*," in Rudolf E. Kuenzli, ed., *New York Dada*, and Dickran Tashjian, *Skyscraper Primitives: Dada and the American Avant-Garde*.

252. Maxwell Bodenheim, "Transfiguration," *The Soil* 1:3 (March 1917), 125.

253. See Dickran Tashjian's *Skyscraper Primitives* for an analysis of the evolution of *Broom*'s commitments to modernism.

254. Alice Halicka (c.1895–1975) was an impressionist and cubist painter who was born in Poland but lived most of her life in France. She did two covers for *Broom*.

Edward Nagle (1893–) was an American painter who, in addition to the cover reproduced here, also wrote reviews for *Broom*.

In his essay on El Lissitzky (1890–1941) that opens the catalogue for a 1987 exhibit of his work at Harvard University, Peter Nisbet begins as follows:

> To introduce El Lissitzky is to make a list: Lissitzky the architecture student in Germany before the Great War; Lissitzky the participant in the revival of Jewish culture around the time of the Russian Revolution in 1917; Lissitzky the passionate convert to geometrical abstraction and coiner of the neologistic title *Proun* for his paintings, prints, and drawings; Lissitzky in Germany in the 1920s as a bridge between Soviet and Western avant-gardes; Lissitzky as a founder of modern typography; Lissitzky as architect of visionary skyscrapers and temporary trade fairs; Lissitzky in the Soviet Union in the 1930s as trusted propagandist for the achievements of Stalinism" (p. 13).

The catalogue, *El Lissitzky* (Cambridge: Harvard University Art Museums, 1987) includes an extensive bibliography. Lissitzky's correspondence with Harold Loeb, editor of *Broom*, is at the Princeton University Library.

255. For a detailed essay on *VVV* see Dawn Ades, *Dada and Surrealism Reviewed*.

256. Jacob Burck (1907–1982) was born in Poland. He did numerous illustrations for *The Daily Worker* in the late 1920s and later joined the staff of the Chicago *Sun-Times* as an editorial cartoonist. He received the Pulitzer Prize for one of his editorial cartoons in 1940.

257. For rather persuasive evidence that feminism did not disappear in the 1930s, see Charlotte Nekola and Paula Rabinowitz, eds., *Writing Red: An Anthology of Women Writers, 1930–1940* (New York: Feminist Press, 1987). The anthology is divided into genres—fiction, poetry, and nonfiction prose—and includes introductions to each section as well as a general introduction.

258. For a concise alternative history that covers many of these events—a history that I have found useful to assign to students in American literature classes—see Howard Zinn, *A People's History of the United States* (New York: Harper & Row, 1980).

259. Morrison Isaac Swift was a prolific writer in several genres. His many pamphlets include *Anti-imperialism* (1899), *Capitalists Are the Cause of the Unemployed* (1894), and *The Evil Religion Does* (1927). His novel, *The*

Monarch Billionaire (1903) is severely critiqued in Walter Rideout's *The Radical Novel in the United States.*

260. Robinson Jeffers, "The Coast-Road," *The Selected Poetry of Robinson Jeffers* (New York: Random House, 1938), p. 581. John Elder opens his *Imagining the Earth: Poetry and the Vision of Nature* (Urbana: University of Illinois Press, 1985) with a reading of "The Coast-Road" and makes Jeffers a central part of the rest of the book. For another important reading of Jeffers see Robert Zaller, *The Cliffs of Solitude: A Reading of Robinson Jeffers* (Cambridge: Cambridge University Press, 1983).

261. Robinson Jeffers, "Staggering Back Toward Life," from the section of previously suppressed poems added to the 1977 expanded edition of *The Double Axe and Other Poems*, p. 162.

262. For an extensive collection of contemporary reviews of Eliot's work, along with a substantial introduction, see Michael Grant, ed., *T. S. Eliot: The Critical Heritage*, 2 vols. (Boston: Routledge & Kegan Paul, 1982).

263. See Taffy Martin, *Marianne Moore: Subversive Modernist* (Austin: University of Texas Press, 1986).

264. Jacques Derrida, in *The Ear of the Other: Otobiography, Transference, Translation*, ed. Christie V. McDonald, trans. Peggy Kamuf and Avital Ronell (New York: Schocken Books, 1985), restates this textual reversibility in terms of the dominant political binarism:

> We are not, I believe, bound to decide. An interpretive decision does not have to draw a line between two intents or two political contents. Our interpretations will not be readings of a hermeneutic or exegetic sort, but rather political interventions in the political rewriting of the text and its destination. This is the way it has always been—and always in a singular manner—for example, ever since what is called the end of philosophy, and beginning with the textual indicator named 'Hegel.' This is no accident. It is an effect of the destinational structure of all so-called post-hegelian texts. There can always be a Hegelianism of the left and a Hegelianism of the right, a Heideggerianism of the left and a Heideggerianism of the right, a Nietzscheanism of the right and a Nietzscheanism of the left, and even, let us not overlook it, a Marxism of the right and a Marxism of the left. The one can always be the other, the double of the other. (p. 32)

265. See Leonard W. Doob, ed. *"Ezra Pound Speaking": Radio Speeches of World War II* (Westport, Conn.: Greenwood Press, 1978).

266. See Lawrance Thompson, *Robert Frost: The Early Years, 1874–1915* (New York: Holt, Rinehart and Winston, 1966), and *Robert Frost: The Years of Triumph, 1915–1938* (New York: Holt, Rinehart and Winston, 1970), as well as Lawrance Thompson and R. H. Winnick, *Robert Frost: The Later Years, 1938–1963* (New York: Holt, Rinehart and Winston, 1976).

267. Readers interested in thinking through the relationship between

Pound's politics and his poetry might begin with *Charles Olson and Ezra Pound: An Encounter at St. Elizabeths*, ed. Catherine Seelye (New York: Grossman, 1975), a book whose record of Olson's struggle with these issues, while hardly definitive, at least shows more depth than any academic has been able to muster. They might then proceed to E. Fuller Torrey, *The Roots of Treason: Ezra Pound and the Secret of St. Elizabeths* (New York: McGraw-Hill, 1984), a book by a psychiatrist that has either been influential or controversial, depending on the politics of the reader. Despite the history of public debate, academic critics have not until recently begun to tackle these issues in a credible way. For a provocative effort to open up some reflective critique of Pound's various biases see Paul Smith, *Pound Revised* (London: Croom Helm, 1983).

On the other hand, those academics wishing to minimize the importance of Pound's political and social beliefs are also hard at work. On the issue of Pound's anti-Semitism, Wendy Stallard Flory in "The Pound Problem," in Daniel Hoffman, ed., *Ezra Pound and William Carlos Williams: The University of Pennsylvania Conference Papers* (Philadelphia: University of Pennsylvania Press, 1983), argues the rational apologist position, suggesting that Pound's anti-Semitism cannot be understood apart from a historical knowledge of forms of anti-Semitism prevailing in America at the time. Yet she ends by finding texts like Pound's January and February 1913 *New Age* essays basically harmless ("if any work is done 'interdenominationally' the Jew overruns it and gradually pushes out the others") and finally sees Pound as largely a victim of common prejudice. Actually, there is extensive scholarship on American anti-Semitism, none of which Flory cites, and much of which might lead us to conclude that Pound was sufficiently committed to his prejudice to be inventive about crossing ordinary class and ethnic lines to find and combine different anti-Semitic discourses. See, for example, Ben D. Kimpel and T. C. Duncan Eaves, "Ezra Pound's Anti-Semitism," *South Atlantic Quarterly* 81 (Winter 1982), 56–69. Among those who find Pound's fascism and anti-Semitism to be substantially constitutive in his work is Robert Casillo, who has undertaken a difficult, probably unresolvable, but altogether necessary project of tracing conscious or unconscious parallels between Pound's writing and contemporary fascist publications. See his *The Genealogy of Demons: Anti-Semitism, Fascism, and the Myths of Ezra Pound* (Chicago: Northwestern University Press, 1988). For sensitive reviews of the overall issue, see Alfred Kazin, "The Fascination and Terror of Ezra Pound," *New York Review of Books* (March 13, 1986), 16–24; and Jerome J. McGann, "The *Cantos* of Ezra Pound, the Truth in Contradiction," *Critical Inquiry* 15: 1 (1988), 1–25.

Finally, one story that needs to go into print illustrates one generally taboo element of academic avoidance of discussion of Pound's politics: anti-Semitism. At the 1984 annual meeting of the Modern Language Association, the organizer of a December 29 session on Pound's fascism related the following story to the audience: When the printed program was published, he received a call from a "senior Pound scholar" expressing dismay that such a topic would be addressed at the convention. The caller also asked whether one panel member, Charles Bernstein, was Jewish, and regretted, if so, that a Jew would be given a chance to speak on this topic. The organizer of the session, Carroll Terrell, reported that he had not asked the panelist about his religion.

268. Donald Davie, *Ezra Pound: Poet as Sculptor* (London: Routledge & Kegan Paul, 1965), p. 146.

269. See Hugh Kenner, *The Pound Era* (Berkeley: University of California Press, 1971).

270. Cf. Jane Tompkins, *Sensational Designs*: "The struggle now being waged in the professoriate over which writers deserve canonical status is not just a struggle over the relative merits of literary geniuses; it is a struggle among contending factions for the right to be represented in the picture America draws of itself" (p. 201).

INDEX

Page numbers in italics refer to illustrations.

Cary Nelson is Professor of English and founding director of the Unit for Criticism and Interpretive Theory at the University of Illinois. He is the author of *The Incarnate Word: Literature as Verbal Space* and *Our Last First Poets: Vision and History in Contemporary American Poetry*, the editor of *Theory in the Classroom*, and the coeditor of several books, including *W. S. Merwin: Essays on the Poetry* and *Marxism and the Interpretation of Culture*. His essays have appeared in such journals as *Critical Inquiry, MLN, New Literary History*, and *PMLA*, and in such collections as *The Columbia Literary History of the United States, Psychoanalysis and the Question of the Text*, and *Men in Feminism*.

THE WISCONSIN PROJECT ON AMERICAN WRITERS

A series edited by Frank Lentricchia